ACKNOWLEDGMENTS

Looking back on the development of this book, I am overwhelmed by the generous assistance that I received at every step. Projects of this scope are perilous, and a number of challenges have threatened it at one time or another. Without the support and advice of the numerous individuals and institutions that have sustained my efforts over the years, it is inconceivable to imagine that this book could have been completed. This project also has been a catalyst for friendships and memories that I will treasure for years to come.

Institutionally, I would like to thank the Katholische Universität Eichstätt for improving my German skills by inviting me as a visiting lecturer and scholar in 1996; I thank the Leo Baeck Institute and the Deutscher Akademischer Austausch Dienst for supporting my travel and research to the Horkheimer, Pollock, Marcuse, and Lowenthal archives in Frankfurt am Main; and I thank Boston College for awarding me a dissertation fellowship that made my research in Albany, New Haven, New York, Washington, and La Jolla possible. Without the generous support of these institutions, none of the research contained in this book could have been completed.

I would also like to thank the following archives and archivists who played such important roles in assisting and advising me about the particular collections of papers with which I worked: the German Intellectual Émigré Collection at the State University of New York in Albany; the Manuscripts and Archives Division of the Yale University Library; the Howard Gotlieb Archival Research Center at Boston University; the

Research Center at the Getty; the National Archives at College Park; the Columbia University Archives; the Columbia University Rare Book and Manuscripts Collection; the Columbia University Oral History Project; the Manuscript and Archives Section of the New York Public Library; the Robert D. Farber Archives and Special Collections Department at Brandeis University; and the Mandeville Special Collections Library at the University of California San Diego. I especially would like to thank Jochen Stollberg from Frankfurt's Stadt und Universitätsbibliothek. Without his generous assistance in making the contents of the Horkheimer, Pollock, Marcuse, and Lowenthal Papers available to me throughout my stay in Germany, my time in Frankfurt would have been substantially longer.

The library staffs at Boston College and Harvard's Widener Library proved to be valuable resources. Throughout the research and writing of this manuscript, it has been essential to consult a wide array of materials, which these two library staffs always were able to locate quickly. On numerous occasions, one line of research would raise questions that could only be answered by consulting another book, and frequently I had the good fortune of being able to locate the new book on the same day that the question arose.

As the book's endnotes indicate, numerous individuals have generously shared time with me to answer my questions about the Frankfurt School's exile in the United States. The interviews and correspondences that have arisen from this project have been among its most rewarding and memorable aspects. I would like to thank the following individuals for sharing their memories and thoughts about the Horkheimer Circle: Stanley Aronowitz, Rick Ayers, Daniel Bell, Paul Breines, Paul Buhle, Lewis Coser, Mike Davis, Bernardine Dohrn, Richard Flacks, Peter Gay, Todd Gitlin, Nathan Glazer, Robert Gottlieb, Tom Hayden, H. Stuart Hughes, Robert Merton, Carl Schorske, Trent Schroyer, Jeremy Shapiro, and David Wellman.

Spending time in so many places far away from home was made all the more pleasant by family and friends who hosted me, sometimes for lengthy periods. I thank Ralph and Heike Kreichbaum (my Frankfurt hosts); Gerhard and Elke Kreichbaum (my Munich hosts); Bali Miller, Stuart Klawans, and a newborn Jacob Klawans (my New York hosts); and Rob, Cheryl, and Lindsay Weiner (my Washington hosts). Although it was always nice to return to Boston, all of you helped me feel like I had a home away from home.

Finally, I thank all of the people who inspired, advised, and guided me through this project. When I think back to the first time that I became acquainted with the Frankfurt School at Brown University, I recognize my good fortune in studying with a group of scholars who helped to nurture my early and ill-defined fascinations. In particular, I thank Brian Hayden, Volker Berghahn, Mary Gluck, and Tom Gleason. At this time I first read Martin Jay's *The Dialectical Imagination.* Although I've had limited contacts with him over the years, I do want to thank Professor Jay for the inspiration that both he and his book have represented for me. At Harvard University, I was able to study with Donald Fleming and John McCole, historians who helped me to gain an appreciation for the wider, transatlantic, and Continental picture. Finally, at Boston College, I worked and studied with some of the most generous and inspiring teachers that I have encountered. Not only did they serve as intellectual role models but they helped me to develop my skills as a teacher and to discover my own love for the classroom. While the entire history department constituted an intellectually stimulating and nurturing atmosphere, I particularly acknowledge my debts to Alan Lawson and Paul Breines. Their suggestions and criticisms of this project—throughout its development as a dissertation and during its transformation into a book—have been invaluable. Alan taught me the intricacies of American cultural and intellectual history, while Paul served as an ideal adviser and mentor. On my first day at Boston College, Paul disclosed that my scholarly interests were going to lead him on a journey into his past, and I hope that the trip has been as rewarding for him as it has been for me. I will be forever in his debt.

In recent years, I have come in contact with a wider network of scholars who share my interests in the intellectual migration, Atlantic history, and the history of the social sciences. These acquaintances and friendships have been critical to the development of this book. I thank the following people for their insights regarding our shared areas of interest and for their reactions to my work: John Abromeit, Ben Agger, Peter Baehr, Christa Buschendorf, Christian Fleck, Lawrence Friedman, Lydia Goehr, Uta Gerhardt, Kyra Holland, Jack Jacobs, David Jenemann, Detlev Junker, George Katsiaficas, Will Kaufman, Martin Klimke, Heidi Macpherson, Anthony Marasco, Wilfried Mausbach, Neil McLaughlin, Eric Oberle, Detlev Siegfried, Peter Simonson, Alfons Soellner, Werner Sollors, Michael Steinberg, John Summers, Jeremy Suri, Daniel Tompkins, Eric Weitz, Michael Werz,

Janet Wolff, K. D. Wolff, Jerry Zaslove, and Jack Zipes. I especially thank Detlev Claussen, David Kettler, and James Schmidt for the special interest they have taken in my work: each has been a constant source of encouragement and new ideas, and their generosity and suggestions have been invaluable.

This manuscript benefited from my work in academic publishing and the supportive coworkers I learned from at Harvard University Press. In particular, I thank Paul Adams, Michael Aronson, Maria Ascher, Kathi Drummy, Michael Fisher, Elizabeth Knoll, Mary Kate Maco, Kathleen McDermott, Jennifer Redding, and Annmarie Why.

I want to thank my colleagues in the history department at Assumption College: Stuart Borsch, Leslie Choquette, David Cohen, Deborah Kisatsky, Lance Lazar, John McClymer, Kenneth Moynihan, Irina Mukhina, Chieko Nakajima, Richard Oehling, and Jed Watters. They have been welcoming since my arrival in the spring of 2006, and they have been constant sources of support and advice regarding both my teaching and research. My students at Assumption also deserve thanks for inspiring me to always think and express myself as clearly and compellingly as possible.

The staff at the University of Minnesota Press made the process of publishing this manuscript a painless and exciting endeavor. In particular, I want to thank my acquiring editor, Douglas Armato, for his constant enthusiasm about this project and for his many excellent suggestions that improved it immeasurably. I would also like to thank Andrea Patch, Davu Seru, Danielle Kasprzak, David Thorstad, and Laura Westlund for guiding the manuscript through each phase of the editing and production process.

Finally, I thank my family. Many claim that working on a book project can be a lonely task. I am grateful to my friends and family for their patience with me and the continuous attention that I have directed toward this project. My grandfather, David Wheatland, possessed a deep regard for higher education and the study of the past; he was a constant supporter of my education and scholarly pursuits, and I wish that he could have seen this project reach its full completion. Following in his footsteps, my parents and sister have been valuable sources of encouragement and support. I similarly thank my wife, Rose Ann Miller, and her family, Marge and Al Miller, her siblings, and our nieces and nephews. All of them have brought moments of levity that offered welcome distractions from this project.

Miles and Leo, my newborn twin sons, provided the most joyous diversion from the final editing of the manuscript. Last, but certainly not least, I acknowledge Rose Ann Miller, to whom I dedicate this book. She sustained me throughout my graduate education and the evolution of this project and has been a true collaborator—raising me up when I felt discouraged, providing her expertise and wisdom with every draft of the manuscript, and sharing her constant love and support. I can never begin to repay my debt of gratitude to her.

PREFACE

Critical Theory and the United States

The Frankfurt School, one of Western Marxism's most productive and celebrated intellectual coteries, has received worldwide scholarly attention since the revival of its works in the 1960s. In this country, one can still speak of a Frankfurt School industry. The extensive American literature on Frankfurt School theorizing and, in particular, on Theodor W. Adorno and Walter Benjamin, however, points to an issue that, surprisingly, has received virtually no scholarly attention: the dynamics of reception, assimilation, and confrontation, which were set into motion when the ideas and sensibilities of the Frankfurt School were exported out of their German context and brought into American society and American culture.

This book focuses on Max Horkheimer's Institut für Sozialforschung (more popularly known as the Frankfurt School) as a case study in the recent transatlantic history of ideas. By examining the encounters between German and U.S. thought during one of the most fruitful periods of cross-fertilization, this project charts the rise of our academic Atlantic culture, which has flourished in the wake of the Second World War. No doubt communication and information technology has provided the material basis for this development, but the face-to-face roots of this relationship extend back to the "intellectual migration," when Germans and Americans struggled to learn from the intellectual and cultural differences that separated them. Through this confrontation with foreign modes of thought, some Americans became interested in concepts and perspectives that previously had been limited to German scholars and German speakers, while at the same time Germans came to appreciate the distinctive qualities of U.S. academia and American society.

Like other coteries from Central Europe, the scholars of the Hork-heimer Circle were unwilling émigrés from Hitler's Germany. Settling in the United States in 1934, they charted an uncertain course from isola-tionism to assimilation and in the process became an intellectual phenom-enon—the so-called Frankfurt School. Although a great deal of research has been devoted to the intellectual and institutional history of the Insti-tut für Sozialforschung, relatively little attention has focused on the inter-actions that took place between members of the Horkheimer Circle and the communities of American scholars and readers that came in contact with them. Although Max Horkheimer and the closest members of his cir-cle had dreamed of a future of "splendid isolation," the realities and neces-sities of American exile required a markedly different mode of existence. In the harsh academic market that existed during the Depression and the war years, the group's participation was strongly encouraged by their U.S. hosts and careful diplomacy was frequently necessary. And indeed, the fantasy of working alone without distraction was only fueled by the challenges and uncertainties of the émigré experience.

Our narrative concentrates on the main crossroads of transatlantic exchange in the Horkheimer Circle's history. Rather than looking at this junction as an intersection of one-way streets (such as simply the Frank-furt School's reception in America, or the impacts of U.S. society and cul-ture upon Critical Theory), this book views the transatlantic relationships that it explores as two-way streets. The "intellectual migration" produced broad boulevards of interaction—thoroughfares on which cross-cultural en-counters could result in cooperation, as well as conflict; and assimilation, as well as misunderstanding. The experiences of the émigrés and their U.S. hosts, therefore, resulted in the construction of some bridges across the Atlantic that would significantly pull the two continents closer together during the era of the Cold War. At the same time, however, the "intellec-tual migration" also helped to erect new walls and to strengthen old divi-sions between Europe and the United States.

Although he has become a major figure within the field of Critical Theory, Jürgen Habermas will not be central in this project. Habermas was too young to be a part of the Frankfurt School's exile in the United States, despite the fact that Habermas has had substantive contacts with the United States and its intellectual life after the war. For this reason, our focus exclusively will be on the first generation of Critical Theorists (T. W. Adorno, Erich Fromm, Max Horkheimer, Otto Kirchheimer, Leo Lowenthal, Herbert Marcuse, Franz Neumann, and Friedrich Pollock), which I will refer to as the Horkheimer Circle because they worked under the direction of Max Horkheimer. Substantive American contacts with this group began in 1934, and I will follow these contacts until the 1970s when the Frankfurt School emerged as an international, intellectual phenomenon.

To some extent, the entire intellectual history of the United States is transatlantic. From the moment of the first colonist's arrival on the shores of North America, European legacies have been inextricably bound with the United States and its people. Although such realizations were never absent from the thoughts of European and American historians, they received a different emphasis in the past. History, as a formal academic discipline, achieved its apex and canonization during the nineteenth century at the height of the age of nationalism. It is little wonder that the nation-state has commanded centrality among historians for such a long period of time. Even today, national histories still form the subdisciplinary foundations within history departments. While contemporary historians still group themselves according to their era and region of study, there are simultaneous trends toward more hybrid approaches. At this moment when Europe struggles to transcend its national divisions, cross-cultural and multinational vantage points have emerged as vibrant new approaches to the study of history. Traditional political, social, economic, cultural, and intellectual narratives are transformed when cast in a transnational or transatlantic spotlight. In one sense, this shift in perspective is entirely consistent with poststructural and postmodern criticisms of identities, totalities, and other traditional categories constructed by scholars within the humanities and social sciences. At the same time, however, many of those pursuing transnational and transatlantic studies are entirely conventional. Their embrace of these new historical subdisciplines represents merely an effort to recast one's vantage point on the past.

This project, which focuses on such an innovative and radical group of figures, presents a series of narratives about them that are quite old-fashioned in their approach. Although some thought has been devoted to the concept of reception, literary theory (whether the "Rezeption Theorie" of the Konstanz School or the "Reader-Response Theories" developed by

Stanley Fish and others) is not the primary orientation of this book. Although it would be tempting to speculate on the transmission of Critical Theory (as a narrative genre) in the United States, this manuscript concentrates on institutional relations more than it provides hermeneutic or semiotic analyses of the Frankfurt School's legacy. In part, this choice signals my own preference for the intellectual history written before the linguistic turn that many historians have taken, but the choice also was made for me in part by the sources that I discovered. In particular, as my work in the Max Horkheimer Archive progressed, I became increasingly convinced that my received notion of a "Frankfurt School" or "Critical Theory" obstructed a more complex, dynamic, and contentious Horkheimer Circle of Critical Theorists. By focusing on Horkheimer's Institut für Sozialforschung as an institution maneuvering within the United States during the 1930s and 1940s, it brought me in contact with a less familiar picture of the Horkheimer Circle and disclosed the powerful dynamics unleashed by the experiences of emigration. As my own "Frankfurt School" myth dissolved, I was able to see the Horkheimer Circle as a representative group within the "intellectual migration" of German thought to the United States.

The book's Introduction provides a brief examination of the Frankfurt School's pre-emigration history. While this is a story that will be familiar to readers already acquainted with the vast secondary literature on the origins and history of Critical Theory, it will provide essential introductions to both the institution and the personalities that comprised the Horkheimer Circle. Like so many other coteries of German interwar thinkers, the Frankfurt School and Critical Theory were products of the failed revolutions of 1918–19 and the doomed Weimar Republic. Situating them within the unique sociopolitical and cultural dynamics of this era, readers that are relatively new to the study of Critical Theory will discover its relationships to the events and intellectual trends of the period before arriving in the United States.

The rest of the book is divided into four parts—each one corresponding to a different community, or network, of U.S. thinkers that the Frankfurt School encountered in the United States. In some cases, these networks were framed by institutions and academic disciplines, but in other circumstances the Horkheimer Circle moved into the broader realm of public intellectual networks.

Part I explores the primary institutional relationship that dominated the exile experience of the Institut für Sozialforschung, Columbia University. The Horkheimer Circle spent the majority of its U.S. stay on Morningside Heights during a critical turning point in the history of the social sciences at Columbia. Navigating a perilous course through the departmental feud between Robert Lynd and Robert MacIver, the Frankfurt School was a participant in the revitalization of Columbia sociology that reached its culmination with the rise of Paul Lazarsfeld and Robert Merton. Although the Horkheimer Circle's reasons for settling at Columbia have never been in doubt, little has been known about Columbia's motives for hosting the Frankfurt School or their activities on campus until now.

In Part II, I uncover the web of interrelations that arose between the Horkheimer Circle and the New York Intellectuals. Although difficult to identify and define, the New York Intellectuals inhabited an urban and cultural milieu that was strikingly similar to that of the members of the Horkheimer Circle. The two groups embraced similar visions of cosmopolitanism, internationalism, and modernism. Ultimately, however, the experience of the war and differing assessments of the Cold War pulled the groups apart. Although the "New York Intellectuals" generally accepted many of the Horkheimer Circle's views regarding aesthetics and mass culture, they differed sharply on the topics of Marxism, liberalism, and Pragmatism, anticipating many of the issues that would capture the imagination of the New Left of the 1960s.

Part III explores the complex world of postwar sociology. The recent interest of literary critics and philosophers in the Frankfurt School has often obscured the fact that the Institut für Sozialforschung was devoted first and foremost to social science. When its members arrived in the United States, they almost exclusively worked within the discipline of sociology. The Horkheimer Circle's experiences highlight the sharp divide that separated the theories and methods practiced in Germany versus those in the United States. While Americans were intrigued by the empirical work of the Institut für Sozialforschung, the group's passion for social philosophy was almost entirely lost on its U.S. audience. Until the rest of the Institute was able to adapt to the expectations and tastes of American sociologists, Erich Fromm served as the group's public face. This process of assimilation, however, was not as easy for the other members of the group. It also was not absolute. The Horkheimer Circle's approach to social problems remained significantly different from work being done in the United States. The hybrid approach to sociology that was adopted by the Institut für Sozialforschung had important impacts on U.S. social science and German social science. Thanks to the efforts of the Horkheimer Circle and many other European sociologists that also participated in this transatlantic effort, American sociology generally became more accepting of social theory and more specifically embraced Freudian psychoanalysis and other theoretical tools that had been fashioned on the Continent. German sociology, however, was even more profoundly changed. Although the Horkheimer Circle remained deeply committed to social philosophy, one of the chief tasks that it accomplished in postwar Germany was the introduction of American research methods.

The final section of this book, Part IV, examines the complex relationship between the Horkheimer Circle and the American New Left. Although the postwar Institut für Sozialforschung bore little resemblance to its manifestation in exile, the group of colleagues and ex-colleagues attained the height of their fame and recognition as a historical construction, the Frankfurt School. While most of the members and former members of the Horkheimer Circle had a deeply problematic relationship with the New Left, Herbert Marcuse's enthusiastic support of the student movement solidified the connection between the Frankfurt School and student rebels. The press of the late 1960s heralded Marcuse as the guru of student rebellion. The evidence among the writings of U.S. student leaders, however, presents a more problematic picture. When examining writings from the era, such as *New Left Notes* and the wide array of underground newspapers linked to the counterculture, one is struck by how infrequently Marcuse's name or ideas appear. After the spring of 1968 when Marcuse actively sought to inspire and ally himself with the New Left, there is slightly more discussion, but still not as much as the popular press led people to believe. To some extent Marcuse's thought could not take root within a movement that progressively embraced increasingly extreme actions and enthusiastically touted its own anti-intellectualism. To Marcuse's most substantial audience, graduate students and scholars sympathetic with the many ambitions of the New Left, the Frankfurt School reminded people of the importance of social theory and the dangers of authoritarianism. Such admirers of the Horkheimer Circle emphasized these aspects of Critical Theory to criticize the rise of extremism in the student movement both at home and abroad. At the same time, however, one must at least entertain the notion that desperate acts of violence may be a natural reaction to the kind of negative totality that was the end product of Critical Theory. The Horkheimer Circle, in essence, offered an East/West convergence theory of globalization. Instead of proposing an alternative, their critique of contemporary trends partly was a work of nostalgia—a longing for the simpler and more fragile world of the classical bourgeoisie. Their young admirers, separated by time and place, however, could not share in this nostalgia. The New Left viewed this negative totality without the same cultural and historical reference points, and the result was a pessimism felt among certain segments of the "Movement" that fueled apocalyptic fantasies, acts of terrorism, and (in the words of Habermas) "Left Fascism."

NOTE REGARDING TRANSLATIONS

This book is targeted at both the audience of specialists familiar with Critical Theory and the more general audience that knows less about it. With this in mind, the author has made every effort to direct his readers to all existing English translations of the writings of the Frankfurt School as well as the sizable secondary literature in English. Assuming that not all of these readers may be able to read the work of the Frankfurt School in German, we are fortunate to possess many English translations. While specialists in Critical Theory may debate the wording of some of these translations, they are an important resource for non-German speakers who may want to learn more about the Frankfurt School and its writings. When existing translations were not available, the author translated the original German documents into English.

INTRODUCTION

A Brief History of the Frankfurt School before Its Arrival in the United States

The Frankfurt School in Exile presents an analysis of Critical Theory in the United States as a social history of ideas. It proposes that ideas cannot be evaluated in isolation from the material or sociopolitical conditions that shape the lifeworlds of the people generating them. The book, consequently, offers a new vantage point on the critical theorists and their ideas by focusing on the institutions in which they worked. Although the study of institutions can conjure images of the cold world of bureaucracies, the manuscript approaches institutions as living social networks. The Frankfurt School simultaneously represents two such networks. On the one hand, it constituted a complex and frequently disunited community of émigré thinkers dedicated to a common goal of integrating philosophy and science to develop a comprehensive theory of modern society. At the same time, the Frankfurt School was an institution that operated and interacted within larger social networks, particularly in exile. Thus, the book examines the history of Critical Theory from the vantage point of Atlantic history. Like other émigré institutions, political exile required entry into and immersion in American ideas and social networks. For the Frankfurt School, isolation was not an option for long. Eventually the institution, its members, and its ideas had to enter into a "new world" of academic, cultural, and public intellectual networks. Unlike the networks to which members of the Institute were accustomed in Europe, the scholarly and public intellectual communities they encountered in the United States were governed by different epistemological assumptions and by different sociopolitical interests. Navigating the world of ideas in the United States required significant modifications of both the Institute and its thought, but such maneuvers simultaneously produced opportunities for Americans to encounter Critical Theory and to be influenced by it.

The methodology distinguishes *The Frankfurt School in Exile* from Martin Jay's *The Dialectical Imagination* and Rolf Wiggershaus's *The Frankfurt School*. Both of these classic works develop rigorous intellectual histories of the Institute that convey its complexity and the evolution of its thought. In its general characterizations and interpretations of the theoretical writings of the group, *The Frankfurt School in Exile* follows in the footsteps of Jay and Wiggershaus. But it develops a new perspective on the phenomenon of exile in the Institute's history, development, ideas, and reception. Whereas Jay and Wiggershaus present some dimensions of the institutional and transatlantic histories, their efforts yield different results from the present study. Jay's *The Dialectical Imagination* hints at the complex interrelations between members of the Institute and their American hosts, but focuses on its main task of developing a clear vision of the various intellectual contributions that formed Critical Theory. Jay's access to the surviving members of the Institute provided both a windfall and a shortfall. On the one hand, such access made possible an unparalleled understanding of the Institute's writings and thought. On the other hand, Jay's personal access set limits on his ability to convey the group's messy and contentious institutional relationships.

Wiggershaus's *The Frankfurt School* was written more than a decade later and was unable to benefit from similar oral histories, but Wiggershaus gained access to materials in the Horkheimer and Pollock archives that substantially enhanced the institutional history of the group. Following Horkheimer's notion that the Frankfurt School possessed "exterior" (institutional) interests and "interior" (intellectual) interests, Wiggershaus carried Jay's history further by showing how such institutional and intellectual interests influenced each other. Wiggershaus, however, conducted little research in the United States, which limited his account of the Institute in exile. While it presents a new appreciation for the inner workings of the Institute, it does not explore the Institute's interactions with the communities of scholars that it encountered in the United States. *The Frankfurt School in Exile* thus uses the vantage points of institutional and Atlantic history to develop a new and unfamiliar picture of the Horkheimer Circle.

The present study aims to challenge what I consider to be some pervasive views about the Frankfurt School during its period of exile in the United States and to reevaluate the implications of this time in America. First, like Jay and Wiggershaus, my study challenges the myth of a homogeneous Horkheimer Circle by complicating the picture of Critical Theory and its theorists. By focusing on the Frankfurt School in exile, we glimpse Critical Theory at a moment of crisis and transformation, an era during which competing visions for the future of the Institute and its intellectual program were openly debated. Second, *The Frankfurt School in Exile* dispels the common idea that the Critical Theorists isolated themselves in the United States by documenting the numerous contacts that emerged between members of the Horkheimer Circle and networks of American scholars and public intellectuals. Third, my project evaluates the impacts that American exile had on the Frankfurt School, as well as the influences that the Critical Theorists had on various communities of U.S. thinkers.

The Frankfurt School in Exile details for the first time a comprehensive picture of the Institute's relationship with Columbia University—not only the activities of the Horkheimer Circle on Morningside Heights, but also the expectations of its hosts. Similarly, the book unearths the relationships between the Critical Theorists and the New York Intellectuals. Until now, scholars have only noted the affinities between the two groups, but the present study, relying on archival evidence, oral histories, and a systematic analysis of the writings of the New York Intellectuals, uncovers the points of contact between the two communities and the debates and mutual influences that ensued. It presents for the first time a picture of the extensive networking that resulted from the Frankfurt School's attempts to establish itself within American sociology. Like the efforts of other émigré communities, those of the Frankfurt School resulted in intellectual assimilation that gained eventual recognition in the United States and simultaneously prepared the Critical Theorists to return to Europe as experts in American sociological methods and theories. Ironically, their efforts at grantsmanship simultaneously fueled the Frankfurt School's critiques of Positivism and the "culture industry," suggesting that the experiences of intellectual entrepreneurialism were necessary steps in the emerging critique of the "totally administered society." Finally, the present study reexamines the relationship between Herbert Marcuse and the New Left, arriving at a conclusion that contradicts traditional accounts. Through a thorough analysis of the archival records of the Students for a Democratic Society (SDS) and the underground newspapers of the 1960s, *The Frankfurt School in Exile* shows that Marcuse's presumed reception by the American student movement and counterculture was largely a construction by the mass media in the spring of 1968.

Some scholars engaged in the continued project of Critical Theory may find these historical reassessments not directly relevant to their contemporary cultural and political interventions, but this has been a reaction that other historians of the Frankfurt School have faced. When Jay published *The Dialectical Imagination,* Douglas Kellner wrote of the book: "Part of the problem lies in the focus and scope of Jay's work. He is a historian and is more concerned with amassing factual details than in developing an interpretation and critique of critical theory that would relate it to current theoretical and political problems."[1] Thus, I don't expect to be exempt from such criticisms. I am a historian of Critical Theory, not a Critical Theorist. My goal has been to build on the works of Jay and Wiggershaus in an effort to clarify our understanding of the Frankfurt School by situating it in a significant and largely unexplored sociohistorical context that shaped its development and reception—the United States.

Before the reader can begin to appreciate or assess the Institute's time in the United States, it is necessary to know something about the history of the Horkheimer Circle prior to its emigration. For scholars familiar with Critical Theory, such an introduction will not be necessary. After the vigorous reception of Critical Theory during the 1970s and the 1980s, the pre-emigration history of the Institute and the genesis of its ideas have been widely reported. The present study offers the following introduction to those readers who may only be casually familiar with the Frankfurt School and may wish to know more about Critical Theory before they learn about the adventures of the Horkheimer Circle in exile.

WEIMAR ORIGINS

The Frankfurt School was an unmistakable product of the birth of Germany's Weimar Republic. This tumultuous period that has left us with so many treasures of German thought and culture represents a moment of historical discontinuity—a revolutionary instant in which the world was turned upside down. Wilhelmine society crumbled and for a time it seemed plausible to think that anything might be possible. These hopes were gradually and repeatedly dashed as an unstable republic took shape and struggled to survive in an inhospitable political environment. Crippled by debt, inflation, and the legacy of the war, the Weimar Republic became an unpopular compromise that never went far enough to satisfy the Marxists and socialists of the German Left but went too far to be tolerated by the nationalists and conservatives that constituted the German Right.

The politics of the group that gathered around Max Horkheimer at the Institut für Sozialforschung was shaped by both the First World War and the collapse of Wilhelmine society that followed on the heels of Germany's surrender. These were pivotal events that molded the moral and political beliefs of the men who populated the Frankfurt School. These experiences made them acutely aware of suffering and the barbarism that human beings were capable of inflicting on each other. Yet at the same time, the popular uprisings that followed the war filled them with hope about the possibilities of a new world that might take shape. This sense of possibility and promise led the members of the Frankfurt School to join Marxist study groups and even to flirt with revolutionary politics. With time, all of them became disillusioned with politics and abandoned activism—but they remained intellectually committed to understanding the world that was emerging after the world war and why a working-class revolution had failed to materialize in Germany.

Intellectually, the Frankfurt School also bears the imprints of the Weimar era. Although the group sought expertise from scholars in nearly every field within the social sciences, the group collectively shared an awareness and concern for philosophy. The Frankfurt School carefully monitored and commented on the intellectual debates of this period occurring within both German philosophy and Marxian theory – debates sparked by Neo-Kantianism, Irrationalism, Phenomenology, the revival of Hegel, and the discovery of the young Marx. As the Frankfurt School pursued the ambitious task of developing a comprehensive theory of contemporary society, Max Horkheimer and his colleagues carefully studied these debates in order to formulate a philosophical position that would guide their social research and enable them to generalize from the data that they collected.

In the realm of culture, the Frankfurt School again manifests the imprints of its Weimar origins. Modernism, and particularly Weimar modernism, was not simply a matter of taste. The Frankfurt School found aesthetic and intellectual modernism to be central to the emerging Critical Theory of society. Moving well beyond the traditional roles of sociologist or critic, the members of the Frankfurt School sought to incorporate aspects of Weimar modernism into their emerging social theory. This led members of the group to study psychoanalysis, modernist literature, and atonal music, as well as to develop a more general theory of art that concentrated on its capacity to criticize contemporary reality and to offer fleeting glimpses of utopian possibilities.

But the formation of the Frankfurt School during the era of the Weimar Republic is not simply important for enabling one to grasp the forces that shaped the creation of Critical Theory. Focusing on the Frankfurt School's origins also helps one to see the way in which the experiences of Weimar were magnified by the experience of exile. The historical discontinuity of the Weimar era was repeated and reinforced by the experience of exile in America. Exile also created a break with the past. Weimar society, like the Wilhelmine society that they experienced before it, vanished with the move to the United States. Max Horkheimer and his colleagues again were faced with a new world filled with uncertainties. Thus exile, like the Weimar period itself, represented a sharp break with the past that was accompanied by terrifying realizations, new hopes, the formation of new political commitments, and intellectual confrontations with new modes of thought.

Like many other figures of the German Left, Felix Weil, the founder of the Institut für Sozialforschung, found himself disillusioned and perplexed by the tremendous turn of events that had occurred during the first years of the Weimar Republic. During the dramatic year of 1919, Weil had participated in Frankfurt's council movement. However, his commitment to the Left was exemplified less by his political participation and more by his support of socialist thought. Weil found the realm of Marxian theory more appealing than the realm of revolutionary practice. In fact, many years later, Weil looked back at his Weimar days and concluded that he had been more of a "salon Bolshevik" than anything else.[2] As a student at Tübingen, Weil was introduced to the theoretical issues surrounding socialism, and he completed a doctoral dissertation on the methods for socialization at the University of Frankfurt in 1920. In the reactionary aftermath of the government's policies against the radical Left, Weil took it upon himself to become a financial benefactor to the political and theoretical forces that were in retreat.

The wealth of Weil's family allowed him to assume this role. He came from a prosperous and highly assimilated Jewish family. His father, Hermann Weil, was an international merchant who made his fortune exporting grain to Europe from Argentina. Felix Weil's politics were similar to those of many other university students flirting with socialism and Marxism during the early days of the Weimar Republic. The politics of these young men was sparked by the war and its aftermath, and some have claimed that there may have been an element of Oedipal rebellion involved too—as the children of many wealthy industrialists, merchants, and financiers were drawn to the radical political movements that flourished following the war. Hermann Weil, however, may not have been the typical bourgeois, German father. Instead of discouraging such political interests, he supported his son, as well as his son's interests. Consequently, the two became philanthropists of the Left. In addition to founding and supporting the Institut für Sozialforschung, the Weils supported everything from publishing houses to individual artists.[3]

One of their early ventures, which helped provide Weil and his friends with the idea of forming an institute for the study of Marxism in Germany, was the Erste Marxistische Arbeitswoche that was held in the summer of 1923 at Geraberg near the Thuringian Forest. The event was intended to build unity among the various theoretical positions that German-speaking Marxists had adopted in response to the situation in Germany, as well as in response to recent events in the Soviet Union. In attendance were a large number of scholars and thinkers who would become involved with the Institut für Sozialforschung. In addition to Felix Weil and his wife, the Erste Marxistische Arbeitswoche included Karl and Hedda Korsch, Georg Lukács, Karl and Rose Wittfogel, Friedrich Pollock, Julian and Hede Gumperz, Richard and Christiane Sorge, as well as more than a dozen other participants. The highlights of the event were the papers presented by Korsch and Lukács that encapsulated many of the ideas that they had recently published in their famous books of the same year (1923)—Lukács's *Geschichte und Klassenbewusstsein* and Korsch's *Marxismus und Philosophie.*[4] Both books proposed new understandings of Marxism that emphasized the role of consciousness in relation to praxis. This new focus led both back to the roots of Marxism and ultimately back to Hegel. Seeking to imagine a similar stage of self-consciousness within the Marxian dialectic, Korsch and Lukács embraced the Hegelian identity theory. Their main revision was that the proletariat, not the philosopher, was the only historical entity capable of realizing itself as both a subject and an object.

Initially, Weil anticipated that the Erste Marxistische Arbeitswoche would be just the first of a series of gatherings for Marxist intellectuals and scholars in Germany. However, as the "Summer Academy" reached its conclusion, Weil felt convinced that a more permanent organization was necessary.[5] At this point, Weil first began to consider the possibility of founding an institute for the purpose of addressing the kinds of questions and issues that the Geraberg group had been exploring. When Weil returned to Frankfurt from the Thuringian Forest, he kept in touch with many of the contacts that he had made there—particularly with those participants who lived in close proximity to Frankfurt. Of particular importance for the future of the Institut für Sozialforschung was the relationship that Weil maintained with Richard Sorge. Sorge was a research assistant to Kurt Albert Gerlach, who was an economist with a radical temperament similar to Weil's. Gerlach had just received a professorship at the University of Frankfurt and was therefore an ideal candidate for the directorship of the institute that Weil had in mind. Because the German Education Ministry required the director of this proposed institute to hold a position at the local university, Weil approached Gerlach with his idea.

Gerlach received the proposal with tremendous enthusiasm, and he set to work with Weil to convert the plans into reality. Although they sought to make the Institute affiliated to the University of Frankfurt (and more specifically connected to its department of social science), Weil and Gerlach also wanted to ensure that their creation would be largely independent and be able to function autonomously. They needed a relationship with the University of Frankfurt more for the sake of official formalities, but they aimed to restrict this relationship to the bare essentials in order to prevent any outside interference in the internal affairs of the Institute. This arrangement was guaranteed, for all practical purposes, when Felix Weil and his father established the endowment. By all standards, this endowment was sizable for the time period and particularly for an unusual institution of this kind. The Weils funded the costs for the building and other facilities required by the Institute, they pledged a yearly grant of 120,000 marks for operating costs, they financed the university chair in social science that would be held by the Institute's director, and they even provided a further inducement for the social science department by making the first floor of the Institute available to it.[6] Weil also established a Society for Social Research in Frankfurt to oversee the operation of the Institute. The Institute's director was given complete control over the day-to-day operations of the Institute, but the Society for Social Research was granted the power to approve all nominations for director. Because Felix Weil and his father Hermann presided as cochairmen of the Society and the Society was composed of no one but friends and associates of the Weils, Felix was always able to maintain some degree of control and involvement in the affairs of his Institute.[7]

THE GRÜNBERG YEARS

Felix Weil's plans were thrown into jeopardy in October 1922 when a tragedy took the Weils and their associates by surprise. Kurt Gerlach died at the young age of thirty-six from diabetes. At first, Weil was so shaken and stunned that he debated whether or not to continue with his plans for the Institute. His Frankfurt friends came to his aid. They bolstered his spirits and convinced him to locate a new director for the anticipated Institute. As a result of this encouragement, Weil eventually found a suitable successor in Vienna. Carl Grünberg, the notable Austro-Marxist, officially became the first director of the newly founded Institut für Sozialforschung on 3 February 1923.

Like Weil and his friends in Frankfurt, Grünberg was from a highly assimilated Jewish family. Born and raised near the Carpathian Mountains, Grünberg was sent to Vienna to study law at the age of twenty.[8] It was there that Grünberg first became familiar with Marxism, and he began work that combined his study of law with sociology. Having completed a doctoral dissertation on the abolition of the manorial system and having published a few short articles dealing with Marxism and socialism, he received his first university appointment in 1899 to the University of Vienna. As he gained the support of other left-wing academics in the city, Grünberg ended his part-time legal practice and gained prominence when he founded an academic journal titled *Archiv für die Geschichte des Sozialismus und der Arbeitsbewegung*. Grünberg gained a reputation in Vienna as a Marxist scholar (one of the key architects of Austro-Marxism), and also did not shy away from political activism.[9] Despite his reputation as a radical, he was granted a chair at the University of Vienna in political economy.

At the time that Weil approached Grünberg to see whether he might be the right man for the directorial post in Frankfurt, Grünberg had already been exploring the possibilities of establishing a similar institution in Vienna. To Weil's good fortune, these plans failed to materialize, and Grünberg accepted Weil's offer. In January 1923, Grünberg was unanimously appointed to a chair in the Department of Economics and Social Sciences at the University of Frankfurt, and he simultaneously became the first director of the Institut für Sozialforschung.

On 3 February 1923, a decree from the Education Ministry signaled the official birth of Felix Weil's Institut für Sozialforschung. Although the organization had no building or offices at the time of this decree, temporary space was soon located as a new building was constructed to house the Institute at 17 Victoria-Allee.[10] Initially, Grünberg, Weil, and their small circle of associates were preoccupied with organizing the library and papers that would be housed in the new building. Later, as the construction was concluded, Grünberg began to reflect on his own vision for the fledgling Institute. He made these thoughts known at the official opening of the Institute's Victoria-Allee offices on 22 June 1924. Much like Max Horkheimer's inaugural address several years later, this was a significant event in the early history of the Institute because it provided Grünberg with the opportunity to share his personal agenda as director with his associates, friends, colleagues, and the members of the Society for Social Research.[11]

Grünberg made it very clear at this opening address that he envisioned the Institut für Sozialforschung as a research organization. Consequently, he drew a sharp distinction between the Frankfurt Institute and the other organizations for social research that were more committed to professional training. To Grünberg, the Institute's primary function was to follow Marx and to struggle with the task of comprehending contemporary society. It followed that there could be less room for the training of young social researchers, because he feared that this might jeopardize the more significant and demanding work that he had in mind.

Grünberg also made his own position in the Institute quite clear to his colleagues, as well as to the members of the Society for Social Research. In harmony with Weil's original intentions, Grünberg proclaimed the dictatorial powers of the director. Once appointed by the Society for Social Research and approved by the University of Frankfurt, the director would control the daily affairs of the Institute. Consequently, Grünberg would be in the position to approve or reject all research projects supported by the Institute, and he would control all publications released by it. The Institute would become a collective embodiment of the interests and concerns of its director.

The last major topic in Grünberg's address was Marxism, and he attempted to describe the role that he felt it would play in the Institute's future work. Unlike Horkheimer and his associates who would later constitute the Frankfurt School of Critical Theory, Grünberg maintained a commitment to the materialist conception of history that was consistent with the traditional notions of materialism that had been pervasive among Social Democrats and Communists since the end of the nineteenth century. One consequence of this was that Grünberg had little interest in the epistomological issues underpinning Marxian materialism—he was interested in the promotion of Marxism as a scientific research method. Grünberg insisted that his associates should focus on the "real objects" of social research in order to uncover the structural transformations taking place within capitalist societies. Like so many Marxists before him, Grünberg sought to grasp the material laws of capitalism and the structural contradictions that pointed to its eventual collapse. Thus, the time and energy of the Institute under Grünberg were directed toward better comprehending classical Marxism and the class struggle that were at the heart of German Communist politics during the years of the Weimar Republic. It was an approach to social research that was markedly different from the Critical Theory of society that made the Institute famous under the leadership of Max Horkheimer.

Under the directorship of Carl Grünberg, the Institut für Sozialforschung grew to fit its director's image. Although it published a few explicitly philosophical works by Marxian theoreticians such as Korsch and Lukács, the main work of the Institute's associates reflected Grünberg's passion for history. As Rolf Wiggershaus explains, during the Grünberg directorship, Weil's creation became "an Institute for research on the history of socialism and the labor movement, on economic history, and on the history and criticism of political economy."[12]

Although the Institute's interests and projects are fairly easy to describe during this period, its structure and composition are not. It is quite clear that Grünberg assumed the dictatorial position that he had proclaimed for himself; it is harder to discern the pyramid that was established beneath him. During this period, there were many scholars coming and going. Besides Friedrich Pollock and Henryk Grossmann, who served as Grünberg's assistants, Rose Wittfogel, who served as the Institute's librarian, and Richard Sorge and Karl Wittfogel, who worked as research associates of the Institute, other scholars were far more transient. Of the larger group who had brief and informal connections to the Institute, nearly all of them had close associations with the German Communist Party (KPD). However, the commonalties end with the KPD. While all of these part-time associates were social scientists, they spanned the spectrum of German academia. Some were graduate students, and others were visiting scholars or fellowship recipients from the University of Frankfurt.

As a result of Grünberg's fading health, the number of projects that were completed by the Institute under his directorship was fairly small. The most widely discussed of these efforts was the contribution that the Institut für Sozialforschung made to the preparation of a new edition of the complete works of Marx and Engels.[13] The Institute participated in this endeavor by assisting the Marx-Engels Institute in Moscow by acting as an intermediary between that organization's head, David Ryazanov, and the German Socialist Party, which was entrusted with all of the manuscripts and archival materials of Marx and Engels. The project proved to be of great significance because it unearthed many documents that had remained unpublished.[14] In addition to this collaborative work, the Institut für Sozialforschung also produced some original studies reflecting Grünberg's interests. Among the most prominent of the original works were Grossmann's study of political economy, Pollock's analysis of the planned economy in the Soviet Union, and Wittfogel's social and economic exploration of Chinese society.[15]

MAX HORKHEIMER AND HIS CIRCLE

Grünberg's directorship ended in 1927 when he suffered a stroke. Although he lived for many more years, the damage caused by the stroke made it impossible for him to return to his old duties. Grünberg passed the administrative responsibilities to his assistant, Friedrich Pollock—a longtime friend and close confidant of Felix Weil. Consequently, it was Pollock who became a kind of interim director of the Institute while everyone waited to see what would become of Carl Grünberg. Once it became clear that a replacement for Grünberg would be necessary, Weil and the Society for Social Research turned their attention to the internal ranks of the Institute.

At this point, there were several scholars connected to the Institute who were all capable and qualified to receive full professorships at Frankfurt, and Weil was content to not look elsewhere because he felt more comfortable appointing someone from within the Institute's circle of friends and associates. Initially, Pollock seemed to be the front-runner for the position. After all, he had been entrusted with the care of the Institute during this traumatic period. However, when Grünberg retired in 1929, his replacement was a man who had close ties to Weil but had been less involved in the day-to-day operations of the Institut für Sozialforschung. His name was Max Horkheimer. Horkheimer was especially close friends with Pollock, and the two had met Weil during their early student days in Frankfurt. But where Pollock had become actively involved in the activities and operations of the Institute, Horkheimer had focused his attention on his education in philosophy. Backed by some powerful supporters in the philosophy department such as the theological philosopher Paul Tillich, Horkheimer had recently received a chair in social philosophy at the University of Frankfurt.

Max Horkheimer was born in Stuttgart in 1895.[16] Like Felix Weil and nearly all of the other figures who would eventually round out his circle, he came from a prosperous and assimilated Jewish family. Like so many German Jews of the era, his parents considered themselves thoroughly German and were not orthodox in their religious practices. Horkheimer's father, Moritz, was a prominent member of the community. He owned several textile factories and was a well-known philanthropist. Initially raised and educated to run his father's business, Max Horkheimer's upbringing made him an unlikely candidate for becoming a philosopher—let alone for emerging as the director and chief architect of the Frankurt School's Critical Theory of society. Moritz Horkheimer was not educated in the German *Gymnasiums* and universities, and thus he was not steeped in the high culture of Wilhelmine society. Max Horkheimer, initially, followed a similar trajectory. He attended a *Realgymnasium,* where he was prepared for the practical career that he was destined to inherit at his father's factories. Horkheimer was a devoted son, but grew to be an intellectually and emotionally rebellious youth as he became increasingly unhappy about the course that had been set for his future.

The initial spark for Horkheimer's escalating rebelliousness was his friendship with Friedrich Pollock. The two met in 1911 and soon became close friends. Together, each contributed to the moral and political development of the other and became a cultural bohemian in the process. Of particular importance were their readings of the various literary and philosophical critics of bourgeois society—such as Ibsen, Zola, Tolstoy, and Schopenhauer—as well as an eighteen-month sojourn that the two took to Brussels, Paris, London, and Manchester prior to the outbreak of the First World War. These experiences cemented the friendship and led both young men to see themselves as rebels against middle-class society with its narrow and alienating values. By contrast, Horkheimer and Pollock committed themselves to higher ideals such as love, compassion, and spiritual renewal.[17]

Upon his return from his travels with Pollock, Horkheimer was made a junior partner in his father's firm but found the work unbearable and stifling. Although the job exempted him from military service for most of the war, the new sensibilities that Horkheimer had developed through his relationship with Pollock colored every experience that he had in the business world. His personal wealth and his experiences as part of his father's management team generated feelings of guilt and led Horkheimer to speculate about the circumstances and psychology of the workers who staffed the factories. These inner conflicts erupted into an open breach with his parents when Horkheimer fell in love with his father's secretary, Rose Riekher. In addition to not having the proper social background, Riekher was not Jewish—a factor that played an equally important role in heightening his parents' displeasure with the romance. As Horkheimer's relationship with Rose grew, his bond with his parents deteriorated. Finally, in an attempt to force the two lovers apart, Moritz Horkheimer fired the young secretary, thus creating a rift between father and son that would last for approximately a decade.

The First World War served as a dramatic interruption to the family struggles that had enveloped Max Horkheimer's personal life. Horkheimer was conscripted by the German army in 1916, but, to his good fortune, he was never mobilized because of his failure to pass the army physical. Thus, he spent the last weeks of the war on the home front, where he beheld the unraveling of Wilhelmine society. The events were particularly dramatic for a young man with Horkheimer's moral and political sensibilities. The world of capitalist injustice and narrow bourgeois worldviews seemed to be crumbling, and what would replace them was not yet clear—but the rise of the soldiers' and workers' councils seemed to indicate that socialist transformation was inevitable. For idealists like Horkheimer and Pollock, these temporarily hopeful circumstances formed the backdrop for their transition to university studies, and this atmosphere would shape the trajectory of their further intellectual development.

With the conclusion of the war, Horkheimer and Pollock went to university in Munich, where they witnessed the formation of the short-lived soviet republic. They moved in many of the same social circles with the bohemian intellectuals and artists who surrounded the republic's new leadership, and they were deeply affected by the sense of hopefulness that they experienced with these people. They also remained in Munich for the destruction of the soviet republic. As the forces of reaction rose up against the renegade city, Horkheimer and Pollock came to the realization that it was too dangerous to continue their studies there. The brief time in Munich, however, left both friends disappointed with the trajectory of recent events but eager to use their studies to discover what was going wrong. The two friends transferred to the University of Frankfurt after only one semester in Munich.

At Frankfurt, Horkheimer fell under the sway of many of the Gestalt psychologists who had settled at the relatively new university. Together with Pollock, he had already completed preliminary readings in German philosophy. Psychology, however, initially attracted Horkheimer because it was a concrete social science that might offer insights regarding the tragic causes for the First World War, as well as explain the failure of socialist revolution in the wake of the war. With its emphasis on consciousness and the mediation between subjects and objects, Horkheimer's initial fascination gradually nurtured his philosophical interests in epistemology and materialism. Hans Cornelius, the noted neo-Kantian, was the professor who ignited Horkheimer's passion for philosophy and showed him how much it had in common with the psychological questions that preoccupied Horkheimer. Under Cornelius's guidance, Horkheimer grew to develop his lifelong commitment to the idea of critical reason that emerged from the writings of Kant. It was also during these early years in Frankfurt that Horkheimer began to study Marxism with friends outside of the classroom. Although he never joined any Communist organizations, Horkheimer was enthralled by his readings of Marx. In Marx, he found a sophisticated justification for the moral and emotional opposition that he had been feeling toward bourgeois society since he was an adolescent. However, inside of the classroom, Horkheimer became such a promising philosophy student that Cornelius sent him to Freiburg to study with the famous father of phenomenology, Edmund Husserl, and his assistant, Martin Heidegger. Despite his clear talent for philosophy, Horkheimer returned to Frankfurt with the intention of writing a dissertation in psychology. However, when a student at another university published a dissertation on the same topic that he had selected, Horkheimer gave way to Cornelius's suggestions to write a dissertation in philosophy on Kant's *Critique of Judgment*. He completed the dissertation, which exhibited both the influence of Cornelius and Gestalt psychology, in 1925. Although Horkheimer's attraction to Cornelius's unique approach to Kant through the principles of Gestalt psychology was short-lived, Cornelius was a mentor that left a lasting impression on Horkheimer. Cornelius insisted that Horkheimer continually stretch himself as a scholar—exposing himself to subjects well outside of his particular scholarly interests, such as physics, chemistry, and the visual arts. For Horkheimer, this exposure to other disciplines formed the foundation of not only his versatility as a scholar but also his commitment to interdisciplinary scholarship.

Upon the project's completion, Horkheimer began a teaching career as a *Privatdozent* at Frankfurt and married his forbidden love, Rose Riekher. He taught several courses in modern philosophy and was disappointed to be passed over for promotion. These years of professional frustration nevertheless were a period of important intellectual growth. In addition to amassing lecture notes on the history of philosophy, Horkheimer also documented his more private thoughts. The latter would later be published as a collection of aphorisms titled *Dämmerung*.[18] The writings demonstrate Horkheimer's continuing concern for social justice, his growing interest in Marxism, and his emerging criticisms of bourgeois society.

Despite Horkheimer's qualifications and recommendations, historians of the Institute have still wondered about his appointment to the position of Institute director—especially if one considers that he had never worked for the Institute in either a research capacity or an administrative capacity. Concern for the Institute's image within the community seems to be one plausible explanation for Horkheimer's otherwise puzzling appointment as director of the Institute.[19] At the time of the search for Grünberg's successor, many scholars and government authorities in Frankfurt looked upon the Institut für Sozialforschung with great suspicion as a Communist organization. According to many who did not share the political convictions of those in the Institute, Weil's group engaged in suspicious activities and an unusual brand of nepotism based more on ideological consistency than on personal loyalty. Weil and his associates might have seen Max Horkheimer's appointment as a way of combating this image. After all, Horkheimer could be perceived as a fringe figure in their group, and he had no formal political affiliations with the Communists or any other radical political party in Germany. More recent research indicates that Horkheimer, while never formally working within the Institute, was a major figure behind the scenes.[20] He had been friends with Weil since the beginning of his studies in Frankfurt, and he had played a critical role in the discussions during which the idea for an institute emerged. Nevertheless, by the time of his appointment as director, the Institute was being viewed with great scrutiny by the community, and Max Horkheimer was a safer choice than the other members who had more radical credentials that could not be disguised or hidden.

Regardless of Weil's motives, it also remains clear that Friedrich Pollock helped make Horkheimer's appointment possible by stepping aside for his good friend. This kind of selfless behavior on the part of Institute associates became a common feature of the Institute. In the years to come, nearly all of the figures connected to the Institut für Sozialforschung made remarkable sacrifices for Horkheimer. Naturally, Horkheimer's position as director could induce this type of behavior. Horkheimer controlled the professional fate of each group member. Nevertheless, much of this behavior (as in this case with Pollock) goes beyond internal politics. Horkheimer possessed the kind of charisma, intelligence, and character that elicited such devotion and personal loyalty.

Max Horkheimer was officially installed as the second director of the Institut für Sozialforschung on 24 January 1931. His inaugural address proved to be as significant as Grünberg's speech at the opening of the Institute in 1924. As Grünberg had done years before, Horkheimer used the opportunity to describe his vision for the group. Although he made no mention of either issue in his talk, it is clear that Horkheimer shared Grünberg's views regarding the emphasis on research, as well as the extraordinary powers of the director. The majority of Horkheimer's talk, however, drew some sharp distinctions from Grünberg's theoretical and methodological perspectives.

As the title of the talk suggests, Horkheimer's main topic was social philosophy and its role in both determining and shaping the fate of man.[21] Far from embracing the scientific Marxism that had shaped the sociological, economic, and historical investigations of the labor movement and political economy that had typified the interests of the Institute under Grünberg, Horkheimer outlined a theoretical and methodological framework that would establish the future course of the Institute and the early history of Critical Theory. The early portion of the talk signaled Horkheimer's relationship to Marxism, but Horkheimer rejected the assumptions that had shaped Grünberg's historical determinism. Instead, Horkheimer outlined a vision of Marxism that embraced its roots in German Idealism.

While expressing his commitment to the notion of critical reason that emerged so forcefully in the writings of Kant, Horkheimer also shared his reservations about the dualism that remained unresolved by Kant. Kant provided a model for the self-examination of reason, but his social philosophy remained restricted to the "isolated subject." By constituting a gulf between the autonomous self and the object realm of "things-in themselves," Kant had built his social philosophy around the "closed unity of the rational subject." Hegel, while preserving the idea and methods of critical reason, was able to take the first step toward bridging the Kantian gulf by establishing a concept of reason that was grounded in history. As far as social philosophy was concerned, this was the first significant step beyond the Kantian subject and the first move toward the materialist conception of history that would be so important to the Left Hegelians and the young Marx. Hegel shifted the direction of German Idealism away from Kant's highly introspective notion of reason that was based on the conception of an autonomous subject, relocating reason within history's "bacchanalian whirl." By understanding society as an essential object of history, Hegel was able to locate a framework for reason that existed beyond the self. However, Horkheimer's debt to Hegel did not stop there.

Hegel also provided the impetus for Horkheimer's social-philosophical methodology. As Horkheimer made clear in his address, Hegel developed the notion that philosophy transfigures historical reality by making it rational. For Horkheimer, this is what made Hegel's philosophical method superior to the empirical methodologies of traditional social science as it was being practiced during the era of the Weimar Republic. Most of his contemporaries in the social sciences and social philosophy had ventured into the realm of Positivism. The obsession with analytic science had led his contemporaries to concentrate on gathering facts, which were then not questioned or integrated by philosophy. Hegel's methodology, by contrast, took facts and gathered them to build rationally historical observations about individuals and societies. By remaining true to the concept of critical reason and by interpreting social facts historically, Hegel and the Left Hegelians had demonstrated that social philosophy guided people toward greater freedom.

Even though Hegel's methodology appeared to hold the key to human freedom, Horkheimer acknowledged that nineteenth-century Positivism and capitalism destroyed the promise that the Left Hegelians and Marx had recognized in Hegel's legacy. Whereas the Left Hegelians and the young Marx had discerned conceptions for more ideal societies, the history of the late nineteenth century had not only led to a more limited view of the social world but also had led to the rise of a more highly individualistic society and worldview. Philosophically, this led to the various brands of nihilism and despair that became so prominent by the end of the nineteenth century. Nevertheless, Horkheimer did not believe that Hegel's dream was completely dead in the twentieth century. He believed, therefore, that one of the chief tasks for the Institute was to try to reorient both philosophy and the social sciences.

This does not mean, however, that Horkheimer was completely opposed to the applications of various methodologies from the social sciences. On the contrary, he was willing to utilize many different forms of information that were gathered by empirical methods. His fundamental caution was that his researchers never mistook this empirical data for the "facts." Horkheimer called upon the Institut für Sozialforschung to combine empirical research with philosophy, just as Hegel had advocated. He challenged the Institute's research associates to convert the "facts" of more traditional social research into philosophical essences. "Facts" were only tools to be used to discover the philosophical realities of social existence that lay beneath mere appearances. As Horkheimer explained:

In short, the task is to do what all true researchers have always done: Namely, to pursue their larger philosophical questions on the basis of the most precise scientific methods, to revise and refine their questions in the course of their substantive work, and to develop new methods without losing sight of the larger context. With this approach, no yes-or-no answers arise to the philosophical questions. Instead, these questions themselves become integrated into the empirical research process; their answers lie in the advance of objective knowledge, which itself affects the form of the questions.[22]

Rather than limiting the horizons of the Institute to a small set of predictable social phenomena (as Grünberg had done), Horkheimer sought to make sense of the broad spectrum of social reality by examining the world through the prism of philosophy. Empirical data would be collected, but it would be understood and interpreted from a theoretical standpoint that was shaped by a notion of critical reason that transfigured historical reality by making it rational. Realizing that such a mission could not be performed by the Institut für Sozialforschung as it had been constituted, Horkheimer welcomed new figures into his circle. Meanwhile, many of those who had been closer to Grünberg and his vision for the Institute went their separate ways. Horkheimer's goal was to assemble a collection of specialists whose fields differed widely but who all shared his philosophical orientation that would best be described as Hegelian Marxism.

Horkheimer's closest associate was Friedrich Pollock—his lifelong friend. Both shared somewhat similar backgrounds. Pollock also came from a prosperous family (his father owned some leather-goods factories), he was expected to take over the family business, and he grew up in a highly assimilated German-Jewish household. Pollock's parents, however, were unlike the Horkheimers in their religious and political outlooks. As Pollock grew up and matured, his father took the more radical step of renouncing Judaism. Similarly, in the wake of the First World War, his parents grew to sympathize with the political Left. Whereas Horkheimer remained independent from organized Weimar politics, Pollock became an avowed Marxist. Although he studied philosophy like all of the other figures in the Horkheimer Circle, economics became Pollock's real vocation and area of expertise. Thus when he became a member of Weil's Institut für Sozialforschung, he worked as an economic research assistant to Grünberg. When Pollock's dissertation on Marx's monetary theory was completed at Frankfurt, Grünberg's journal *Archiv für Geschichte des Sozialismus und der*

Arbeiterbewegung published it.[23] Also as a result of his connections to the Institute, Pollock received an invitation from the Marx-Engels Institute to travel to the Soviet Union only a few years after the completion of his dissertation. The trip provided him with the raw data that served as the basis for a second book, which Pollock submitted as his *Habilitationsschrift*—an economic analysis of the planned economy in Russia. The book was sympathetic to the economic efforts that had been undertaken in the Soviet Union, but Pollock did not shy away from pointing out some of the terrible mistakes that had been made by Russian economic planners. This study, *Die planwirtschaftlichen Versuche in der Sowjetunion,* was also published by the Institute as a monograph.

Pollock had proven himself to be one of the most productive figures around Felix Weil, and a loyal friend of Max Horkheimer. Although Pollock did not remain a central contributor to the intellectual work of the Horkheimer Circle, he remained a steadfast supporter who assisted Horkheimer with nearly all of the administrative responsibilities connected with running the Institute—in particular, using his training as an economist to manage the group's finances.

While Pollock was of great value to Horkheimer as a result of his loyalty and administrative guidance, Erich Fromm was a primary contributor to the theoretical work of the group and the chief architect of its social research projects. Fromm came from an orthodox Jewish family in Frankfurt, and he maintained a strong religious identity into adulthood. Fromm had been academically trained as a sociologist at Heidelberg. While teaching during the 1920s at Frankfurt's Freies Jüdisches Lehrhaus, Fromm grew increasingly interested in psychoanalysis and eventually received the requisite training to become an analyst. At the same time that he pursued the study of psychoanalysis, Fromm fell under the sway of socialism. When he had completed his training in psychology, he rapidly began to make a name for himself as a Freudian revisionist who was seeking to combine the insights of psychoanalysis with Marx's theory of class consciousness. Fromm received a lectureship from the Frankfurt Institute of Psychoanalysis, which is where he first came into contact with Max Horkheimer and the Institut für Sozialforschung. At the same time that Fromm was looking for ways to unite the ideas of Freud and Marx, Horkheimer was becoming increasingly interested in psychoanalysis as a tool for uncovering the motivations that lay behind the human declarations or actions that were the focus of social research. As the two men's interests grew closer together, Fromm was hired by the Institute to add his expertise to a new study on the German working class.

Leo Lowenthal's role fell somewhere in between that of Friedrich Pollock and Erich Fromm. He served as a central contributor to the arena of literary studies as a sociologist of literature, and he held an important administrative duty as editor of the Institute's *Zeitschrift für Sozialforschung*. Lowenthal was born in Frankfurt and raised in a totally assimilated Jewish household. As in Pollock's family, Lowenthal's father renounced Judaism and reared his son in a completely secular home. Despite this upbringing, Lowenthal was drawn to Judaism on his own through his early political commitment to socialism—becoming involved with socialist student groups at the University of Heidelberg that were committed to Judaic humanism and Zionism. Eventually, he joined the circle of intellectuals surrounding Rabbi N. A. Nobel and thus became acquainted with Erich Fromm and other socialists in Frankfurt (such as Theodor Wiesengrund-Adorno, Ernst Bloch, and Siegfried Kracauer). Consequently, Lowenthal began to develop contacts with different people connected with the Institut für Sozialforschung. He received his doctorate in philosophy at Frankfurt with a dissertation on Franz von Baader. Lowenthal hoped eventually to study for his *Habilitation* with Horkheimer's old mentor, Hans Cornelius. Ironically, he realized that his main competition for Cornelius's attention was another young friend of Horkheimer, Theodor Wiesengrund-Adorno.

Herbert Marcuse was brought into the Institute to assist Horkheimer with the philosophical work that was central to Horkheimer's conception of Critical Theory. Although Pollock, Fromm, and Lowenthal had all studied philosophy as students, each had migrated into other fields. Marcuse, by contrast, remained a philosopher for his entire academic career.[24] Marcuse, born 19 July 1898, was the eldest of three children. His father provided the family with a comfortable lifestyle through his successful textile business and later through real estate. Marcuse was academically trained at Humboldt University and the University of Freiburg, receiving a PhD in German literature, philosophy, and political economy. His political education, however, took place as a result of his experiences in the First World War. He served in a German reserve unit during the last years of the war, after which he joined the Social Democratic Party (SPD). Marcuse remained a relatively inactive member of the party, but his experiences in it caused him to begin systematically exploring socialist thought.[25] With the murders of Rosa Luxemburg and Karl Liebknecht, Marcuse left the SPD, never to join a political party again—but these experiences during the Spartacist winter of 1918–19 left permanent imprints on his political imagination. As a Berliner, he had been closer to the revolution than any of his other colleagues from the Institute—a factor that might explain his very different relationship to the student movement of the 1960s. Whereas his colleagues from the Frankfurt School largely grew increasingly suspicious of the masses and political activism, Marcuse vividly recalled the liberatory potential that he experienced at the end of the war.

With the completion of his dissertation and his continued interest in Marxism, Marcuse returned to the University of Freiburg in 1928. He was employed as a philosophical assistant to Martin Heidegger. Marcuse was drawn to Heidegger because he sought to combine his Marxist ideas with Heideggerian existentialism. Like Sartre, years later, Marcuse sought a recovery of the individual, philosophical subject that many perceived to be threatened as a result of Marxism's emphasis on objective, social forces.[26] His time in Freiburg was productive, but it was also frustrating. Marcuse developed a more profound understanding of contemporary philosophy, but became disenchanted with Heidegger because Heidegger did not share Marcuse's affinities for Marxist thought.[27] But the work with Heidegger did generate Marcuse's book *Hegel's Ontology*,[28] which alerted Horkheimer to Marcuse's work. Marcuse was quickly hired by the Institute to assist Horkheimer.

The final key figure from the Horkheimer Circle who began collaborating with the Institute before exile was Theodor W. Adorno. Initially, Adorno's primary responsibilities were in the field of aesthetics. However, as his involvement with the group increased, he also began to make significant contributions to the sociological and philosophical work that was being undertaken. Adorno was a tireless worker who intimidated others with his remarkable intellectual output and his challenging writing style. As Adorno's younger colleague, Jürgen Habermas, recalled years later:

> Adorno was a genius. I say that without a hint of ambiguity. In the case of Horkheimer or Marcuse, with whom, by the way, I had a less complicated and, if you like, more intimate relationship, no one would have ever thought

of saying such a thing. Adorno had an immediacy of awareness, a sponta-
neity of thought, and a power of formulation which I have never encountered before or since. One could not observe the process of development of
Adorno's thoughts: they issued from him complete—he was a virtuoso in
that respect. Also, he was simply not able to drop below his own level; he
could not escape the strain of his own thinking for a moment. As long as
one was with Adorno, one was caught up in the movement of his thought.
Adorno did not have the common touch, it was impossible for him, in an
altogether painful way to be commonplace.[29]

Although he did not become an official member of the Institute until
1938, Adorno would eventually become one of Horkheimer's most trusted
and productive collaborators. However, his loyalty to Horkheimer was
tainted by a powerful desire to exclusively monopolize Horkheimer's
favor—a drive that led Adorno, on occasion, to undermine the relationships between Horkheimer and other members of the Circle.

Adorno was born Theodor Wiesengrund-Adorno (later, in exile, he
dropped the first half of the hyphenated name and became known as
Theodor W. Adorno).[30] His father was a wealthy wine merchant who converted to Christianity, and his mother was a Corsican Catholic. Adorno
was provided with not only a first-class academic education but also with
superb training in the arts, developing an early love for music and becoming an accomplished pianist. He also was a great proponent of modernist
music—particularly the work of Arnold Schoenberg. In fact, after receiving a doctorate in philosophy from the University of Frankfurt, Adorno
abandoned academia to study in Vienna with Schoenberg's star pupil, Alban
Berg. However, he remained in Vienna for only three years. Although it is
difficult to ascertain Adorno's reasons for returning to academia, there seem
to have been a number of interconnected reasons. Adorno wrote music
criticism throughout his time in Vienna, and these writings were not received warmly by Schoenberg. It also appears that Adorno's return to philosophy was neither abrupt nor absolute. A man with many interests and
talents, Adorno sought to keep his options open.[31]

Adorno returned to Frankfurt in 1928 to complete his *Habilitation*. His
first attempt on Freud and Kant was abandoned, and he briefly left academia again to be a part-time music critic in Berlin.[32] The time in Berlin
was fruitful because it enabled Adorno to befriend Walter Benjamin, who

became an important influence on the young scholar. It was also significant because it gave Adorno the chance to develop some ideas for a new
project on Kierkegaard. This second *Habilitation* project proved to be a
success and Adorno became a *Privatdozent* at the University of Frankfurt
just as the Nazis were preparing to come to power. In addition to attain-
ing this all-important *Habilitation,* Adorno's return to Frankfurt also re-
acquainted him with Max Horkheimer (whom he had met in one of
Cornelius's seminars as a student). Horkheimer, who was now the director of the Institute, was impressed by Adorno's knowledge of aesthetics
and invited him to contribute some essays on music for the Institute. Thus
began Adorno's long career with Max Horkheimer and the Institute to
which his name will always be linked.

Almost immediately after the promotion to the directorship of the
Institute, Horkheimer began to combat the organization's reputation for
Communist sympathies and nepotism by maintaining close ties with his
colleagues in the philosophy department, as well as with sociologists and
economists. By encouraging members of the Institute to engage in joint
endeavors and to participate in university programs with members of the
university faculty who shared their general political outlook, the Institut
für Sozialforschung became an identifiable entity within the broader spectrum of the academic left in Frankfurt.[33] The change greatly enhanced the
Institute's reputation and established a standard that remained constant
throughout the history of the Institute—despite the common perception
that the Frankfurt School remained an isolated coterie, the Institut für
Sozialforschung always encouraged collaboration with a variety of scholars and institutions. They were indisputably a tight-knit group, but they
cooperated with a myriad of intellectuals.

The Institute also began work on a major piece of scholarship that fully
demonstrated its hybrid approach to social philosophy and empirical research. The study's subject matter was the German working class during
the Weimar Republic, and its goal was to determine the psychological
makeup of German workers from this period and the social forces affecting them. Viewed from the broader perspective of Western Marxism (as
developed by Georg Lukács and Karl Korsch), the Institute's study sought
to understand and describe the "real" consciousness of workers, as opposed
to the uncritical acceptance of assumptions regarding the inevitability
of Marxian class consciousness. Underlying this project was a belief that

capitalist society was changing in dramatic ways and that working-class jobs were drying up as industry became more mechanized and consolidated. Workers, who suffered the main brunt of contemporary capitalism's transformation, were more at the mercy of industry's masters than ever before. It was reasonably suspected that this lack of economic and political control would have significant psychological impacts on working-class people.

Horkheimer and the project's primary supervisor, Erich Fromm, proceeded with detailed questionnaires that were distributed to German workers. The questionnaires dealt with a myriad of subjects intended to generate a broad yet comprehensive psychological picture of the respondents. However, no interviews were performed to verify the psychological findings because the costs of such a procedure were prohibitive. Instead, Fromm subjected the actual questionnaire responses to careful psychoanalytic analysis. This methodology represented a major breakthrough in the German social sciences. Until this point, psychoanalysis had never been used in this manner to complement empirical research. It was also a notable study in the overall history of the Institute because it served as a model and testing ground for a number of other empirical studies that would be pursued in later years. On a more practical level, the project also was significant to the Institute's future because it enabled Horkheimer to develop professional contacts in Geneva, Switzerland. Horkheimer traveled to Geneva on several occasions, initially because the International Labor Office was located there. Once the Nazis came to power in 1933, these Geneva contacts would prove to be of great value to the members of the Institut für Sozialforschung.

Ultimately, however, this first study of the German working class was a failure. Horkheimer was never completely satisfied with the execution of the questionnaires, and he was even more troubled by the preliminary findings that Fromm reported to the Institute. Fromm's conclusions suggested that the working classes were not developing any form of class consciousness and that there were no signs of a widespread revolutionary potential among German workers. Instead, Fromm uncovered clear signs of passivity and psychological escapism. From a historical standpoint, these results were extremely significant. After all, they suggest an important set of reasons for the working class's failure to block the rise of Nazism. In retrospect, it seems tragic that Horkheimer did not publicize the findings. However, the Institute and its political allies on the Left believed that news of these results would serve to boost the confidence of Nazis, as well as other conservative and nationalist parties in Germany.[34] For these reasons, the Institute withheld its data on the German workers, but Fromm continued to tinker with it until he split from the Institute in 1939.[35]

The other major project that began during the final years that the Institute spent in the Weimar Republic was its journal, the *Zeitschrift für Sozialforschung.* With Leo Lowenthal installed as the journal's editor, the *Zeitschrift* became a testing ground for the Institute's nascent Critical Theory of society. Whereas Grünberg had remained content to focus upon economic, social, and labor history, the *Zeitschrift für Sozialforschung* contained a wide variety of articles and reviews reflecting the diversity of interests that Horkheimer had elected to incorporate into the mission of his Institute. Most editions of the *Zeitschrift* combined a dizzying array of subject matter. It was not unusual for a single copy to contain a philosophical essay by Horkheimer, an economic piece by Pollock, a psychoanalytic study by Fromm, and an examination of classical or popular music by Adorno. Although the Institute continued to pursue large research projects, its true style came to be embodied in the *Zeitschrift für Sozialforschung*—a style that is polished, demanding, and economical. The Horkheimer Circle reached its greatest theoretical and literary heights in the short essay formats that its periodical demanded.

The theoretical contours of the early contributions to the Institute's *Zeitschrift* were consistent with the mission statement that Horkheimer had outlined in his inaugural address as director. They demonstrate a shared commitment to critical reason, the Hegelian dialectic, and the writings of the young Marx. Collectively, these essays aimed to develop a materialist history of contemporary society that was derived from the specific fields of expertise in which each member of the Institute's core specialized. They provide one with a clear (but patchwork) picture of the early Critical Theory of society that was emerging during the first years of the Institute. Written at a time when Marxian terminology was not yet stripped from the group's vocabulary, the first volumes of the *Zeitschrift* exhibit the Frankfurt School's efforts to grapple with the social, political, and cultural world of the Weimar Republic. They demonstrate the lingering political optimism that was present among the Weimar Left, and they point to some of the more troubling discoveries and realizations about contemporary society that would preoccupy Critical Theory during its exile and after.

In the economic arena, the Frankfurt School's economists noted the trend toward centralization. But, rather than pointing to this development as clear evidence of the inevitable collapse of capitalism or of the necessary rise of more progressive economic planning, writers like Friedrich Pollock acknowledged that capitalism was transforming its systems of production. Large-scale mass production had become an economic reality within the advanced capitalist economies, but its implications were far from clear. On the one hand, such centralization seemed to verify the Marxian belief that capitalism would build the tools of its own demise; yet, on the other hand, Pollock was far from certain that centralization would provide the basis for more developed socialist economies. He recognized that centralization could just as easily lead to capitalist planned economies. Rather than toppling monopoly capitalism, capitalist centralization could consolidate itself and preserve its existence indefinitely—thereby weakening the working class.[36]

Meanwhile, in the field of psychology, Erich Fromm and Max Horkheimer both sought to utilize the instinct theories from Freudian psychoanalysis to grasp a better understanding of individual drives, motives, and consciousness. As a result of Critical Theory's reliance on Hegel and Marx, the origins and nature of human drives were highly significant. Orthodox Marxists had arrived at a position of historical determinism, because they limited their concept of psychology to a mere reflection of a historical epoch and the material conditions underlying that epoch. Historical change and revolution were thus a matter of self-conscious recognition of historical circumstances combined with the inherent flaws of the existing capitalist system. This Marxian thesis had to be more carefully studied in light of Freud's contributions to psychology—especially the deep structures of consciousness and ego development that psychoanalysis had uncovered. Fromm and Horkheimer used the thought of Freud to reconsider Marxism in an effort to broaden Marxism's understanding of human drives and consciousness, and by the same token they aimed to use Marx to reexamine psychoanalysis in order to better recognize the penetration of socioeconomic forces within the psychological terrain of the id, ego, and superego.[37]

Even the early contributions to cultural criticism from the *Zeitschrift* shared the same goal of contributing to the emerging picture of contemporary society. Rather than traditional art criticism, the first forays into aesthetics rigorously aimed to link social developments with artistic developments. Thus, Theodor W. Adorno's essay on Schoenberg was not merely an analysis of the latter's technical achievements in modern music— Adorno was constantly indicating how the music was a reflection of broader social forces. In Adorno's hands, Schoenberg came to represent the apex of bourgeois identity and consciousness. The failure of Schoenberg's contemporaries to recognize the composer's genius pointed to a flaw within the audience and society in general. It pointed to widespread alienation and irrationalism that were pervasive in society. Similarly, Leo Lowenthal's first contribution to the *Zeitschrift* aimed to rigorously combine social and artistic criticism to forward the broader theory of contemporary society. Lowenthal wrote a manifesto for a sociological approach to literary studies that would be attentive to the socioeconomic forces that shaped the production of literary works, as well as their interpretation and reception. Like Adorno's use of Schoenberg, Lowenthal used Balzac's *Comédie Humaine* and Zola's *Les Rougon-Macquart* to illustrate his historical-materialist approach to art and to show how the bourgeois worldview of the nineteenth century shaped the constitution of these works—in particular, how the mercantile economy affected the imagination of Balzac, while the emerging capitalist economy impacted Zola.[38]

EXILE—GENEVA

The Institut für Sozialforschung was uprooted by the Nazi seizure of power that took place on 30 January 1933. Although this political development was very sudden, it did not catch the members of the Institute by surprise. For several years, it had been aware that if the Nazis ever gained a majority in the government, left-wing institutions like it would be in grave danger. Further jeopardizing Horkheimer's circle was the fact that nearly all of its members were Jewish. With the events of 30 January, most members of the Institut für Sozialforschung felt that their time in Germany was at an end.

The members of the Frankfurt School (with the exception of Adorno, who remained in Germany for several years and eventually fled to Oxford University in England) made their way to Switzerland, where Horkheimer had already developed the necessary contacts that permitted the Institute to relocate to Geneva. Although the Institute's building in Frankfurt was searched and closed by the police on 13 March 1933, the Nazis could not seize the bulk of the Institute's property or wealth. Most of the library had been shipped out of Germany during the previous months, and all of the Institute's financial holdings had been moved out of German banks. Therefore, the Institute still maintained control of the assets that guaranteed its future existence. The members left behind most of their personal property in Germany, but the foresight of Horkheimer and Pollock did permit them to survive in exile and to continue the work that they shared together. There is no question that exile was an extremely disruptive force in the personal lives and work of the Institut für Sozialforschung. However, it also functioned to bind the members of Horkheimer's circle more tightly together. As Martin Jay noted:

> It had been the intent of the founding members to create a community of scholars whose solidarity would serve as a microcosmic foretaste of the brotherly society of the future. The *Zeitschrift* . . . helped cement the sense of group identity; and the common experience of forced exile and regrouping abroad added considerably to this feeling.[39]

In February 1933, the Institute marked a break with its former history and began its new existence in exile. To reflect its new existence in Geneva, Horkheimer elected to modify the name from German into French—thus, the Institut für Sozialforschung became the Société Internationale de Recherches Sociales. Of greater consequence were important changes in the research priorities of the Frankfurt School that accompanied the temporary move to Geneva. The unsatisfactory German workers project pointed it in the direction of its next major area of research—the topic of authority and its relationship to the contemporary European family.[40] The workers' questionnaires suggested that serious changes in the family were taking place, and the Institute wanted to explore these more thoroughly. Thus a new study of the family was envisioned—a social research project that would examine how family units were being structurally affected by the economic dislocations caused by a capitalist system that was either on the brink of collapse or, alternatively, on the brink of monopoly capitalist transformation. Horkheimer and Fromm were interested in whether unemployment affected the structures of family authority—in particular, they wanted to know whether traditional patriarchal authority was eroding and giving way to matriarchal authority, as well as the possible social and psychological consequences of such a change.

Members of the Institute proceeded by developing surveys with the aid of various research groups throughout Europe in order to gain different perspectives on the phenomenon. The first surveys were circulated among urban French workers who had been unemployed for at least six months. These surveys were meant to develop a profile of the types of families that the Institute believed were most likely experiencing structural changes—because these same socioeconomic groups were suffering the most severe effects of the depression. Next, the Institute surveyed "professionals" who were best positioned to provide expert commentary on the changes they were witnessing within the structure of families. This second set of questionnaires was given to "expert observers" such as professors of social science, teachers, social workers, judges, and other government officials who dealt with family matters on a regular basis. These family professionals were selected from a variety of countries such as Switzerland, Austria, France, Belgium, and Holland. The last set of surveys focused on the group that was thought to be most affected by structural changes in the family—children. A final set of questionnaires was sent, therefore, to Swiss children who were asked to disclose their perceptions and attitudes about their own families.

Because only the design of the study and the research commenced while the Institute was based in Switzerland, its publication and findings will be reserved for the subsequent chapters on the Frankfurt School's years at Columbia University in the United States. However, it should be noted that this research represented another example of empirical sociology's enhancement through the use of psychoanalytic theory—this project became more significant from the perspective of the Institute's reputation because it was actually completed and published.

Despite this productive flurry of activity, it was clear to everyone in the Institute that Geneva could only be a temporary home. Only Horkheimer had a Swiss residency permit, and the other members of the group had to keep renewing their tourist visas. Because the Swiss authorities had little desire to grant residency permits to the others, it was only a matter of time before the Horkheimer Circle would again have to move its base of operations. Furthermore, on experiencing the political situation in Switzerland, many members of the Institute feared that the Alps might not offer enough of a barrier between themselves and the spreading tentacles of Nazism. Consequently, throughout their time in Switzerland, Horkheimer and his associates kept their attention fixed on locating a more permanent home for the Institute. Although they established branch offices for their Institute in both Paris and London, Horkheimer did not entertain serious thoughts about relocating to either of these cities for fear of the spread of fascism. He did, however, allow the Institute's German publisher to terminate its relationship with his group, and the Frankfurt School established a new publishing arrangement with Alcan in Paris.[41] Nevertheless, a new base of operations was needed by the Frankfurt School—someplace far from the dangers that were growing in Europe. Horkheimer sought a location that would offer protection from all manner of interference, and he particularly sought an institutional partner such as the University of Frankfurt had been. Affiliation with a major university both sheltered the Frankfurt School and provided it with the prestige and respectability that would be needed in exile.

PART I

CRITICAL THEORY ON MORNINGSIDE HEIGHTS

chapter 1

NEW YORK TRANSIT

An Invitation to Columbia University

It is puzzling that the Frankfurt School's relationship to Columbia University has been somewhat neglected by its many historians. It is not hard to understand why the Horkheimer Circle would have desired to settle at Columbia, but it is peculiar that the Frankfurt School would have received an invitation from Columbia. After all, why would Columbia University's conservative president, Nicholas Murray Butler, and its sociology department extend an invitation to a group of predominantly German-speaking social theorists with strong links to the Marxian left?

Regrettably, the one time that questions were raised about the Horkheimer Circle's connection with Columbia University, a debate ensued in which the focus shifted away from Morningside Heights and a Cold War polemic regarding the Institute's motives and political leanings became the only result. By 1980, when this controversy erupted, the Frankfurt School had become a popular topic for academic study within departments of philosophy, history, comparative literature, and German in the United States. It particularly appealed to younger scholars sympathetic with the then declining New Left. Consequently, when Lewis Feuer's article appeared in *Survey* during the summer of 1980,[1] it caught the attention of many Frankfurt School analysts.

Feuer not only attacked the Institute for Social Research, but also attacked those who had written historical studies of the Horkheimer group and its thought. Martin Jay was the most prominent of these historians, and his account of the Institute's move to New York was rejected for its "pleasant naïveté" (156). According to Feuer, the Institute was far less politically or morally innocent. The move to Columbia was not a happy accident, but instead the result of a complex plot in which the faculty and administration were duped into offering space and an affiliation with the university. By focusing on the presidential papers from the Columbia Archives, Feuer attempted to disclose precisely how the Institute approached the university, as well as Columbia's reasons for extending an offer to the Institute.

By uncovering the extent of Julian Gumperz's involvement in the negotiations with Columbia, Feuer was able to raise the specters of Communist infiltration and nefarious motives. Although Gumperz's connections to Communist organizations in Europe had been common knowledge among the Frankfurt School's commentators, Feuer surprised many of his readers by proposing that Gumperz had followed the strategies of Willi Muenzenberg, an infamous Bolshevik spymaster, in his negotiations with Columbia University (166). By approaching politically sympathetic members of the sociology department, such as Robert Lynd, Gumperz was able to attract allies to the Institute's cause. According to Feuer, Lynd and virtually all of the other members of the Institute's advisory board were left-leaning liberals or fellow travelers who were exploited by the Horkheimer Circle in an attempt to cloak itself from political scrutiny. During its earliest years in Germany, the Institut für Sozialforschung maintained close relations with the Communist Party. By the time it was run by Max Horkheimer and had become connected with Columbia, however, the Marxism of its members had become more muted—"a more amorphous variety of fellow-traveling" (169). The newer members "criticized bourgeois culture and society, while preserving at least a common denominator of silence with regard to all such phenomena as the purges, 'trials,' labour camps, and 'liquidation' of Old Bolsheviks and Trotskyists, geneticists, and the more productive peasants" (ibid.).

Although it's true that the Horkheimer Circle was often relatively quiet regarding Stalinism, Feuer's account lacked a credible motive and also developed wild speculations from scant evidence and creative interpretations of existing documents. Even if the Institute masked its political underpinnings and Gumperz appealed most directly to the Institute's natural allies on the Columbia faculty, Feuer failed to provide any compelling reason for developing a plan to infiltrate Columbia in the first place. By Feuer's own admission, the Institute did not lack money, thereby taking away any financial motive. Furthermore, as Feuer admitted, the Horkheimer group engaged in no form of political or ideological recruitment, which eliminated the only other potential motive (169–70). With so many holes in his argument, it would have seemed as though Jay and other historians of the Frankfurt School could easily dispense with Feuer's charges. All they had to do was offer a more accurate account of the Institute's relationship to Columbia. The retort that was published in the next issue of *Survey,* however, left much of the mystery unsolved.

Instead of offering new evidence to defend the Institute's affiliation with Columbia University, Jay refuted the political substance of Feuer's arguments.[2] Clearly, this represented the more damaging set of accusations. However, the strategy proved to be an ineffective way of dispensing with Feuer's assertions. Although Jay set the record straight regarding the Institute's theoretical accomplishments and activities, his retort only opened the door for more outrageous accusations from Feuer.[3] As Jay provided evidence that countered Feuer's red-baiting attacks, Feuer, in turn, gathered more evidence for a counterstrike that suggested further Communist and fellow-traveling condemnations.

Although Jay was able to defend the Frankfurt School's theories and politics, this controversy with Feuer illuminated little about the Horkheimer Circle at Columbia. In its wake, many key questions remained unanswered. Crucial pieces of the story remained cloudy. For example: How did the Institute approach Columbia University in the first place? Why did it wish to be on Morningside Heights? Why did Columbia want to become involved in a relationship with the Horkheimer group?

COLUMBIA'S SOCIOLOGY DEPARTMENT

The field of sociology was not represented among the disciplinary divisions within the original Faculty of Political Science at Columbia, which meant that sociology did not become a distinct academic field until later. This resulted partly from the perceptions and lack of knowledge regarding sociology during these years. President John Burgess divided the Faculty of Political Science into four parts: history, political science, constitutional and international law, and political economy and social science.[4] At this early point in the Faculty's history, sociology was subsumed within the field of social science. Its methodologies remained poorly defined and understood in United States, causing many Columbia trustees and administrators to balk when a chair of sociology was proposed in 1891.[5] Were it not for the efforts of President Seth Low, who offered to fund the new position personally, the establishment of Columbia's first chair in sociology may have taken years longer to achieve. Low was a true public intellectual who loved New York as much as he adored his university. In his eyes, sociology was a much-needed addition to the Faculty of Political Science. He believed that sociology's insights would result in the most tangible contributions to the university's surrounding community.

Low's appointee, Franklin Giddings, was the ideal candidate for forming a lasting department of sociology at Columbia. Although it took several years to break away from Burgess's departmental coupling with political economy, Giddings managed to satisfy the dual aims of his sponsors. He directed the University Settlement in New York, proving his commitments to social reform and the scholar's civic duties, while he simultaneously made some of the most significant contributions to the academic establishment of sociology in the United States.[6] Giddings was a positivist and was strongly inclined toward establishing sociology as a scientific discipline; however, he was also an astute social theorist. His own scholarly output helped define the field of sociology in the United States during the turn of the century, and his prominence helped place Columbia's emerging department at the forefront of the discipline.[7]

Excited by his early success, Giddings began to become more concerned with laying the academic foundations of American sociology. He remained committed to social reform, but he strongly supported separating the training of social workers from his department of sociology. By 1900, after years of nudging, his goal was accomplished. Social work moved to the New York School of Philanthropy, enabling Giddings and his colleagues in social economics, Samuel Lindsay and Edward Devine, to concentrate on the scientific study of society. Collectively, the trio continued to maintain Columbia's reputation on the cutting edge of American sociological study, and all three strongly supported efforts to incorporate the use of statistics and empirical research into the field. At Columbia, the department's drift toward empiricism was signaled by the appointment of a statistician, Robert Chaddock.[8] By the 1920s, the entire field of sociology in the United States had made the leap from social work to scientific discipline, and Columbia had helped blaze the trail. Now that the entire subject matter had begun to model itself on the natural sciences and their methodologies, Giddings and the Columbia sociologists struggled to distinguish themselves and to maintain their lofty status.[9]

Intense competition for top students and outside funding from the newly formed social-science foundations distinguished American sociology in the 1920s. Money became available to researchers like never before. Giddings and his colleagues must have viewed the development with mixed feelings. On the one hand, their discipline was gaining notoriety, making new and important work more feasible; on the other hand, these same conditions made it harder for Columbia to maintain its status in the discipline. Fears about the department's future prospects increased as the decade drew to a close. By 1928, Giddings was too old to continue leading the department, and the importance of locating a successor was magnified by the perception that sociology at Columbia had been surpassed by the University of Chicago. Bolstered by huge Rockefeller grants and directed under the careful scrutiny of Robert Park, the University of Chicago took American sociology into a new and fruitful direction—into the study of local communities. These community studies captivated the imaginations of social scientists throughout the country, who saw endless possibilities for regional applications of Park's work.

It took nearly a year to find a suitable replacement for Franklin Giddings, and it was clear that his would be almost impossible shoes to fill. In retrospect, this makes the university's choice a bit surprising. At a time when the entire discipline was pursuing empirical applications, Columbia selected a new department chair who was firmly committed to social theorizing. Giddings's replacement, Robert MacIver, originally came from Scotland. His main specialty was political theory, but his Oxford education had enabled him to be extremely knowledgeable about the entire European sociological tradition. After teaching briefly in Europe, MacIver joined the faculty of the University of Toronto, where he taught for twelve years. Instead of focusing his attention on societal maladies, like so many sociologists in the United States, MacIver was more interested in theorizing about social processes and cohesion. This orientation, however, did not preclude him from serving on important governmental projects—most notably Canada's War Labor Committee during World War I.[10] After publishing a series of important theoretical texts following the war, MacIver arrived on Morningside Heights in 1927. He had been offered the chairmanship of Barnard's Department of Economics and Sociology, as well as an appointment to Columbia's Department of Public Law and Government. After teaching sociology to Barnard undergraduates and political theory to Columbia graduate students for only a year, MacIver came to the attention of the sociology department's search committee. He was hired to lead the new phase of Columbia sociology in the winter of 1928.

COLUMBIA'S MOTIVES FOR AFFILIATING ITSELF WITH THE INSTITUTE FOR SOCIAL RESEARCH

As prestigious as Columbia's sociology program was, the department was lucky to hire Robert MacIver. By 1928, its very existence had come into question. As MacIver recalled, members of the Columbia community had many reasons to shake their heads. Some were still hesitant to support a field that aspired to do the work of all the other social sciences combined, while others lamented the woeful state of the department following Giddings's departure. Were it not for support from respected scholars such as John Dewey, President Nicholas Murray Butler might have followed his initial instincts and abolished sociology at Columbia.[11] Instead, the department survived under MacIver's direction, and it developed a long-range plan for the future with the help of the entire Faculty of Political Science. In an internal memorandum, members of the Faculty of Political Science agreed that the pursuit of empiricism was of the utmost importance.[12] Columbia's social scientists agreed that the quantitative method was the best way of positioning the social sciences on the same firm footing as the natural sciences, but they went on to recognize:

> the rise of the quantitative method means, from the administrative and budgetary point of view of the universities, revolutionizing the concept of research. The quantitative method is expensive, and must, distinctly, be seen on this plane. It is a big idea and needs to be treated in a big way. Just as the laboratory in the physical sciences was a big idea and meant large appropriations for equipment, materials, care, assistants, etc. If the universities do not meet this need in a proper way, they must inevitably become insignificant in a function which is properly their own. The achievement and prestige will pass to government such as the Bureau of Labor Statistics, the Department of Commerce, or to private bureaus such as the National Bureau of Economic Research and the National Industrial Conference Board, or to private industries such as the banks and the large corporations.[13]

A minimum budget of fifty thousand dollars was required from Columbia University to create the kind of social research bureau that the Faculty aspired to create on Morningside Heights. Such an institution would not need a great deal of technical equipment, but a large sum of money was needed to pay for calculators, travel and field research costs, and salaries to pay graduate students and to enable faculty members to leave their normal teaching assignments. To underscore the great task ahead of them, the Faculty of Political Science concluded its memorandum with the following warning:

> The situation with reference to research through quantitative measurement may really be described as a crisis. If this crisis is not met in a large way, achievement on the part of universities cannot be expected. Research of a *truly scientific nature* in the social sciences in America is far from being what it should be expected to be. The recent recognition of realizable possibilities in quantitative measurement puts the issue squarely up to the universities.[14]

The proposal was daring for an academic department of social science. Chicago's great achievements had largely been funded by Rockefeller money. The Faculty of Political Science was proposing something entirely different. By liberating itself from the government and private interests, Columbia obviously believed that it could pursue unique studies that would provide value in both their findings and pedagogic merits. It is impossible to say how this proposal would have fared on its own, because the stock market crash in the fall of 1929 made such an ambitious program impossible.

The Depression had mixed consequences for Columbia's Department of Sociology. Columbia, like all other institutions in the United States, was vulnerable to the economic dislocations of the 1930s. This led to the acceptance of new fiscal realities and limitations. MacIver had to regularly remind the department of the economic restraints imposed by the university. He emphasized the need for economy within the department.[15] During some years the fiscal crisis was so severe that MacIver and members of the department were forced to shift regular course offerings to the extension program in an effort to expand the teaching day so that all of the necessary courses could be offered without expanding the number of instructors.[16] At the same time, however, the Depression raised new questions about society, thus enhancing the role and prominence of social science.[17] The combination of these factors, the scaling back of activities matched with the growing demands for scientifically based social interventions and economic planning, must have caused tremendous frustrations for Columbia's sociologists throughout the 1930s. New York was an ideal vantage point for the study of the new social challenges in the United States during the Depression, but the Columbia sociologists were limited in their capabilities.

Despite the budgetary restraints imposed by the new economic realities, Columbia did enable the Department of Social Science to make one stride toward its goal of achieving a bureau for quantitative social research. Robert Lynd, the famous sociologist who had tarnished the image of the Rockefellers in Wyoming and who had coauthored the best-selling *Middletown,* was appointed to a professorship of sociology. Although MacIver recognized the importance of offering empirical social research at Columbia, he was personally opposed to the positivist trends in U.S. sociology that sought to model the discipline on the natural sciences.[18] Someone else would be needed to accomplish the task at Columbia. It was hoped that Lynd might lay the foundations for such work on Morningside Heights by initiating community studies similar to *Middletown.* At the time of his appointment in 1931, this may have been a reasonable expectation. Lynd's interests, however, began to shift after his arrival on Morningside Heights. As MacIver recalled, "I hoped he [Lynd] would initiate a program on the sociology of the metropolis, but he turned his interest in other directions."[19] By the time of the Horkheimer Circle's arrival in New York, pressing needs still remained for the sociology department of Columbia University.

Three essential conditions were in place at Columbia that played a role in the negotiations with the Institut für Sozialforschung. First, Columbia's social sciences were in a state of decline after a legacy of dominance. The complete abolition of the department had been narrowly averted, but the threat still hung in the air. Second, the entire Faculty of Political Science agreed that the most promising strategy for strengthening social science at Columbia was the formation of a bureau for quantitative methods in sociology. Such a plan held the promise of scientific certainty, as well as the facilities for the proper training of social researchers. Third, the Depression made the Faculty's proposal impossible. Robert Lynd was hired in an attempt to move in the direction of quantitative studies, but he was both

disinterested and overwhelmed by the task that lay ahead. If only an existing bureau that employed quantitative research methods and that was eco-
nomically self-sufficient were willing to place its services at Columbia's
disposal. How could the university's sociology department receive something for nothing?

THE INSTITUTE FOR SOCIAL RESEARCH INTRODUCES
ITSELF TO U.S. SOCIAL SCIENTISTS

There was really only one motive behind Horkheimer's desire to move
the Institute from Europe to the United States and that was the threat of
fascism's spread throughout the Continent. As members of the Horkheimer Circle surveyed the political situation from their new headquarters
in Geneva, they could not avoid the realization that fascist organizations
existed in nearly every European country. To Germany's first wave of exiles
it appeared as though all of Europe could succumb to the psychological
and political malady that had driven them from their homes.[20] The entire
group was unreservedly European in their tastes, attitudes, and mind-sets.
Consequently, the United States was not a place where they wished to relocate. They foresaw the terrible isolation and homesickness that would
inevitably lie ahead if they left the shores of the Continent. Nevertheless,
a second emigration seemed increasingly necessary as they monitored the
swirling forces of reaction enveloping them.

The Institute's move to the United States might never have been possible were it not for the efforts of two figures within the Horkheimer Circle. From start to finish, Erich Fromm and Julian Gumperz directed every
step of the Institute's campaign for affiliation with an American social-
scientific institution. The job fell to these two men partly as a result of
their preexisting contacts with Americans, but also because of their abilities with the English language.

Their first step was to develop contacts between the Institute and
American scholars. The Horkheimer Circle realized that their work would
not be familiar to the American academic community, and they set out
to rectify the situation by introducing themselves and their writings. The
Frankfurt School put together a series of mailings. Enclosed with copies
of the *Zeitschrift für Sozialforschung* and with preliminary reports on their
studies of authority and the family was an English letter written by Fromm
and Gumperz introducing the Institute and its work. Few packets were

sent to the United States, and it appears that Fromm and Gumperz were highly selective about the individuals and institutions that they approached. They tended to concentrate on U.S. social scientists or departments of sociology with interests similar to those of the Institute. Specifically, they sent mailings to scholars who were intrigued by topics such as authority, the family, social psychology, economics, and labor. Among the individuals receiving these materials were Lewis Lorwin of the Brookings Institution, Pitirim Sorokin of Harvard University, W. F. Ogburn of the University of Chicago, and Robert MacIver of Columbia University, as well as the departments of sociology at the University of Wisconsin, the University of North Carolina, the University of Michigan, UCLA, Yale University, and Bryn Mawr.[21] As the mailings were sent out from Geneva, Fromm and Gumperz traveled to the United States in order to meet in person with the interested recipients.

As one of Germany's prominent Freudians, Fromm had contacts with members of the psychoanalytic network that circled the globe. Consequently, most of Fromm's American contacts were analysts. His closest associates in the United States were Karen Horney and Franz Alexander of the Chicago Psychoanalytic Institute.[22] Before Horkheimer had even begun to seriously consider a move to the United States, Fromm was invited to the Chicago Institute by Horney. He traveled to the United States in 1932 with plans of being affiliated with Horney and Alexander for a semester or two: however, he left after an abbreviated stay in Chicago. The hasty departure was partly due to serious illness (Fromm suffered a bout with tuberculosis at this time, forcing him to enter a sanitarium),[23] and was partly the result of major disagreements with his hosts about Freudian orthodoxy.[24] Nevertheless, Fromm did have time to develop contacts with social scientists and social psychologists at the University of Chicago. By the fall of 1933 and the spring of 1934, when Horkheimer was pursuing the establishment of an American bureau for the Institute for Social Research, Fromm returned to Chicago to approach his old friends about a possible affiliation with the Horkheimer Circle.[25] The primary contacts at Chicago were Karen Horney, Harold Lasswell, W. F. Ogburn, and Donald Slessinger, who were particularly interested in the Horkheimer Circle's use of social psychology in their studies of authority and the family.[26] Although Fromm may have privately hoped that Horkheimer would select Chicago as a base of operations, he quickly backed down when he learned that his counterpart, Julian Gumperz, had negotiated an extremely desirable relationship with Columbia University.[27]

JULIAN GUMPERZ AND THE NEGOTIATIONS WITH COLUMBIA UNIVERSITY

It is surprising how little is known about Julian Gumperz, especially when one considers that he enabled the Institut für Sozialforschung to move to the United States. The histories of the Horkheimer Circle typically mention him briefly with regard to the group's Atlantic crossing, but little else is ever reported. He played a prominent role in Feuer's accusations about the Frankfurt School's Communist connections and fellow traveling, but only a narrow picture of the man's political life was uncovered. Who was Julian Gumperz and how did he make the Horkheimer Circle's affiliation with Columbia possible?

Sociologically, Gumperz fit the profile that is so common to the members of the Horkheimer Circle. His family was Jewish, and he was raised as a member of the upper-middle class. The one distinguishing characteristic that set his childhood apart was the fact that he was born in the United States, and his father made a fortune as an industrialist. The family remained in the United States until after the First World War, but Gumperz left for Germany fluent in the English language and maintaining his American citizenship. Like Horkheimer and the other members of the Institute, Gumperz was drawn to Marx as a student. Originally, he was attracted to the Communist-sponsored arts councils and eventually edited journals such as *Der Gegner* and *Rote Fahne,* but his travels in the USSR during the spring of 1923 stimulated a burning interest in economics and sociology.

His contacts with the Institut für Sozialforschung date back to before its formation. Gumperz and his wife attended the Marxist Study Week sponsored by Felix Weil and maintained cordial relations with the group while he studied for his PhD at the University of Heidelberg. After receiving his degree, Gumperz became a formal research associate of the Institute and served as an assistant to Friedrich Pollock. When Horkheimer began the *Zeitschrift für Sozialforschung,* Gumperz supplied many of the reviews of American contributions to the social sciences, helping to add to the journal's international orientation. By 1932, however, Gumperz began to drift out of the Institute's orbit. He had never been one of the central figures in the new Horkheimer directorship, and he was growing weary with his small role. He moved away from the Institute to Berlin, where he began to formulate the basis for a monograph on the sociology of the American political party system. The proposed project did not interest the hierarchy of the Institut für Sozialforschung, and Gumperz became angry about his lack of financial support. Meanwhile, Horkheimer also began to grow tired of the estranged associate in Berlin. Horkheimer required the utmost loyalty and diligence from the members of his circle, and Gumperz's increasingly erratic behavior troubled him. By the spring of 1932, Gumperz turned to other organizations in an effort to finance a research trip to the United States. Despite his apparent misgivings, Horkheimer did succumb to bullying from Gumperz and provided the former research associate with references.[28] Gumperz's most promising lead was a fellowship from the Brookings Institution. He mailed his application to Lewis Lorwin, a member of the faculty, and Horkheimer enclosed an accompanying letter of recommendation in which he wrote:

> Dr. Julian Gumperz is a scientific worker of the highest quality. He has a thorough knowledge of methods and economics and also has a very high opinion of the responsibility of scientific activity and a serious discipline of work. He combines those qualities with a real ability for independent analysis of different economic problems. I am convinced that the decision of the Fellowship Committee in favor of Dr. Gumperz would only bear the best results. Therefore I recommend Dr. Gumperz very heartily.[29]

Despite Horkheimer's succinct endorsement, Gumperz's application was rejected, and he returned to writing book reviews for the *Zeitschrift für Sozialforschung*. Gumperz now looked for an alternate means of getting to the United States to pursue his study of its political party system.

When Horkheimer began to consider establishing a U.S. branch of the Institute to escape to if the political situation worsened in Europe, Gumperz recognized the possibility for pursuing his own ambitions. Horkheimer clearly wanted Gumperz's assistance. Of all of the people connected with the Institute, Gumperz was the most familiar with the recent developments in American social science. Fromm knew many American psychoanalysts and social psychologists, but he did not yet know the important sociologists and economists in the United States. Gumperz knew these people's work and was fluent in their language. As Horkheimer viewed it, his participation in any negotiations would be essential. In an attempt to guarantee Gumperz's involvement, Horkheimer and Pollock promised that he would be hired as the director of the resulting American bureau.[30] What they failed to tell him was that Horkheimer would assume control if the headquarters of the Institute was moved from Geneva to the United States. Gumperz, however, was likely more enticed by the possibility of having the Horkheimer Circle pay for him to live in the United States. Negotiating a future home for the Institute in the United States would enable him to carry out his research on the American party system.

There are few records of the Institute for Social Research's contacts with Columbia University prior to the summer of 1934 when Horkheimer personally traveled to New York to negotiate the final arrangements with the school's administration. We do know that by January 1933 Robert MacIver received the group's mailing and was intrigued by what he found.[31] There are, however, no other records of activity or communication between the Horkheimer Circle and Columbia after this point. We can assume that Gumperz must have visited with members of the Columbia sociology department during the winter of 1933–34, but there is no record of any contact. Further clouding the picture is the fact that those who knew them agree that neither MacIver nor Lynd read German well enough to have entirely grasped the Institute's work.[32] If these assessments are true, it means that Columbia's social scientists must have been influenced largely by their contact with Gumperz, and they also must have sought an outside assessment of the Institute. Based on the department's precarious position within Columbia University, it is highly unlikely that MacIver and Lynd would have stuck their necks out for the Horkheimer Circle without endorsements from other U.S. scholars. But who could have been familiar with the Institute's work and also been a close ally of the social sciences at Columbia?

Many people could certainly fit the description. Members of the New School's University in Exile would have been familiar with both groups, but there are no records of any such connections until after the Frankfurt School's arrival in New York. Furthermore, there is evidence suggesting that when the faculty of the New School did share their opinions on the Horkheimer group, the assessments were generally negative.[33] The people from the University of Chicago might have been an intermediary, but there is no evidence suggesting this either, and it is unlikely that Chicago would have encouraged its Columbia rivals to host the Horkheimer Circle.

Paul Lazarsfeld is another possible candidate. He was a longtime acquaintance of the Frankfurt School and had even collaborated with it in
Europe. Lazarsfeld was a brilliant empirical researcher with impeccable
credentials. Born and raised in Vienna, he shared a background similar to
the members of the Horkheimer Circle. His family was Jewish and highly
assimilated, and his upbringing was distinctly upper-middle class. At a
young age, Lazarsfeld became a devoted student of both psychoanalysis
and Marxism, although his formal academic training was in mathematics.
When he finished his studies at university, Lazarsfeld combined his interest
in psychology with his training in math. Initially, he began working with
several prominent Viennese psychologists to assist with their empirical research, but he eventually founded Vienna's Economic and Psychological
Research Group. Based on the outstanding reputation that Lazarsfeld made
for himself with several studies of adolescents in particular, the Rockefeller
Foundation took an interest in the Austrian researcher. Lazarsfeld was in
the United States under the auspices of the foundation when the troubles
in Austria began. When Lazarsfeld learned that the constitution in his native
country had been eliminated, thereby endangering socialists and Marxists,
he made his decision to remain in the United States. He extended his
scholarship and with the help of Robert Lynd established a research group
at Newark University. He thus was in a fortuitous position to assist the
Frankfurt School during the moment that negotiations with Columbia
University were occurring. Not only was he friends with Robert Lynd during his first years in the United States, but also he had recently completed
his own study of the family in Vienna. He certainly knew the Frankfurt
School's work and he may have even met Gumperz in New York during
the winter of 1933–34. Again, there are, however, no records of any such
connections in either the Institute's extensive archives or among Lazarsfeld's papers.

The only name that does come up frequently in conjunction with both
the Horkheimer group and Columbia's sociology department is Lewis Lorwin. Lorwin, formerly known as Lewis Levine, was a product of Columbia's Faculty of Political Science. Born in Kiev in 1883, his family traveled
throughout Europe, enabling the young boy to be educated in Russia,
Switzerland, and France. Lorwin's primary interest was sociology, and he
enrolled in Columbia's PhD program in the social sciences.[34] He received
a scholarship and his adviser was none other than Franklin Giddings, the

patriarch of Columbia sociology. When asked by his famous mentor about his projected thesis topic, Lorwin ambitiously disclosed vague plans about a project on social evolution. Giddings steered him toward a dissertation on French Syndicalism in an effort to give focus and direction to the study. Lorwin acquiesced, and the shift in subject matter had significant consequences for the student's subsequent career.[35] Lorwin grew close to Edwin Seligman, one of the department's early social economists, and he discovered his passions for the study of economics and the labor movement—two subject matters that dominated his attention throughout a long and distinguished career in the social sciences.

Lorwin's early professional life was extremely varied. He briefly taught at Wellesley College and Columbia and then moved to a more permanent position at the University of Montana. The move west fascinated Lorwin, and it also transformed the man of science into a public intellectual. Lorwin became outraged when he discovered the unfair tax practices being exploited by Montana mining companies. Because of various loopholes in the laws, wealthy mining companies were paying lower taxes than poverty-stricken farmers. Much to the horror of the university's president, Edward Elliot, Lorwin joined the political fracas by helping the Montana legislature draft two tax reform bills and publicized the case in newspapers throughout the country. The controversy became quite famous, like Robert Lynd's early battle over mining with the Rockefellers in Wyoming. The major difference in Montana was that Lorwin lost his war with the mining industry. The bills failed to be passed, and Lorwin was suspended from his teaching duties. Lorwin took the University of Montana to court, but eventually decided to leave after teaching for only three years.

After these adventures in Montana, Lorwin experimented with a number of different careers before returning to academia. His first new job was as a journalist. He began as a reporter in the field of economics with the *New York World* and later embarked on one of the great adventures of his life—a trip to the Soviet Union as a writer for the *Chicago Daily News* during 1921 and 1922. The trip to Russia enabled Lorwin to witness the social and economic conditions firsthand. Although Lorwin remained a man of the Left with strong sympathies for the labor movement, his travels in the Soviet Union led to a complete and thorough rejection of Russian Communism. He returned to New York's Greenwich Village after the death of his wife's father in 1923 and found a new job that led him back into the world of academia. He was hired by the International League of Garment Workers' Unions to write the history of the organization for its twenty-fifth anniversary. Because there were no precedents for such a project, Lorwin completed a vast amount of research and produced a study that made him a highly visible figure in the field of labor history.[36]

The fame led to Lorwin's appointment with the Brookings Institution. During the fall of 1924, Harold Moulton, the head of the Brookings, hired Lorwin as a specialist in its labor division. His first major project for the Brookings was a study of the international labor movement, titled *Labor and Internationalism*. He began his research in 1926, and it brought him to every major European nation. His first task was to study the labor movements in all of the countries of Europe, particularly looking for international connections between the various organizations. He then looked at the handful of international labor groups and examined the obstacles facing them. During these years, it is likely that Lorwin first met many of the people connected with both the Horkheimer Circle and the International Labor Organization, which hosted the Institut für Sozialforschung years later in Geneva. Although enthusiastic about the promise of an international labor movement, Lorwin was critical of the efforts he witnessed. He found that European labor was poorly organized and that the international institutions were too small to be effective. When he returned to the United States to write his monograph, Lorwin had to resort to his own imagination in order to conceptualize the kind of effective labor movement that he one day hoped to see.[37] The resulting book received international acclaim, and Julian Gumperz was among its many European reviewers. As Lorwin later recalled:

This [referring to a press clipping that Lorwin showed the interviewer] appeared in Leipzig, Germany, by a man called Julian Gumperz, now an investment consultant in New York City and making lots of money. At the time he was a left-wing Socialist and editor of a Marxist magazine. I saw him a year or two ago at a luncheon, and he's sort of forgotten the old days but still it's in his blood. He says: "Louis [*sic*] Lorwin, as a result of his two books on Syndicalism in France and the women's garment workers, is already well-known to large circles as a writer who combines wide knowledge of history and theory of the labor movement with a scientific objectivity quite unusual in this field of study." I've always prided myself that people have recognized that I was objective. Then he says, the importance of this book and so on, which I won't read on. (157)

Gumperz's high regard for Lorwin may explain why the latter's name topped the Frankfurt School's mailing list. It is also clear, however, that Gumperz left an equally lasting impression on the Brookings Institution's young star.

Labor and Internationalism represented a new turning point in Lorwin's career that led to closer affiliations with the International Labor Organization in Geneva (159–65). The book alerted him to the importance of monitoring international economics, and he felt the need to focus on international history and international relations. It also signaled the beginning of Lorwin's interest in economic planning (168–69). The International Labor Organization became an important resource for Lorwin because of its similar focuses. Although his plan to pursue these new concerns by taking up residency in Geneva with the international labor organizations was put on hold until 1935 because of deadlines with his second Brookings monograph on the American Federation of Labor (AFL), Lorwin kept close contact with colleagues in Geneva and probably visited during trips to Europe throughout the early 1930s. This is the only way to explain the numerous contacts between Lorwin and the Horkheimer Circle.

Evidence suggests that both parties were extremely familiar with one another during the early 1930s. We already know about Lorwin being one of the first recipients of the Institute's mailing, we are aware of Gumperz's review of Lorwin's book on labor and internationalism, and we also have noted that Gumperz directed his application for a Brookings fellowship to Lewis Lorwin. In addition, the Horkheimer Circle seriously considered translating and then publishing Lorwin's book on the AFL. After the success of *Labor and Internationalism*, Lorwin felt that his new book also needed a worldwide audience. He evidently contacted Pollock in the fall of 1932 while the Institute was still based in Frankfurt—suggesting that the two became acquainted with one another during the German phase of Lorwin's research for the labor book.[38] Apparently feeling that the AFL book had merit, Pollock wrote to the Institute's best translator of English, Julian Gumperz, and asked whether he wanted to translate it. Gumperz, who perhaps was still wounded by his rejection from the Brookings, refused the project on the grounds that it would take up too much of his

time and would cut into his own work, which he incidentally viewed as
being similar to Lorwin's.[39] Pollock renewed the offer by sending Gumperz
an overview of the book and its table of contents, but the assignment
was again rejected because of concerns about the manuscript's length—
Gumperz suggested cutting it by more than a third.[40] Although the collaboration between the Institute for Social Research and Lewis Lorwin
did not bear fruit in terms of a translated edition of the AFL book, it may
have served as the basis for a relationship between the two parties. The
Institute tried to come to Lorwin's aid, and it may be the case that Lorwin
attempted to return the favor by helping the Institute settle in the United
States.

Of greatest significance is evidence suggesting a face-to-face meeting
that took place between Lewis Lorwin and Friedrich Pollock.[41] Pollock
sought Lorwin's advice about possibly moving the Institut für Sozialforschung to the United States. Because Pollock didn't arrive in the United
States before August 1934 and Lorwin wrote to Horkheimer about meeting Pollock in a letter dated 3 July 1934, we must assume that the conference took place in Europe. We can further narrow the date and location
of the rendezvous by considering the agenda. Because Horkheimer did not
even consider moving the Institute to the United States until the group
had resettled in Geneva, we must assume that Lorwin and Pollock met in
Geneva, probably during one of Lorwin's visits to the International Labor
Organization. But did Lorwin act as the intermediary between Columbia's
social scientists and the Frankfurt School?

Lorwin's new focus on internationalism put him in touch with one of
the future key figures of Columbia's sociology department. James Shotwell, the chair of the international relations committee of the Social Science Research Council (SSRC), sought to involve Lorwin in the group's
activities. In particular, he sought Lorwin's expertise in arranging an SSRC
trip to the Soviet Union. Lorwin, who was planning a second visit to
the USSR in preparation for *Labor and Internationalism,* was evidently a
valued expert on Russian affairs.[42] During the time of this collaboration
with the SSRC, Lorwin became friends with the organization's permanent
secretary, Robert Lynd. Lynd, who after the completion of *Middletown*
was offered the SSRC job by friends within the organization, first worked
with Lorwin on the Russian expedition. The two later renewed their friendship during the Great Depression. Lorwin, who became a well-known

proponent of economic planning while serving on LaFollette's Committee on Manufacturing, attracted Lynd's interest again. Lynd, who in 1931 was appointed to a professorship of sociology at Columbia, invited Lorwin frequently to New York, where the two discussed the merits of planned economies.[43]

An examination of Columbia's administrative files on the Institute for Social Research suggests that Lewis Feuer was correct in noting the central role played by Robert Lynd in the negotiations between the Horkheimer Circle and the university.[44] There is, however, no evidence of his involvement being motivated by fellow-traveling zeal. In fact, there is strong evidence suggesting that Lynd was a staunch opponent of Russian Communism. As Lewis Corey reported to Lynd in a letter of 12 December 1950:

> [S. M.] Lipsett told me you were not a fellow-traveler; that for two years you had been outspokenly anti-communist and opposed communists as professors on the ground that they could not teach with integrity.[45]

Clearly, Lynd's close friends and colleagues realized the true nature of his political convictions. Lynd became a suspected fellow traveler after signing up as a sponsor of the Cultural and Scientific Congress for World Peace in 1949. For Cold War anti-Communists like Lewis Feuer, such acts were clear causes for suspicion. In the hysterical environment of Cold War America, Lynd, like many other American intellectuals, was unfairly scrutinized and attacked on the grounds of his moral and intellectual positions. By focusing only on possible political motives for Lynd's involvement with the Frankfurt School, Feuer ignored the more compelling reasons for Lynd's interest in the Horkheimer Circle. One must carefully consider Robert Lynd's sociological interests during the time of the Institute for Social Research's negotiations with Columbia.

During the late 1920s and early 1930s when Lynd and Lorwin were meeting to discuss SSRC business and planned economies, Lynd was involved with a number of inquiries that he viewed as some of the most urgent tasks facing American social science. It is striking how many of these projects overlap with the interests and orientation of the Horkheimer Circle during the early years of Horkheimer's directorship.

During an SSRC conference at the Brookings Institution held during

February 1931, Robert Lynd gave a talk titled "Possibilities of Cooperation among Research Institutions." Lynd stood before his colleagues (and Lorwin is likely to have been one of them because the meeting was at his institutional home) and surveyed the social sciences in America. His central message was that increasingly complex studies must be encouraged, but lone researchers were increasingly becoming less able to carry out such research. The only solution was to foster cooperation between researchers and even between research teams. While exploring the various possibilities for cooperative work, Lynd reserved his greatest admiration for the form of collaboration practiced by the Horkheimer Circle. As if having the Institut für Sozialforschung in mind, Lynd said:

> There are different patterns of cooperation in research, some of them amounting only to a kind of pseudo-cooperation. At its simplest, cooperative research may consist in giving the expert a corps of pick-and-shovel junior assistants to speed along his labors. A more complicated pattern involves the association of a group of specialists in a single discipline for mutual inter-stimulation and, in some cases, joint attack upon a common problem. Still a third pattern, the most complicated of all, is the association of men from radically diverse disciplines for joint action upon some problem sprawled across all their fields. The first two of these patterns are fairly common and the third as yet largely a matter of occasional experimental forays.[46]

As if echoing Horkheimer's own inaugural address given during his appointment as the new director of the Institut für Sozialforschung, Lynd emphasized the importance of gathering experts across different disciplines and working together in the singular goal of producing a unified theory of society.[47] When Horkheimer had outlined the new design for his Institute, he proclaimed that

> the question today is to organize investigations stimulated by contemporary philosophical problems in which philosophers, sociologists, economists, historians, and psychologists are brought together in permanent collection to undertake in common that which can be carried out individually in the laboratory in other fields. In short the task is to do what all true researchers have always done: namely, to pursue their larger philosophical questions

on the basis of the most precise scientific methods, to revise and refine their questions in the course of their substantive work, and to develop new methods without losing sight of the larger context.[48]

Intellectually, Robert Lynd was a kindred spirit who would have been highly attracted to the Institute's brand of social research. If his German was good enough to understand the Horkheimer Circle's writings, he must have realized this while he read through the packet sent to Robert MacIver. If, however, he could not read German adequately, Julian Gumperz, and quite probably Lewis Lorwin, made him better aware of the Institute and its program.

In addition to sharing similar methodological attitudes regarding the practice and structure of effective sociological institutions, Lynd also shared specific research interests with the Horkheimer group during the time that an affiliation with Columbia was being considered. Like the research teams led by Erich Fromm, Lynd was also studying the effects of the Depression on families. As MacIver had noted, Columbia expected Lynd to continue his work in community studies, but Lynd's interests had shifted to a new subject—the family. Instead of studying other "Middletowns," Lynd had become intrigued by the smaller institutional units that formed the basis of communities. This fascination was stimulated further by the Depression. Like Fromm, Lynd saw the family as a crucial social site from which to view the effects of economic dislocation, because the family was the institution mediating the relationship between individuals and society.

On 14 March 1933, Lynd submitted a memorandum to the SSRC and Columbia University's Research Council outlining his program for studying the family during the Depression.[49] According to Lynd, the timing was perfect for his research plans:

> The unusual opportunity which the depression affords for the study of the interaction of personality and culture in this fundamental institution derives from three things: (1) The extraordinary catholicity of the current financial depression which is touching directly or indirectly all classes, including the well-to-do who are ordinarily cushioned against most sorts of sudden cultural pressure; (2) the fact that we can as a result study families of all types and incomes simultaneously placed under single centrally-derived

sources of strain, almost as if by design in a laboratory; (3) the testimony of investigators in many fields touching the family that it is actually notably easier to get intimate family data from "normal" families than it was prior to the depression.[50]

The research plan called for three synchronized approaches: first, a statistical study of the internal and external functions of families and their members derived from data regarding participation in public organizations (recreations, schools, churches, etc.), delinquency rates, marriage and childbirth rates, and trends in wage earning; second, the use of questionnaires and oral interviews to survey the broad effects of the depression; and third, the use of case studies.[51] The program, consequently, entailed the kind of close collaboration between sociologists and psychologists that the Horkheimer Circle's own studies of the family involved.

There is no record of the SSRC's initial response to Lynd's proposal, but there is evidence suggesting that Lynd's colleagues at Columbia disapproved of the project. In a memorandum dated 1 May 1933 attached to the original research proposal, Lynd pleaded with the members of the university's subcommittee on sociological and anthropological projects (composed of Robert MacIver, Samuel Lindsay, and Franz Boas).[52] All three apparently disapproved of Lynd's cross-disciplinary approach and were particularly troubled by his planned reliance on psychology. Lynd protested that the subcommittee "condemned out of hand an entire discipline and made no effort to inquire into the capacity of the specific psychiatrist involved."[53] He alerted his opponents to the fact that both the SSRC and the Social Science Division of the Rockefeller Foundation had been promoting cooperation between psychology and the other social sciences for several years. Sensing the uselessness of his pleas and counterarguments, Lynd concluded by suggesting that the Columbia Council only fund five thousand dollars for the sociological portion of the project. Meanwhile, he would seek the additional $1,400 necessary for the psychiatric portion of the study from less hostile sources. By supporting an affiliation with the Horkheimer Circle, Lynd might have sensed that he was striking back at the opponents of his proposal. By supporting the Institute, he could expect to have new allies on Morningside Heights that shared his sociological orientation and research interests. Additionally, he could finally complete the task that MacIver had set for him. Perhaps through cooperation with the Institute, he could fulfill the expectations that had been placed on his shoulders at the time of his hiring—the achievement of a social research bureau.

The Institute had a natural ally in Robert Lynd. In order to appeal to the rest of the sociology department, it would need to convince the other faculty members of the Horkheimer Circle's commitment to quantitative methods. We cannot be certain about whether Lorwin and/or Lynd ever made this known to the Institute. Perhaps chance played a role. Whatever the case, Gumperz and the Institute convinced Columbia. Although there are no records or notes from Gumperz's meetings with members of the university faculty and administration, we do know how the Horkheimer Circle represented itself in legal documents drafted only months before the move to the United States. In the Constitution for the International Society of Social Research drawn up by the New York law firm of Mitchell, Taylor, Capron and Marsh, the Institute's U.S. legal team proclaimed:

> The sole object of the corporation shall be to render social service. It will study problems of international welfare, and will endeavor to solve the same by means of social research, the application of scientific knowledge, and by assembling necessary data and other appropriate means.[54]

This only represents, however, a small part of the picture that must have been presented to Columbia. Although we cannot be entirely sure of the other pieces of this image, we can be reasonably certain about how the Institute introduced itself to the American public just after its arrival in New York during the summer of 1934. By the fall of that year, Julian Gumperz had been assigned the task of fund-raising. For this purpose, a speech was prepared.[55] The presence of editorial markings in the handwritings of both Pollock and Horkheimer suggests that the leaders of the Institute had been closely involved in the writing of this talk. Because it is unlikely that the Horkheimer Circle would have had much time to prepare an entirely new strategy for appealing to American social scientists, it seems reasonable that the speech is a good representation of the way in which the group approached Columbia. If the text of Gumperz's talk is any indication of the content for his negotiations with Columbia, the Institute for Social Research must have appeared to be the answer to the sociology department's prayers.

Gumperz's fund-raising speech emphasized the role of science in the Institute's agenda. Appealing to the orientation of American sociologists in the audiences, Gumperz concluded his introductory paragraph with the promise: "I intend to start with an analysis of the scientific aims of this organization [the Institute for Social Research], and the methods by which we hope to achieve them." What was new and significant about the Institute's approach was that its members promised to go beyond the mere gathering of social facts that typified so much of American social research. Instead, they proclaimed their determination to never lose sight of the relationship of social data to the social totality. Gumperz insisted that too many American social scientists were guilty of surrendering the whole to its component parts. As Gumperz explained:

> as soon as you approach the problem as a whole,—as soon as you try to interrelate the accumulations of social facts stored away in the safe-deposit boxes of the different specialized social science disciplines,—as soon as you attempt to deal with the problems of society as a whole,—you find that the social sciences have no answer to your problems on hand.

The Institute for Social Research, Gumperz insisted, had been conceived with the goal of circumventing this flaw. It would accomplish this task by formulating a common set of theoretical assumptions about social structures and their development over time. Gumperz failed to elaborate on any of this. Instead, he attempted to set the Institute's work apart from other research organizations in the most general fashion. As he explained to the Horkheimer Circle's potential patrons:

> So when, in the beginning of the 20s, a group of German scholars set themselves the task of organizing a new enterprise in their field—the Institute for Social Research—(then at the University of Frankfurt)—the ideas they had in mind were to further with their efforts a theory of present society as an integrated and moving body, and to conduct the research work proposed in light of a unifying principle that would differentiate the work done from a mere description and enumeration of facts, and would guard it at the same time from the danger that threatens every abstract theory,—namely, of failing when put to the test of practical application.

Of course, political critics of the Frankfurt School, such as Lewis Feuer, would see the Institute's hesitancy in only the worst light. Its members did not elaborate their abstract theory, because it was Marxist in orientation. Their refusal to describe their theory of society is one of their many acts of treachery. The text of Gumperz's speech, however, does not bear this out. Although the theory is left undeveloped, Gumperz did signal the group's political sympathies:

> The present period in which we live is not only a period of extremely un-settled economic, social and political conditions the world over, but appears to me to be characterized also by a deep and fundamental crisis that has affected the scientific activities of mankind in their broader aspects. While there are in the world today more elements of material wealth available than ever before in history, there seems to exist, on the other hand, insuperable barriers to utilizing them correspondingly for the benefit of the large masses of humanity.

As this suggests, there was nothing ambiguous about the group's basic attitude toward the modern industrial society of the 1930s. They abhorred the inequitable distribution of wealth in the world, especially when juxta-posed against the vast material prosperity of bourgeois elites.

Although the group's ideas were generally presented as left of center, Gumperz did insist on the Institute's respectability as a social research organization. He made a great point of emphasizing the Horkheimer Circle's ties with the International Labor Office in Geneva, as well as with the small bureaus established by the Sorbonne and the Institute of Sociology in London. Clearly, the implication being made was that the Institute did have cordial and close relations with a number of prestigious sociological institutions in Europe. If it were good enough for the likes of the Sorbonne, it certainly would be able to meet the needs of an institution in turmoil like Columbia.

In his conclusion, Gumperz emphasized the main selling points of the Institute. He divided its projects into four basic categories. First, he briefly outlined the individual research projects being pursued by members of the Horkheimer Circle. In particular, he mentioned the economic studies of planning in the Soviet Union, Horkheimer's sociological analysis of the history of philosophy, a study of criminal justice by Georg Rusche that was subsidized by the Institute, and Karl Wittfogel's analysis of Chinese society. Second, he called attention to the Institute's collaborative effort to study authority and the family. This was perhaps the Institute's greatest asset from the perspective of Columbia's needs. Gumperz, as if fully aware of this fact, stated:

> there is an effort to organize on a cooperative basis the scientific work of students working in the different fields of the social sciences—economics, history, psychology, social philosophy, and so on,—and to coordinate the work of these different scientists in tackling a special problem. At present, the problem of the family in present day society has been selected for this purpose, because the family, as one of the basic units of the social organization, lends itself to that type of scientific approach that I have been trying to outline.

Lynd, in particular, must not have believed his ears when he heard that a group of German sociologists not only were carrying out the style of collaborative research that he valued so highly but also were studying the same subject matter. Third, Gumperz briefly outlined the program for a second cooperative study of economic planning. He admitted that the study was indefinitely on hold owing to a lack of sufficient funds. Even though this proposal never moved beyond the early stages, it would have attracted tremendous interest from Lorwin, Lynd, and many other American social scientists. It was one of the most hotly debated topics in the United States and was sure to have caught Columbia's attention. Fourth, Gumperz concluded by mentioning the *Zeitschrift*. The magazine provided a constant outlet for Institute publications. Collectively, this represented an enormous set of research projects and writings. If Columbia was presented with all of this information, it is no wonder that it quickly loaned the Institute a building at 428 West 117th Street. This was an arrangement that could not be passed up under any circumstances. The potential benefits were enormous and there were almost no downsides for Columbia University.

chapter 2

FAILURE AND THE MYTHOLOGIES OF EXILE

The Frankfurt School's Years at Columbia University

The Frankfurt School's first years on Morningside Heights progressed smoothly. In addition to achieving an almost uninterrupted continuation of the Institute's past activities—such as the publication of the *Zeitschrift für Sozialforschung* and the data gathering and analysis for the research begun in Europe—the circle of researchers surrounding Max Horkheimer expanded during the first years in exile. The most notable additions to the Institute's core were Theodor W. Adorno, Otto Kirchheimer, Franz Neumann, and Walter Benjamin. The latter thinkers contributed to the evolution of Critical Theory that took place during the Frankfurt School's U.S. sojourn, and also assisted Horkheimer with the academic diplomacy and grantsmanship that became necessary in the United States (the one notable exception in this administrative capacity was Walter Benjamin, who never escaped Nazi Europe). These scholars were completely new to the Institute and brought new talents and insights with them.

Theodor W. Adorno was an exception in that he had been corresponding with Horkheimer ever since they had worked together in Frankfurt. Consequently, when Horkheimer finally made a serious job offer to him, Adorno snatched up the opportunity, abandoning his study of Husserl, which surely would have earned him a DPhil from Oxford University—where Adorno had fled after the situation in Germany became too dangerous for him. Upon his return to the Institute, Adorno discovered that Horkheimer had new plans as to his role within the group. In addition to his duties as the Institute's expert on music, Adorno was also invited to get involved with the philosophical work being pursued by Horkheimer and Marcuse.

Further facilitating Adorno's emigration to the United States was a job offer arranged by Horkheimer but extended by Paul Lazarsfeld, who had become an important contributor to the Institute's sociological work of the late 1930s and 1940s.[1] The job was working on Lazarsfeld's Radio Research Project, which represented the first serious study of radio as a means of mass communication and culture. Through his skills as both a talented researcher and a shrewd administrator, Lazarsfeld rapidly established a reputation in the United States and was approached (again with the recommendation of Robert Lynd) by Hadley Cantril to direct a major study of the effects of radio on the American public.

Partly because of their shared links to Robert Lynd and partly as a result of their past collaborations, Lazarsfeld was also a friend and adviser of the exiled Institute for Social Research. Horkheimer was impressed with Lazarsfeld's empirical background, and he began to seek consultation with Lazarsfeld with regard to a number of studies that Horkheimer and the Institute had undertaken during the 1930s.[2] The informal relationship developed into a professional one by 1938. By this point, Lazarsfeld was included as a research associate within the Institute for Social Reasearch. But, although Lazarsfeld remained an important adviser on research methodology and empirical matters, he was never a central figure within the Institute. Part of this was a result of personality differences, and the rest was owing to the fact that Lazarsfeld was assembling his own research institution devoted to the study of radio.

Another figure who played a modest role in the Institute and was only loosely affiliated during the exile years was Otto Kirchheimer. Like nearly all of the other members of the Horkheimer Circle, Kirchheimer was a German Jew. However, unlike most of them, he was trained in law and social science. A longtime supporter of the SPD, Kirchheimer completed his dissertation with Carl Schmitt on constitutional theory and Bolshevism. He wrote articles on constitutional law and taught courses at the trade union colleges during the late years of the Weimar Republic while working as a lawyer in Berlin.[3] When the Nazis rose to power in 1933, Kirchheimer left Germany for Paris. Once in France, he shifted his area of expertise to criminal and French law. He continued to publish and soon became involved with the Parisian branch office of the Institut für Sozialforschung. As a result of these contacts, Kirchheimer came to Horkheimer's attention. Consequently, when Kirchheimer decided to emigrate to the United States in 1937–38, Horkheimer assisted with the legal formalitites required by the American government. Horkheimer, however, who was beginning to grow concerned about taking on too large a staff at the Institute, only offered Kirchheimer a minor position with a modest salary.

Also during the late 1930s, Franz Neumann became the other legal expert at the Institute. Socially and culturally, Neumann shared the same German Jewish roots that were so common in the Institute, but socioeconomically he came from a more modest background. Politically, Neumann was also different from the rest of Horkheimer's associates. He had been active within the reform-minded wing of the SPD for many years. He was a champion of trade unionism, and he envisioned a socialization of the state that would progress through peaceful, slow, democratic means. His academic training was in philosophy and law, and he became a trade-union lawyer in Berlin following the completion of his dissertation. He remained a tireless worker and supporter of the SPD throughout the Weimar years. In fact, he achieved the highest-ranking legal position in the party when he was promoted to serve as its head legal consultant. When the Nazis came to power, Neumann attempted to remain in Germany and to continue his legal and political work. As the atmosphere became too dangerous, he fled to England, where he received a grant to study political science with Harold Laski.[4] While working toward his degree, he was hired by the London branch of the Institut für Sozialforschung to protect its library and financial assets in Europe. The legal services to the Institute were neither glamorous nor interesting, but Horkheimer was grateful for Neumann's efforts. They met in London in 1936, and Neumann volunteered to promote the *Zeitschrift* among English academics as well as to write contributions. That same year, the Institute brought Neumann to the United States and attempted to find a university post for him. Because of the tight job market, they settled on hiring him as a lawyer to handle many of the Institute's legal affairs, and they also appointed him as a research associate.

The final figure of influence, who entered the Horkheimer Circle during the years of exile in the United States, is Walter Benjamin. Although Benjamin was primarily a friend and associate of Adorno's and despite the fact that he was never part of Horkheimer's inner circle (or a resident

member of the Institute), his thought had important implications for Horkheimer and Adorno, as well as for the future direction of Critical Theory.
Benjamin came from a prosperous German Jewish family in Berlin. Since
his days in Gustav Wyneken's student movement, he always exhibited a
radical and romantic sensibility. He received his doctorate in philosophy,
although his innovative *Habilitationsschrift* on the tradition of German
Trauerspiel was a failure. Unable to pursue a career as an academic, Benjamin
became a freelance translator, essayist, and critic. His introduction to Marxism resulted from a love affair with the Russian revolutionary Asja Lacis.
This commitment to Marx was only reinforced by his lifelong relationship
with the playwright Bertolt Brecht. However, Benjamin's Marxism was
filtered through a complex affinity for Judaic messianism that was fueled by
his friendship with the famous Kabbalistic scholar Gershom Scholem. Benjamin developed an approach to philosophy and art that was an extremely
unconventional blending of Marxian insights with theological motifs.[5]

When the Nazis rose to power, Benjamin left Germany for France, where
he was planning a massive project on the Parisian arcades. Once in Paris,
he was drawn to the Institute's French branch by Adorno, who believed
that his friend Benjamin would be a welcome addition to Horkheimer's
group. Benjamin's relationship with the Institute was turbulent during
the 1930s. The Horkheimer Circle financially supported Benjamin with
his research, but it was concerned about his submissions to the *Zeitschrift*.
Adorno, who felt responsible for Benjamin's involvement with the Institute, took it upon himself to reprimand Benjamin for the idiosyncrasies in
his work. Benjamin submitted to the criticisms, but was clearly troubled
by the unpleasant correspondences. His contributions to the *Zeitschrift*
were few, but their impact was significant. The project on the Parisian
Arcades was cut short by the fall of France in 1940 and by Benjamin's
tragic death on the Franco-Spanish border while attempting to flee to the
United States. One can only speculate on the history of the Institute had
Benjamin safely made this journey.

WRITINGS, RESEARCH, AND INSTRUCTION AT COLUMBIA UNIVERSITY

Based on the Frankfurt School's early activities and accomplishments in
the United States, it is clear that its members had not misrepresented
themselves to Columbia's sociologists and administrators. The emphasis

that had been placed on scientific social research had not been an empty marketing scheme. Members of the Institute for Social Research were busy with a myriad of social research projects throughout the 1930s. Although members of the Horkheimer Circle later emphasized their anonymity and isolation at Columbia, evidence suggests that such claims were exaggerated.

For many commentators, the image of isolation in exile is bolstered by the fact that the Frankfurt School's journal, the *Zeitschrift für Sozialforschung,* continued to concentrate on distinctively European themes and topics within the arena of social theory, as well as by the fact that the journal continued to be published in German. The rationale for these decisions was complex, and they do not simply indicate Horkheimer's desire for autonomy that was bought at the expense of seclusion and academic anonymity. There were three major reasons for the continued German orientation of the journal. First, few members of the Horkheimer group were comfortable enough with English to begin fashioning their ideas in it. Second, Horkheimer and the members of his circle felt that German was the most authentic language for the expression of their ideas and philosophical orientation. Their own use of immanent critique and dialectical logic was rooted not only in the methods of Kant and Hegel, but also in the language and style of classic German Idealism. Consequently, their collective work was concerned as much with form as it was with content, and the use of German was essential to the crafting of this form. Third, Horkheimer and several of his colleagues viewed their journal as one of the last bastions of authentic German thought and culture.[6] While Germany degenerated under the rule of the Nazis, the Horkheimer group hoped to preserve the intellectual and artistic traditions through the continuation of the periodical and the support of other German thinkers.

Despite these powerful motives for preserving the original spirit that had formed the *Zeitschrift,* it did undergo significant changes as a result of exile. Outstanding American contributions to philosophy, aesthetics, and social science had always been reviewed in the *Zeitschrift;* however, the journal naturally began to examine American contributions to social research and social theory more frequently during the group's stay in the United States. This was partly a result of the diminished contact between the Institute and European social scientists remaining in Europe (as well as the disruptions of research and publishing that were caused by the spread of fascism), but it also represented an attempt by the group to reach out to their American audience.[7] In addition to increasing the number of reviews of American scholarly works, the Institute also began to publish articles by U.S. scholars in English by the late 1930s. Charles Beard and Margaret Mead were perhaps the most famous of the American contributors to the *Zeitschrift* during the early years that the Institute spent at Columbia.[8] Attracting such notables to the *Zeitschrift* helped to build connections between the Institute and established academic figures in America.

The major impetus leading to the journal's cultural and intellectual assimilation was the fall of France in 1940. With the onset of the Vichy regime, the Alcan press could no longer handle the Institute's publishing needs. Consequently, Horkheimer decided to transform the *Zeitschrift* into an English-language periodical titled *Studies in Philosophy and Social Science*. The new journal could be published in the safe environs of New York, and at the same time it could be used to carve out an intellectual home in the United States for the Horkheimer group.

The research activities of the Frankfurt School present an even clearer picture of the Horkheimer Circle's intentions to fulfill the expectations of their new colleagues at Columbia University. Despite the fact that little was accomplished during 1934 because of the logistics of moving across the Atlantic, the Institute for Social Research renewed its many research projects in 1935. Throughout the mid- to late 1930s, the Institute completed its major study initiated in Europe by Erich Fromm—the study on authority and the family, which "attempted to analyze the actual role of the family in Western Europe in educating the individual for the acceptance or rejection of authority in society."[9] In March 1936, Horkheimer reported to Columbia's president that *Studien über Autorität und Familie* was completed and ready for publication.[10]

The research for *Studien über Autorität und Familie* largely had been completed in Geneva, but a great deal of work still remained with regard to the analysis of the raw data. The writings that were finished in New York can be divided into three sections: a theoretical section, an empirical section reporting the findings from the research projects and questionnaires, and a final section devoted to related studies that were prompted by the preliminary research that formed the core of the project. The entire book coveys a hurried and unfinished quality. The Institute was eager to share its preliminary thoughts and findings with its new friends and sponsors at Columbia, but the published book was unpolished.

The research studies, which embodied the final two sections of the project, were presented in a fairly raw state. Results had not been fully generalized and few statistically conclusive findings could be drawn from questionnaires because so many of them had been interrupted or lost owing to the political instability in Europe. Yet, as incomplete as the empirical sections were, they did demonstrate the Institute (and particularly Erich Fromm) to be an innovative force within the field of social research. For American sociologists interested in the possible applications of psychoanalysis and social psychology, *Studien über Autorität und Familie* was a demonstration of several new and fruitful directions for future research.[11]

The most polished section of the book was the first, which contained the theoretical writings on authority. The section began with Horkheimer's introduction, which provided a general examination of the historical development of authority in the bourgeois world—a topic that echoed themes and ideas that had already been expressed in earlier writings, particularly in "Egoismus und Freiheitsbewegung: Zur Anthropologie des bürgerlichen Zeitalters" and in "Beginnings of the Bourgeois Philosophy of History."[12] Despite these echoes from past work, Horkheimer made the central concept of the study quite clear—socioeconomic factors were conspiring to undermine paternal authority that was typical in the bourgeois family. With the demise of the bourgeois family, the focus of familial authority was shifting from the father to social forces and authorities outside of the family. The primary outcome of this development was the rise of fascism in both Germany and Italy.

The second piece of the theoretical section was written by Erich Fromm and presented the social-psychological concepts that underpinned the group's theory of authority and its operation in society. Although the essay echoed many of Fromm's revisions of Freud that had appeared in the pages of the *Zeitschrift* previously, it was the most original and significant of the three pieces because it articulated the group's notion of the "authoritarian character."[13] This early model of the authoritarian personality differed significantly from the same notion that Fromm would later develop in *Escape from Freedom*.[14] Instead of linking authoritarianism firmly with alienation as he would later do, Fromm's first thoughts on this character type were derived from Freud's theory of sadomasochism. Following Freud, Fromm believed that the sadistic and masochistic traits were joined in a unified dynamic. With regard to authoritarianism, masochism manifested itself in the surrender to authority, and sadism was evident in the acceptance of social hierarchy. In the developmental and sexual sense, the authoritarian character had suffered a regression from genital sexuality to infantile sexuality. Accompanying this regression of libidinal energy, Fromm also expected a shift from heterosexual to homosexual behavior among authoritarian personalities. Fromm's prognosis for Western civilization, however, was not as gloomy as Horkheimer's. Fromm believed that the nurturing of well-developed, rational egos could protect people from psychological regression and equip them with the ability to remain unswayed by authoritarian character types and social structures.

The third essay of the theoretical section was written by Herbert Marcuse and was an intellectual history of authority within the bourgeois worldview. Beginning with the Reformation, there emerged a long tradition of idealizing internal freedom over external freedom—and, in fact, seeing the sacrifice of external freedom as a necessary prerequisite for achieving individual autonomy. The same attitude toward inner freedom persisted long after the birth of Protestantism, Marcuse noted, and found its way into the thought of major social and philosophical thinkers such as Kant and Hegel—a topic that Leonard Krieger, a colleague of Marcuse's during the Second World War, similarly examined in his book *The German Idea of Freedom*.[15] Marcuse's main aim was to demonstrate that authority and domination had always been components of bourgeois thought and had grown to be entangled with conceptions of autonomy and individual freedom. With such assumptions lying at the core of the bourgeois worldview, the transition to totalitarianism and Nazism could be seen as a continuation of bourgeois sensibilities rather than a rupture with them. Echoing the main argument that Marcuse had first developed in a contribution to the *Zeitschrift* titled "Der Kampf gegen den Liberalismus in der totalitären Staatsauffassung," he proposed that totalitarianism was not simply consistent with liberalism but had arisen within it.[16]

The results of the empirical research tended to corroborate the basic theoretical assumption that Horkheimer, Fromm, and Marcuse had all made—namely, that patriarchal authority structures within the families from the research pools were in fact eroding. Because of the lack of responses to many of the questionnaires, however, the Institute was unable to theorize about the latter development's implications. One possible outcome, which

Fromm later took up, was the development of an authority that was "matri-archal." In the mid-1930s, however, there was not enough data to specu-late about either the existence or the dynamics of matriarchal authority in families.

What Fromm and his collaborators on the empirical studies were able to generate were character models. They were derived from all the informa-tion that had been generated by the questionnaires that had been circulated to the parents of "at-risk" families. Based on his analysis of the responses, Fromm was able to develop three character types—authoritarian, revolu-tionary, and ambivalent. Although the authoritarian character was clearly developed and generalized from the research, the other two types were sketched far more generally. The authoritarian character type displayed the kind of sadomasochistic psychological and sexual traits that Fromm had already explored in his theoretical essay. On the other pole of the politi-cal and psychological spectrum was the revolutionary character, which embodied antibourgeois traits. Revolutionary character types were indi-viduals who would conflict with every society, whether authoritarian or not. The last type, which seemed to serve as a kind of psychological "un-decided," was the ambivalent character. As Fromm's concept suggests, the ambivalent character would be susceptible to persuasion by the other two characters. Although all three types seemed as though they easily could have been derived from the political forces that the Institute had witnessed only years before while they lived in Germany's Weimar Republic, Fromm had carefully examined the empirical findings. Exercising caution to make use of his data, Fromm utilized every response to each question to provide confirmation for his character models.

Although the Institute was unable to give concrete answers regarding the fate of the family or about the development of fascism, *Studien über Autorität und Familie* served as an important stage in the Institute's evo-lution as a research group.[17] The study's use of psychoanalysis was a sig-nificant innovation in sociological research, and the models it developed would play an important role in later projects, such as the five-volume *Studies in Prejudice*. This subsequent series of books would accomplish what *Studien über Autorität und Familie* could not. Not only were the character types better developed, but the empirical data was generalized so that one could also detect authoritarian tendencies based on responses to only a few questions.

The other project carried over from Europe was the study of the German working class. Fromm remained the principal architect of, and caretaker for, the project, which had been largely abandoned shortly after the move to Geneva. The data, consisting of 750 questionnaires, had not been properly organized or analyzed, but Fromm convinced Horkheimer that something could be salvaged. From 1935 until his 1939 departure from the Institute for Social Research, Fromm continued to ponder the workers' questionnaires and might have published his findings had he not left the group.

Two new, extensive studies were also formulated and directed by Fromm during the late 1930s. One, conceived as an American accompaniment to *Studien über Autorität und Familie*, focused on unemployment and family life in Newark, New Jersey. Because the majority of the Institute's members spent most of the 1930s preparing theoretical work for the *Zeitschrift für Sozialforschung*, Fromm turned to Columbia's faculty and students for help, as well as bringing in Paul Lazarsfeld to assist with the study's direction. Based on his experience with the previous two European projects, Fromm provided the research team with guidance in creating the interview protocols and in analyzing the case studies. Despite his significant involvement with the project, the actual task of writing up the results was passed on to Mirra Komarovsky, who published the study as *The Unemployed Man and His Family*.[18] Although no individual member of the Horkheimer Circle was credited with the project, all of those familiar with it understood the Institute's involvement and credited the Institute for Social Research with publishing the work.

The second original study suffered a similar fate. Begun under Fromm's direction, the analysis of postadolescent attitudes regarding authority was never completed or credited to the Institute for Social Research. The study took place at Sarah Lawrence and was conducted in conjunction with the college's reevaluation of the purposes and functions of education. Fromm offered to teach the Sarah Lawrence researchers to organize and produce case studies and other projective tests.[19] While much of the project concentrated on establishing new goals for collegiate education that would help develop the "whole student," it also uncovered attitudes regarding authority by examining student–teacher relationships. As Horkheimer explained to President Butler in March 1937:

[t]he object of our study of the attitude of students in a women's college in New York towards the authority of teachers and of the college, is the fixation of definite types of attitude and the accomplishment of an understanding of the relations between this typical attitude, on the one hand, and the social and cultural situation and the family background of the student, on the other, and further, of the relations between this attitude and a distinctive characterological structure.[20]

Because of substantial commitments of time and finances to both the Newark unemployment study and the German workers project, the Sarah Lawrence project moved slowly out of Fromm's control.[21] Based on his angry reaction to a book published by one of the project's leaders at Sarah Lawrence, it is clear that Fromm had planned to write up his findings, eventually, as a book of his own. Ruth Munroe's *Teaching the Individual* was a terrible blow because it reported many of the discoveries that Fromm had planned to disclose in his future monograph.[22] In response to an irate letter Fromm sent to Sarah Lawrence inquiring about the development, Beatrice Doerschuk, the college's director of education, wrote:

May I assure you . . . that in the report Miss Munroe is making we have every wish to maintain the cooperative relationship with you and your material as it has stood the past three years, without encroachment upon the purposes of your own study. Her report is one we have had in mind for several years as one of perhaps several analyses of the educational implications of teacher–student relationships. The intention is a practical one: to be of use to teachers, on the basis of our own experience in working out procedures in education. We are greatly indebted to you both for focusing our attention upon this particular aspect of the problem and for new insights about the relationships involved. It is our intention and desire to give full recognition for this, as also for insight and stimulus gained from several other sources. I believe, however, that our intent in the present study is different from yours. I have conceived the studies as independent enterprises.[23]

Despite these assurances, the published study did make use of Fromm's ideas and findings on authority. Munroe simply invented a new name for

Fromm's "authoritarian character," calling her type the "rigid student."[24] Although she did not use the concept for the same purposes that Fromm had in mind, he decided not to publish his findings.

Even with Fromm's efforts throughout the 1930s, the Horkheimer Circle was only credited with one completed study by those unfamiliar with all of the group's collaborations. As anticipated by sociologists at Columbia, the Horkheimer Circle brought many new social research projects to Morningside Heights, and most of these involved complex quantitative methods. The problem was that the Institute was rarely credited for the publication of these projects. It has always been crucial for scholars to publish. Clearly, by the 1940s, the Institute's lack of research publications became a problem, but there were other contributing factors to the Horkheimer Circle's decline, such as the departure of Erich Fromm.

When it came to relations with members of the Columbia sociology department, the Horkheimer Circle was guarded. It seemed uncomfortable about disclosing details about the Institute's finances. Considering that its leaders lived comfortably during the Depression in America while so many U.S. citizens and scholars struggled to make ends meet, the group's secretiveness is understandable. Yet, the way inquiries into the Institute's background were handled left many members of the department puzzled. As Theodore Abel recorded in his journal:

> Went up to Columbia for lunch with Horkheimer and Pollock of the Institute for Social Research. They have beautiful quarters and a magnificent library. We talked about the founding of the Institute with the money of an Argentine German, whose name is not even remembered by these directors, who are sitting pretty on account of the endowment which they exchanged into gold francs before Hitler came to power.[25]

The other reason for the group's occasionally reclusive tendencies was concern about the reception of their political beliefs. During the last years of his life, Herbert Marcuse recalled that members were forbidden to engage in any type of political activity. As he explained in an interview with Jürgen Habermas:

> HABERMAS: Did the Institute ever establish, shall we say, relationships with local, more strictly political groups in emigration?

MARCUSE: That was strictly forbidden. From the beginning Horkheimer had insisted that we were guests of Columbia University, philosophers and scholars. Any organizational ties could have shaken the Institute's precarious administrative foundation. Such ties were out of the question.[26]

Although it is easy to mistake such concerns as paranoid, one must remember the political circumstances facing a group of German-Jewish émigrés during the 1930s and 1940s. The Institute was a frequent target of government investigations, and its members knew this. During the early years at Columbia, the offices on 117th Street were visited by German-speaking New York police detectives searching for Nazi sympathizers within the German community.[27] Later, the Institute was frequently monitored by the FBI as a result of anonymous accusations regarding Communist sympathies among the group's members.[28] The sheer bulk of the FBI files on this matter suggests that Horkheimer had good reason to forbid political activity. Even though Institute members followed the director's instructions, the group was still the target of numerous investigations. Harsher repercussions likely would have resulted had Horkheimer's warnings been ignored.

Despite the hesitations, the Horkheimer Circle did mingle with the faculty on Morningside Heights. It is not surprising that Robert Lynd became one of the group's closest friends during the first years in New York. He was probably responsible for their invitation to Columbia and shared many scholarly interests in common with the Horkheimer Circle. Once Horkheimer had finished negotiating the Institute's arrangements with the university, Lynd was the first to congratulate him. As Lynd wrote:

I want to express my delight that the arrangement for the 117th Street house has gone through and that your Society is to be part of the Columbia family. You will find the atmosphere there of the freest, an easy scientific camaraderie that will interfere at no point with your work and yet will stand ready to assist at any time that you need such assistance.[29]

Horkheimer reciprocated Lynd's warmth and did not recoil from the offers of assistance and cooperation. In the director's mind, Lynd was an important friend who needed to be included in the Institute's activities. As Horkheimer explained to Friedrich Pollock:

I am sending you the enclosed copy of writings by Lynd, the author of *Middletown*. You see that the present atmosphere for us is really positive and extraordinarily friendly. I had negotiated with Lynd, like I wrote to you earlier, and he is especially interested in our work. He already offered his and his wife's help with our academic work. I think that later we should offer him entry into our established Society here.[30]

Lynd and his wife were not simply a source of support for the Horkheimer Circle. They also helped the Institute develop important contacts with other social scientists, Lynd's reintroduction of Paul Lazarsfeld to the Institute for Social Research being a prime example. Lazarsfeld, who had worked with Lynd since the time of his arrival as a Rockefeller Fellow in 1933, continued to maintain close contact. Once the members of the Institute arrived, Lynd quickly recognized how valuable collaboration between both parties might be. As early as 1935, Lynd notified Horkheimer:

I gather that Paul Lazarsfeld may stay in this country next year at the University of Pittsburgh. If he does, it occurs to me that it might be useful to you to make some arrangement with him for a few days a month of his time to advise with the Institute regarding its program. This note is an impertinence on my part, but I am truly fond of Lazarsfeld and regard him highly.[31]

Lynd's foresight proved to be correct. Fruitful collaborations resulted from the reintroduction. Members of the Horkheimer Circle were active in Lazarsfeld's research projects for many years, and Lazarsfeld provided invaluable assistance to Horkheimer's colleagues on projects as varied as the Newark unemployment study and projects on anti-Semitism. Were it not for Lynd's role, the Institute might never have developed such significant contacts in the United States. Without his early support, the Institute for Social Research might likely have been as alienated in the United States as it later claimed to have been.

Another early faculty friend of the Frankfurt School was Samuel Lindsay, Columbia's famous social economist. Although he was nearing the end of an extraordinary career in the social sciences, Lindsay became involved with the Institute's studies on the family. He had always had a keen interest in social legislation and social work. During his first years at Columbia, he worked together with Franklin Giddings in the more academic pursuit of sociology, but he also oversaw the training of social workers at Columbia, functioning as director of the New York School of Philanthropy for five years. When the Horkheimer Circle arrived at Columbia and began considering a study of American families to complement its work in Europe, Lindsay offered his assistance. Although he never sought formal acknowledgment, he worked closely with the research teams in Newark, devoting his time and energy to the unemployment study that was eventually authored and published by Mirra Komarovsky. His intellectual contributions are impossible to determine, but his personal papers suggest that he was consulted in all aspects of the project.[32]

The other members of Columbia's sociology department had more limited contact with members of the Horkheimer Circle. During the Institute's first five years on Morningside Heights, most of the department remained outside of the Institute's orbit, instead pursuing its own interests. Robert MacIver wrote a sociology textbook and later a critical study of Marxism's social and political implications, yet showed no inclination to be involved with the Horkheimer Circle's research.[33] Similarly, Theodore Abel, who shared MacIver's preference for political theory, spent this time struggling to find a topic for his first major sociological monograph. Robert Chaddock and Frank Ross, functioning more as statisticians than as sociologists, continued to provide undergraduates and graduate students with the fundamental tools necessary for quantitative research. William Casey, meanwhile, concentrated on teaching undergraduates and popularizing sociology. Even though none of these figures became closely involved with the Horkheimer group and its work, all of them developed social contacts with members of the Institute for Social Research through office visits or faculty club luncheons.

More substantial and intellectual contacts with department members were developed through monthly Sunday-night seminars at MacIver's home. Although the structure was casual and friendly, the Sunday gatherings represented an important bond that held the department together and enabled its members to share ideas with one another. As MacIver later recalled:

I particularly enjoyed a Sunday evening symposium held at our apartment on Riverside Drive to which I invited a group of advanced students and department members. I arranged for someone, not infrequently a visiting professor, a behaviorist or positivist, or, say, a classical authoritarian such as Mortimer Adler, to introduce a controversial subject. And then the discussion would become fast and furious, and at times rather heated, into the midnight hours.[34]

From the time of their arrival on Morningside Heights, members of the Horkheimer Circle participated regularly in the department seminars.[35] Horkheimer clearly understood the importance of such gatherings. The discussions were often fruitful, and the participation of Institute members helped the group maintain a presence within the department. In fact, it was not unusual for members of the Horkheimer Circle to lead discussions, especially when they dealt with topics in which the Institute for Social Research excelled.[36] Because of the important contacts afforded by the gatherings, Horkheimer insisted that new members of the Institute attend them.[37] The Sunday seminars remained an essential ritual for members of the Horkheimer Circle for the duration of their stay in the United States. Even during the 1940s, after Horkheimer and Adorno had relocated to California, the members remaining in New York still found it essential to have at least one representative from the group attending the meetings.[38]

Of all the Horkheimer Circle's members, Fromm became the most visible and popular at Columbia during his first years in the United States.[39] He was less guarded than his colleagues, and he was in a position, as the group's functional director of social research projects, to develop strong contacts with U.S. social scientists.[40] The more Fromm encouraged collaborative efforts with American researchers, the more he became a recognizable figure in the field. His closest friend and colleague in New York was Robert Lynd. Because he was primarily interested in its research techniques and studies of the family, Lynd frequently consulted with Fromm. He respected Fromm's abilities as a researcher and was fascinated by his skills as a psychoanalyst.[41] In particular, Lynd sought to learn more about how Fromm seemed to incorporate the two disciplines so effortlessly. As a result of his own enthusiasm for Fromm and the Horkheimer Circle's empirical research, Lynd began introducing Fromm to others on the Columbia campus who might benefit from his unique abilities and expertise.[42] As this practice continued, Fromm's reputation on Morningside Heights

grew. By the time a temporary lectureship was available to a member of
the Institute for Social Research, the sociology department's logical choice
was Fromm.[43] In the eyes of Columbia's faculty, he was the central figure
guiding the Horkheimer Circle's most significant work.

The Horkheimer Circle's activities on the Columbia campus, however,
were not limited to the university faculty's involvement. Institute members also served as teachers during the group's initial five years in the
United States. Although no member was offered a position on the sociology department's staff roster during that time, the group taught in the
extension school and offered casual evening seminars that were open to
faculty members and graduate students. Although none of these peda-
gogical activities compared to the offerings of an institution like the "University in Exile," the Horkheimer Circle became a recognizable part of
New York's intellectual milieu. As Daniel Bell explained years after he
studied sociology at Columbia, the Institute was more self-contained than
the New School for Social Research and consequently had less resonance
among students.[44] Nevertheless, Horkheimer and his colleagues were generally known to those students possessing strong interests in European
social theory.[45] For graduate students such as Bell, the Institute for Social
Research represented a component of Columbia's unique collection of
European-trained sociologists.[46]

The Institute's more formal and official contributions to Columbia's
curriculum were the extension courses titled "Authoritarian Doctrines and
Modern European Institutions." The courses met once a week for two
hours and collectively spanned the duration of an academic year. Arranged
with the help of Robert MacIver, the courses were first offered in 1936–
37.[47] Although the enrollment was not always high enough to justify offering the courses, the pairing was listed in every subsequent extension
course catalog until 1949.[48] Horkheimer was the principal instructor, but
all members of the Institute presented lectures in their fields of specialization. Horkheimer delivered the initial introductory lectures on the topic
of authority, its importance in the modern world, and the Institute's general approach to it. The course examined authority by critically dissecting it. Marcuse presented lectures on the changing forms of authority
throughout the history of Western Europe; Lazarsfeld devoted a group of
lectures to empirical research and its methods for examining authority;
Pollock addressed the relationship between different economic systems and

authority; Julian Gumperz examined American economic institutions in an attempt to differentiate them from their European counterparts, thereby enabling a comparison of different attitudes toward authority; Fromm explained the authoritarian character pattern, locating it firmly within Freudian theory; Franz Neumann developed his theories of authority and the development of the totalitarian state; and finally, Leo Lowenthal drew from his experience as a schoolteacher in lectures on authority and education, and then on the role of authority in contemporary literature.[49]

The courses must have presented a challenge for the students. Horkheimer admitted the language barrier that still existed for members of his circle, and students like Daniel Bell confirm the point.[50] In addition, Horkheimer alerted his young listeners to the fact that the German academic style would be unfamiliar and awkward for many.[51] He pointed as well to an even more serious difficulty—the fact that his circle presented an approach to social research that would be unfamiliar to American-trained students of the social sciences:

> We do not maintain that we are able at the outset to formulate principles which give a definite insight into the very essence of things. We do not claim to have at our disposal such simple definitions that any further treatment of the subject would merely be in the way of differentiation, application or amendment. If this were true, I should only have to give in my next lectures definitions of authority, of society, the family, etc., later to illustrate these definitions by means of specific cases and to show their interrelation, and on your part you could look forward, after a few lectures, to taking home definite insights and preserving the finished product forever after. We are of the opinion, however, that clarity comes at the end, not at the beginning. In the beginning, naturally, we must make use of abstract definitions, but such definitions, when tested by reality, always remain isolated notions, distorted and untrue. Such untrue statements, which are necessary in all abstract definitions, are only overcome by slow and progressive proximity to concrete objects and by keeping a watchful eye for the essential.[52]

In addition to the challenges posed by the clash of two languages and intellectual cultures, the Horkheimer Circle's students had to struggle with the complexities of Critical Theory. For the Americans (and émigrés) in attendance, this must have been a perplexing encounter, because the intellectual underpinnings of the Horkheimer Circle's approach would have been largely unknown to U.S. students of sociology.

The lectures, however, show that Institute members were not entirely timid in their dealings with Americans. Participation in politics may have been forbidden, but their radical approach to social science was presented to students and colleagues in an unadulterated form. It is impossible to adequately summarize the circle's extension lectures, but the point that was emphasized throughout the courses was that forms of authority had been transformed by historical changes. Although modern man was no longer subjected to naked coercion by the elite of a community, he deferred to a more invisible and insidious form of authority. Perhaps Horkheimer expressed the point most clearly in his second lecture, when he explained:

> In former times the needs and wishes of society were voiced through certain privileged personages and corporations. Today these needs make themselves known through economic and social conditions, through the "language of facts," as it were . . . All is regulated indirectly by market conditions and the whole structure of the economy. Authority is no longer an immediate relationship, but a *Sachverhältnis,* a relation mediated through objective facts, and the dependence on impersonal facts has taken the place of dependence on persons . . . All the secondary emanations of authority, which have been mentioned before, namely, newspapers, advertising, radio, etc., are but the amplification and intensification of the "language of facts." These factors of modern life are surface phenomena only and presuppose a highly developed veneration of facts. The resignation to the higher will of God or of his representatives on earth, has been replaced by resignation to the exigencies of life.[53]

What Horkheimer referred to at Columbia as the "language of facts" slowly evolved under Adorno's influence into the notion of instrumental reason that would subsequently form the basis for *Dialectic of Enlightenment.* Reason, blunted by the realities of modern civilization, had lost the ability to view the world critically. The exigencies of modern life forced the new "language of facts" to become the basis for a "means–ends" rationality that was incapable of breaking the continuous cycles of social injustice and domination.

Although some of the Horkheimer Circle's students became well known in later years, archival records provide little information about their relationships with their teachers. No substantive correspondence exists between any of the students and members of the Institute for Social Research, and consequently little can be said about the immediate reception of these courses. Partial class lists from the first four years of the courses still exist among the Max Horkheimer papers, and they show a varied student population.[54] One is immediately struck by the large number of women enrolled, as well as the number of foreign students. Many enrolled because of personal acquaintances with members of the Institute, and in other cases students were simply curious about the subject matter and the Institute's reputation, both of which became increasingly important as the dangers and realities of fascism became more obvious.

Whereas the Columbia University extension courses were intended to meet the Horkheimer Circle's professional obligations, the Tuesday evening seminars were directed toward satisfying the group's own intellectual needs. Instead of tailoring the presentations to the audience of faculty members and graduate students, members presented their ideas for one another.[55] Typically, members would present papers at each of the weekly gatherings. At times, the papers were part of broader collective investigations of topics prearranged by Horkheimer.[56] On most occasions, however, the presentations came from articles that were in production for the *Zeitschrift für Sozialforschung* or that dealt with an aspect of a larger project being carried out by a member of the group.[57] Nonmembers attending the seminars were welcome to comment, but it was understood by all participants that the occasions were primarily for members of the Horkheimer Circle. As Daniel Bell recalled, the Institute resembled the type of authoritarian family that occupied the imaginations of so many Institute members.[58] The group assembled around a long rectangular table during the seminars, while visitors looked on from locations around the perimeter of the Institute's library. Horkheimer, as paternal authority figure, occupied the table's center seat and never smiled. To his left sat Theodor W. Adorno, who—unable to contain his intellect or excitement—flitted about the room like a hummingbird, constantly conversing with people. On Horkheimer's right sat Friedrich Pollock in a state of perpetual solemnity. Herbert Marcuse and Franz L. Neumann, two of the wittiest and most personable members of the group, were assigned the next pair of seats beside Adorno and Pollock. Leo Lowenthal and Henryk Grossmann occupied the last two interior spaces at the table, and Otto Kirchheimer and Arkady Gurland sat at the ends of the table, occupying the most hazardous position at the seminars. After each paper, Institute members would address it in turn. Horkheimer would speak first, followed by Pollock, then Adorno, and so it would proceed until the floor was turned over to Kirchheimer and Gurland. Because both were always the last to speak, their comments often seemed unoriginal or wildly speculative, formulated in a desperate attempt to say something new. As Bell recalls, both received the frequent derision of their colleagues.[59] Especially for graduate students interested in European social theory, the Tuesday seminar was a significant event at Columbia. Although largely limited to a small group, it provided an important contact with the European traditions begun by Marx, Freud, and Max Weber. For members of the Horkheimer Circle, it provided another source of contact with Columbia faculty and students.

CHANGING FORTUNES:
THE DEPARTURE OF ERICH FROMM

One might think that, based upon the talent at his disposal within the Frankfurt School, Horkheimer would have been very pleased about the state of the Institute by the late 1930s. He was not. Instead of being concerned with the collective work of his circle, Horkheimer had begun to formulate the idea for a book that he hoped would become his philosophical masterpiece. Instead of wanting to manage the talented team of researchers and thinkers that he had at his disposal, he actually longed for the solitude of private scholarship. His dream was to disentangle himself from the Institute, but to have the financial resources to work with only a few collaborators, such as Marcuse and Adorno.

The book he initially planned to write on dialectical logic eventually became *Dialectic of Enlightenment*. Part of the book would concern itself with the limits of scientific knowledge—a topic that initially appeared most clearly in his first monograph on the bourgeois philosophy of history and then later resurfaced in many of his essays for the *Zeitschrift*. While Horkheimer dreamed of subjecting scientific reason to a thorough critique, he wanted to avoid the celebrations of irrationalism and metaphysics that had accompanied similar efforts that had preceded his. He believed that such pitfalls could be avoided by deploying a dialectical

critique that simultaneously displayed the utility of dialectical logic. Ultimately, the project was intended to serve as a vindication of the type of
social research that Horkheimer had been advocating since his inaugural
address of 1931. The work on dialectical logic was to rescue scientific rationality from its own inherent flaws, thereby establishing the basis for a social
theory that could then function as the necessary backbone of any and all
future social research at the Institute. Consequently, Horkheimer viewed
his project as a necessary next step in the Circle's development. Without
taking this step, the group was destined to suffer disappointments similar
to those with the study of the German working class.

Just as Horkheimer formulated his project, however, the Circle's relations
with Columbia began to unravel when tensions grew between Fromm and
the Institute's leaders. By the end of the 1930s, moreover, the Circle's endowment was greatly depleted. During the initial years in the United States,
Institute members, particularly Horkheimer and Pollock, lived comfortably. The Institute employed a large staff, including translators and permanent secretaries, and it still had enough money left over to generously
support other European refugees dislocated by Nazism.[60] Starting in 1937,
however, the Société Internationale de Recherches Sociales began suffering a series of significant losses. Poor investments in the stock market,
combined with several disastrous real-estate deals, caused the group's assets
to shrink, forcing the directors to draw from the endowment's capital.[61]
According to the Institute's bylaws, however, dipping into principal was
prohibited. Horkheimer needed to find a solution to the group's financial
setbacks. His anxieties only increased as he had also begun to envision the
grand project on dialectics. If he did not find a way to cut back on the Institute's expenses, his own future and work would suffer. He could potentially
lose everything. The director briefly considered altering the Institute's
legal structure by changing it to a private foundation, but he instead opted
to cut salaries and personnel.[62] The first salary subject to these decreases
was Fromm's.

Subtle tensions had existed between Fromm and the Institute's other
members for a long time. Basic differences had arisen as a result of Fromm's
revisions of Freud.[63] Although theoretical disputes obviously played a role
in the deteriorating relations between both parties, personal and financial issues became the major causes of the eventual split. As we have seen,
the gregarious Fromm never hesitated to network with other scholars, and

had become the Institute's best-known member during the early years at Columbia. Instead of enjoying the notoriety Fromm brought to the group, Horkheimer remained extremely suspicious of his associate.[64] This attitude came across most clearly in a letter written in 1934, in the midst of Institute's migration to the United States. Horkheimer complained:

> [Fromm] does not particularly appeal to me. He has productive ideas, but he wants to be on good terms with too many people at once, and doesn't want to miss anything. It is quite pleasant to talk to him, but my impression is that it is quite pleasant for very many people.[65]

Horkheimer's fears regarding the personal loyalty of his associates prevented him from appreciating Fromm, and he failed to recognize the considerable benefits that his colleague's work and personality brought to the Institute in the United States. Although the personality conflict did not cause the final break with Fromm, it played a role in Horkheimer's decision to cut Fromm's salary—as did the fact that Fromm had a lucrative therapeutic practice in Manhattan. Of the Circle's members, Fromm was the only one who would not suffer significantly from the elimination of his Institute salary.

In May 1939, Horkheimer and Pollock informed Fromm of the Institute's dire financial straits and insisted that they would not be able to pay his salary after October of that year.[66] Fromm was asked to agree voluntarily to the arrangement based on his ability to survive solely on his psychoanalytic practice. Instead of deferring to Horkheimer's decision, Fromm, outraged, fought back. He had passed up high-paying positions out of loyalty to the Institute and had scaled back his practice in an attempt to devote more time to the group's empirical studies.[67] Sacrifices had been made for the Institute, Fromm emphasized, and he would not leave without receiving a severance package. While the Institute dragged its feet deciding how to handle the situation, the October deadline came and went. True to his word, Horkheimer discontinued Fromm's salary checks. Enraged by this development, Fromm accused the Institute of a breach of contract.[68] Horkheimer, apparently fearful of the legal allegations, proposed sweeping the plan under the rug and offered to resume salary payments. Fromm, however, insisted that relations were irreparably damaged. Although he was sent salary checks for November and December, he returned them to the Institute and demanded the severance package. The eventual settlement to Fromm, which clearly escalated because of Horkheimer and Pollock's mishandling of the dispute,[69] was twenty thousand dollars.[70]

In addition to its substantial dollar cost to the Institute, Fromm's exit also resulted in the evaporation of the group's empirical research projects. In a series of miscalculations, Horkheimer surrendered the sizable severance package, as well as the German workers' project and the Sarah Lawrence study. No other Institute members had been involved in the latter projects. Their activities tended to focus on publications for the *Zeitschrift für Sozialforschung*. Instead of tackling large-scale social research projects, nearly all of these writings focused on social theory, philosophy, and culture. With Fromm's departure, the Institute could be seen for what it really was—a collection of social theorists and philosophers. The only reason Columbia's social scientists had mistaken the Institute for Social Research for a group of empirical researchers was owing to the work of Erich Fromm. Now that he was gone, the Institute had little to offer the university.

Former Columbia friends of the Horkheimer Circle almost immediately recognized the significance of the events with Fromm and were enraged by them. In particular, Robert Lynd became disenchanted with the Institute, while maintaining close and cordial relations with Fromm.[71] Lynd was irate not only because a productive, talented member of the group had been callously cast aside, but also because of the loss that the move entailed for both the Horkheimer Circle and Columbia. It clearly signaled an elimination of empirical research for the sociology department. Members of the Circle clearly sensed Lynd's disappointment. Although they had been accustomed to relying on Lynd as a close friend, Institute members began to fear him as a possible enemy. In paranoid fashion, they suspected a united front forming among Fromm and other former associates of the Circle (such as Karl Wittfogel and Julian Gumperz).[72] Mutual friends of both parties insist that no such conspiracy ever existed;[73] nevertheless, Horkheimer remained convinced of nefarious dealings behind closed doors.

It is certainly plausible to suspect that Lynd was aware of various grievances between former associates and the Institute. Furthermore, his personality would have provided some justification for Horkheimer's suspicions. Lynd's impatience and temper were well known among his associates and friends. As his wife recalled:

he was impatient about a lot of things. He was impatient about Paul's [Lazarsfeld's] double dealing. He was impatient about people pussyfooting when they might speak out. He was impatient about somebody who was going to meet us at the 8:15 train, to climb the Rampapos and missed the train. All kinds of things. He got so angry and impatient with people who wouldn't do things his way.[74]

Although it is possible that Lynd took Fromm's departure very personally, he was equally (if not more) frustrated with the Institute's failure of nerve. All attempts at empirical social research had been abandoned with Fromm's departure. Lynd had supported Columbia's offer of the 117th Street house to Horkheimer's group based on his assessment of the Institute as it had been characterized by Julian Gumperz. After Fromm's departure, such a characterization was no longer apt.

Compounding the problem, and undoubtedly further angering Lynd, was the fact that the Horkheimer Circle refused to publish its theoretical work for a U.S. audience. As Marcuse, recounting a conversation with Lynd, explained:

[Lynd] immediately took off on a nearly one-hour speech about the Institute. Basically the same old story: that we had wasted a great opportunity. That we had never achieved a true collaboration in which we might have confronted our European experiences with conditions in America, for example to analyze monopoly capitalism, fascist tendencies and so forth . . . He said he had the greatest respect for your [Horkheimer's] theoretical undertakings and had, even back then, encouraged you to publish them, but that you were always apprehensive about being viewed as a Marxist and therefore had always presented your thoughts in an incomprehensible, garbled manner . . . Every time I tried to get him to be more concrete he countered that it really didn't matter what we actually studied and wrote about if we would just be truly collaborative in our work. He also said we shouldn't always wait for American aid and impetus but rather should first create something on our own, by our own efforts. Even though he said all this in the friendliest manner and in a tone of genuine concern, I felt his enmity was not to be overcome, indeed not even neutralized. Irrational hatred is doubtless involved.[75]

By 1941, when Marcuse reported the encounter, Lynd had to encourage the Institute's publication of theoretical work. Whereas previously he had pushed members to pursue quantitative research methods, he scaled back his expectations and hoped for "grand and vital theoretical perspectives."[76] He no longer worried about the group's inability to carry out empirical research because he had already found a replacement for the Institute for Social Research.

Lazarsfeld's Office of Radio Research replaced the Horkheimer Circle at Columbia University. With Lynd's recommendation, Lazarsfeld had been offered the directorship of a Rockefeller-funded project on radio research during the summer of 1937 by Hadley Cantril of Princeton University. His research team, having grown out of a previous group at the University of Newark, soon became well known within the field of American social science. Lynd, who had been a longtime admirer of Lazarsfeld and his research efforts, volunteered to serve on the advisory board for the Rockefeller Foundation. During the spring and summer of 1939, as relations between Horkheimer and Fromm soured, Lynd became entwined in an equally serious dispute regarding the future of the Princeton Radio Project. The renewal of the Rockefeller grant was approaching, and Cantril sought greater involvement in the project's administration. The direction of radio research would have transferred to Cantril if the project remained at Princeton.[77] Lynd rescued Lazarsfeld's job by moving the Office of Radio Research from Princeton to Columbia. By the fall of 1939, Lynd had gathered enough support from his colleagues at the Rockefeller Foundation to approach Princeton's President Harold W. Dodds.[78] The result was the turnover of the radio project to Columbia University.

The new Columbia Office of Radio Research, which later evolved into the Bureau of Applied Social Research, met the sociology department's new needs in the wake of Fromm's departure. In Lazarsfeld and his research team, it found a new self-supporting proponent of quantitative methods in social research. Again, Columbia risked nothing but office space. As with the Institute, the bills were paid by someone else, and yet the sociology department could involve its faculty and graduate students in Lazarsfeld's projects.

Although Columbia's sociologists grew disappointed with the Institute's lack of productivity and collaboration, they got more than they bargained for from the Office of Radio Research (and later the Bureau of Applied Social Research). As Lazarsfeld recalled:

I think that the difficulties [with the Columbia people] were in no way that anyone was opposed to social research—they appeared to want research. But it is conceivable to say that what they hadn't realized is that what had happened was—I wouldn't say a collision, but a convergence, of two existing units. I think this is probably the way to put it, as a problem from his side (MacIver's). The programs MacIver and Lynd and everyone pictured were, (after all I know now what with being head of department),—they hire a man who has experience and is interested in empirical research, and let him build that up. That's how it would happen now—if Rockefeller wanted empirical research, that would be their picture, that someone can build it up. That wasn't the case. Here was an existing organization with its own people, its own tradition. Now what happened is: the two now have to live together. So much difficulty, of which you certainly were aware as a student, came from this misunderstanding: that MacIver definitely wanted empirical research and called a man in to build it up, but what they really got is a rather strong social system which was transformed into his social system. And at this point, I think he didn't frankly like it . . . it was like somebody who was invited to dinner and brings all his relatives with him: that is somewhat disconcerting.[79]

As Lazarsfeld grew to realize, Columbia had high expectations for whichever research organization it sponsored on its campus. Despite the difficulties, Lazarsfeld turned Columbia's dreams into a reality, and the Bureau of Applied Research remains an important part of the university's history. The Institute for Social Research, however, was unable to achieve its expected potential. Although it later made a major contribution to American social science with its innovative *Studies in Prejudice,* its fame came too late to make a difference at Columbia.

THE FAILURES OF THE 1940S

Fromm's departure, and the consequent elimination of social research at the Institute, would have been devastating at any point during the group's exile in the United States. The state of the group's finances, however, exacerbated the problem. Economic insecurity created desperation and eventually pulled the group apart.

Initially, Horkheimer attempted simply to replace the loss of Fromm's research studies by developing new projects. Concerned by the political developments in Europe, Horkheimer's first proposal was for a study of anti-Semitism. As early as the spring of 1939, Institute members were seeking Lynd's support and involvement with the project. The Institute planned to draw from previous discussions regarding human rights and the parallels between anti-Semitism and the persecution of aristocrats during the French Revolution.[80] The study would first examine the representative texts of contemporary European anti-Semitism, grounding them in their historical context. They would then design a set of experiments to identify the basic features of the anti-Semitic mind, thereby enabling social scientists to monitor latent anti-Jewish sentiments among various populations.[81] Although Lynd supported the basic concept, he was unwilling to make the necessary time commitment.[82] Horkheimer also approached other American friends of his group and must have received similar responses. The Institute's inner circle came to realize that the chances of receiving grant support were slim. By 1940, the anti-Semitism proposal was postponed, and the Frankfurt School shifted its attention to German culture.[83]

The Horkheimer Circle was passionate about its ideas regarding its homeland and the rise of Nazism there. At first, the German project was intended to be largely historical. Designed in the spirit of the *Flaschenpost* (or message in a bottle) by which the Institute imagined its writings to be intended for future generations, the original aim was to explore the various aspects of German culture prior to the Nazi seizure of power as both a cautionary tale and a salvage mission.[84] By focusing on the culture of the prefascist period, forbidden and outlawed cultural products could be preserved and linked to the nation's earlier artistic traditions. As Horkheimer approached American scholars to seek advice and support for the project, he came to recognize that a reorientation was necessary. Consequently, the project began to shift toward a study of the origins of National Socialism.[85] The Institute lined up American sponsors, as well as a codirector, for the project, and valuable time and resources were devoted to a campaign to secure external funding. Other émigrés, however, were pursuing similar studies, and the Institute's efforts resulted in bitter failure.[86] A team of rivals from the New School earned the available grants. They had pondered the issue longer and devoted more energy to adapting to U.S. academic standards. While Horkheimer and the inner circle of the Institute interpreted the result, again, in a paranoid fashion—the fallout of old Frankfurt rivalries and the betrayal of former members and supporters—the New School won the funding for its research fairly.

By the summer of 1941, the Horkheimer Circle's schemes for alleviating its financial burdens through the external funding of social research projects had failed. Although creative independence and autonomy had remained the group's primary objectives throughout its previous history, such goals came to seem unaffordable luxuries. Although the lack of serious empirical studies made a tighter relationship with Columbia unlikely, the Horkheimer Circle began to explore the possibility. Horkheimer began drafting a plan that would lay out the first steps toward a closer relationship with the university.[87] It called for at least one group member to be appointed as a permanent member of the sociology department's faculty. The department could select whomever it deemed fit for the position, and the Institute would reimburse the university for the cost of the salary. The Institute also offered its intellectual services and resources to the university in return for recognition as a formal university affiliate and faculty privileges. Although the initial relationship clearly benefited Columbia, there were possible future benefits to the Institute. If the Horkheimer Circle sufficiently pleased Columbia, it might be able to expect future financial support. If the tighter relationship yielded no assistance, moreover, the Institute would at least have Columbia's name behind it in other dealings with American scholars and academic institutions in future searches for grant support.

Negotiations between the Institute for Social Research and Columbia's sociology department took place during the spring and summer of 1941, and they seem to have included talks about multiple lectureships, which would have enabled more than one associate to join the university's faculty.[88] Two significant obstacles stood in the way, however. The first was the pervasive anti-Semitism on Morningside Heights.[89] An undisclosed quota system limited the number of Jewish faculty members.[90] Since nothing could combat this first obstacle, the Institute concentrated on the other, which was far more serious. By 1939, Columbia's sociology department was embroiled in a civil war between its two principal figures, Robert MacIver and Robert Lynd. The tensions arose from MacIver's review of Lynd's book *Knowledge for What?*[91] In the book, Lynd bemoaned U.S. social science and its drift toward Positivism and specialization. The pursuit of the social totality was being sacrificed to narrower approaches, he argued.[92] As MacIver viewed it, Lynd's book called for a more progressive, utilitarian approach to sociology that would be capable of training public-service professionals to solve the problems facing modern society.[93] MacIver attacked Lynd's ignorance regarding the epistemology of social theory and criticized his restricted view of the discipline.[94] Lynd criticized the neutral and disinterested observer of social phenomena and seemed to advocate for a more engaged orientation.[95] MacIver, by contrast, argued in favor of pursuing knowledge for its own sake. He accused Lynd of a sociological Pragmatism and a political bias that equally endangered the kind of grand theoretical view of society that Lynd claimed to favor.[96] While Lynd attempted to defend himself in the scholarly journals,[97] the department became split into factions supporting each combatant. Abel and Casey rushed to MacIver's defense, while the other members of the department allied themselves with Lynd. The Horkheimer Circle carefully monitored the situation, attempting to court both sides while simultaneously antagonizing neither of them. MacIver, who no longer had enough support to remain chairperson of the department, resigned. Perhaps motivated by revenge,[98] he became the Institute's strongest supporter at Columbia and told members of the Horkheimer Circle that he wanted it to become the university's social research Institute.[99] By supporting the Horkheimer Circle, MacIver created competition for Paul Lazarsfeld (who Lynd desired as a replacement for the Institute for Social Research).[100] As MacIver's support of the Horkheimer Circle increased, Lynd's dissatisfaction with the group escalated.

Despite such considerable obstacles, the proposal was brought before the Faculty of Political Science's Committee on Instruction.[101] Horkheimer, elated by the progress, became convinced that the group's future lay with Columbia.[102] Pollock believed the twin keys to the proposal's success were patching up relations with Lynd and allowing Neumann to act as the group's primary representative on campus.[103]

By the fall, however, emotions were dampened by fears of treachery. As Neumann moved ahead with the Institute's plans for incorporation, Horkheimer and Pollock feared that their colleague was increasingly promoting his own career at the expense of the Institute.[104] In particular, they feared that Neumann would be the department's first choice for the potential lectureship.[105] In January 1942, the fears were realized when Neumann was offered the position in the sociology department.[106] Neumann's popularity at Columbia, however, had nothing to do with duplicity on his part. Evidently, Neumann was impressive. He was a versatile and tireless worker who was able to collaborate with his American colleagues. Neumann's impact on Morningside Heights was strong enough to make him a candidate for a permanent position once the war was over. Nevertheless, the Institute leaders refused to see the decision as a positive evaluation of one of their colleagues. Instead, they took the defeat personally and consequently adopted a more radical solution to the economic crisis. They decided to begin downsizing the Institute and its staff.[107]

The major triumph of the 1940s was the project on anti-Semitism that resulted in the book series *Studies in Prejudice*. Before Neumann's departure from the Horkheimer Circle, he had managed to convince the American Jewish Committee (AJC) of the study's merits.[108] The AJC's generosity dramatically changed the Institute's finances but did not change the strategy adopted by the group's leaders. Although recently dismissed Institute members participated actively in the new work, Horkheimer insisted that the financial commitments remain temporary. He did not wish to repeat the process of eliminating associates.[109] The project's success brought greater visibility to the Horkheimer Circle[110] and led to renewed talks about incorporating the Institute into Columbia University.

In the spring of 1945, following the war's conclusion, the Faculty of Political Science's Committee on Instruction sought to clarify the relationship between Columbia and the Institute for Social Research. The investigation, led by Arthur MacMahon, lasted more than a year and resulted in a final arrangement between the two parties. Circumstances differed significantly from those surrounding earlier discussions in 1941 and 1942.

The first issue affecting MacMahon's evaluation was the state of the Institute. According to Horkheimer's grand design, the members were scattered throughout the country. Horkheimer and Adorno spent the war on the West Coast, completing *Dialectic of Enlightenment,* overseeing the entire anti-Semitism project, and working on *The Authoritarian Personality.* Marcuse, Neumann, and Kirchheimer worked for the Office of Strategic Services, which limited their involvement in the AJC studies. Only a tiny group remained in New York, and they divided much of their time between *Studies in Prejudice* and Paul Lazarsfeld's Office of Radio Research. Columbia's sociologists, perplexed by these unexpected and unannounced developments, struggled to balance their ethical views regarding Columbia's obligations to the Institute and the administrative needs of the university.[111] At the end of 1943, the navy, clamoring for space on Morningside Heights, set its sights on the Institute's offices on 117th Street.[112] The administration, puzzled by the lack of activity at the Institute for Social Research, felt tempted to evict it, but Pollock, with the aid of faculty allies, managed to free up enough space in the building to satisfy the navy's needs.

The other development affecting MacMahon's evaluation was the creation of Lazarsfeld's Bureau of Applied Social Research. In November 1944, the sociology department met with Lazarsfeld in the hopes of establishing a more formal relationship with him and his associates. Lazarsfeld was given a position on the university's faculty, and the bureau was established to meet the needs of the sociology department—the very same needs that had faced the department since the 1920s. Once Lazarsfeld joined the Faculty of Political Science, relationships with Horkheimer and the Institute were no longer pressing. A compelling need for affiliation with the Horkheimer Circle no longer existed.

During the lengthy evaluation process of 1945–46, Lazarsfeld became the Institute's strongest supporter on the Columbia faculty. Although he pointed out the "idiocy of the Institute group" for not publishing more in English, he credited them with publications that were easily ignored by other faculty members.[113] In particular, he described his own role in the Newark unemployment study and explained that the main force behind the project was the Horkheimer Circle, not Mirra Komarovsky. Although Lazarsfeld did the group a service by defending them before the department, his motives might not have been selfless. He hoped to benefit from a relationship with the group, which he wanted to see split into what he referred to as "theoretical" and "empirical" branches.[114] The two categories were idiosyncratic (for example, the peculiarity of lumping Marcuse into the "empirical" branch), but they were designed to serve a purpose. Lazarsfeld saw the impossibility of collaborating with Horkheimer and Adorno, but he recognized that the other members of the Institute might be valuable team members within his Bureau of Applied Social Research. By creating the distinctions between a "theoretical" and an "empirical" branch, Lazarsfeld capitalized on the ambitions of the sociology department, convincing his colleagues to jettison the theorists while retaining the empiricists. The bureau would facilitate the move by hosting the group's empirical branch (composed of Lowenthal, Massing, Marcuse, Neumann, and Pollock) as a separate division. Some members and financial resources would join in studies of mass culture, while others would be devoted to

Lazarsfeld's industrial sociology team. Yearly payments of thirty thousand dollars would be required from the Horkheimer Circle's endowment. Of the total sum, four thousand dollars would go to the bureau's budget to pay the overhead, while the remaining amount would pay staff salaries. No provisions, however, were made for Horkheimer or the theoretical wing of the Institute for Social Research.

As a result of Lazarsfeld's interventions, the MacMahon committee produced a positive report on the Horkheimer Circle.[115] After summarizing the group's specific contributions to the study of National Socialism, Chinese society, the family, prejudice, philosophy, and the arts, Columbia's sociologists made their general evaluation of the Institute for Social Research. They concluded their report by stating:

> The books and articles published under the auspices of the Institute rank high from the point of view of originality, thoroughness and logical clarity. Some of the studies that were mentioned are undoubtedly lasting contributions to the social sciences. Many of the articles are monographs in which the authors have either opened up new perspectives of study or achieved a penetrating and many-sided analysis of their subject matter. Throughout the publications show awareness of the requirements of modern developments in methodology. In initiating large-scale research projects and in opening up new fields of study the Institute during the ten year period of its association with Columbia University has been an important factor in promoting the growth of the social sciences in the United States.[116]

The MacMahon committee, recognizing that the final decision lay with the two primary parties involved, authorized Lazarsfeld to negotiate with Horkheimer on the university's behalf.[117] The issue had become a matter to be settled between the Bureau of Applied Social Research and the Institute for Social Research. Columbia, in a decision consistent with its original aims, would only accept an affiliation with the Horkheimer Circle that promoted empirical research and quantitative methods. Horkheimer must have realized that he had no room to negotiate, because he broke off his talks with Lazarsfeld at the beginning of June. It would have been unimaginable for Horkheimer to hand over so much control of his Institute. Citing theoretical tasks that lay before the Institute, Horkheimer respectfully thanked Columbia and declined its offer.[118]

The Institute, following Horkheimer's decision, vacated its offices at Columbia but did not yet leave Morningside Heights. Lowenthal and Marcuse taught occasional courses at Columbia during the late 1940s; Neumann was eventually hired by the department of government in 1949; and the Institute maintained a residential apartment at 90 Morningside Drive that was frequently occupied by Alice and Joseph Maier. Relations between Columbia and the Institute's leaders became cool but not hostile. Horkheimer still sought the occasional recommendation or contact from his former colleagues in the sociology department,[119] but he concentrated on the completion of *Studies in Prejudice*. When he received an offer to return the Institute to Frankfurt in 1949, he did not hesitate. The remaining core of Horkheimer, Pollock, and Adorno returned to the University of Frankfurt, leaving behind most of the group's former members. With the exception of Neumann, and later Kirchheimer, the group members who remained in the United States eventually left Columbia for teaching positions at other American universities, such as Brandeis, the University of California, Berkeley, and the University of California San Diego. By the 1960s, no traces of the Horkheimer Circle could be found at Columbia, except those buried deep within the university's archives.

PART II

THE OWL OF MINERVA COMES TO NEW YORK

c h a p t e r 3

JOHN DEWEY'S PIT BULL

Sidney Hook and the Confrontation between
Pragmatism and Critical Theory

Max Horkheimer knew relatively little about New York City at the time that it was selected to be the new base of operations for the diasporic existence of the Frankfurt School. The members of the Institut für Sozialforschung wanted to leave Europe and get as far away from the Nazis as possible, and a wide array of North American cities had been considered. Particularly because of its proximity to Europe, Manhattan was deemed a desirable new home for the group. Horkheimer failed to note, however, what an ideal location he had selected for the group's new headquarters. Although Horkheimer recognized what a prestigious institution Columbia University was, he also understood that New York City was not a typical American college town. Perhaps no American city could have provided as exceptional an environment for Horkheimer and his colleagues, but the Frankfurt School would never allow itself to take advantage of all of the opportunities that New York City had to offer.

Horkheimer and the other members of the Institute uprooted their lives with their departure from Frankfurt am Main. They left family and friends behind, and they also were retreating from a city that had grown to be a comfortable home. Although members of Frankfurt's Goethe University faculty may have questioned the political and intellectual orientations of the Institut für Sozialforschung, the progressive atmosphere within the university and its environs allowed Horkheimer to build alliances with other scholars and institutions. In addition to recruiting a cohort of younger associates from the Goethe University (such as T. W. Adorno, Erich Fromm,

97

and Leo Lowenthal), Horkheimer also nurtured collegial (if sometimes competitive) relations with other scholars in Frankfurt that remained outside of the Institute's orbit—most notably Kurt Riezler, Paul Tillich, Karl Mannheim, and Adolf Löwe, who all met regularly with Horkheimer at the Café Laumer. Outside of the lecture halls of the university and its surrounding neighborhood, the city of Frankfurt had also grown to be a good home for Horkheimer and the other members of the Institute. Although one could never mistake either the political or the cultural atmosphere in Frankfurt for Berlin, Frankfurt had developed numerous outlets for left-leaning intellectuals and for supporters of aesthetic modernism. During the years of the Weimar Republic, Frankfurt am Main became a key arena for Germany's avant-garde. George Swarzenski built the Städel Gallery into a showplace for German expressionists such as Max Beckmann; architects from the Bauhaus such as Ernst May received commissions for projects in Frankfurt; and the city's theaters and concert halls offered a wide array of modernist dramas, musical programs, and operas. Furthermore, the *Frankfurter Zeitung* and Carl Schleussner's Südwestdeutsche Rundfunk had emerged as important outlets for intellectuals sharing interests that overlapped with the Institut für Sozialforschung. Siegfried Kracauer, a close friend of Adorno and the Institute, was a regular contributor to the *Frankfurter Zeitung,* and both Walter Benjamin and T. W. Adorno presented lectures and radio addresses for the Südwestdeutsche Rundfunk.

The members of the Horkheimer Circle missed Frankfurt a great deal during their years of exile, and they struggled with the unique homesickness brought on by political exile throughout their years in Manhattan. Nostalgia for home and accompanying fears of political persecution caused members of the Frankfurt School to enter New York warily. Under other circumstances, the staff of the Institut für Sozialforschung more quickly might have been able to recognize the unique environment and opportunities that existed in New York City. As Thomas Bender points out, the "New York intellect" had long-standing, firm ties to the European mind.[1] For years, New York served as the primary point of entry for European immigrants arriving in the United States. As a consequence, New York also became the central passageway for European ideas entering the country. As William Barrett recounted in his memoir from his years working for *Partisan Review,* "New York was not really an American city—it was 'the last outpost of Europe' on these shores—and the intellectual life does not fit with our native American habits."[2] Europe's intellectual traditions, however, were not simply assimilated by the inhabitants of the city. Instead, a unique process of cultural blending took place. The result was an unusual atmosphere unlike any in the "New World." Manhattan became a mixing bowl and an intellectual battleground for ideas, culture, and intellectuals. The Institute for Social Research, therefore, entered an environment that potentially was more open to its legacy than perhaps any location outside of Europe. Furthermore, the Horkheimer Circle arrived in an urban landscape that was teeming with vitality. New York's intellectuals shared similar interests—they were captivated by modernism, as well as innovative approaches to the culture and politics of the Left. The Institute for Social Research, therefore, overlooked an enormous number of potential allies that its new home offered. By choosing to remain silent about the major political questions of the day and by concealing its Marxism almost completely, the Horkheimer Circle unwittingly abandoned the opportunity to play a larger role in New York's intellectual universe. As we noted in our examination of the Institute's relationship with Columbia University, the Horkheimer Circle struggled to satisfy the expectations of its hosts following Erich Fromm's departure from the Institute. Ironically, the broader intellectual atmosphere in New York may have held more promise for the group—but Horkheimer remained unwilling to risk the possible repercussions of political activism or even political engagement with the major topics of the era.

As the members of the Horkheimer Circle attempted to prove their worth at Columbia and endeavored to participate within the world of American social science, a remarkably similar coterie of writers took shape among the "little magazines" of Greenwich Village—the "New York Intellectuals." Although they diverged more sharply with the passing of time, there is a surprising correspondence between the two groups during the 1930s and early 1940s. The New York Intellectuals and the Frankfurt School inhabited a strikingly similar intellectual terrain, employing their "dialectical imaginations" to symmetrical sets of interconnected issues such as Marxism, alienation, conformity, mass culture, aesthetic theory, modernism, and totalitarianism. Sharing such a vast array of resemblances, the question of influence is not only reasonable but also essential. Is it possible that each group affected the views and ideas of the other? Or, in a similar vein, is it possible that each simultaneously encouraged the intellectual development of the other?

Intellectual historians of both groups have noted the similarities, but none have pursued the questions of contact and influence.[3] All point out the intellectual correspondences between the two coteries, but none have attempted to connect the dots and to get to the bottom of these similarities. The current and subsequent chapters seek to unravel the true nature of the relationships between the Frankfurt School and the New York Intellectuals. The striking resemblances between the two coteries aren't simply coincidental. Both groups knew of each other and at times interacted, but to what extent did they make use of each other? What was the nature of their interactions? What were the results of their intellectual and personal contacts?

The New York Intellectuals need little introduction. Over the past three decades, they have probably received more attention from American intellectual historians than any other comparable twentieth-century community of thinkers in the United States. Members of the group have assisted in the prolonging of this fascination by periodically stirring up controversies in memoirs and reminiscences. The group's story is compelling, because it documents and anticipates so many of the major political, cultural, and intellectual trends of the twentieth century. Founding and then coalescing around a number of small-circulation journals, the New York Intellectuals placed both themselves and their ideas at the center of America's cultural and political map.

Whether one loves or hates the writings and thought of the New York Intellectuals, both supporters and detractors must acknowledge the group's remarkable dexterity at uncovering the most interesting and important questions facing American society in the twentieth century. This collection of brash and controversial New Yorkers has always been a few steps ahead of American public opinion—before modernism had found a strong and vibrant audience in the United States, the New York Intellectuals were its champions; in the midst of the Depression, the group helped bring the intricacies of Marxism to the attention of highbrow and middlebrow reading audiences; and during the years prior to the inaugural hostilities of the Cold War, the New York writers had laid claim to a powerful anti-Stalinist position that anticipated the shocking disclosures of the Gulag Archipelago, as well as the birth of the neoconservative movement in American politics. Although it's true that most intellectuals worthy of the title remain a few steps ahead of their contemporaries, this group consistently and correctly dissected the emerging social and cultural trends within postwar society.

Adding to their reputation and notoriety is the fact that so many of the
New York Intellectuals carved out a living outside the proverbial ivory
towers of the academy. With time, many eventually entered the ranks of
university faculties, but all of them remained, first and foremost, public
intellectuals. In fact, as Russell Jacoby has famously suggested, they may
be America's *last* generation of public intellectuals.[4]

While many of the New York Intellectuals offered their services to a
wide array of magazines for which they expounded and developed a shared
set of sensibilities, four functioned as the central organs of the group. *Partisan Review,* founded as a platform for the critical support of modernism
and leftist radicalism, became the primary outlet for aesthetic theorizing
and art criticism. Dwight Macdonald's *Politics,* born from the disillusioning
realizations of World War II, explored the first outlines of a post-Trotskyist
radicalism and mounted the first assaults against mass culture. *Commentary,* the creation of Elliot Cohen and the American Jewish Committee,
transcended its initial purpose—locating a uniquely Jewish-American consciousness—and became an intellectual forum for the major political and
sociological debates of the postwar period. And Lewis Coser and Irving
Howe's *Dissent* took shape in response to fears of intellectual Cold War conformity and became the house magazine for America's social-democratic,
anti-Stalinist, anti-McCarthy Left. There were many other magazines with
which the New York Intellectuals became involved (most notably, *Encounter,* the *New York Review of Books,* and *The Public Interest*), but none commanded the same respect or attention. *Partisan Review, Politics, Commentary,*
and *Dissent* were the institutional and intellectual stars that New York writers such as Philip Rahv, William Phillips, Lionel Trilling, James Burnham,
James Rorty, Meyer Schapiro, Clement Greenberg, Harold Rosenberg,
Dwight Macdonald, Elliot Cohen, Mary McCarthy, Hannah Arendt, Sidney Hook, Irving Howe, Irving Kristol, Daniel Bell, Leslie Fielder, Seymour
Martin Lipset, Nathan Glazer, Robert Warshow, and Norman Podhoretz
orbited.

SIDNEY HOOK AND THE FRANKFURT SCHOOL'S
INTRODUCTION TO THE WORLD OF THE
NEW YORK INTELLECTUALS

The first New York Intellectual to have direct contact with the Horkheimer
Circle was probably Sidney Hook. Sidney Hook (1902–89), in addition to

being an early participant in the circle around *Partisan Review,* also served
as an intellectual and political mentor to the group. During the 1930s,
Hook distinguished himself as perhaps the foremost American authority
on the writings and legacy of Karl Marx. As such, Hook helped the New
York intellectual community grapple with the intricacies of Marxian theory and the dialectic. Combining Marxism with Deweyian Pragmatism,
Hook fashioned a unique interpretation of Marxism that combated the
rigid notions of truth that had been envisioned by the architects of the Second International and that were subscribed to by the American Communist Party, as well as the American Socialist Party. Through his work with
John Dewey, Hook gained an appreciation for the ever-changing nature of
reality that science was best equipped to grasp, as well as the role played
by subjectivity in the pursuit of knowledge. Perhaps more important, however, Dewey's Pragmatism also enabled Hook to reformulate Marxism with
regard to its relationship with democracy. William Phillips and Delmore
Schwartz, two of *Partisan Review's* central figures who both studied with
Hook at New York University, credited his teachings as a crucial inspiration for their own understanding of Marx. Consequently, when *Partisan
Review* took shape and gave rise to the "New York Intellectual" pedigree,
Hook's Pragmatic Marxism predominated as the radical philosophical ori-
entation of the new magazine and its group of young writers.

Archival records indicate that Sidney Hook was among Max Horkheimer's earliest correspondents from the United States. With their mutual
interest and expertise in Marxian theory, it is not surprising that a brief exchange of letters and publications took place in 1935.[5] While Horkheimer
introduced Hook to the Institute's *Zeitschrift für Sozialforschung* and in
particular his article titled "Zum Rationalismusstreit in der gegenwärtigen
Philosophie" ("The Rationalism Debate in Contemporary Philosophy"),
Hook similarly passed along a copy of a recent article titled "Experimental
Logic."[6] As cordial and benign as this preliminary series of contacts were,
they nevertheless established the groundwork for the subsequent confrontations that took place between the critical theorists of the Frankfurt
School and U.S. supporters of Pragmatism—a topic that we will revisit in
depth later in this chapter.

Meyer Schapiro, one of Hook's friends and associates from the 1930s,
also came in contact with the Institute at this time. Schapiro (1904–96), by
contrast, played a more modest role within New York's radical, intellectual

community. Although he earned a reputation as a learned art historian and critic, he was also a public intellectual deeply engaged in the political struggles of the American Left during the 1930s and 1940s. Personally, Schapiro was a well-known and well-liked figure in New York. Splitting his time, however, between the New York Intellectuals and the artists of Greenwich Village made him a more limited and part-time member of the circles surrounding *Partisan Review, Commentary, Politics,* and *Dissent.* His position at Columbia on the faculty in art history gave him a prestige and reputation that few others achieved. Although he shared similar political passions with the other New York Intellectuals, Schapiro remained less boisterous in expressing his views and he did not undertake the path toward deradicalization that became commonplace among so many other members of this community. Schapiro sympathized with the Communist Party much longer than many of his friends in New York. Even once he had joined the ranks of the anti-Stalinists, his views remained out of step with the New York mainstream, as Schapiro became one of the first to move toward Social Democracy.

Although Schapiro may have encountered members of the Institute for Social Research on Morningside Heights through his faculty position at Columbia, we possess no archival sources that would indicate this. Yet we can be certain that Schapiro, together with Hook and the philosopher of logic Ernest Nagel, definitely participated in a pair of meetings with the Horkheimer Circle during 1936 and 1937.[7] Hook recalled that the gatherings were assembled as a result of an article he published in the fledgling journal *Marxist Quarterly* titled "Dialectic and Nature."[8] Again, like the mistake about the date of the gathering, Hook's memory was not entirely correct. Although Horkheimer did have objections to Hook's description and analysis of the dialectic, Horkheimer invited the New Yorkers to the Institute's headquarters on 117th Street in the company of Otto Neurath—the Austro-Marxist and member of the Vienna Circle who was visiting New York at the time of the first meeting that took place during the fall of 1936. The second meeting, which occurred in 1937 and did not include Otto Neurath, likely was a direct confrontation with Hook's article, as well as the fallout from the first meeting. These face-to-face encounters not only represented some of the earliest substantive contacts between members of the Frankfurt School and the New York Intellectuals, but also anticipated and precipitated many of the subsequent conflicts and misunderstandings that erupted between the first generation of Frankfurt School Critical Theorists and the school of Pragmatism that originated from John Dewey.

HOOK'S PRAGMATIC MARXISM AND HORKHEIMER'S CRITICAL THEORY: THE NARCISSISM OF SMALL DIFFERENCES?

Throughout his lifetime and after, Hook was a powerfully polarizing figure.[9] As Nathan Glazer recalled, Hook did not merely argue tirelessly in some very controversial debates during a highly polemical era, but also galvanized other intellectuals to his cause in the same way that a general rallies his troops.[10] Thus, the Horkheimer Circle not only found itself embroiled in debate with a formidable adversary who threatened the foundations of Critical Theory, but also engaged in a dialogue that would shape the attitudes of many within the community of New York Intellectuals. Hook was the acknowledged expert when it came to the intricacies of Marxism, and simultaneously was a figure of substantial power and influence in the center of the intellectual networks that tied New York's little magazines together.

By now the contours of the debate between the Critical Theory of the Horkheimer Circle and American Pragmatism are familiar to students of both philosophical orientations, but a cursory glance at these two schools of thought might lead one to expect less friction between them. In fact, some might be tempted to see the controversies between Sidney Hook and the Frankfurt School as an ideal case study in Freud's "narcissism of small differences."[11]

By the early 1930s, both philosophies responded to the crisis of modernity following World War I by seeking to locate a middle road between radical subjectivism and materialism. Critical Theory and Pragmatism, therefore, were equally hostile toward metaphysics, Idealism, phenomenology, and the various manifestations of irrationalism that arose during the 1920s. Simultaneously, both were similarly hostile toward the pure mathematical formalism of logic and Positivism—although Dewey and Hook were more sympathetic students of Logical Positivism, individual experience still remained the basis for their Pragmatic Instrumentalism. Pragmatism, like Critical Theory, avoided the epistemological whirlpools that had been left behind in the wake of the Cartesian dualism between subject and object. Pragmatists, like the Critical Theorists, did not concern themselves with questions concerning the actual nature of reality and also did not retreat into an empirical copy-theory of knowledge that removed moral and ethical matters from philosophy. Instead, Pragmatists, like John Dewey and Sidney Hook, formulated a philosophy that was grounded in individual scientific experience and thus yielded observations that disclosed practical rather than eternal truths about the world. Comparable to Critical Theory, the primary goals of Pragmatism were to identify social and natural problems that blocked human actions and potentials and then to develop ideas that could overcome these obstacles. Pragmatism, therefore, like Critical Theory, shared an overarching goal of making our understanding of the world more rational through a scientific methodology. In addition, the Horkheimer Circle and John Dewey were inspired by the legacy of G. W. F. Hegel. While similarly rejecting the identity theory that emerged within Hegel's philosophy, both the Frankfurt School and Dewey embraced historicism and a belief in the social constructedness of reality. Knowledge of the present shed light on both the past and the future, and thereby moved humankind toward a realization of its own freedom through rational analysis of the world.[12]

As Marxists of the 1930s, the resemblances between Sidney Hook and the Horkheimer Circle were even more pronounced. Operating in the shadows of the Second International, the revisionism of Eduard Bernstein, and the Russian Revolution, another mediated position needed to be found by Hook and the Frankfurt School—this time navigating between the dialectical materialism subscribed to by orthodox revolutionaries, the accommodation politics of mainstream socialist parties, and the vanguard strategies of the Bolsheviks. The Horkheimer Circle and Sidney Hook returned to the writings of the young Marx and the Hegelian legacy that inspired him in order to locate alternatives to the forms of Marxism that were popular in the 1930s. Following in the footsteps of Karl Korsch and Georg Lukács, the Frankfurt School and Hook tried to reorient Marxism as a social-scientific and philosophical method rather than as a quasi-Social Darwinian faith in the inevitability of revolution or as a mere political tool for political reform (or coup d'état). Both Hook and the Institute for Social Research, thus, understood Marxism as a sociophilosophical methodology that united social theory together with scientific analysis for the purpose of promoting rational and progressive social change through action. At a moment when Marxism was finally free of legal repression and gaining in popularity, Sidney Hook and the Frankfurt School continually retreated from Marxian political organizations (such as the Communists, the Popular Front, the Trotskyists, and the Socialists) to chart their own independent paths.

Subtle but significant differences, nevertheless, separated Sidney Hook and the Frankfurt School. As intellectual descendants of Marxism, both were concerned with action (or praxis)—yet action played a far more prominent role within the Pragmatic Marxism of Sidney Hook than it did for members of the Institute for Social Research (who grew to see critical reason as a form of practice and resistance from a totally reified and authoritarian society). Similarly, both recognized that scientific innovation and reason were providing humankind with the potential for constructing more just and free societies—but Sidney Hook, like his mentor John Dewey, was far more comfortable with conceiving of this development as the exercising of human power and will over nature (a conclusion that grew to be at odds with the Horkheimer Circle's concerns about instrumental rationality). Unquestionably, the most divisive issues for Sidney Hook and the Frankfurt School related to their differing notions about dialectical logic, the value of Hegel's legacy for both philosophy and social science, and their conceptions of science itself.

It is important to remember that Critical Theory sought to recover the Hegelian roots of Marxism. By returning to Hegel, Critical Theory de-emphasized the economic dogmatism and scientism that pervaded Marx's late work and the thinking of the Second International, and it thereby sought to renew the quest to decipher the social and intellectual totality of contemporary, Western society. Instead of reducing all social and cultural life to their roots in the economic means of production, Critical Theory recovered Hegel in an attempt to rethink alienation, consciousness, and their relationships to the history of late-industrial society. Perhaps more importantly, they also sought to revive Hegel's emphasis on reason. Social theory should uncover whether social organizations and social values are as reasonable as they believe themselves to be. While the Horkheimer Circle was open to inspiration from a variety of complementary social theories (particularly those of Freud and Weber), its thought remained firmly fixed within the tradition of historical materialism. Reality was not fixed or static. It was, instead, dynamic and perpetually in a state of becoming. The Hegelian dialectic provided the Critical Theorist with the only adequate means of assembling specific observations and grounding them in the social totality, and the technique of immanent criticism was the method by which the Frankfurt School kept its theory historical rather than transcendent. Also, immanent critique was the tool by which the Frankfurt School exposed contemporary civilization to the light of reason.

Sidney Hook, by contrast, grew to object to this Western Marxist trend of reviving Hegelianism. Although he similarly sought to reexamine the social-scientific methodology of the young Marx, Hook was wary of backtracking too far into Hegel's legacy. For Hook, the study of Hegelian Marxists such as Georg Lukács and Karl Korsch had been useful for the same reasons that studying Lenin and Rosa Luxemburg had been important—they helped to justify the same emphasis upon human action that attracted Hook to Deweyan Pragmatism. Lukács and Korsch interested Hook less because of their methodological return to the philosophy of Hegel, and more because of their contributions to Marxian philosophy that liberated it from the stagnant determinism of the Second International.[13] This is not to imply that Sidney Hook misread or misunderstood Western Marxism, nor to suggest that he was not adequately familiar with the philosophical legacy of German Idealism, which had inspired Western Marxists such as Lukács or Korsch; instead it points to the conclusion that Hook was a very selective student of Western Marxism. Like the Western Marxists, Hook was a knowledgeable reader of Kant, Hegel, and the Young Hegelians. He had studied in Germany on a Guggenheim fellowship in 1928 and developed grave suspicions about the philosophical traditions that he encountered there. Instead of discovering a philosophical system as he had from John Dewey, Hook felt that he had stumbled upon a lay religion—in which philosophers were deferred to by academics from other fields, and yet the philosophers spoke of "eternal truths" that were ignorant of or in contradiction with social facts. The predominant philosophical tendency that Hook identified was a broadly defined idealism, which was fixated on formulating coherent and totalizing worldviews that grossly deemphasized specific details in favor of the whole.[14] Furthermore, sounding much like our contemporary critics of deconstruction, Hook also was frustrated by the jargon that was common in German philosophical discussions. Instead of clarifying social theory, Hook felt that German philosophical discourse clouded reason in a thick veil of linguistic virtuosity that obfuscated and prevented others from understanding contemporary reality. Although Hook agreed that the dogmatic acceptance of Marx's theories was undesirable, a return to Hegel was not particularly promising either. In Hook's view, Hegel's thought was deeply embedded in the theological struggles of his day and was suffused with the conservatism of Restoration Europe.[15] Hegel, in Hook's view, remained grounded within the tradition of metaphysics. The concepts of "absolute knowledge," "totality," the preference for *Vernunft* (reason) over *Verstand* (understanding) were evidence of metaphysical residues within Hegel's philosophy. Marx, by contrast, was a vast improvement over Hegel because Marx's thought was grounded in materialism and was oriented toward action. While Marx proposed "practical" improvements for the world, Hegel remained a "pure" thinker and resorted to philosophical absolutes to justify his thought.

Sidney Hook's interpretation of Marxism, by contrast, was distinctly American, and he proposed it as an alternative to the growing number of Western Marxist attacks against the orthodoxy of the Second International. Hook's Marxism embraced action, democracy, and the United States' main contribution to philosophy—Pragmatism. While still a graduate student at Columbia, Hook began attending some of John Dewey's lecture courses and became an intellectual convert to Instrumentalism. Initially, Hook had discredited Pragmatism, believing falsely that it evaluated all thought according to the dictates of utility.[16] After hearing Dewey speak, however, Hook discovered that Instrumentalism's notion of practicality did not imply utility, but rather evoked the action and practical experimentalism of science.[17] As Hook began to blend this new enthusiasm with his older commitment to Marxism, he inserted Dewey's Instrumentalism into Marx's thought to provide the latter with a clearer "scientific" component. Marxian orthodoxy therefore was flawed because it embraced a nonscientific view of reality that mimicked the blind faith of religious zeal. Hook's newly constituted Pragmatic Marxism continually subjected reality to scientific investigation. The ultimate purpose was to derive new and more progressive social changes for contemporary society through objective, value-free analysis. While the Horkheimer Circle attempted to reconfigure Marx as a historical materialist (firmly rooted within the legacy of Hegel's logic), Hook's Marx was a "scientist-activist."[18] In Hook's opinion, the Horkheimer Circle's Hegelianization of Marx represented a return to the conservatism, authoritarianism, and obscurantism that were at the very roots of German Idealism.[19] Hook's Pragmatic Marxism avoided such elitist and antidemocratic pitfalls and presented a version of Marx that was consistent with democracy. Both Dewey and Hook were strongly influenced by the writings of C. S. Peirce and recognized the democratic and egalitarian principles that pervaded his notion of a scientific community.[20] Each individual could participate in and contribute to Pragmatist philosophy. Any person, like any scientist, was capable of generating new and creative ideas about the world that could be tested and evaluated according to practical experience. Knowledge and reason then could be refined as the discoveries within this scientific community were shared and consensus began to take shape. Hook's Marx, consequently, was a champion of private thought and reason, and he was a proponent of collective action.[21] Hook's Pragmatic Marxists made up their own minds based on their own scientific evaluations of contemporary reality. If consensus could be reached among these private evaluations, collective action was possible, and its democratic course was assured.

Scientific rationalism, and particularly the form of instrumental logic that formed the basis for the Pragmatism of John Dewey and Sidney Hook, was a topic that Max Horkheimer had criticized during his early academic career. Throughout his lectures at the University of Frankfurt, Horkheimer offered not only a material history of the development of philosophy during the bourgeois era but also included a sustained critique of Positivism in the natural and social sciences.[22] By failing to grasp the historical nature of reality, by excluding critical reason (*Vernunft*), and by contenting itself with uncovering practical solutions to practical problems (and thus concentrating its energy on technical innovation and refined methods for describing existing reality), Positivism and science failed the live up to their full potential. Horkheimer's early analysis of Pragmatism grew out of this analysis of Positivism and scientific logic in the bourgeois era. In 1932, before his arrival in the United States and his first contact with Sidney Hook, Horkheimer addressed the topic of Pragmatism for the first time in an article titled "Notes on Science and the Crisis."[23] Judging Pragmatism's instrumentalist doctrines to be symptomatic of science's integration within the bourgeois means of production, Horkheimer stated:

> The fact that science contributes to the social life-process as a productive power and a means of production in no way legitimates a pragmatist theory of knowledge. The fruitfulness of knowledge indeed plays a role in its claim to truth, but the fruitfulness in question is to be understood as intrinsic to

the science and not as usefulness for ulterior purposes. The test of the truth of a judgment is something different from the test of its importance for human life. It is not for social interests to decide what is or is not true; the criteria for truth have developed, rather, in connection with progress at the theoretical level.[24]

Horkheimer, arguing from the standpoint of historical materialism, pinpointed the Pragmatic theory of knowledge as a symptom of the more general crisis that he had diagnosed within scientific logic. Recognizing the incorporation of science within bourgeois civilization's means of production, Horkheimer pointed to Pragmatism as a distortion of scientific logic that derived its criteria for knowledge from utility. At this moment in time, Horkheimer's familiarity with Pragmatism was minimal. With time, it would expand to become a significant piece of his broader critique of Positivism.

During the early 1930s following the Institute's emigration to the United States, the Horkheimer Circle was aware of Sidney Hook and American Pragmatism—but the confrontation between the two philosophical schools initially was conducted entirely by reviewers for the Institute's *Zeitschrift für Sozialforschung*.[25] In 1934, Paul Mattick (a fellow German émigré and temporary friend of the Frankfurt School) contributed a review of Hook's *Towards the Understanding of Karl Marx*. Mattick, who was a personal friend of Karl Korsch and an active participant and organizer of the Council Communist movement (in contrast to revisionism and Leninism, Council Communism looked back to the direct democracy of the spontaneous workers' and soldiers' councils as the most natural and ideal form of working-class organization), praised Hook's book for the important discussions that it would stimulate in the United States, but his overall judgment of the manuscript was entirely negative.[26] Mattick defended the Marxian theory of value and the premise of revolutionary inevitability by attacking Hook's Pragmatic conception of dialectical materialism and his philosophical defense of Leninism. Whereas Hook emphasized consciousness and voluntary action, Mattick emphasized the pervasive but nondeterministic role that objective socioeconomic relations played within Marxism. Social activity, argued Mattick, was conditioned by human needs and necessities arising from biological, social, and historical drives. The dialectic would not end with the overcoming of socioeconomic conflicts in the Soviet Union or anywhere else, because the development of humanity was endless. Although it is likely that the Institute for Social Research would have been uncomfortable with the political implications of Mattick's judgments, it is important to note how well camouflaged they were within the review. The important point that Mattick and the Horkheimer Circle shared in relation to Hook was a rejection of his Pragmatic reinterpretation of the Marxian dialectic—a point that Horkheimer would begin to develop as he underwent preparation for his article "On the Problem of Truth."[27]

The article, which appeared in the third installment of the 1935 *Zeitschrift für Sozialforschung*, presented Horkheimer's most devastating comments (until this point) regarding Pragmatism. Explicitly identifying it as a product of Positivism, Horkheimer examined the distortions that both philosophies inflicted upon reason and reality. As in 1932, Horkheimer framed his analysis as an immanent critique of bourgeois science:

> Analysis carried through to the end and skeptical distrust of all theory on the one hand and readiness to believe naively in detached fixed principles on the other, these are characteristic of the bourgeois mind.[28]

Whereas Critical Theory relied on historical materialism and critical reason to integrate specific observations within a theoretically comprehensive interpretation of contemporary society (and similarly relied on particular observations to help modify the theory), Positivism and Pragmatism rejected the theoretical impulse and instead favored the isolation of scientific disciplines and the "facts" that they uncovered. The unfortunate result was the rise of highly developed critical attitudes in specialized fields but naive views about social life more generally. This willful ignorance and its accompanying distortions of reality led Horkheimer to the ironic conclusion that Positivism and Pragmatism had more in common with metaphysics and Idealism than one would gather from their rhetoric.[29] To bolster this argument, Horkheimer concentrated on William James's "mysticism" and "mediumism" within his Pragmatic methodology to illustrate an "inclination toward spiritualism [that] can be followed through the later history of Positivism."[30] This choice by Horkheimer, however, disclosed an ignorance of Deweyan Pragmatism. Dewey and Hook, by extension, were highly critical of the emotional and spiritual impulses that had shaped the Pragmatism of William James.[31] Contrary to Horkheimer's characterizations, Dewey and Hook's Pragmatism was focused on general social life and represented neither a retreat from history into the specificity of social facts nor a spiritual escape within subjective individualism.[32]

Whether fair or not, Horkheimer's analysis of Pragmatism continued to rely heavily on the writings of William James throughout the article. Repeating the interpretation of James that had become common in Germany following the 1908 translation of *Pragmatism*, Horkheimer echoed his own judgment about Pragmatism from "Notes on Science and the Crisis":

> According to this view [Pragmatism], the truth of theories is decided by what one accomplishes with them. Their power to produce desired effects for the spiritual and physical existence of human beings is also their criterion.[33]

James, who had never been adequately clear about his concepts of truth, meaning, and utility, was partly responsible for the reception of his thought in Germany. Other philosophers, in addition to Horkheimer, had perceived the same link between truth and utility within his writings.

John Dewey, however, did eventually enter into Horkheimer's analysis. After spending several years in the United States, Horkheimer was more aware of Dewey's contributions to Pragmatism. Some of Dewey's work had been reviewed in the *Zeitschrift für Sozialforschung*,[34] but also Horkheimer was in contact with "Dewey's bulldog," Sidney Hook. If Horkheimer was unfamiliar with or unclear about Dewey's own writings on Instrumentalism, he had received a copy of Sidney Hook's "Experimental Logic" in 1931 from the author himself.[35] This essay would have provided Horkheimer with an accurate description of the practical, scientific action theory that Dewey had formulated as the essential criterion for knowledge—as well as a road map for making sense of Dewey's *Reconstruction of Philosophy*,[36] which Horkheimer cited in his text. Horkheimer wrote:

> The corroboration of thoughts in practice is identical with their truth, and indeed pragmatism, especially in its most recent development, places the principal emphasis not so much on the mere confirmation of a judgment by the occurrence of the predicted factual situation, as on the promotion of human activity, liberation from all sorts of internal restraints, and the growth of personality and social life.[37]

Although Horkheimer acknowledged Dewey's apparent concern for social life, which he accused other Positivists and Pragmatists for lacking, the director of the Institute was sharply critical of Dewey's instrumental linkage between truth and practice. While this "most recent development" freed Dewey's philosophy of truth from the obvious pitfalls that arose from James's reliance on the notion of utility, practicality led to other traps that anticipated Horkheimer's later critiques of Pragmatism and Positivism. By requiring thoughts to be tested against their practical outcome, Dewey formulated an epistemology that could not move beyond the natural or social status quo. As Horkheimer explained:

> The pragmatic concept of truth in its exclusive form, without any contradictory metaphysics to supplement it, corresponds to limitless trust in the existing world. If the goodness of every idea is given time and opportunity to come to light, if the success of the truth—even after struggle and resistance—is in the long run certain, if the idea of a dangerous, explosive truth cannot come into the field of vision, then the present social structure is consecrated and—to the extent that it warns of harm—capable of unlimited development.[38]

The necessary criterion for truth that Deweyan Pragmatism lacked was a comprehensive theory of society that Critical Theory and historical materialism provided. What seems somewhat unfair about this judgment is that Critical Theory, as an immanent critique, did not offer the kind of comprehensive theory that Horkheimer criticized Deweyan Pragmatism for lacking. The Frankfurt School worked with a general theory of bourgeois society that was used to provide context for specific social facts, but it too was continually being revised as theoretical assumptions were undermined and revised by social research. In fact, at the time that Horkheimer was attacking Dewey, the results of the Horkheimer Circle's German workers project were raising disturbing questions about many of the assumptions that had guided the historical materialism of the early 1930s and the growing threat of fascism was generating hypotheses that would eventually transform Critical Theory.

By 1936, the topic of naturalism, which had become a central component of the Pragmatic conception of science that both Hook and Dewey developed, similarly was subjected to analysis and exposition within the

Zeitschrift für Sozialforschung. A review of *American Philosophy Today and Tomorrow* (edited by Horace Kallen and Sidney Hook) was contributed by Robert Marshak—a brilliant philosophy and mathematics student at Columbia University during the early 1930s who later changed his major to physics.[39] Unlike Mattick's review, Marshak's contribution was not an attack on the concept of naturalism within Pragmatist philosophy. Instead it was a clear and concise summary of the function that naturalism played within the concepts of science that the disciples of John Dewey utilized. As Marshak explained:

> The naturalism of these men [John Randall, Ernest Nagel, Sidney Hook, and Irwin Edman] embodies a theory of nature, a specific kind of analytic method, and a generally applicable apparatus of evaluation. Their method demands that the world of common-sense functions throughout as the source and referent of the complex instruments of the understanding, and that an analysis of nature begins with what is beheld and not with what we wish to find nor what the fact of analysis is assumed to create. The application of this method by philosophy itself, they claim, will reveal nature as a logical structure, as a field of action, and as a scene where values may be generated and understanding made possible by the character of its own setting, and made actual by the thinking, acting, and appreciative characteristics of man.[40]

Horkheimer and his associates familiar with his correspondence with Sidney Hook would have been entirely unsurprised by Hook's increasing reliance on naturalism to form the basis for his Pragmatic epistemology. This dimension of Hook's philosophy would have become readily apparent to the Frankfurt School when Hook mailed them a copy of his essay "Experimental Logic."[41] Like the contribution to *American Philosophy Today and Tomorrow,* this article from 1931 made the argument that "logical validity was grounded on natural facts."[42] Hook, therefore, rejected nominalism and denied that forms had any essence or meaning until appearing within an inferential inquiry. He argued in favor of the "continuity between the methods of thought and the world in which thoughts go on" that was established "by defining the meaning of ideas operationally and their validity in terms of anticipated consequences."[43]

Following in the footsteps of Peirce and Dewey, Hook was in the process of formulating an instrumental and practical logic that could surpass formal logic and dialectical materialism. Toward this end, Hook more aggressively was formulating a concept of reason (or logic) that relied exclusively on *Verstand* (practical understanding) and degraded *Vernunft* (critical reason) as a metaphysical artifact from Hegelian philosophy—related to the faulty metaphysical distinction between appearance and essence. Hook wished not only to leave behind Hegel's reliance on "totality" but also to dispense with Hegel's overreliance on "concepts." Uncomfortable with the Idealistic implications of both, Hook sought to reconsider dialectical logic. The logic that he desired should be grounded in social facts that were understood historically. Hook's notion of the dialectic, thus, was becoming increasingly more reliant on an instrumental concept of reason, but his notion of a scientific community equipped him with the confidence that his dialectical method was not as limiting as the Horkheimer Circle and other Western Marxists might argue.[44] By 1937 when Hook came face-to-face with the Horkheimer Circle, he was on the verge of abandoning the notion of dialectical logic altogether. His understanding of the scientific method had entirely displaced the need for dialectics.

Faced with the simultaneous encounters with Logical Positivism and Pragmatism, the Horkheimer Circle found it necessary to more clearly articulate its critical theory of society. Having developed its intellectual identity in opposition to the metaphysical philosophies that it had left behind in Germany, the criticisms directed at Hegel and dialectical logic were correctly perceived as threats. At the same time as the Frankfurt School sought to mount a defense of itself and an attack on these new enemies, the Institute was growing increasingly preoccupied with the topic of Nazism. Gradually, the Critical Theorists began to experiment with the emerging concept of totalitarianism and to develop the concept of state capitalism. Thus, the critiques of Positivism and Pragmatism grew to become entwined with the theoretical formulation of a new social totality. Instrumental rationality grew to become a transhistorical critique of modernity that functioned as the ideology of state capitalism (which admittedly was a Weberian ideal type rather than a product of historical materialism and immanent critique).[45] As these developments within the Horkheimer Circle progressed, the philosophies of Sidney Hook and his mentor, John Dewey, would emerge as significant targets for the increasingly ideological criticisms of the Horkheimer Circle. Unlike in 1932 or 1936 when Horkheimer was able to identify the Pragmatist theory of knowledge as merely a symptom of capitalism's distortion of scientific thought, Horkheimer was beginning to see the eclipse of the classical bourgeois world and had begun to commence with his speculations about the fate of reason under this new totalitarian social order. As Critical Theory began to change during the late 1930s, Horkheimer hoped to further develop his critiques of scientific reason and Pragmatism.

It is little wonder that Sidney Hook (accompanied by friends Ernest Nagel and Meyer Schapiro) was invited to join the Vienna Circle positivist, Otto Neurath, as a guest of the Institute for Social Research in the autumn of 1936. Neurath had been hired as a contractor by the Institute for work that he was pursuing regarding the standard of living,[46] but Horkheimer was simultaneously using his contact with Neurath to gain a better understanding of logical empiricism.[47] Hook and Nagel, in particular, were invited to join the meeting because of the philosophical affinities that the Horkheimer Circle had grown to perceive between Pragmatism and Logical Positivism.[48] What none of the guests realized was that Horkheimer sought to use the gathering to help him formulate his most devastating critique yet against Positivism.[49] Simultaneously, Horkheimer wished to interrogate Hook about his article "Dialectics and Nature"—thus enabling the Institute to initiate a critique of Hook's Pragmatism and to finally address the topic of dialectical materialism that had been raised years before by Paul Mattick.

To our great misfortune, transcripts from these meetings either were never produced or were not preserved. Such a resource would have provided a great deal more clarity about the relationship between Critical Theory and Pragmatism at this critical juncture—the era when the Institute for Social Research began to formulate some of the most significant revisions of Critical Theory, and a moment when Hook began to make his slow but steady departure from the world of Marxism. It is tempting to wonder about the information that could be gained from a more precise record of this meeting: How much headway did Horkheimer gain with the lines of attack that he had formulated in "On the Problem of Truth"? Perhaps more important, were any of the parties able to recognize the amount of ground they shared? What, if any, consequences arose from these meetings that may have influenced the future development of either Pragmatism or Critical Theory? Although we can only speculate about the answers to such questions, we do possess enough resources to develop an educated guess about what might have taken place during these significant confrontations.

The substance of the encounter with Otto Neurath is perhaps easier to discern because Horkheimer recounted the meetings in an exchange of letters with Neurath, as well as in correspondence with other members of the Institute for Social Research. Although he politely yet evasively minimized the philosophical and sociological differences that arose between Neurath and the members of his circle, Horkheimer was clear about the difficulties he had with Logical Positivism.[50] Horkheimer felt that Neurath had not adequately articulated the distinction that Logical Positivism drew between the concept of science and the concept of metaphysics. Similarly, Horkheimer admitted that he would need to more carefully examine the criteria that were operative within his own group's concept of science. Horkheimer expressed his belief that the meaningful correspondences and differences could be more clearly identified if a conceptual common ground could be established between the two parties.

At the same time, however, Horkheimer was beginning to probe the implications of Logical Positivism more deeply and consequently to develop greater reservations about his earlier position. In a letter to Theodor W. Adorno, Horkheimer admitted:

Already here in the Institute we have led some extensive seminar discussions for the purpose of our orientation. The last time Otto Neurath reported on the latest fate of the school [Logical Positivism], something he knows well. Basically the whole thing is only a miserable rearguard action by the formalistic epistemology of Liberalism, which, also in this area, segues into open fawning in the service of Fascism. If an important function of Neo-Kantianism has been to glorify the society whose preservation it serves through apologetics for the dominant scientific enterprise, all spheres of culture are shamelessly now sacrificed to irrationalism. It can mean nothing else but that only those thoughts, which are expressed by means of logic, can count as knowledge. It now emerges ever more clearly that one can express basically nothing with it, and in the end it reveals itself entirely as part of the fight against the application of thought to society and history generally. Leave us only in our posts as physicist and chemist, as modest servants of industry, and in return science will deliberately keep its mouth shut about all human concerns! This sounds like the confessions of middle industry in Germany: Let us tend to our modest shops, and we will give you *plein pouvoir* [full power] politically. What appears here is just what I indicated in the truth article ["On the Concept of Truth"]: the pre-established harmony of science and barbarity.[51]

Long before the despairing formulations of *Dialectic of Enlightenment,* Horkheimer's encounter with Logical Positivism (set against the backdrop of mounting Nazi aggression) was leading him toward the critique of instrumental rationality and its ideological link to the theory of the totally administered society. Philosophy, socioeconomic analysis, and ideology critique were all coming together to generate a nightmarish vision of domination and conformity in the postbourgeois world.

In the two articles that followed the meetings with Neurath, Horkheimer refined his attack on Positivism and modified his conception of Critical Theory. Although Neurath, like the early Frankfurt School, sought a philosophical unification of the sciences, Horkheimer attacked this ambition by drawing a sharp distinction between philosophy and science—a strategy that contradicted his own conception of historical materialism that had guided the early activities of the Institute. Science and Positivism, in their attempt to eradicate any form of metaphysics, restricted attention to only the empirically verifiable. Consequently, all forms of Positivism and empiricism focused on the perceptions of appearances of the world. By retreating from Idealism's emphasis on active cognition and the construction and utilization of concepts, Logical Positivism and modern science had impoverished philosophy and knowledge. Statements of fact were deprived of their social utility and transformative capabilities because they were not the same as statements of value. Positivism could merely describe the existing world, but it could not evaluate it or appreciate the constructive role that human beings played within it. Dialectical theory—now formulated without the same emphasis on social research—was offered as the antidote. As Horkheimer explained, "The facts of science and science itself are but segments of the life process of society, and in order to understand the significance of facts or of science generally one must possess the key to the historical situation, the right social theory."[52] Dialectical theory was crucial to social knowledge because it could historically account for the continuous changes that occurred within human communities and the rational process of concept formation and concept development. Instead of being mobilized to refine our understanding of the status quo, dialectical theory was mobilized to refashion society. While empiricism had grown to perceive the established order as the natural one, oppositional thinking was proposed as the key feature that helped to distinguish between "traditional" (scientific and instrumental) theories and "critical" theories. Horkheimer wrote: "The viewpoints which the latter [Critical Theory] derives from historical analysis as the goals of human activity, especially the idea of a reasonable organization of society that will meet the needs of the whole community, are immanent in human work but are not correctly grasped by individuals or by the common mind."[53]

With this new distinction between the active, critical analysis of dialectical logic and the passive perceptions of scientific logic, Horkheimer moved closer to the thought of the American Pragmatists. Dewey and Hook were not antihistoricist and therefore could not be guilty of the same blindness that the Logical Positivists suffered from. More important, Deweyan Pragmatism saw the philosopher and individual as active thinkers who tested ideas and formulated conclusions based on scientific and historical experiences. Last, but not least, neither Dewey nor Hook could have been mistaken for defenders of the status quo in the 1930s. Dewey, during this era, was identified as a new liberal, a progressive, a radical democrat, and a socialist, while Hook briefly affiliated himself with Leninists, Trotskyists, and Social Democrats. Horkheimer would not be able to make the same arguments against Pragmatism that he had unleashed on Otto Neurath, making the mystery of his encounter with Hook all the more intriguing.

Hook was invited to clarify the arguments that he had made in "Dialectic and Nature." This essay marked Hook's final repudiation of dialectic logic. The declared purpose of the article was to examine the concept of dialectics and to determine whether this methodology represented an improvement over the scientific method. Concentrating on the writings of G. W. F. Hegel, Friedrich Engels, Georgi Plekhanov, Karl Kautsky, V. I. Lenin, and Franz Mehring, Hook argued that the proponents of dialectical materialism understood its laws to be objective and universal. He, by contrast, saw this as grotesque exaggeration—the dialectic was not the only method of uncovering truth. In fact, Hook insisted that much of dialectical materialism's methodology was inconsistent and illogical. There were no clear rules for the confrontation or reconciliation of concepts, and he observed that reality was not composed of such sharp and static polarities. More important for the Horkheimer Circle, Hook repudiated the concept of totality, arguing that it was meaningless to say that all things were interrelated, unless Hegel and his followers were able to illustrate the interrelatedness of all objects and all knowledge in the world. Science could be offered as an alternative to dialectical logic, because a hypothesis underwent a similar pattern of conceptual development and modification—but science had formulated more rigorous and systematic methods for testing the validity of its hypotheses. Furthermore, science was able to recognize functional relationships among a limited number of variables without taking the metaphysical leap and trying to take into account the rest of the universe. Echoing his previous criticisms of Hegelian philosophy, Hook argued that dialectical logic projected theology into the analysis of reality through the role played by consciousness and the concepts it formed. By reducing all phenomena to their conceptual existence within consciousness, dialectics endowed the schemata of all things with a pervasive purpose or system of purposes. The scientific method avoided this pitfall by "a transformation of materials, an intervention into natural processes, and introduction of *redirective activities* upon what is given to hand in order to achieve the tested knowledge necessary for prediction and control."[54] Hook concluded his essay with a deceptively simple challenge:

> If we have established anything so far, we have shown that the only sense in which the dialectic is applicable to nature is the sense in which it is an abbreviated synonym for scientific method. And as a confirmation of this conclusion we need only ask of those who deny it, to point to a single case of knowledge discovered by, or explicable in terms of, the dialectic method which cannot be more simply certified by the canons of scientific method.[55]

Seated together with Neurath, Nagel, and Schapiro, Sidney Hook was undoubtedly questioned in the same collegial way that Horkheimer had made inquiries regarding Logical Positivism. Hook, though, was a more combative figure and was arguing in favor of a position that posed a far more serious threat to the Frankfurt School's program than anything that Neurath appears to have said. In a reminiscence of the encounter (published forty-four years later), Hook repeated his central conclusion: "either the dialectic method was synonymous with what passed ordinarily as scientific methods or that it was a kind of hocus pocus."[56] Hook then claimed that Neurath had made the argument that dialectical logic was a piece of the metaphysical Hegelian legacy that was incompatible with Marxist thought and the empirical discoveries of scientific sociology.

In response, Horkheimer, with the aid of Pollock, Marcuse and Lowenthal, accused Hook and Neurath of misunderstanding dialectical logic. We can only imagine that Horkheimer and his colleagues must have begun an initial attempt to articulate the defense of Hegelian philosophy that would later appear in "The Latest Attack on Metaphysics" and "Traditional and Critical Theory." This perhaps explains why Horkheimer was so insistent about requesting that Neurath provide a clearer distinction between science and metaphysics. If Hook and Neurath were proclaiming that no functional difference separated their concept of dialectics from scientific method yet saw dialectical logic as a vestige of metaphysics, it is no wonder that Horkheimer perceived how essential it was for his critics to clarify their arguments. For his own part, Horkheimer tried to elucidate the significant differences that separated the Institute's understanding and use of dialectical logic from those expressed in Hook's article. What made this job infinitely more complex was that Hook, following up on the challenge he threw down at the culmination of his essay, sought to clarify the issues (as well as to provoke his hosts) by demanding "an illustration from any field of a statement that was scientifically true but dialectically false or one that was dialectically false but scientifically true."[57] Judging by Hook's account of the discussion, it sounds as though Horkheimer tried to rely on his immanent critiques of the intellectual history of early modern bourgeois thought that had formed the core of his lecture courses in Frankfurt and been a powerful tool in his articles for the *Zeitschrift*. Concentrating on contradictions within the realms of philosophy and political theory, Horkheimer tried to show how subsequent intellectual and material developments arose from the reconciliation of these contradictions. Hook, however, recalls arguing that Horkheimer's examples were "commonplace cases that required the modification or the elimination of hypotheses."[58] With this path in the dialogue blocked, Horkheimer tried to turn the tables.

Perhaps in an attempt to put his interrogators on the defensive, Horkheimer and Pollock began to elaborate their critique of Positivism. This strategy, of course, had been used rather effectively in Horkheimer's essay

"On the Problem of Truth." Hook, however, remained unconvinced by this new line of argument. Thinking back to that evening in 1936, he recalled:

> they had no clear or coherent notion of what positivism was. It seemed as if they identified it with "worship of the facts," and opposition to theory. They were nonplussed when we pointed out that facts by themselves were not significant in the process of acquiring knowledge except with reference to some theory and the real problem was to distinguish between testable theories and speculative fancies.[59]

Although at times the Horkheimer Circle was guilty of treading close to the simple equation of Positivism with blind empiricism, the critique of Positivism that Horkheimer had published only months earlier was far more complex than this. In "On the Problem of Truth," Horkheimer had formulated some criticisms of Pragmatism that Hook easily would have dismissed—such as equating Pragmatic logic with utility—but there were other lines of attack that would have been harder for Hook to overcome. What, for example, might have been Hook's reply to the Frankfurt School's historical-materialist analysis of science in the bourgeois era? Certainly, Hook would not have seen this issue in the quite the same way. Following in the footsteps of Peirce and Dewey, Hook was evoking the idea of a scientific community that was too vast to become unconscious contributors to the reification of late-capitalist society—but Horkheimer could have pointed to any number of examples (including his Institute's research on the German working class) to point out that such faith in the typical reasoner had tragic consequences in Germany. More significantly, Horkheimer could have repeated his critique of Dewey's linkage between truth and practice. Last, and perhaps most significantly, Horkheimer could have made the argument, which he was only beginning to formulate, that both Positivism and Pragmatism revived metaphysics. Although he had initially raised this point with the example of William James, he would eventually shift his approach to interrogate the unproven correlation that Positivists and Pragmatists saw between scientific progress and the emergence of a more just and improved society. Critical Theory, with its reliance on dialectical logic, was able to question the social totality and to determine how it failed to live up to these promises.

THE FAILURE OF NERVE AND CRITICAL THEORY'S
RENEWED DEBATE WITH SIDNEY HOOK

In the wake of this encounter with Sidney Hook, the Horkheimer Circle began attacking and undermining the pillars of Hook's scientific optimism throughout the late 1930s and early 1940s. Beginning with the Circle's studies of authority and then sustained throughout its analyses of Nazism and mass culture, it documented the decline of individual autonomy and private Reason, and it followed the rise of mass conformity and technological rationality. According to the Institute's work, Hook's democratic faith in free and independent men and women was thoroughly naive—such people were rapidly becoming extinct. Furthermore, largely as a result of Horkheimer and Adorno's work on *Dialectic of Enlightenment,* the Institute for Social Research aggressively proposed the idea that experimental science, or Positivism, was one of the primary culprits for modernity's mental enslavement. By attempting to transpose the models of the natural and physical sciences into the arena of the social sciences, Positivists, like Hook, had removed the essential critical element that had propelled Western science since its inception. Without this critical impulse, Positivism mistook the status quo for reality. Instead of viewing the social world as a series of potentialities, Hook and other Positivists simply reduced social science to empirical replications of what already existed. Hegelianism, with its emphasis on the historicity of social reality and the continual unfolding of all concepts, was again proposed by the Horkheimer Circle as the only antidote to the new orthodoxy of Positivism.

The unresolved conflict between Critical Theory and Pragmatism erupted again in 1943, when Sidney Hook and several of his friends launched an assault on all proponents of philosophical and moral absolutisms. Evoking Gilbert Murray's notion of "the failure of nerve," Hook provocatively proposed that there was a dangerous symmetry between the United States in the 1940s and the Classical World on the eve of its precipitous decline. A large number of intellectuals from both societies grew fascinated with "asceticism, mysticism, pessimism, and despair."[60] Instead of maintaining their faith in the logic and values that represented the foundations of their worlds, they engaged in irresponsible panic and abandoned responsibility in favor of false supernaturalisms. According to Murray, this shift was a main cause for the collapse of Greek and Roman civilizations. It represented a clear and unambiguous warning for Hook and his friends, who all insisted that the recent, parallel trend threatened Western liberalism. The central element in the contemporary "failure of nerve" was a loss of confidence in science. Instead of recognizing the continuous reliability and success of science, the new intellectual cowards sought to propose alternative "methods" that privileged subjectivism and "private truths." They failed to offer a legitimate option to the scientific method and ultimately promoted different modes of obscurantism (5). Science was a disciplined and organized search for truth that relied on public verification to gain its consensus. The "new failure of nerve," by contrast, was arbitrary, exclusionary, and biased.

According to Hook and his colleagues, the causes for the contemporary, intellectual crisis were clear. Despair and disappointment were natural reactions to the failures of the postwar world (8). The peace process that ended World War I had not enabled it to be the war that ended all wars. Furthermore, postwar society had suffered severe economic setbacks and had witnessed the rise of a new and frightening political reality—totalitarianism. Nevertheless, intellectuals needed to remain calm in the face of such hardships, and they were not entitled to allow their private fears to contaminate the public's confidence. According to Hook, the anticipated construction of a free and stable welfare state would put a permanent end to the conditions that had given birth to the "new failure of nerve" (ibid.). Patience was required until this welfare state was built.

The intellectual culprits that Hook directed his attack against were primarily theologians, such as Reinhold Niebuhr and Jacques Maritain, who sought religious renewal by counterposing faith against science (10–23). These pious proponents of the "failure of nerve" insisted that reliance on the scientific method had dealt a serious blow to human values and was thus largely responsible for the rise and growth of totalitarianism. Hook sought to counter such assertions by emphasizing the value-free nature of the scientific method (10). He also raised the point that the church had attempted to improve the world for nearly two thousand years, and its efforts had failed. Science represented a new, secular effort toward the same general goal (ibid.). Perhaps most important, however, Hook raised the uncomfortable fact that fascism had sprung into existence within Germany and Italy—two of the West's most strongly religious and metaphysical countries. If totalitarianism were linked to the scientific erosion of values, how did theologians explain its rise in these two places? Why did it not instead emerge in more Positivistic nations such as Great Britain and the United States? (22).

The secondary targets of Hook's attack were disappointed socialists, such as the members of the Horkheimer Circle, who had begun to lose faith in the promises of their movement. In response to socialism's failures to take root and in reaction to the frightening realizations regarding Bolshevism, leftist thinkers abandoned their own ideology's roots in modern science (8–9). Instead of continuing to target the intellect, desperate socialists had begun denigrating science and were borrowing religion's rhetoric of salvation to generate a more emotionally compelling appeal. This betrayal of the scientific method became complete when these same intellectuals blamed science for totalitarianism and the Second World War. Proclaiming that Positivism's basic impulse was for total control of reality, socialists endeavored to demonstrate its complicity in the formation and trajectory of German Nazism, Italian Fascism, and Russian Bolshevism. According to Hook, there was absolutely no evidence for such claims. In fact, a casual perusal of humanity's most egregious social failures illuminated the fact that scientific considerations were absent or poorly deployed (ibid.). Hook's mentor, John Dewey, bolstered his student's claims by insisting that the proponents of the "failure of nerve" were the real totalitarians. The theological and secular "anti-Naturalists" substituted their own private dogmatisms for scientific reason. The result was supernatural fanaticism and philosophical absolutism that had far more in common with the cultural and intellectual authority wielded within totalitarian societies.[61]

Partisan Review's "The New Failure of Nerve" series was not simply a defense of American Pragmatism and its reliance on the scientific method. Although this series of articles published by Sidney Hook, John Dewey, and Ernest Nagel was consistent with the Marxian Instrumentalism that Hook had constructed during the 1930s, "The New Failure of Nerve" also marked an important shift in Hook's political allegiances and self-identification. During the 1930s, his enthusiasm for Marx had been diminished (as it had been for many of the other New York Intellectuals) by his realizations about Stalinism, the Popular Front, and the Communist Party's tragic policy of "Social Fascism."[62] Together, these three discoveries highlighted the inconsistencies between the Marxian politics of the 1930s and the ideal of liberalism that was so central to Hook's Marxist Pragmatism. Hook temporarily rectified his situation by abandoning his ties with the Communists

and by gravitating toward the Trotskyist factions in New York. The expul-
sion of the Trotskyists from the Socialist Party and the coming of World
War II, however, forced this tenuous solution to give way. The necessities
of the war, coupled with Hook's tremendous disillusionment with the
Left, led to a total disappointment with Marxism. As Christopher Phelps
convincingly demonstrates, Hook came to recognize that the elements of
Marx that he valued the most were already components of Dewey's Instrumentalism. It therefore became possible to abandon Marx and to solely
endorse Pragmatism.[63] Upon making this realization, Hook's main enemies became his former allies of the Left. While he attacked those who
uncomfortably condoned, excused, or remained silent about the horrific
course that Leninism had taken, Hook became a vigorous defender of the
United States and of scientific reason. "The New Failure of Nerve" thus
served to defend the assumptions underlying his faith in Pragmatism,
while at the same time attacking those who rejected the United States' participation in the war on moral and metaphysical grounds.

Although "The New Failure of Nerve" was not directed specifically at the
Critical Theorists of the Institute for Social Research, they clearly saw the
series as a partial attack against themselves. In large part, this may have had
to do with Hook's review of Herbert Marcuse's *Reason and Revolution,* which
appeared in the summer of 1941. Marcuse's book, which rescued Hegel's
Anglo-American reputation from the taint of Nazism, also represented one
of the clearest and most thorough analyses of the foundations of Critical
Theory. Surveying the legacies of German Idealism and Marxism, Marcuse
helped to clarify and defend the definition of Critical Theory that had been
the source of such tension during the face-to-face meetings with Hook in
1936–37. Hook's review, however, returned to many of these sore spots and
poured salt into the wounds by calling Marcuse's interpretations "highly
dubious and on basic questions definitely wrong."[64] Hook went on to con-
tradict Marcuse's view of Hegel's philosophy as an expression of the liberalism of the French Revolution (an opinion that had been commonplace
within the Institute since its formation) by reminding Marcuse to consider
the reactionary role that nationalism played within Hegel's thought. Hook
similarly ridiculed Marcuse's characterization of early Positivism (associated with Saint Simon, Comte, and Stahl) as a counterrevolutionary reaction to Hegel's liberalism. Revisiting the major points of controversy that
had arisen during the face-to-face meetings of 1936–37, Hook proclaimed:

The least common denominator of this inclusive positivism is apparently the refusal to accept the idealist principle "that the matters of fact or experience have to be justified before the court of reason." The refusal to accept this principle means to Mr. Marcuse either accommodation to the status quo or mere reformism. It [Marcuse's interpretations of Positivism] shows that he [Marcuse] does not come within hailing distance of understanding positivism. Positivism in social thought does not take its point of departure from ready-made facts but seeks to discover by scientific, not dialectical, methods what the facts are. It is only by testing our ideals and principles by available facts that we can tell whether our choice of them has been intelligent. As for Mr. Marcuse's dissatisfaction with positivist reformism, "reform" is just as much an ideal as "revolution," and positivists can be and have been revolutionists just as dialecticians can be and have been reformists and even stand-patters. The irony of the situation is that on Mr. Marcuse's own formulation of the idealistic principle, the use of the ambiguous term Reason makes it easy to sanctify the status quo . . . Whoever wins, is right.[65]

Hook's review not only undermined the core of Marcuse's book and the traditions on which Critical Theory was built, but also now subjected the concept of critical reason to the same harsh treatment. This concept had been the cornerstone of Horkheimer's 1937 essays that came out of the meetings with Otto Neurath and Sidney Hook. Horkheimer had turned to a defense of the Hegelian dialectic and its basis in critical reason to point out the shortcomings of Positivism in general. By concentrating his most devastating remarks on this portion of Marcuse's book, Hook was again questioning the entire basis for a critical theory of society.

In the wake of this review, the subsequent actions of the Frankfurt School become clear. Despite the Institute's consistent policy of maintaining a relatively low profile within New York's extremely political public intellectual community, Max Horkheimer lifted the ban on political engagement and took aim at Hook and his colleagues. Clearly, the responses to "The New Failure of Nerve" came at a time when the Institute for Social Research had abandoned its strategy of isolation. The group was actively seeking integration within Columbia University, and it was vigorously pursuing grant support from a variety of American institutions. Nevertheless, leaping into the midst of this particular controversy remains a bit odd when one considers the broader context. By the time "The New

Failure of Nerve" appeared, nearly all of the New York Intellectuals embraced the war effort and therefore would be a more receptive audience to
the case Hook was making. More important, "The New Failure of Nerve"
was not simply a series that would be discussed by the typical readers of
Partisan Review. The main provocation for the series had been a conference held at the Jewish Theological Seminary in 1940.[66] Many scholars
from Columbia University, as well as from the ranks of American sociology, attended the conference and thus substantially would have increased
the audience for Hook's *Partisan Review* articles. The Frankfurt School
took a significant risk by entering this public intellectual debate, and it
risked antagonizing many of the same scholars and administrators who
it hoped to solicit for support. Perhaps, in addition to desiring one final
confrontation with Sidney Hook, it wanted to seize the opportunity that
"The New Failure of Nerve" created in an effort to circulate its views on
Positivism, which formed such a crucial component of Horkheimer and
Adorno's *Dialectic of Enlightenment.* With both factors in mind, however,
it is interesting to note that among the many samples of American Pragmatism that the Horkheimer Circle could have chosen from, it chose to
attack a highly visible defense of Positivism that simultaneously lumped
together the theological and political opponents of American thought and
policy. By attacking Hook, the Horkheimer Circle could lay the groundwork for the American reception of *Dialectic of Enlightenment,* it could
justify the Hegelian, historical-materialist basis for Critical Theory, and it
could defend the theological motifs that were emerging within its own
thought. By attempting to pull the intellectual rug out from beneath Hook,
the members of the Institute sought to defend their theoretical assumptions and preferences.

At first, the Horkheimer Circle moved surreptitiously against Hook and
the other authors of the *Partisan Review* series. Instead of a central figure
from the Institute's inner core presenting a response for the next edition
of Phillips's and Rahv's journal, the task was passed off to Norbert Guterman, a Polish-born translator and writer who had emigrated to New York
in 1933 and had become an associate of the Frankfurt School in 1936.[67]
Guterman's contribution, titled "Neither-Nor," was a cleverly crafted retort
against Hook that carefully shielded the theoretical perspective of both
Guterman and the Institute.[68] The piece focused on the legacy of Søren
Kierkegaard, and it simultaneously shifted between critiquing and praising

the Danish philosopher. By rejecting Hegel's system of abstract thinking (which obliterated the individual thinker by displacing him within the World Spirit), Kierkegaard proposed radical subjectivism as the only path to concrete existence. On the one hand, Kierkegaard's proto-existentialist position uncovered some of the most basic flaws of Positivism (the reduction of the world to observed phenomena), but, on the other hand, his privileging of the internal paralleled the same type of uncritical bias that the metaphysical critics of Positivism had perpetrated (the reduction of the world to the internally consistent). By analyzing Kierkegaard in this way, Guterman ultimately sought to illustrate that *neither* Positivism *nor* radical subjectivism was a solution to the basic epistemological argument that Hook had initiated. In opposition to both of these options, Guterman carefully resuscitated Hegelianism and the historical-materialist orientation that lay at the heart of Critical Theory:

Any theory that comforts us through the implicit or explicit negation of the historical context in which our lives are caught, any theory that negates the reality of the struggle as though the full realization of man were possible in the immediate present, involves a degrading abandonment of lucidity. In our time, military virtue is part of the individual's self-realization, even though it exposes him to the risk of losing his own unique life. But the claim that such virtue can be the result of only blind faith, that to achieve it our awareness of the actual condition of the world must be dulled, is a further example of religious opportunism. Philosophy and experience teach us that the opposite is true: the best fighters are not those who cultivate sacrifice as an end in itself but those who even in the face of voluntary death preserve the conviction that a world is possible in which men will control history instead of being controlled by it.[69]

A more direct response to "The New Failure of Nerve" was not published by the Horkheimer Circle until 1947.[70] It had, however, been prominent within Horkheimer's early plans for a series of lectures that he delivered at Columbia University's philosophy department in February and March 1944.[71] The lectures, following shortly on the heels of "The New Failure of Nerve," became a source of controversy and animated debate when Horkheimer presented his attack on Pragmatism. By the time the lectures were transformed into a book, *Eclipse of Reason*, the furor had died down, but the issues surrounding Critical Theory and Pragmatism remained unresolved. While most of the book reexamined many of the arguments that had been originally formulated in *Dialectic of Enlightenment,* the chapter "Conflicting Panaceas" returned to "The New Failure of Nerve" controversy.[72] Just as Guterman had written years before, Horkheimer expressed his concern about much of the reactionary resuscitation of metaphysical absolutes and outdated values (60–62). Such historically invalid dogmas were indeed dangerous, but so was the scientific dogmatism that Hook defended. As Horkheimer explained:

> The adversaries of Neo-Thomism justly point out that dogmatism sooner or later brings thought to a standstill. But is not the neo-positivist doctrine as dogmatic as the glorification of any absolute? (70)

Positivism, like dogmatic faith, required the conformity of thought. Instead of seeking conversion to the catechism of a theological system, science demanded absolute faith in the observable facts that formed the basis of the experimental method. The correlation, however, between method and truth had never been developed. Lacking the elaboration of this concrete relationship, science represented a new authoritarian mythology (76–77). The resulting scientific preference for commonsense observation and description justified and legitimated the censorship of all complex and abstract ideas. The Positivist bias against complex words and phrases disclosed a pervasive anti-intellectualism present in American society (85):

> The expertly processed mentality of this century retains the cave man's hostility toward the stranger. This is expressed in hatred not only of those who have skin of a different color or wear a different kind of suit, but also of strange and unusual thought, nay, even of thought itself when it follows truth beyond the boundaries delimited by the requirements of a given social order. (86)

Ultimately, Positivism was consistent with the socioeconomic order of monopoly capitalism. Although Hook and some of the other New York Intellectuals may not have realized it, Horkheimer was proclaiming their faith in science to be totalitarian. This was implied through all of Horkheimer's references to its dogmatism, authoritarianism, and conformity.

Linking Positivism to monopoly capital, however, represented a veiled way of disclosing its totalitarian tendencies. Throughout the late 1930s and 1940s, members of the Institute had struggled to make sense of Nazism. In the end, they arrived at the conclusion that it represented "state capitalism." Consequently, when Horkheimer included Positivism in his overall analysis of Western society, the implication was clear to his colleagues and other Americans familiar with the work of the Institute for Social Research (71). The only epistemological alternative apparent to the members of the Institute and their friends was Critical Theory. In a brief statement that greatly surpassed the clarity of Guterman's earlier attempt, Horkheimer briefly outlined the virtues of the Institute's theoretical method and disclosed its Hegelian and historical-materialist roots:

> The task of critical reflection is not merely to understand the various facts in their historical development—and even this has immeasurably wider implications than positivist scholasticism has ever dreamed of—but also to see through the notion of fact itself, in its development and therefore in its relativity. The so-called facts ascertained by quantitative methods, which the positivists are inclined to regard as the only scientific ones, are often surface phenomena that obscure rather than disclose the underlying reality. (82)

Social science could not freeze its observed facts in time, and it could not reduce them to static entities. As Hegel, the young Marx, and the early Western Marxists had insisted, all facts were mediated by history. They were dynamic and pregnant with possibilities.

Hook did not respond to the Horkheimer Circle's criticisms either publicly or privately. "The New Failure of Nerve" had not been directed at the Circle in the first place, and Horkheimer's *Eclipse of Reason* was not widely read or discussed in the late 1940s. Furthermore, the appearance of this attack by the Institute for Social Research came in the waning years of the institution's American exile. Even if Hook had wanted to revisit this debate, there was little point once Horkheimer returned to Germany. Thus, there were no published responses to either Guterman or Horkheimer, and Hook made no public mention of the Institute for Social Research until the rise of the New Left during the late 1960s. With Herbert Marcuse's rise to media prominence, Hook returned to the topic of Critical Theory in connection with his broader hostility to student radicalism. Consequently, in the 1980s, when the Horkheimer Circle no longer existed and nearly all of its founding members were deceased, Sidney Hook reexamined his debates and commented generally on the Institute for Social Research. These writings represent his summation on the topic of Critical Theory. By this moment in time, Hook had changed a great deal and the reputation of Critical Theory was significantly different. Nevertheless, these retrospective analyses do recapture the energy and revisit the crucial differences that arose in the confrontations of the 1930s and 1940s. In addition to providing the Addendum (about his 1936–37 meetings with the Horkheimer Circle) to accompany Lewis Feuer's historical investigation of the Frankfurt School at Columbia,[73] his more comprehensive statement was made in *Marxism and Beyond*.[74] In an essay titled "Reflections of the Frankfurt School," Hook looked back on the two major questions that the Institute raised for him—first, to what extent was it Marxist?; and second, did it make any significant contribution to our understanding of man and society?

To the first question, Hook claimed that the members of the Frankfurt School thought that they were Marxists, and (from his perspective) they maintained a suspiciously ambiguous position regarding Stalin and the Soviet Union. Nevertheless, Hook insisted that the Frankfurt School had Hegelianized Marxism so radically that its "revisionism" was more substantial than that of Eduard Bernstein (120). The second question, however, was far more clear-cut. In Hook's view, the Frankfurt School was an unmitigated failure. Not only had it not contributed to our understanding of the individual or society, but it had created some dangerously false illusions that required combating. Although it was unlikely that Hook would have liked the group any better if its views had been more consistent with Marx's, Hook exploited the inconsistencies—ironically, emphasizing what failures the members of the Horkheimer Circle were as Marxists. By downplaying the mode of production, the Frankfurt School obliterated Marx's concept of society and substituted Hegel's model of the social totality with its confounding series of interconnected parts (121). By rejecting naturalism, the Institute undermined Marxian materialism (122). By emphasizing the conformity and late-capitalist integration of the proletariat through consumerism, it rejected Marx's theories on working-class consciousness and paved the way for Marcuse's embrace of the counterculture (125–27). Although Hook correctly recalled that Critical Theory was rooted in reason and the dialectic, he also pointed out that the members of the Horkheimer Circle had never been able to publicly or privately demonstrate the superiority of their method over science. It was absurd to assume, as the Frankfurt School had, that facts were inherently dangerous. Facts, Hook insisted, were only meaningful when they were incorporated into theories of reality (122–25). The most devastating criticism, however, was reserved for last. In addition to claiming that members of the Horkheimer Circle were inadequate Marxists and social scientists, Hook also asserted that the Frankfurt School was elitist. According to Hook, Marx may have been mistaken about a great many things, but at least his heart was in the right place. He loved universal suffrage and had great faith in the masses. The Institute for Social Research, by contrast, had contempt for these very same people (127–29). The group's theories of authority, conformity, and mass culture all betrayed a lack of faith in liberalism as both a creed and a practice. Instead of embracing democracy, as the New York Intellectuals had learned to do, the Frankfurt School maintained an antidemocratic paternalism that was condescending and overly pessimistic.

Although Hook's views represent only one set of opinions about Critical Theory and the Horkheimer Circle, they were important to the other New York Intellectuals. The vast majority of writers and critics in the New York Intellectual community were oriented toward literature and/or sociology. Although their interests and expertise were extremely diverse, they were not professional philosophers like Sidney Hook. In fact, when it came to Marxism, Hook was the group's recognized expert and his influence was enormous.[75] The New York Intellectuals' introduction to Marxism may have occurred in their families and neighborhoods, but their academic introduction to Marx was filtered directly and indirectly through Sidney Hook. It began with the first generation that encountered Hook at New York University and around Greenwich Village and then was passed along to a second generation. As European as the New York Intellectuals' literary and artistic tastes may have been, their Marxism was unique. Specifically, it was inspired by Hook's fusion of Marx and Dewey. Although not all of the New York writers abandoned Marxism at the same time or in the same way that Hook did, the majority eventually embarked on similar paths toward deradicalization. Whether because of Stalin, the theory of social fascism, the purge trials, the Nazi–Soviet Pact, the Second World War, the Cold War, the rise of the Warsaw Pact, postwar American prosperity, or

the repression of Hungary, almost all of the New York Intellectuals grew
to embrace American democracy and to be suspicious of radical rhetoric.

For nearly all who joined Hook in his accommodation with the United
States, radical Marxian programs such as Critical Theory grew to become
quaint but outdated reminders of their younger days. For others, the
Horkheimer Circle took on more sinister characteristics—as it had in
Hook's mind. Late in the *Politics* group's fascination with the Horkheimer
Circle's contributions to the theory of mass culture (a topic that will be
examined in the next chapter), Daniel Bell and Edward Shils repeated the
accusations of antidemocratic paternalism that Hook had hinted about
in his review of Marcuse's *Reason and Revolution*.[76] Both Bell and Shils
ridiculed the leftist defenders of high culture and insisted that their stance
was actually conservative. The Horkheimer Circle, Dwight Macdonald,
and the many others who had joined the bandwagon were hopeless elit-
ists. Instead of fearing kitsch and mass culture, these critics needed to re-
assess the phenomenon and recognize that it marked the democratization
of culture and not the totalitarian leveling and control of art. To others
still, as the Cold War progressed, the Institute for Social Research took on
insidious Communist characteristics. Suspected connections with various
German Communists and Soviet spies easily arose and then spread because
of the group's secretiveness, paranoid behavior, and failure to speak out
against Stalin during the years of exile in New York.[77] The rise of the
student movement in the 1960s and its embrace of the Frankfurt School
undoubtedly only fed these rumors, but much of the true opposition had
already begun years earlier.

IRRECONCILABLE DIFFERENCES AND
MISSED OPPORTUNITIES

Before examining the details of the confrontation between Critical Theory and American Pragmatism, one might be tempted to see it as a case of
Freud's narcissism of small differences. The stubborn bitterness of both
sides, the inability of either party to recognize any common ground, and
the mutual desire to revisit an argument that was moving nowhere might
indicate that this intellectual feud was fueled by a neurotic compulsion.
Without denying the existence of powerful psychological dynamics within
such debates, it would be a mistake to rely solely on this psychoanalytic
interpretation. From a transatlantic, historical perspective, there was more

at stake in this controversy than might be readily obvious. Some observers from the immediate postwar era pointed to the significant cultural barriers that separated Europeans and Americans. Ludwig Marcuse, for example, saw Europhilia and jealousy at the core of émigré hostility toward the United States.[78] Although this explanation accounts for much of the animosity and conflict that emerged between the émigrés and their hosts, it does not adequately describe the controversy between Pragmatism and Critical Theory. Although the Horkheimer Circle, by all accounts, was particularly Eurocentric in its taste and thought, this does not help to explain its hostility to Sidney Hook. Hook presented a legitimate threat to the Frankfurt School, and vice versa.

Francis Goffing's postwar analysis of the transatlantic dynamic, by contrast, gets us much closer to the heart of the matter. Concentrating on the intellectual contrasts, Goffing argued that Americans and Europeans thought differently about the world.[79] Repeating a claim that has become pervasive in the literature concerning the "intellectual migration," Goffing insisted that the European mind was hierarchical, systematic, and abstractly conceptual in its analysis of the world, whereas the American mind was lateral, free-wheeling, and concretely empirical.[80]

At the very core of the debate between Sidney Hook and the Frankfurt School were two competing epistemological methodologies—scientific reason and critical reason. Ironically, each side made the same claim about the other—that the methodology formulated by the opponent represented a revival of metaphysics—and it was this accusation of metaphysical thinking that fed the bitterness and led to the circularity of the discussions. Why did this association with metaphysics provoke such hostility, and is there any significance to the fact that both parties used the taint of metaphysics to uncover totalitarian tendencies within the thought of the other party?

In his analysis of the wartime and postwar intellectual landscape, David Hollinger convincingly demonstrates the rise of a cultural program that was built around a cult of science. In the struggle against totalitarianism, the ideal of scientists arose as a role model for the democratic citizen. The scientific community and healthy civic communities were encouraged to live by "the code of honest, free inquiry, the code of critical, inter-active, evidence based, universalistic, antiauthoritarianism, and hence 'scientific conduct.'"[81] The secular, cosmopolitan Jews forming the community of the New York Intellectuals constituted one significant faction in this *Kulturkampf* against all transcendent and totalizing thought systems. Science slowly emerged as a new cornerstone for the cosmopolitan identity of the New York Intellectuals. Like Marxism, science represented a vision of social and political emancipation from prejudice and injustice through the democratic application of reason and critical analysis. Like the French revolutionaries, this new breed of philosophes sought to combat the mental absolutisms of the past that were rekindled in the new totalitarian systems. Whereas the Enlightenment had fought the metaphysical systems that affirmed the authority of the church and the monarchy, the opponents of totalitarianism saw themselves as "the guarantors of a particular vision of democracy: one authentically Jeffersonian, but being subverted by the perpetuation of old-fashioned religious and ethnic prejudices and being inhibited by a psychologically immature and socially provincial predilection for absolutes that portended an authoritarian political culture for the United States."[82]

What is striking about this formulation is how well it could be applied to the self-images of both the Horkheimer Circle and the Deweyan Pragmatists. Critical Theory and Pragmatism had both taken shape to combat similar enemies who deceived themselves with forms of irrationalism that were spawned in reaction to science. At the same time, both philosophies sought to reexamine the scientific heritage in order to negate the legitimate criticisms that had been hurled at the naive Positivisms of the early twentieth century. Hollinger's scientific *Kulturkampf,* therefore, would appear to be a transatlantic phenomenon before it became the dominant intellectual culture of the postwar West. In different political contexts, it might include Hegelian and Marxian dimensions, but its proponents saw this *Kulturkampf* as trying to facilitate similar aims.

This is why the accusations that Hook and the Horkheimer Circle hurled at each other were so offensive to both sets of combatants. Both sides saw themselves as critical thinkers who enriched their knowledge of the world through scientific investigation. Like the young Sidney Hook, the Frankfurt School saw its application of the Hegelian dialectic to be not only consistent with science but an heir to the liberatory legacies of the scientific revolution and the Enlightenment. Of course, the early scientists were concerned with effecting practical results within the world, but their application of science was also directed toward the progressive transformation of society. Similarly, John Dewey and Sidney Hook understood Instrumentalism to be a method that clarified knowledge and thus liberated individuals to make more rational decisions. The Pragmatic view of science also was consistent with the democratic knowledge community that Peirce had envisioned and that the colonial Americans had established. Thus, both the Deweyan Pragmatists and the Critical Theorists could see themselves as the philosophical heirs to the same historical forces that had progressively transformed Western civilization.

The rise of totalitarianism, however, led each side to view the other as enemies rather than as allies. Surveying the wreckage of the Weimar Republic, the Frankfurt School believed that the intellectual community had failed Germany—and the reasons for this failure were complex and led to a series of interrelated explanations that evolved as the members of the Institute continually pondered the question. At first, Horkheimer and his colleagues believed that Positivism had allowed the scientific community to be co-opted by the economic means of production. With time and considerable analysis, the Frankfurt School grew to see that the productive relationships had changed under totalitarianism. As the economy and society became increasingly coordinated by the state, the domination of nature became the central focus of Critical Theory. Once this theoretical transition had been made, science and its reliance on instrumental logic was identified as the source of totalitarianism—and thus the threat was not restricted to Germany or the Soviet Union, but was evident in the United States as well. Positivism in all of its varieties, as well as Pragmatism, not only became symptomatic of the crisis facing knowledge, but also was understood to be a cause for the spread of barbarism directed against nature and humankind. Pragmatists, like Sidney Hook, had dragged philosophy back into metaphysics and thereby crippled it. In an effort to combat this menace, Critical Theory devoted itself to recovering and preserving the noninstrumental mode of reasoning that was a part of the scientific legacy. Philosophy, and particularly Hegelian philosophy, provided the tools that Critical Theory needed for this effort.

Totalitarianism had a similar impact on Sidney Hook. As he scrutinized the Marxian legacy in the shadow of Stalinism, Hook struggled to comprehend why the Revolution had failed. Initially, this caused him to reinterpret Marxism. Based in part on his experiences in Weimar Germany, Hook jettisoned the Hegelian legacy and relied on Dewey's Pragmatism to supply his Marxism with a critically rigorous methodology that retained historicism and emphasized practical action. At the same time that Hook examined his philosophical assumptions, he strained against the dogmatism and the authoritarianism of the Communist Party. Like the other New York Intellectuals, it did not take long for him to recognize the antidemocratic and nonegalitarian behavior of the Communists. Philosophy and life experience converged. The problem with Hegel was that his logic relied on categories that Hook judged to be metaphysical. Hegel's views about concepts, totality, and absolute knowing not only distorted the world, but also were the source of the intellectual elitism and authoritarianism that he witnessed in Germany in 1928 and among the Communists during the 1930s. The Hegelian legacy could be used to justify reactionary politics in Germany and could be used to defend the dictatorship of the proletariat in Russia. As Hook warned Marcuse, Hegel's logic permitted philosophy to proclaim that "whoever wins, is right." Pragmatism and the scientific method offered the only promising alternative, because they preserved the objectivity of knowledge and facilitated egalitarian democracy by forming a scientific community with the aim of clarifying knowledge for the purposes of just and practical action. The Frankfurt School's Hegelianization of Marx caused Critical Theory to arrive at undemocratic and elitist conclusions about the world. The Horkheimer Circle abandoned the working class and criticized it for its conformity and lack of aesthetic taste. The members of the Frankfurt School grew to see themselves as the only revolutionary subject, because only they had achieved a state of self-conscious reflection that transcended the reified world of the totally administered society.

Perhaps witnessing a parallel between the commissar and the Critical Theorist, Hook interpreted the Institute for Social Research's silence about Stalin as an indication of support. This suspicion would not remain isolated. Other public intellectuals from the community of New York Intellectuals also harbored this fear. We have already examined how Hook's friend Lewis Feuer accused the Frankfurt School of being a Soviet spy ring. Perhaps, however, the more powerful example emerges from the correspondence of Edmund Wilson. Wilson, a hero of the New York Intellectuals and a knowledgeable analyst of Marxism, wrote:

> I have just thought of somebody else who ought to be a perfect model of an
> orthodox Marxist: Norbert Guterman. When I saw him some months ago,

he told me that the trouble with Marxism was that it had too little instead of too much Hegelian Dialectic.[83]

Norbert Guterman was only a temporary associate of the Institute, but he did cowrite *The Prophets of Deceit* with Leo Lowenthal and did cast the first stone at Sidney Hook's "The New Failure of Nerve." Furthermore, Wilson's judgment of Guterman would have been similarly true for the entire Horkheimer Circle. Sidney Hook and the New York Intellectuals could entertain the idea that this organization was a front for Stalin, because their judgment of its philosophy led them to this conclusion.

chapter 4

CROSSTOWN TRAFFIC

The New York Intellectuals
Encounter Critical Theory

There are few questions about Sidney Hook's early and sustained contacts with the Frankfurt School. Hook was one of the first public intellectuals in New York to approach the Institute for Social Research, and the differences of opinion that he discovered between himself and the recent émigrés probably influenced the reputation of the Institute among New York's anti-Stalinist radical community. But what of the other New York Intellectuals? Were there other substantive contacts between these two intellectual networks?

Determining when and how the New York Intellectuals first came into contact with the Horkheimer Circle is a more complex question than it might seem. In fact, it is far easier to locate and examine the traces of their mutual receptions than it is to pinpoint precisely when the first literary and face-to-face encounters took place. Archival material, typically one of the most trusted and reliable tools of the historian, yields little information. Instead of offering a clear picture of the contacts between the two groups, the archival evidence offers only a disjointed mosaic. Most letters and manuscripts provide us with a limited, retrospective view of the contacts between these two groups. Such documentation clearly suggests that each party was well aware of the other's work (in some cases there is even unambiguous acknowledgment of influence), but there are few indications of precisely when and how the relationship came about. Although one might be tempted to use this dearth of solid archival material to minimize the impact that each coterie had on the other, the lack of

140

preserved written records does not justify such an interpretive leap. Where the archival sources have offered more questions than answers, oral histories and published memoirs fill in the gaps. Although both suffer from the same reliance on memory, they have often provided a welcome degree of clarity regarding the blossoming relations that emerged in the late 1930s and early 1940s between the New York Intellectuals and the Horkheimer Circle.

Max Horkheimer placed extensive restrictions on the independent contacts and political affiliations that members of the Institute were permitted to pursue in the United States.[1] Horkheimer insisted that his personnel, as guests of Columbia University and as political exiles seeking refuge in a foreign land, refrain from any activities that might jeopardize the security or reputation of the group. Based on their previous experiences in Germany, Horkheimer's particularly "authoritarian" repression may have seemed justified. The Frankfurt branch of the circle had, after all, been closed and its property confiscated by the Nazis because of prior political connections and the public disclosures of radical beliefs. To then pack up these fears and to import them into the United States, however, created serious repercussions for the subsequent history of the Institute in America. As noted in the preceding chapter, New York City provided a unique intellectual milieu for the members of the Horkheimer Circle that would have been particularly hospitable to their interests and concerns. By following Horkheimer's instructions, however, the Institute for Social Research existed in a state of relative "splendid isolation" throughout the 1930s, because the Institute was able to dictate and control the nature of the collaborations that it undertook with Americans.[2]

During this early period of the Institute's history in Manhattan, the only American scholars that came into contact with the Horkheimer Circle did so by chance or were either connected with Columbia University or contracted by the group for editorial assistance and translation services. Through these official and formal relations, word of the Institut für Sozialforschung gradually began to spread among the New York Intellectuals. Although most formal introductions between the two coteries did not take place until the 1940s (at which point, financial necessity had required an end to Horkheimer's earlier timidity, and the sociological and philosophical work of the Institute became actively publicized), the reputation of the Horkheimer Circle quietly became established among New York's radical, scholarly community through the various interlocutors that were drawn into the Institute's small and protected world.

INROADS TO THE WORLD OF THE
NEW YORK INTELLECTUALS

Although never more than fringe figures in the world of the New York Intellectuals, several of the Institute's associates during the 1930s brought news of the Horkheimer Circle to City College and other hotbeds of intellectual radicalism around the New York vicinity. Moses Finkelstein (who later changed his name to M. I. Finley), Benjamin Nelson, and George Simpson all worked closely with members of the Horkheimer Circle in the late 1930s and thereby became informal "students" and interlocutors of the Institute.[3] All three drifted into the world of the Horkheimer Circle through its formal ties with Columbia University, as well as the involvement of some Institute members in Paul Lazarsfeld's Office of Radio Research. Few members of the Horkheimer Circle arrived in the United States with expertise in English. They could certainly communicate, but they were not prepared to participate in the intellectual life of the country. Even after living and working in the United States for more than nine years, Horkheimer admitted to his close confidants that the language barrier between German and English remained a formidable obstacle between Critical Theory and its American audience. In a letter of November 1943, he wrote about an early report of the Frankfurt School's research into anti-Semitism that grew to become the five-volume book series *Studies in Prejudice* and candidly indicated his continued discomfort with the English language:

> Since I cannot get rid of the impression that in addition to the usual dullness and naivety of such documents, our presentations express a certain perplexity due to our inability to master the English style of thinking and writing, I strongly advise [you] to have a good American writer assist you in formulating and organizing the final edition of this text.[4]

Serving primarily as translators, Finkelstein, Nelson, and Simpson were among the first to struggle with converting the Horkheimer Circle's dense Germanic prose into comprehensible English. As a result of their efforts, the work of the Frankfurt School gradually began to emerge from its isolated, Teutonic cocoon.

Finkelstein, who received his master's degree in ancient history from Columbia in 1929, had become a freelance intellectual and instructor in New York during the early 1930s. Although his formal training was as a classical historian, he combined these interests with a strong commitment to and fascination with social science. In fact, one of his first academic jobs was as a consultant on Edwin Seligman and Alvin Johnson's famous *Encyclopedia of the Social Sciences* (1931–35). Upon the completion of the project, Finkelstein was hired as a history instructor at City College, where he became an important mentor to many of the young New York Intellectuals who were studying there.[5] Although he began to spend increasing amounts of time uptown in connection with his new teaching duties, Finkelstein did maintain contact with his friends and colleagues at Columbia. By 1937, his presence on Morningside Heights was dramatically changed when Horkheimer hired him as an associate of the Institute for Social Research. Finkelstein was initially brought in to assist Otto Kirchheimer with the completion of *Punishment and Social Structure.*[6] The book, which had been contracted by the Institute, was the brainchild of Georg Rusche. Conditions in Europe had made its completion impossible, and Kirchheimer and Finkelstein had been assigned the task of completing and polishing the manuscript.[7] The book became one of the first English publications of the Institute in the United States, and it brought a small degree of fanfare to the Horkheimer Circle.[8] Anticipating many of the same issues that Michel Foucault explored in *Discipline and Punish,* Rusche and Kirchheimer offered analyses of different penal structures and legal systems by linking them to the sociohistorical dynamics of the eras that spawned them. Their pathbreaking discovery, which was meticulously supported with carefully gathered data, was a conclusion in harmony with the historical materialism of Marx and the other members of the Horkheimer Circle—that different forms of punishment conformed to the needs and interests of a society's productive forces. Thus, different methods of punishment changed over time to safeguard social values that had their basis in the interests of a society's evolving socioeconomic structure. Provocatively, the book further argued that the crime rates within contemporary societies were not deterred by harsh regimes of punishment or by elaborate schemes for character reform. These rates remained unchanged because the underlying structure of the contemporary socioeconomic order was hostile and unjust. A substantial decline in criminality, therefore, could only be expected with the socioeconomic transformation of modern society.

With the completion of *Punishment and Social Structure,* Finkelstein was rehired as a translator until he decided to stop dividing his time between City College and Columbia in 1939. In addition to his contribution to the Rusche and Kirchheimer book, Finkelstein helped the Horkheimer Circle translate and edit various articles for the English version of the *Zeitschrift,* the periodical that came to be known as *Studies in Philosophy and Social Science.* He also carried out work on an uncompleted project for the WPA's translation series that would have resulted in an English version of *Autorität und die Familie.*[9] Although his collaboration was brief, Finkelstein found a community of kindred spirits on the staff of the Institute for Social Research. Like himself, these visitors from Germany were committed to bridging the gulfs between historical analysis, philosophy, and the social sciences. For the Horkheimer Circle, the result of this project was Critical Theory. For Moses Finkelstein, however, the result was pioneering work in the previously untapped social and economic history of Ancient Greece, in which a social-scientific approach was deployed to shed new light on the intellectual history of the Classical World.[10]

Benjamin Nelson, another historian trained at Columbia, joined Finkelstein at the Institute in 1937 as a translator and editor. A few years younger than his Classicist colleague, Nelson juggled his tasks for the Horkheimer Circle with his graduate studies and a part-time teaching position at City College.[11] Trained as a medieval historian, Nelson's historicism was influenced, like Finkelstein's, by a strong interest in the social sciences. Max Horkheimer, who was well aware of the natural affinities between Nelson's own interests and the work of the Institute, actively supported the work of the young medievalist and grew to view him as a possible protégé. As Horkheimer reported in a letter of recommendation that he wrote on Nelson's behalf:

> We have met many students in the three years that the International Institute of Social Research has been in the United States, but I do not think that any of them reveals greater scholarly abilities and philosophical understanding than Mr. Nelson. I have frequently discussed various historical problems with him in connection with my own work, and his suggestions and opinions have always been stimulating and valuable . . . He is a very

hard and rapid worker, but not a grind in the invidious sense of the term. He has broad interests in philosophy, literature, and the arts, and shows balance and discriminating taste. I understand from others that he is also a popular teacher, and that merely confirms my own surmise based on the ability to analyze and develop ideas which he displays in our conversations and discussions.[12]

In addition to collaborating with Finkelstein on translations for *Studies in Philosophy and Social Science* and the WPA work on *Autorität und Familie,*[13] Nelson wrote a number of book reviews for the Frankfurt School and even translated and edited Horkheimer's Columbia lecture series titled "Society and Reason."[14] The relationship, which mutually benefited both parties throughout the late 1930s and early 1940s, came to a bitter end, however, in 1944–45 because of a dispute over finances. Nelson, who had agreed to provide editorial assistance for Horkheimer's *Eclipse of Reason,* backed out of the contract at the last minute. Horkheimer, who was traveling hurriedly between New York and California in conjunction with his managerial duties over the anti-Semitism project of the American Jewish Committee, had no time to consult with Nelson about the manuscript. In the past, members of the Institute had worked closely with their translators to ensure the accurate rendering of their ideas. Under the circumstances created by *Studies in Prejudice,* however, Nelson was forced to struggle alone. Recognizing the futility of his position, he pulled out of the project rather than submitting a manuscript that inevitably would not receive Horkheimer's approval. Horkheimer, however, failed to see the dangers of Nelson's predicament and took this rejection as a betrayal and vigorously demanded the return of a cash advance that Nelson had received for the translation. The two parties thus parted ways under ugly circumstances. Nelson took a position at the University of Chicago and later moved on to distinguished tenured positions at the University of Minnesota, Hofstra, SUNY Stony Brook, and the New School, while much of the Horkheimer Circle returned to Germany. Generally, Horkheimer and Nelson ignored one another, with the notable exception of a bitter feud over the legacy of Max Weber that took place in 1964.[15]

George Simpson, the last of the triumvirate of translators from the late 1930s, worked with Theodor Adorno on his project for the Office of Radio Research. Noted for his translations of Durkheim, Simpson came into contact with Adorno through his studies at Columbia. Unlike Finkelstein and Nelson, Simpson was a graduate student in the sociology department and worked closely with Robert MacIver.[16] Unable to locate a permanent academic appointment following the awarding of his PhD in 1937, Simpson received a job as a research assistant to Theodor Adorno, who had recently arrived in the United States and was working for Paul Lazarsfeld. According to friends who knew him during this period, Simpson was undergoing political and philosophical transformation. Theodore Abel believed that the stress and frustration of being without a teaching position had driven the young sociologist into the arms of Communism.[17] Whether such political sentiments ever entered into Simpson's relationship with Adorno is unclear (and unlikely considering the strict prohibitions Horkheimer placed on the Institute's associates); however, Simpson's flirtations with Communism may have brought him into contact with various people connected with the world of the New York Intellectuals. Although political collaboration between Simpson and Adorno was probably nonexistent, their intellectual collaboration was an acknowledged success. Adorno found Simpson to be an invaluable contributor to his own work and thought. As Adorno recalled many years later:

> Officially, Simpson functioned as "editorial assistant." In fact, he did a great deal more by making the first attempts to transform my distinctive efforts into American sociological language. This process was accomplished in a way that was very surprising and instructive for me. Like the burnt child that dreads the fire, I had developed an exaggerated caution and hardly dared to formulate my ideas as undiguisedly and emphatically as required to make them stand out. But it appears that such caution is not appropriate to a philosophy as remote from trial and error as my own. Now Simpson not only encouraged me to write as radically and uncompromisingly as possible, he also gave me his all to make it succeed.[18]

These early translators and editors for the Institute for Social Research played significant dual functions as the interlocutors of Critical Theory. First, these three men were largely responsible for literally converting the work of the Horkheimer Circle into English. By carrying out this important role when they did, they helped fashion many of the English writings of the Horkheimer Circle that then attracted the attention of American scholars, such as the New York Intellectuals. At a time when the Hork-heimer Circle was desperately trying to break out of its cocoon and make itself known in the United States, these scholars played the crucial inter-mediary role between émigré culture and indigenous American intellectual life. Second, the collaboration of these American translators created word-of-mouth news about the Horkheimer Circle and its writings. Nelson and Finkelstein were both history instructors at City College and brought news of the Institute to their eager students who were interested in European social theory and philosophy.[19] Similarly, George Simpson, who entered the world of radical politics during these years, also is likely to have brought news of the Institute to young New York Intellectuals moving within Manhattan's Communist, Socialist, and Trotskyist circles. Daniel Bell, who did not come into direct contact with the Horkheimer Circle until he entered Columbia as a graduate student in 1938–39, recalled that the New York Intellectuals generally knew of the Institute for Social Research. Like the more famous figures connected with the New School, Max Hork-heimer's Institute for Social Research attracted the attention of young, pre-cocious radicals who were interested in European thought and culture.[20]

As a result of these early contacts in the 1930s—through important fig-ures such as Hook and Schapiro, and through linguistic and intellectual mediators such as Finkelstein, Nelson, and Simpson—the larger commu-nity of New York Intellectuals became aware of the Horkheimer Circle in the 1940s. The gregarious Daniel Bell became the first central writer within Manhattan's literary milieu to make firm and lasting contact with the Horkheimer Circle.

Daniel Bell (born 1919), although a second-generation member of the New York Intellectuals, was one of the best connected and most success-ful. Juggling careers in journalism and sociology, Bell possessed a vast net-work of associates. Politically, they included trade unionists, Socialists, Trotskyists, liberals, and later neoconservatives. In addition to contribut-ing to the central journals of the New York Intellectuals, Bell also worked closely with the *New Leader* and *Fortune*. As a sociologist, his provocative theoretical writings were prophetic. They anticipated the cooling of ideo-logical ardor in the 1950s and the rise of the current information age.

Bell formed the central bulwark of the younger, "second generation" of New York Intellectuals that came out of the infamous "Alcove 1" at City College in the late 1930s and early 1940s. Meeting in one of the many alcoves within the school's dining hall, Bell met regularly with other students interested in the non-Communist Left. Composed of Trotskyists, socialists, and Social Democrats, the students of "Alcove 1" gathered each day to discuss current events, politics, and culture. Keeping a healthy distance from the Communists at City College, Bell and his lunch mates explored Marxian theory and radical alternatives to Stalinism and the emerging Popular Front. Thus, "Alcove 1" became an important reception point for a wide variety of social and cultural theories emanating from Europe, and its members became enthusiastic audiences for the "intellectual migration" that was bringing so many alternative perspectives into New York City. As a history student with Finkelstein and Nelson at CCNY, Bell arrived at Columbia's sociology department in the fall of 1938 already curious and interested in the generally reclusive group of German émigrés on 117th Street. During this one year as a full-time graduate student on Morningside Heights, Bell became a regular visitor to the Horkheimer Circle's weekly Tuesday night seminar. His days at Columbia, however, proved to be short in number. Sensing that a future in academia was risky, he abandoned graduate studies after his first year to join the masthead of the *New Leader*, where he took up the cause of the social-democratic labor movement. As an editor and journalist, he soon became a major contributor to the magazines of the New York Intellectuals. Bell's contact with the Horkheimer Circle, however, did not end with his departure from Columbia. Like most of the other New York writers, he eagerly accepted freelance work. The Horkheimer Circle thus became one of his many contractors. At first working with Finkelstein and Nelson, Bell entered the small ranks of the Institute's translators and editors. Once the anti-Semitism project started up, Bell, who through his work with the *New Leader* also played an important role within the Jewish Labor Committee (JLC), became the crucial intermediary for the JLC-funded project "Anti-Semitism among American Labor." As a result of Bell's frequent dealings with the Horkheimer Circle throughout the 1940s, he brought news of the group to others in the New York intellectual community—sometimes even helping friends locate temporary work with the Institute.[21]

Another important writer who helped establish relations between the New York Intellectuals and the Frankfurt School was the young sociology student Lewis Coser (1913–2003). After completing his doctorate in sociology, Coser went on to a successful career. He taught at Brandeis (with

Marcuse) and SUNY Stony Brook, and his contributions to conflict theory led him to become one of the great rivals of Parsonian Functionalism. Instead of building models of social cohesion based on functional integration, Coser showed how conflict just as effectively bound groups together. Together with his friend Irving Howe, Coser was a founder of the journal *Dissent*.

Coser, who arrived in the United States in 1941 by way of Germany and then France, received some of the financial assistance necessary for his emigration from the Institute for Social Research. Determined to thank those responsible for his rescue, he visited the International Relief Association (where he met Rose Laub, who later became his wife) and the Institute for Social Research (where he was offered part-time work on a variety of projects). Perhaps his most notable project for the Horkheimer Circle was an institutional history of the group that was circulated to American colleagues, administrators at Columbia, and grant committees titled *Ten Years on Morningside Heights*.[22]

At the same time Coser was working alongside Horkheimer, Pollock, Marcuse, and Lowenthal, he also spent much of his free time with various new friends that he had met in the radical political circles of New York. Coser, who had contacts with Trotskyists in Paris before his departure for the United States, sought out like-minded radicals after his arrival in New York. Through the Schachtmanites, Coser came into contact with Dwight and Nancy Macdonald (who he'd already heard of from his Trotskyist contacts in Europe), who subsequently became Coser's key point of entry into the world of the New York Intellectuals.

Dwight Macdonald (1906–82) was one of the early editors of *Partisan Review*. Following his political break with the journal, he remained a powerful literary voice and influence within the world of the New York Intellectuals. He founded *Politics* with his wife, Nancy, to voice concerns about bureaucratic collectivism, the Second World War, and the rise of mass culture. Although his politics and opinions fell out of favor with most of the New York Intellectuals, Macdonald was embraced by the New Left at the end of his life.

At various gatherings organized by the Macdonalds, Coser met a vast array of New York's radical, literary community: Irving Howe, Philip Selznick, Seymour Martin Lipset, Irving Kristol, Nathan Glazer, Daniel Bell, Paul Goodman, Harold Rosenberg, and Meyer Schapiro. In addition,

Macdonald, who had only recently broken with the editors of *Partisan Review*, recruited Coser to contribute pieces for his new magazine, *Politics*.[23] Coser, like Bell, had a foot in both the world of the Horkheimer Circle and the domain of the New York Intellectuals. As a native German speaker who had worked on short-term projects for the Institute for Social Research, he was able to introduce the work of the Horkheimer Circle to Dwight Macdonald and his other new friends. Coser functioned, therefore, as a major intermediary between the Critical Theory of the Horkheimer Circle and the radical thought of, specifically, the group around *Politics*.[24]

Through Bell and Coser, Dwight Macdonald's young friends at City College—Irving Howe, Nathan Glazer, and Irving Kristol—first came into contact with the work of the Frankfurt School. Through these personal and professional networks, familiarity with the thought of the Horkheimer Circle spread in New York among writers who would become major public intellectuals.

Irving Howe (1920–93) became one of the country's most tireless supporters of Social Democracy. Best remembered for his contributions to *Dissent*, the journal he founded with Coser, and his writings on literature, Howe remained one of the few New York Intellectuals to sustain his commitment to an anti-Stalinist Left. While many of his colleagues drifted toward moderation and conservatism, Howe remained committed to achieving the aims of Social Democracy in the United States.

Nathan Glazer (born 1923), like his contemporary Daniel Bell, remains an important sociologist. Similarly, like Bell, he arrived at sociology along a circuitous path. He worked on the editorial board of *Commentary*, he was an editor at Anchor Books, and he collaborated with David Riesman on *The Lonely Crowd*. Although he has studied a wide array of topics as a sociologist, his work on race and cultural assimilation is perhaps best known.

Irving Kristol (born 1920), perhaps more than any other figure, is largely responsible for the neoconservative label that has become entwined with the reputations of the New York Intellectuals. Like his friends from City College, Kristol flirted with Trotskyism and was a man of the Left during his early days writing for *Commentary*. With the conclusion of World War II, Kristol began a sharp turn to the right and distinguished himself in his candid support of McCarthyism. By the 1980s, he had become a key supporter of Ronald Reagan.

Throughout the late 1930s and early 1940s, these students from "Alcove 1" discussed many topics, including Critical Theory. Glazer, who drifted into the anti-Stalinist Left at City Collge through the socialist, Zionist group Avukah, also recalled that Zellig Harris (a key intellectual mentor to the group's newspaper, *Avukah Student Action*) played a significant role in introducing City College radicals to the Horkheimer Circle.[25] In addition to reading "important" writings from *Partisan Review* and the *New International,* the study group of "Alcove 1" also dipped into the *Zeitschrift für Sozialforschung,* as well as writings by Bukharin and Rosa Luxemburg. Initially struggling to translate the German volumes of the Horkheimer Circle, the "Alcove 1" members were relieved to read Fromm's *Escape from Freedom* and the Institute's English journal, *Studies in Philosophy and Social Science.* Although no member of "Alcove 1" ever became a "follower" of Critical Theory, they were all deeply impressed by the Institute's innovative work in sociology and particularly its writings on mass culture.[26] In later years, largely with the help of Daniel Bell, many of the same members of these "Alcove 1" study groups went to work on a variety of projects for the Horkheimer Circle. Glazer, for example, briefly functioned as a research assistant for Horkheimer during the early stages of the anti-Semitism project by reading and reporting on the most recent breakthroughs by American sociologists.[27] Similarly, Irving Howe served as a ghost editor for Leo Lowenthal and Norbert Guterman's contribution to *Studies in Prejudice*—the volume titled *Prophets of Deceit.*[28]

Ironically, the "leaders" of the New York Intellectuals—William Phillips and Philip Rahv (the chief editors of *Partisan Review*)—were among the last to come into contact with the Horkheimer Circle. Long after many of the younger contributors to their magazine had been reading the *Zeitschrift* and doing editorial work for the Institute, the editors of *Partisan Review* encountered the Frankfurt School and became exposed to their work for the first time.

William Phillips (1907–2002) was one of the founding editors of the *Partisan Review,* which arose as a vehicle for the fusion of modernist sensibilities and radical consciousness but which grew into a major forum for discussing contemporary society and innovations within the world of art and thereby served as a launching pad for the successful literary careers of some leading twentieth-century writers, such as Saul Bellow, Bernard Malamud, and Delmore Schwartz. In addition to being one of the central editorial and administrative figures at *Partisan Review,* Phillips also was a keen literary critic and professor of literature at Rutgers University and Boston University.

Philip Rahv (1908–73) was the other founding editor of *Partisan Review.* Famous within New York's intellectual culture as an autodidact and for his powerfully intimidating personality, Rahv also made his personal mark as a literary critic who was versatile enough to examine Europe's modern literary masters in their original languages while also being a keen analyst of the American literary canon.

Although it is extremely difficult to date the first encounters between the leaders of *Partisan Review* and the Frankfurt School, the scant evidence suggests that they took place around 1944, when Phillips was invited to help Horkheimer edit some of the "Society and Reason" lectures that became *Eclipse of Reason.*[29] It is similarly challenging to determine the extent of the contact between the two groups. Based on Phillips's retrospective comments, it seems likely that relations were extremely limited and formal. Intriguingly, the archival records of *Partisan Review* suggest that Phillips and Rahv were more keen on having Erich Fromm contribute to the pages of their magazine than any of the other figures that were associated with the Institute for Social Research. As on Morningside Heights, Fromm's successful transition to the world of American intellectual life made him a more alluring figure to New York's leading public intellectuals. In 1944, following Fromm's publication of *Escape from Freedom,* Phillips invited him to contribute to a cultural discussion that *Partisan Review* had planned.[30] Later during the same year, Phillips again approached Fromm to review Sander Leonard's anthology *Psycho-Analysis Today.*[31] Later in 1948, Rahv inquired about whether Fromm might want to write a review of the Kinsey report.[32] With the exception of Herbert Marcuse, who caught the eye of the editors of *Partisan Review* following the publication of *Eros and Civilization,*[33] none of the other members of the Horkheimer Circle were approached for submissions until the era of the New Left when the Frankfurt School became famous.[34] To the heads of *Partisan Review* during the 1940s, Max Horkheimer and the Institute for Social Research may have been a perplexing curiosity, and probably little else. From Horkheimer's perspective, however, Phillips and *Partisan Review,* like other influential American editors and journals, were important contacts to be developed. At the same time that Phillips edited Horkheimer's lectures, "Society and

Reason," the Institute hoped to nurture the relationship so that it might seek future support from *Partisan Review* for the renewed publication of *Studies in Philosophy and Social Science.*[35]

The last but certainly one of the strongest bonds forged between the Horkheimer Circle and the New York Intellectuals originated with the birth of *Commentary* in November 1945. Of all of the journals linked to the world of the New York Intellectuals, *Commentary* was arguably among the most significant in terms of promoting the work and the reputations of the figures affiliated with the Institute for Social Research. *Commentary* publicized the Frankfurt School's pathbreaking work in the study of prejudice,[36] and became a forum in which members and former members of the Institute were able to share their analyses of postwar Europe and offer contributions to the exploration of postwar Jewish identity.

The reasons behind this relationship are not hard to discern. Institutional and intellectual needs overlapped. Together with the Horkheimer Circle, the new magazine and its editor, Elliot Cohen, shared an affiliation with the American Jewish Committee, as well as office space in the same building. In fact, Nathan Glazer recalled that he was invited to join the editorial team for *Commentary*, in part, because he had been working across the hall for Max Horkheimer in 1944 as a consultant and reader of American social-scientific literature for the studies regarding prejudice that the Institute for Social Research had been hired to undertake. This placed Glazer in precisely the right place at the right time when the AJC decided to transform its earlier journal, the *Contemporary Jewish Record,* into *Commentary.* Having worked for Horkheimer in the AJC's Department of Scientific Research and having served as the editor for CCNY's Zionist student journal, Glazer was among the first group of contributors and editors recruited to join the new masthead of *Commentary.*[37]

In addition to being neighbors and sharing close institutional affiliations with the AJC, both the Horkheimer Circle and the contributors to *Commentary* embraced similar intellectual concerns during the final years of the Horkheimer Circle's American sojourn. The two groups grappled with the sober and stark realizations that faced American and exiled European Jews following the shocking revelations of the Holocaust. The AJC hired the Frankfurt School not simply to combat anti-Semitism, but to combat prejudice more generally—thereby reflecting the AJC's commitment to safeguarding civil and religious rights for more than simply the

Jewish community. Rather than simply fulfilling Jewish aims that had been dramatically highlighted by the Holocaust, the *Studies in Prejudice* were envisioned to be a broader contribution to American society and culture—efforts consistent with the AJC's desire to promote pluralism and Jewish cultural interests within the United States. *Commentary* was created by the AJC to promote parallel aims. Unlike *Partisan Review,* which self-consciously promoted an ideal of cosmopolitan universalism that was framed by the influences of Marxism and modernism, *Commentary* as a distinctly postwar creation was designed to reflect the changing needs felt by the leadership of the AJC. *Commentary* was envisioned to be a distinctly Jewish magazine, but also to be a vehicle for demonstrating how comfortably the American Jewish identity fit within the broader culture of the United States.[38] Like the work of the Horkheimer Circle, *Commentary* grappled with issues that had special resonance for Jewish readers during the postwar era but also transcended the boundaries of this constituency by demonstrating how vital such topics were to the broader reading public. As Cohen wrote in his first editorial statement, "[In] the search for light on the basic issues of peace and freedom and human destiny which challenge all mankind, *Commentary* hopes to be of service."[39]

The mission that the AJC and Elliot Cohen envisioned for the new magazine was fully appreciated by members of the Institute for Social Research. Horkheimer and his colleagues recognized the affinities between their own work and the material that was appearing in the newly reconfigured journal of the AJC. Horkheimer and the members of the Institute were clearly intrigued by what was taking shape across the hall at *Commentary.* In March 1946, only months after the first appearance of the magazine, Horkheimer wrote an encouraging letter to Cohen, in which he stated:

> I am following the development of *Commentary* with great interest and enthusiasm. The February issue is a model of how pertinent questions of the various fields of culture can be treated on a high literary level and still make good and easy reading. The Jewish viewpoint makes itself felt as a principle which keeps the diversity of articles from tilting over into mere plurality. Also it is handled with true finesse. Yet, this may be one of the reasons why we feel that the Jewish idea can still be very much alive.[40]

Self-interest and opportunism, however, may have been further reasons for Horkheimer's enthusiastic praise for *Commentary*. By 1946, Horkheimer's goals had become increasingly complex. First, he was embroiled in a struggle to protect and safeguard his control over the anti-Semitism project. As the project grew in size, Horkheimer was forced into conflict with rivals (such as Samuel Flowerman) as he sought to preserve his position of leadership on the AJC's Department of Scientific Research. Second and perhaps more important, Horkheimer was determined to use the anti-Semitism project as a springboard for the reputation of his Institute and the work of its members. By seeking allies from the masthead of *Commentary*, Horkheimer not only hoped to recruit some potentially powerful allies within the world of the AJC, but also to gain some much-needed publicity for his group and its work.

In chapter 6, when we turn to the execution and reception of the Horkheimer Circle's book series *Studies in Prejudice,* we will explore the specific role that *Commentary* played in publicizing and promoting the achievements of the Frankfurt School. For the purposes of our current discussion, it is only essential to indicate that *Commentary* helped build an audience for *Studies in Prejudice* by reporting on some of the findings that later appeared in all five of the books. Although Elliot Cohen, *Commentary*'s editor, was legitimately intrigued by Horkheimer and the Institute's research regarding anti-Semitism,[41] it is also clear that his public support of the Frankfurt School and its members may have represented an instance in which Cohen was able to gain favor with his sponsors at the AJC. None of the parties connected with *Commentary* wanted to create an impression that the magazine was a tool of the AJC. Such a reputation would have undermined the journal and alienated the New York Intellectuals that *Commentary* sought to attract to its pages. Instead, Cohen was granted absolute authority to control everything published in the magazine. Nathan Abrams, however, has unearthed evidence from the files of the AJC that suggests that Cohen's autonomy may have been more of an illusion than a reality. Abrams confirms that Cohen dominated his editorial staff and the contributors to *Commentary*, but proposes that Cohen's behind-the-scenes dealings with the AJC were markedly less dictatorial. Although Cohen shared the same vision for the magazine as his sponsors, he was occasionally reprimanded for editorial decisions that conflicted with the aims of the organization and on other occasions was pressured to promote agendas and projects that the AJC supported.[42] Thus, Cohen's backing of the Frankfurt School and its contributions to the study of anti-Semitism may have not simply reflected his own interests, but also may have demonstrated his desire to curry favor with his sponsors at the AJC. Regardless of motives, however, Cohen continually encouraged members of the Institute for Social Research to contribute articles to *Commentary*, and the magazine eventually became one of the significant places where the views of the Institute for Social Research gained access to a broader American audience.

In addition to the topic of anti-Semitism, associates of Horkheimer branched out and submitted articles on broader issues that resonated with the more general goals of *Commentary*—in particular, the aim of monitoring and analyzing developments throughout the world that had relevance for both Jewish and non-Jewish readers, and, more important, the aim of surveying Jewish culture to establish a postwar Jewish identity. Toward the first end, former members of the Institute such as Franz Neumann and Arkadij Gurland (who had specialized in the Horkheimer Circle's analyses of Nazism) offered contributions on the situation in postwar Germany. Neumann's article "Re-educating the Germans" warned *Commentary*'s readers about the differing views regarding denazification efforts that existed between the United States and the Soviet Union. In a fairly balanced critique of both sets of policies, Neumann recognized the problems and dangers inherent in each. While the Western allies risked a repeat of the Weimar Republic by focusing their attention on the restoration of democratic institutions and the training of democratic citizens, the Soviets dismantled the socioeconomic system that they believed had made the Weimar Republic so unstable but were executing their destruction of monopoly capitalism through the dictatorial rule of a single-party political system.[43] In a similar vein, Gurland's article "Why Democracy Is Losing in Germany" picked up on the fears and concerns Neumann had expressed and echoed them in the wake of the German elections of 1949, warning his readers that the new German republic likely was doomed in the same way that the Weimar Republic had been. Again concentrating on the challenges inherent in democratization and denazification efforts, Gurland illuminated the persistence of nationalism and authoritarianism.[44] Like George Orwell's reports from postwar Britain, these contributions on the German situation provided informed analysis to American readers puzzled and worried about the future of Europe. In addition to the Jewish audience concerned about postwar events in Germany, both articles reached out to the broader American audience that shared the same concerns.

Leo Lowenthal, by contrast, contributed an article that addressed the more central mission of *Commentary* during its early years. His piece, "Heine's Religion," was a powerfully crafted example of the kind of Jewish self-exploration that Cohen and the rest of the editorial board at *Commentary* were encouraging.[45] The figure of Heinrich Heine functioned for Lowenthal as a symbol for the problems faced by the entire New York Intellectual community and by many German-Jewish exiles as well. Lowenthal's focus was the Christian conversion of Heinrich Heine, German Jewry's famous exiled poet. In searching for Heine's motivations for converting to Christianity, Lowenthal unearthed an urge that resonated for both himself and for the entire world of the New York Intellectuals. Heine, like so many German Jews after him and like the New York Intellectuals, had sacrificed his Jewish traditions in order to embrace the same ideal of cosmopolitanism—embodied by the Enlightenment and the French Revolution—that the Frankfurt School and the prewar writers for *Partisan Review* adopted. Heine, like Germany's Jews and the young New York writers, abandoned the parochialism that he perceived in traditional Judaism and sought to fashion a new identity founded in universal reason. As Lowenthal explained, "To him [Heine], Christianity is only the outer garment, the husk of modern European culture . . . To Heine, European culture meant the Europe of the French Revolution, the chance for a happy, free, earth-bound existence."[46] As an early example of German Jewry's embrace of *Bildung*, Heine's motives and values were consistent with those of both the Horkheimer Circle and the New York Intellectuals. For both groups, Marxism embodied the yearning for a repaired and redeemed humanity— a world in which racial prejudice and socioeconomic injustice were overcome. The tragedy and cautionary tale that Lowenthal discovered in Heine's biography thus was deeply relevant to those reading *Commentary* in the wake of the Holocaust. Toward the end of his life, Heine discovered that his conversion had brought him nothing but despair. The poet grew to despise Christianity, and his cosmopolitan idealism eventually dissipated. In a moment of powerful self-criticism, Heine recognized his desire to return to Judaism. Quoting Heine, Lowenthal reproduced a portion of the poet's *Confessions:*

I never used to care for Moses, probably because the Greek spirit predominated in me. I couldn't forgive the law-giver of the Jews his hatred of
idols and plastic representation. I did not realize that Moses was himself a
great artist and possessed of the true artistic spirit, despite his attacks on
art. Only, his artistic spirit—like that of his Egyptian compatriots—was
directed toward the colossal and indestructible. Yet instead of erecting structures of brick and granite, Moses wanted to build human pyramids and
obelisks . . . My preference for Greece has since declined. I see now that the
Greeks were merely handsome youths, while the Jews were, and still are,
grown men, mighty, indomitable men, despite eighteen centuries of persecution and misery. I have learned to rate them at their true value.[47]

Through Heine, Lowenthal acknowledged that Judaism was a tradition
that need not be transcended in the name of loftier ideals. The quest for a
redeemed humanity lay within the heart of Judaism itself. Reflecting on the
lessons Heine discovered at the end of his life, Lowenthal wrote, "Judaism,
humanity and messianic redemption became for him [Heine] an interrelated unity. He defined the fulfillment of Jewish history as the transition
from the stage of suffering and dire necessity into a truly human stage of
universal liberty." Thus through Heine was Lowenthal able to discover a
distinctly Jewish identity consistent with Critical Theory and the prewar
political impulses that gathered the Horkheimer Circle together. For the
readers of *Commentary,* a similar revelation was offered. Judaism provided
the same vision that the New York Intellectuals had glimpsed in the fusion
of radicalism and modernism that they had imagined. In the wake of the
war, Heine stood as a symbol—perhaps all Jewish exiles could return home.

MARXISM, MODERNISM, MASS CULTURE, AND THE
HOLOCAUST: THE EARLY RECEPTION OF CRITICAL THEORY

Thematically, the most significant and influential contributions that the
Frankfurt School provided to the world of the New York Intellectuals were
their interrelated critiques of totalitarianism and mass society—yet neither
topic had become central to the Horkheimer Circle's analysis of contemporary society until the late 1930s and the transformations that their thought
underwent during the Second World War.

Prior to their arrival on Morningside Heights, the members of the Frankfurt School had followed the vision that Max Horkheimer had established

for the group. Charting a course between metaphysics and naive Positivism, Horkheimer had consistently criticized both the opponents of empirical social science and the empirical social scientists themselves. Having emerged from the ranks of the neo-Kantian revolution in German philosophy and sociology, Horkheimer was aware of the fact that contemporary social research faced the danger of repeating the epistemological illusions perpetrated by the early empiricists that Hegel had criticized in the *Phenomenology of the Spirit*. At the same time, however, Horkheimer was unwilling to embrace the humanistic and phenomenological critiques of Positivism fashionable in the 1920s because he rejected their radical subjectivism and their retreat into idealism. Horkheimer and the Institute sought a mediated position between these two antagonistic trends by embracing the concept of a Marxian materialism that was grounded within a dialectical logic capable of offering an immanent critique of contemporary society. Immanent criticism examined a social system and its ideology on their own terms and thus identified their ideals, but then highlighted how these ideals were in contradiction with the realities of the social system. Social research (including quantitative as well as qualitative analysis) was a necessary component of Critical Theory's materialism, but social research projects were formulated within the context of a continually evolving theoretical understanding of modern society. Whereas the Marxists of the Second International had grown to accept a transcendent critique of capitalist society that no longer was grounded in the material and cultural history of the late-bourgeois era, the Frankfurt School placed all of the scholarly disciplines at its disposal to regain the critical and historical methodologies that lay at the heart of the Marxian tradition. Thus, social research and social philosophy were complementary aspects of investigative procedures, interpretive techniques, and theory formation. Although the logic of this integration was derived from Hegel, the members of the Institute rejected the transcendent nature of Hegel's idealism. By relying on Marx's notion of materially rigorous immanent criticism, the Frankfurt School avoided the pitfalls of transcendent idealism that led the philosophies of Kant and Hegel back into the realm of metaphysics.[48]

Cultural criticism and aesthetic theory, therefore, functioned in a supporting role for the original materialist theory of society that the entire Frankfurt School was seeking to develop. Initially, the Institute's experts on the arts (such as Leo Lowenthal, Theodor W. Adorno, and Walter

Benjamin) worked in harmony with Horkheimer's vision by providing richly sociological analyses of literary and musical trends in contemporary society. Artistic developments, thus, were examined in relation to wider societal trends and helped to generate fundamental critiques of bourgeois culture.[49] By the late 1930s, however, these aesthetic contributions began to undergo a significant change leading to the exploration of links between the concepts of authoritarianism, Nazism, and mass culture. In 1936, Walter Benjamin published his famous essay on art in the age of mechanical reproduction—an article that walked a tightrope between excitement and despair about the transformation of the art object during the age of the assembly line and the consequences this created for revolutionaries and Nazi demagogues.[50] Not long thereafter, Herbert Marcuse wrote a more disparaging article about the links that could be seen between the cultural realm and the authoritarian ideologies that had grown to preoccupy the thought of the entire Horkheimer Circle by the late 1930s. In his 1937 article "The Affirmative Character of Culture," Marcuse assaulted all bourgeois culture for its escapism, repression, and concealment of capitalism's harsh realities.[51] The cultivated realm of *Bildung* that had been produced by the bourgeoisie became a source of danger in the emerging era of totalitarianism. Art, which historically was linked to notions of transcendent beauty and spiritual refinement, simultaneously denied sensual pleasure in the bourgeois epoch, thus disclosing another intellectual realm in which materialism was being obliterated by a revival of metaphysics and thereby further alienating the human subject from the world. While not directed specifically at the concept of mass culture, Marcuse had taken aim at highbrow, middlebrow, and lowbrow art in a comprehensive critique of aesthetics within contemporary society and recognized a general trend in which art was reinforcing the sociopolitical status quo. Similarly, Theodor W. Adorno's article "On the Fetish Character in Music and the Regression of Listening" (published in 1938) recognized a similar dynamic within the entire aesthetic sphere, but he directed his most severe criticisms at mass culture.[52] Like Marcuse, Adorno developed an immanent critique of aesthetics in the age of totalitarianism and uncovered similar conclusions about the alienation and isolation of individuals from one another and from the realities of the world. Where Adorno differed most sharply was in his qualitative analysis of popular culture and his application of the Marxian concept of the commodity fetish to the theme of aesthetic reception—a topic that we will discuss in more detail when comparing the early mass culture criticism of the New York Intellectuals to the analysis of the Frankfurt School.

This shift in the cultural criticism of the Horkheimer Circle, like nearly all other developments within the Frankfurt School, was not isolated. The new focus on mass culture was examined within a broader social theoretical context. As the threat of fascism escalated, the theme of authoritarianism grew to gain a more prominent role within the Critical Theory of society. Like so many of the other émigrés from Europe, the Frankfurt School gradually arrived at a theory of totalitarianism to explain the emergence and spread of fascism. Socioeconomically, Friedrich Pollock was beginning to develop his theory of state capitalism, which formed the foundation of the Frankfurt School's materialist analysis of totalitarianism.[53] Although it met with some opposition, most particularly from Franz Neumann, Pollock argued that economic planning by regimes of the Left and Right was resulting in greater stability and strength from coordination within the economic sphere. Despite the instability created by the Depression, state intervention in all sectors of the economy minimized insecurity by causing individual and group needs to become eclipsed by those of the state. State power now entered into the economic sphere where previously only entrepreneurs and workers had confronted each other. Unlike these prior relations between capital and labor, the state was able to use its power to command and thus to transform the nature and dynamics of the entire market. Where individual political actors had once operated alone or in concert and thus exercised their freedom through reasoned decision making and action, all individuals now found themselves coordinated by managers and bureaucrats. Although such circumstances did not eliminate the contradictions that Marx had diagnosed within capitalism, these developments certainly delayed the possibilities of radical social transformation—and perhaps eliminated such possibilities altogether. The theory of state capitalism, consequently, became the first significant step leading to the late Critical Theory of the Horkheimer Circle.[54] Pollock provided the structural theory about changes in the socioeconomic base of society, which inevitably led to similarly dramatic reformulations of the superstructure. Although the Soviet Union was explicitly absent from this analysis, Pollock and the other members of the Frankfurt School were beginning to develop a theory of East–West convergence in which the totalitarian societies of fascist Germany, Communist Russia, and New Deal America emerged as state capitalist successors to the free-market era of the liberal bourgeoisie.[55] As Moishe Postone has pointed out, the great problem that accompanied this theoretical sea change was that Pollock formulated the concept of state capitalism as an ideal type—and the more that this ideal type became the materialist basis for Critical Theory, the more the work of the Horkheimer Circle became transcendent rather than immanent.[56] No longer was the socioeconomic analysis of the Frankfurt School securely moored within the material conditions and contradictions of existing society. Its revelations were transhistorical, and the consequences this would have for the philosophical and aesthetic dimensions of their critique would become just as dramatic. With the moorings cut, the critiques of instrumental reason and mass culture veered toward pure ideological criticism that had been averted by earlier Critical Theory because of its basis in immanent criticism and historical materialism.

In addition to a series of articles that concentrated on the phenomenon of mass culture as one of the central symptoms of the societal movement toward totalitarianism, the other by-product of these significant intellectual shifts was Horkheimer and Adorno's strange and despairing *Dialectic of Enlightenment*.[57] The book was written almost entirely in California and was the intellectual realization of Horkheimer's older plans for a work on dialectical logic. Although incomplete at the time of its first mimeographed print run of five hundred copies in 1944, the book did accomplish the critique of scientific rationality that Horkheimer had planned for years. Last and certainly not least, the book relied on Pollock's theory of state capitalism as the material basis of its transhistorical analyses of myth and reason.

The book's main message was that enlightenment had more in common with myth than one might assume. The philosophes, in their rhetoric, liked to juxtapose enlightenment and myth to emphasize the progressive rationalism of the former and the superstitious irrationalism of the latter, but Horkheimer and Adorno sought to disclose the "cunning of reason" in both. Before the ages of mythology and enlightenment, there existed pristine yet barbaric nature unsullied by human thought or action. This time before myth and enlightenment was a time of mimesis and magic, in which humans largely communicated awe and wonder about the natural world. Mythology and enlightenment arose to control and penetrate the mysteries of nature. Mythology and enlightenment were opposed to the barbarism of mimesis and magic, and consequently they sought to disenchant the natural world.

According to Horkheimer and Adorno, enlightenment succeeded in its struggles against myth and nature. Superstition gave way to the triumph of reason, and nature gave way to the wishes of man. However, these victories also led to a transformation of enlightenment. As a result of reason's ability to tame nature, reason underwent a transformation from being "critical" to being "instrumental." Critical reason existed since the dawn of the enlightenment, and it embodies the initial impulse behind enlightenment—to question all knowledge and authority. Instrumental reason, by contrast, arose from the successes against nature, and its only aim is utility. Instrumental reason is not driven by a need to inquire but is driven by a need to dominate and conquer. Instrumental reason no longer questions or probes the mysteries of the world; instead it contents itself with controlling and commanding.

The irony of this development is the "dialectic of Enlightenment": enlightenment, after the transformation from critical to instrumental reason, reverts back to myth. The instrumental mind becomes so fixed on the utility of nature's conquest that it posits laws and rules for nature. Nature, however, does not always correspond to these man-made conceptions. Consequently, a situation arises in which the laws of nature represent a new form of myth. While these new scientific myths may contain fragments of Truth, they also entail a reversion to barbarism. This barbarism is particularly evident when one considers the way in which instrumental reason has been deployed in the domination and subjugation of different groups of people—one of the most horrific examples being the Holocaust.

Dialectic of Enlightenment examines different manifestations of this dialectical relationship and focuses on the consequences. The first excursus uncovers the play of these themes in Homer's epic *The Odyssey,* further illustrating the main points by studying the details and implications of story, and the second excursus explores the moral implications of these developments by examining the philosophies of Kant, Sade, and Nietzsche. The remainder of the book is a series of philosophical fragments, with the first group of aphorisms exploring the culture industry—Horkheimer and Adorno's term for contemporary, bourgeois popular culture. For them, the culture industry not only demonstrated the pervasiveness of instrumental thought, it also illustrated the subtle and not so subtle forms of domination that are so prevalent in the lowbrow culture of late-industrial society. The last set of aphorisms presents anti-Semitism as a case study paralleling the analysis of the culture industry—this time with the moral and ethical stakes being higher. In this last set of fragments, the consequences are no longer simply a pliant consumer of popular culture. This time the gas chambers of Auschwitz are the price of instrumental reason. Eugenics presents a perverse example of reason reverting to myth, and the deaths of six million Jews glaringly reminds the reader of the return of myth's barbaric character carried out with technological efficiency.

By the late 1930s and early 1940s when the New York Intellectuals first came in contact with the members of the Horkheimer Circle, this dramatic intellectual shift was taking place within the history of Critical Theory. On the one hand, these changes made the work of the Frankfurt School intriguing to many of the New York Intellectuals. Within a single yet broad theoretical framework, the Horkheimer Circle was putting together a puzzle whose pieces had attracted the attention of the New York Intellectuals for years. Not only were Marxism and Modernism fused together within a broader interpretation of contemporary society, but the new totalitarian menace and mass culture were integrated as well. On the other hand, many of the same flaws that have raised criticisms from more recent commentators on Critical Theory created concern and suspicion among the ranks of New York's intellectuals. Weren't the results of the Horkheimer Circle's efforts too out of step with common appraisals of the United States and weren't they too bleak and negative? Did they lead the radical intellectual into a social-theoretical dead end? Was the transcendent and transhistorical nature of the aesthetic criticism of mass culture inherently elitist?

For the contributors to New York's little magazines, mass culture and Modernism were closely entwined. Generally, these writers were hostile to the mass entertainment industries, which were undergoing substantial growth during the 1930s and 1940s. Modernism, the New Yorkers believed, functioned as an oppositional social and aesthetic force. While mass culture pandered to base desires and provided simplistic reflections of the world, Modernist art was antimaterialist, anticommercial, and capable of conveying the alienation of contemporary society. Modernism sought to communicate the subjective realm of selfhood and to offer unique expressions of consciousness. Modernist writers and artists produced a cultural

legacy that was rigorous, inventive, and highly intellectual. More important, however, Modernism represented not only the apex of Western culture but also an international urbanity that had much in common with
the Marxian internationalism of European, *haut bourgeois* radicalism.[58]
This unique form of cosmopolitanism thus provided the New York Intellectuals with a means of culturally transcending their Jewish, immigrant
milieu, and it signified an inspiring if vague route to aesthetic and intellectual renewal.[59]

The New York Intellectuals' hostility to mass culture was nothing particularly new to American intellectual life. Popular culture had been mass-
produced in the United States since before the Revolutionary War. The
proliferation and consumption of mass art, however, reached new propor-
tions toward the end of the nineteenth century and touched off choruses
of condemnation. The first serious critics of mass entertainment were cultural conservatives (such as Rollin Lynde Hartt, Samuel Hopkins Adams,
and Frederick Winsor), who saw the expansion of popular culture as a challenge to the genteel traditions of high art in the United States. The sudden rise and expansion of the new mass mediums threatened the cultural
leadership of U.S. intellectuals and seemed to represent yet another dangerous development that accompanied modernity. Although the first conservative critics relied heavily on ethnic prejudice to condemn predominantly
Jewish and African-American sources for many of the new mass arts, their
main concern for the American public arose from the belief that popular
culture appealed to the most primitive, physical passions and primal emotions. Rather than stirring the soul and the spirit as high art had accomplished, mass art put the country's culture and character in jeopardy.[60]

Such perspectives, however, did not remain restricted to the conservative
defenders of American traditionalism. Critics from the Left also joined the
attacks against the emerging mass entertainment industries. Progressives,
and later Communists, shared the conservatives' dislike for mass art, but
instead of condemning the consumers of popular culture, they began to
view the masses as passive and innocent victims of ruthless commercial
interests that ignored the welfare of the nation, its people, and its culture.
Industrialization had created leisure time, but it also produced an urban
working class so impoverished by the monotony of labor and harsh living
conditions that this new leisure could be easily exploited by the corrupt
producers of mass culture. Instead of offering the same kind of refinement

that the conservative defenders of high art preferred, mass entertainment corrupted the morality of the nation by appealing to the lowest common denominator. Communists, drawing on the Marxian critique of ideology, likewise but more specifically condemned mass culture as capitalist propaganda that offered psychological escape from the material conditions that bred revolutionary, working-class consciousness and thus subtly bolstered particular aspects of the bourgeois worldview.[61]

The New York Intellectuals began their careers as the heirs of this leftist interpretation of popular culture that had been constructed by Progressives and then modified by U.S. Communists. They combined this political position, however, with the more strictly aesthetic assault of American Modernists. By aligning themselves with the Modernist legacy, the New York Intellectuals were able to create further distance between themselves and the traditional, conservative critics of mass art. Although the Modernists (writing for such magazines as *Seven Arts*, the *Little Review, Broom*, and the *Dial*), hated mass culture for all of the same reasons as the Left and Right critics, they also despised the genteel tradition of high culture that the conservatives and Progressives sought to protect. Hoping to construct a new highbrow culture, the first generation of U.S. Modernists challenged the sensibilities and assumptions of traditional high culture, all the while realizing the rising dangers posed by cultural massification. They successfully achieved a high, countercultural tradition, but their victory came at a high price—retreat and isolation. Although Modernism represented precisely the cultural Renaissance that its producers and allies sought, the artistic result was not appreciated by the majority of Americans, who preferred the greater accessibility of mass art.[62]

The New York Intellectuals emerged during a critical juncture in the history of the two traditions with which they were originally allied. First, they grew out of the American Communist movement at the moment that it was reaching the height of its popularity, but also was simultaneously succumbing to rigid Stalinist control. And second, they attempted to infuse Modernism into the party's Proletarian Culture initiative at a time when the avant-garde was consolidating its formal achievements but simultaneously was drifting toward aestheticism. By attempting to cross-fertilize their political and artistic passions, the New York Intellectuals hoped to invigorate both movements. The fusion of the two, however, proved to be far more complex and problematic than they had anticipated.

The aesthetic theory of the Communist Party took form under the guidance of Mike Gold. His Proletarian Culture movement sought to develop an authentic workers' art that opposed both the high culture of the bourgeoisie and the commercial popular culture that was corrupting the minds of the masses. By encouraging experimentation among working-class artists and their allies, the Communists hoped to fashion true expressions of working-class consciousness that would ultimately transform art into a "working-class weapon."[63] The aesthetic practice, however, resulted in something quite different from what the aesthetic theory indicated. By placing a greater emphasis on the political orientation of the artwork, the Proletarian Culture movement often abandoned artistry in favor of naked propaganda and political agitation. *Partisan Review,* which was formed as a critical/theoretical journal allied with the politics and general aesthetic goals of the Communist Party, was disappointed with the results of Proletarian Culture. As *Partisan Review's* editors, William Phillips and Philip Rahv, pointed out in their formal "Editorial Statement" introducing the magazine, "We shall resist every attempt to cripple our literature by narrow-minded, sectarian theories and practices."[64]

The New York Intellectuals' aesthetic theory was more complex, but also less concrete or developed. Like Mike Gold and the other participants in the Proletarian Culture movement, *Partisan Review* supported the efforts to construct an autonomous, authentic, working-class art. The criticisms of the New York Intellectuals arose only from the particular form that Proletarian Culture took. Proletarian Culture, by strictly accepting the orthodox Marxian orientation of the Communist Party, had embraced a mechanical materialism that was fatal for the production of great art.[65] Mike Gold and his followers believed that culture and all other elements of society's superstructure were products of the economic base. According to the editors of *Partisan Review,* this faulty assumption distorted the other crucial factors that shape art. Instead of grappling with the complexities of consciousness, Proletarian Culture could only tout its slogans and produce shallow pieces of art. A successful proletarian art would require more technically sophisticated renderings of reality and perception, and the key to such results was Modernism.[66] Matters of form and content had to be separated. Proletarian Culture contained the right political content, but the form was a distortion of reality. Effective revolutionary art had to be influenced by more rigorous, theoretical considerations, and it needed to aspire to capture the flux of human experience.[67] Even counterrevolutionary art, like T. S. Eliot's and Ezra Pound's, was an improvement over the unsatisfactory formalism of Mike Gold, but only as long as the forms pioneered by reactionary Modernists presented the harsh realities of capitalism in clear and interesting ways.[68]

During the late 1930s when Proletarian Culture embraced the doctrines of the Popular Front, Gold and his associates committed the graver sin of drifting back toward popular culture. The League of American Writers, which replaced the John Reed Clubs, adopted a nonsectarian approach, which should have pleased the New York Intellectuals. What this meant in practice, however, was not an acceptance of the avant-garde but an accommodation with mass culture and radical folk art. Left-wing Modernists, like the group around *Partisan Review,* were attacked for their intellectualism and their snobbery that seemed out of touch with the masses with whom they claimed allegiance.[69] The New York Intellectuals, not completely surprised by this turn of events, embraced their rejection by the Communist Party. Perhaps more important, their own experiences with the authoritarian dogmatism within the Popular Front led them to immediately perceive a connection between mass culture and the conformity of Stalinist cultural practices—a conceptual coupling that would be developed further to link ideas about totalitarianism and mass art. Modernism, thus, became linked in their minds with an aesthetics that was neither authoritarian nor totalitarian—and this realization strengthened their belief that Modernism and independent radicalism were somehow united. With their formal break with the Communists, the editors of *Partisan Review* celebrated its new sense of independence that separation from Proletarian Culture entailed. Reflecting on the 1930s, William Phillips looked at *Partisan Review's* liberation from the Communists as one of its main sources of strength and vitality:

> But we had no such constraints in the magazine itself, whose role we saw as being open, forthright, and aggressive. Stalinist lies and shenanigans were exposed constantly, as were double-talking liberals, nor were Trotsky and the Trotskyites spared any criticism. At the same time, our opposition to conservatives was always clear . . . False literary reputations were cut down . . . On the whole, the magazine was raucous, impious, and intransigent.[70]

The freedom, however, did not bring a greater sense of clarity to the aesthetic theories and assumptions of New York's radical literary scene.

Released from Communist control, *Partisan Review*'s editors had enabled the magazine and its writers to chart their own independent course in the worlds of American radicalism and Modernism, but their synthesis of Marxism and the avant-garde remained opaque. Perhaps part of the problem was the unique form of dilettantism that has been frequently practiced within Marxist circles. William Phillips himself once admitted that the power of Marxian rhetoric produced an "inflation of one's intellectual pretensions and the shrinking of one's capacities."[71] New York's radical critics clearly suffered from this syndrome from time to time. It was easy to ridicule the ideas of other aesthetic and Marxist theorists, but constructing an alternative—finally delivering the goods, building a bridge between Marxism and Modernism—was a challenge with no easy solutions.

The initial impulse behind the Marxist–Modernist merger seemed natural and simple. The dispositions of Marxism and Modernism appeared to be perfectly suited to one another. Both were hostile to the comfortable world of the bourgeoisie, and the two movements were intellectually critical. They cut deep beneath the apparent realities of society and exposed new, complex interpretations of an unjust world. As Irving Howe remembered:

That the literary avant garde and the political Left were not really comfortable partners would become clear with the passage of time; in Europe it already had. But during the years the New York intellectuals began to appear as writers and critics worthy of some attention, there was a feeling in the air that a union of the advanced—critical consciousness and political conscience—could be forged. Throughout the 30's the New York intellectuals believed, somewhat naively, that this union was not only a desirable possibility but a tie both natural and appropriate.[72]

When the New York Intellectuals set out to build the theoretical basis for their synthesis, the conditions that had previously given them hope in revolutionary change rapidly began to deteriorate. As they sank their pilings for a bridge between Modernism and Marxism, the ground gave way. During the late 1930s, *Partisan Review* had to grapple with the Stalinist purge trials, the consolidation of Nazism and the spread of fascism, and the escalating popularity of mass culture in the United States. They found themselves disillusioned, frightened, and more isolated than they had ever been before. By the end of the decade, they were no closer to theoretically disclosing their artistic assumptions or the philosophical basis for an aesthetic theory. With their faith in Marx rattled, they embraced Modernism more tightly and showed a tendency to mirror the aestheticism to which so many members of the avant-garde had succumbed. As William Phillips explained:

> Of Lawrence or Joyce or Kafka, for example, it can be said that each in his own way was constructing some ideal consciousness, some pure vision that was not only revolutionary but also messianic, and was rooted in the assumption of a moral and intellectual elite. In a Nietzschean sense, literature was conceived as an act of breaking through the accepted categories: which is why so much writing of the 20's was anti-naturalistic, mythic, obsessive, and ultimately moral in its search for a new kind of wholeness and authenticity.[73]

Initially, this liberation of pure consciousness formed the basis for their conception of revolutionary art. In reaction to Stalin and the Communists' accommodation with mass culture, *Partisan Review* began to see Modernism as the only alternative to a tightly controlled cultural sphere of commercial and ideological domination. Their theoretical efforts rapidly reflected this growing awareness. They remained some of the avant-garde's greatest admirers in the United States, and all of their future criticism and aesthetic theorizing continually acknowledged the Modernists as the artistic ideal. Their chief task, however, shifted from examining and developing Modernism's revolutionary role to attacking the new enemy—the mass culture of American capitalists and European totalitarians.

When they made their strategic shift at the end of the 1930s from simply affirming Modernism to actively assaulting popular culture, the writers of *Partisan Review* were novices in the emerging field of mass culture criticism. They had a general sense of what mass culture was, and they dimly perceived connections between the commercial mass art in the United States and the culture of propaganda in Nazi Germany and the Soviet Union. What they lacked, however, were fully developed theories of mass culture, Modernism, and totalitarianism. In this context, the Institute for

Social Research had much to offer. The Horkheimer Circle had been considering these matters for many years. Several initial barriers, however, prevented the two coteries from intellectually coming together. While language and culture unquestionably played a role, Horkheimer's official policy of political isolation was the main obstacle. Terrified that it could again be identified as a political enemy, the Institute allowed its European experiences to color its fears in the United States. Rather than articulating the group's political orientation, Horkheimer insisted that all members refrain from overtly political statements or actions.[74] This nurtured an atmosphere that prevented the Institute's early social and professional contacts from blossoming into more substantial relationships. All of this changed, however, at the end of the 1930s when Horkheimer radically altered course owing to the group's financial crisis. In addition to assuming a more public role at Columbia University and more generally within the field of sociology, the Horkheimer Circle also made its work more accessible to interested American acquaintances by publishing in English and by participating more actively in the intellectual and cultural life of its new home, New York City.

The escalating impact of the Horkheimer Circle is readily apparent in the writings of the New York Intellectuals throughout the 1940s and 1950s. The New Yorkers' early work on mass culture showed only a rudimentary understanding of its form, function, and social significance. This gradually began to shift as the writers of *Partisan Review* drew from the Horkheimer Circle's work on commodity fetishism, conformity, authoritarianism, and negation. At the same time that the Critical Theorists' views on mass culture were taken up by the New York Intellectuals, however, the United States' entry into the Second World War shattered the solidarity of New York's community of little magazines. While some of the New York Intellectuals maintained the new perspectives on mass culture that had been gained with the help of Critical Theory, others, in an attempt to reconcile themselves with the United States, became newly converted defenders of mass culture. This startling turnaround produced a deep rift within New York's literary community and perpetuated a series of intense clashes that lasted far beyond the Institute's stay in the United States.[75]

The first major critique of mass culture by a New York Intellectual was published by Dwight Macdonald in *Partisan Review*. The duo of articles appeared during the summer of 1938. Unlike previous condemnations of

popular culture and proletarian literature that debunked both in favor of
Modernism, Macdonald's pieces presented a sustained analysis of mass art.
While Macdonald's chief aim was to discredit Stalin and his regrettable
impact on Soviet art, the surprising new wrinkle was an insistence that
Stalinist political interference resulted in a debasement of culture paralleling American mass culture. Both phenomena contained an anti-intellectual
regimentation that was anathema to authentic aesthetics.[76] Juxtaposing
examples of Soviet cinema and Hollywood films, Macdonald insisted that
both engaged in an insidious manipulation of the masses. Soviet cinema,
under Stalinist control, sought to control taste in an effort to indoctrinate
the Russian people. In Macdonald's eyes, Hollywood was carrying out a
remarkably similar project. Although the studios were operating indepen-
dently of the state, they still were shaping the tastes of their audiences
and indoctrinating them to accept bourgeois ideology. The interests of
commercial capital, for Macdonald, thus bore startling resemblances to
the authoritarianism of the Stalinist state and its bureaucracy.[77]

Macdonald's series received a positive reception at *Partisan Review*. In
a matter of months, Philip Rahv was echoing Macdonald but expanding
the position to include Nazi artistic practices in Germany. From Rahv's
perspective, the picture was even bleaker than Macdonald had painted it.
Not only was mass culture stripping the average worker of his independence and imagination, but the avant-garde had ceased to offer an aesthetic
alternative. Instead of continuing to provide audiences with a critically liberated consciousness, Modernism opted either to retreat into isolation or
to corrupt its authentic visions of the world by taking political sides in
the final struggle of capitalism's last stages.[78] As powerful and intriguing
as these formulations were, however, Macdonald, Rahv, and the rest of the
Partisan Review circle still accepted a passive model of the masses that
lacked any qualitative analysis of aesthetic reception. Borrowing directly
from the American legacy of mass culture criticism, the writers of *Partisan
Review* repeated the various assumptions and formulations that had been
pioneered by conservatives, Progressives, Communists, and the earlier generation of Greenwich Village Modernists—mass entertainment audiences
were perceived as passive objects of manipulation. No thought was given
to how audiences developed relationships to mass arts or were psychologically affected by them. By constructing such an uncritical and ahistorical
notion of the masses, they unconsciously mirrored the operation of mass

culture that they were describing. While they bemoaned the objectification and passivity of America's masses, they unwittingly accepted an image of the working and middle classes that helped perpetuate the situation that they abhorred and replicated the outcome that they attributed only to mass culture.[79]

The first New York Intellectual to depart from this legacy of mass culture criticism was Clement Greenberg. While working in New York's customs office during the late 1930s, Greenberg moved along the periphery of New York's literary community, but he eagerly followed the work pouring out of *Partisan Review*. Macdonald's articles on Soviet cinema served as the provocation that catapulted Greenberg from the sidelines to the center of Manhattan's literary arena of public intellectuals. Seizing upon Macdonald's failure to account adequately for mass tastes in Russia, Greenberg sought to offer a more rigorous analysis of popular culture that directly confronted the problem of aesthetic reception that had been ignored in the past.[80] His article "Avant-garde and Kitsch" signaled an important shift in American views regarding mass art, and it highlights the convergence between the interests of the Frankfurt School and the New York Intellectuals during the 1930s and 1940s.

"Avant-garde and Kitsch" clearly was inspired by Macdonald's pieces, and Greenberg was a young, well-read man when he wrote the article. Archival materials suggest that, despite his age, Greenberg was familiar with a great deal of German cultural criticism, but these sources contain no references to the work of the Horkheimer Circle.[81] Despite this lack of evidence, Greenberg's biographer and a former colleague insist that he was deeply influenced by Critical Theory and that "Avant-garde and Kitsch" clearly demonstrates this.[82] The article, itself, partly confirms such claims, but in other regards it indicates a gap between Greenberg and members of the Institute for Social Research.

Like Rahv, Greenberg identified the aesthetic and intellectual achievements of the avant-garde, and its retreat into isolation. To Greenberg, Modernism's greatest accomplishment was its superior consciousness of history.[83] Like Lukács, Greenberg valued art that located contemporary civilization within history's flow, thereby representing the social totality. Contemporary Modernists of his day, however, had abandoned revolutionary politics and instead pursued goals of technical innovation and experimentation. In Greenberg's view, this development not only preserved

Modernism's integrity, but also transformed its central thrust from social consciousness to an absolutism of form (36–37). While Modernism still represented high art, its audience grew increasingly limited with the passing of time and the movement's continued retreat from the realm of the social. The masses had rarely cared about high art, but now society's elite were even retracting their support from the avant-garde as the artworks became less accessible (85). The development signaled a potentially severe threat to the future of culture.

The decline of high art did not simply leave an aesthetic void in its wake. Like other writers for *Partisan Review,* Greenberg noted that kitsch, or mass art, was filling the emptiness and actually displacing high art. The article's true innovation was to uncover the formal elements of mass culture and to speculate on their reception. Greenberg recognized that mass culture arose from the industrial revolution and the urbanization that accompanied it. Unlike the previous folk culture that had its roots in the agricultural life of rural communities, kitsch was firmly connected to the boredom and monotony of capitalist civilization (39). Drawing from genuine high and popular culture, kitsch appropriated various elements but debased them through mechanical, formulaic transformations (40). The result was a more immediate and conformist art that was easily consumed by its audiences (44). Unlike high art and Modernism, which both required intellectual effort and cultural refinement, kitsch required nothing of its audiences and provided the escape of pure sensation. Totalitarians in Russia and Germany relied on kitsch precisely because the masses preferred it—not because it enabled them any greater degree of control over their populations. Avant-garde art, in Greenberg's view, was not inherently critical and was consequently not an effective intellectual weapon against totalitarianism. The only reason that Stalinists and Nazis rejected Modernism was that it was less popular and thereby harder to use for propaganda purposes (47).

The picture of mass culture that took shape in Greenberg's analysis bears intriguing resemblances to Theodor W. Adorno's work on the fetish character that had been published only months earlier in the *Zeitschrift für Sozialforschung.*[84] Adorno, like Greenberg, had firmly grounded mass art within the broader social and historical processes of industrialization and modernization. He also emphasized the repetition and eternal sameness inherent in the forms of mass culture. Adorno's formal considerations of the art object's constitution, however, were more fully rooted in Marx's concept of the commodity fetish and Lukács's notion of reification. Adorno would have agreed with Greenberg that kitsch engaged in a ruthless appropriation of high culture, but he also insisted that high art had sunk to the level of mere commodity. As Adorno pointed out, exchange value had overtaken the use value of art.[85] Consequently, certain forms of older high art (Adorno used the example of a Toscanini concert) were consumed to bring the prestige associated with the exchange value of the artistic product. Taste and art therefore became entwined with the wider phenomenon of reified bourgeois reality. For Adorno, the real (and revolutionary) task of art was to interrogate the prevailing societal assumptions and to present alternatives to the status quo. In Adorno's Hegelian terms, art represented one of the most basic and fundamental forms of negation. Mass culture and commodity fetishism, by contrast, offered false pleasure, reaffirmed the status quo, and promoted a pervasive conformity that stripped the masses of their individuality and subjectivity. In Adorno's view, mass art was not something that was simply deployed by fascists and Stalinists for strategic purposes. On the contrary, mass culture was in its very essence totalitarian.

In several respects, Greenberg's analysis was closer to the thought of the Horkheimer Circle than it was to that of his fellow New York Intellectuals. Nevertheless, there was still a wide gulf separating the two. Like the other writers at *Partisan Review,* Greenberg had a different sense of art's role and capabilities. He believed that Modernism offered a glimpse of the social totality—in much the same way that Lukács viewed great realist art. Furthermore, Greenberg was sounding a warning to the Modernist avant-garde—a warning that was consistent with the progressive role that the New York Intellectuals envisioned for art within the Marxian/Modernist synthesis. The Institute for Social Research, by contrast, ascribed a more purely critical and negative role to art. Fondly quoting Stendahl, members of the Horkheimer Circle spoke of art as "une promesse de bonheur"—a notion that evoked the other, the antibourgeois, the negation of the status quo.

While much separated Greenberg's work from the exotic Weimar Hegelian Marxism of Critical Theory, Greenberg's achievement was substantial in its reformulation of pervasive American concerns and assumptions about mass culture. "Avant-garde and Kitsch" was a milestone. It represented one of the most comprehensive Marxian qualitative analyses of mass culture that had ever appeared in English. In his article's wake, surprisingly little was published regarding mass culture for the next few years. Part of the reason was the dramatic events of the era—the Nazi–Soviet Pact and the beginning of World War II. These developments helped to pull the fragmented American Left further apart. Tension pervaded the editorial board of *Partisan Review* during the late 1930s and early 1940s. Its initial source was Dwight Macdonald's commitment to Trotskyism. As the rest of the editors reveled in the new independence brought about by their break from the Communist Party, Macdonald and a small group of similarly predisposed writers (Clement Greenberg, Irving Howe, Lewis Coser, James Burnham, C. Wright Mills, and Paul Goodman) gravitated toward the ranks of the highly polarized U.S. Trotskyist movement. Although commitment to Trotskyism remained short-lived, Macdonald and his younger friends accepted the "third camp" interpretation of World War II by some Trotskyists. The journal's other editors generally shared Macdonald's views at first, but their fear of Nazi victory slowly brought them to a more patriotic stance regarding the American war effort. When Macdonald attempted to inject his pacifist perspectives into *Partisan Review* in the summer of 1941, Rahv and Phillips vigorously attacked him.[86] The conflict swiftly escalated, and both sides began jockeying for control of the journal. When the dust settled in the middle of 1943, Rahv and Phillips claimed victory, while Macdonald pushed forward with plans to start his own little magazine—*Politics*.

From this point onward, *Partisan Review* embarked on its journey of deradicalization and accommodation with the United States. As William Phillips recalled:

> The fact is we did not oppose the war. And this political act, for it was a decisive political act, had far-reaching consequences. It meant the end of traditional radicalism, particularly of the Marxist or Trotskyist variety, which was predicated on the pure idea of internationalism. And it opened the door to the legitimization of nationalist feelings and doctrines, both in the advanced and the "retarded" countries, and to the sanctification of ethnic feelings and aspirations. Old-fashioned Marxism no longer worked, but the new profusion of political creeds was no better: it has brought us to our present state of ideological confusion in which any notion, conventional or crackpot, can find some justification and rationalization.[87]

The more tangible changes evident in this transformation were the acceptance of a vigorous, Cold War anticommunism (emanating from Sidney
Hook—one of the journal's political and philosophical guiding lights) and
an artistic retreat into a form of neo-aestheticism. This end point of the
journal's Modernist odyssey had perhaps been inevitable.[88] From its outset, *Partisan Review* had admired literary achievement at the occasional
exclusion of political considerations, and the group's awkward defenses of
reactionary Modernist writers (such as Eliot and Pound) clearly indicated
this preference. With their gradual abandonment of Marxism during World
War II, however, the magazine and its writers could pursue their adoration
of Modernist styles and forms without struggling to make their criticism
fit within a radical sociological and political framework. Thus, the original goal of theoretically grounding the work of the avant-garde in relation
to social criticism evaporated, and an ethos of "Modernism for Modernism's sake" emerged. Mass culture could still be attacked as a kind of corpo-
rate philistinism, but the more Marxian analyses pioneered by Greenberg
and the Horkheimer Circle lost their appeal as *Partisan Review* moved
toward the Conservative and Progressive traditions of American popular
culture criticism that have been examined already.

DWIGHT MACDONALD'S *POLITICS* AND THE
RECEPTION OF CRITICAL THEORY

Dwight Macdonald's *Politics* consequently became the main recipient of
Critical Theory during the 1940s. Macdonald and his friends eagerly
consumed the writings of the Institute even before the break with *Partisan Review* was complete.[89] In 1941, the Horkheimer Circle released a bar-
rage of material in English that greatly clarified many of its positions and
views. During this brief period, the *Zeitschrift für Sozialforschung* (which
had transformed itself into an American periodical and adopted the new
title *Studies in Philosophy and Social Science*) published a special issue
on mass culture, followed by another on Nazism and state capitalism.[90]
Together, both installments introduced a wider American audience to Critical Theory, and disclosed how the topics of mass culture and totalitarianism
were closely entwined in the thought of the Institute. Complementing all
of these writings was Erich Fromm's masterpiece, *Escape from Freedom*.[91]
The Horkheimer Circle's critiques of popular culture and Nazism were
both deeply influenced by Fromm's psychological contributions to Critical

Theory and his pioneering work in the fields of social conformity and authoritarianism. Before the publication of *Escape from Freedom*, however, Fromm's connection to these matters would have only been known to Americans familiar with *Autorität und Familie*. Early readers of *Studies in Philosophy and Social Science*, consequently, were presented with a sophisticated yet confusing combination of Marx and Freud that seemed to have little precedence or context. Fromm's *Escape from Freedom* rectified this situation by disclosing the assumptions that underlay this synthesis and by more clearly disclosing many similar insights that the Horkheimer Circle relied on in its own writings. In Macdonald's review of *Escape from Freedom*, it is clear that he was beginning to see the connection between authority and conformism that Fromm was discussing and the theories of state capitalism and mass culture that the Horkheimer School published in 1941. As Macdonald wrote:

> Today, for the first time in history, the *technical* means exist to create an economy of plenty for all. The failure to achieve this so far is extremely serious, for it means that the masses of people get from their freedom *from* old authority and restraints, only a deep sense of insecurity and isolation, which forces the individual to seek security in certain psychological compensations. In capitalist-democratic societies like ours, this means what Fromm terms "automaton conformity," that is, the individual "adopts entirely the kind of personality offered to him by cultural patterns, and he therefore becomes exactly as all others are and as they expect him to be." In the authoritarian societies of Germany and Russia, this means "the tendency to give up the independence of one's own individual self and to fuse one's self with somebody or something outside of one's self in order to acquire the strength which the individual self is lacking."[92]

Thus, even in the case of the circle of New York Intellectuals that gathered around Dwight Macdonald and that briefly formed the magazine *Politics*, Erich Fromm functioned in much the same way as he had on Morningside Heights—Fromm was the first highly accessible public intellectual transmitter of Critical Theory in the United States.

To Dwight Macdonald and his allies, the writings of Erich Fromm and the Frankfurt School provided stimulating new directions for rethinking radicalism. Attacking the totalitarianism of the Stalin regime in the USSR had been common among the New York Intellectuals since the founding of *Partisan Review,* but the concept of totalitarianism grew to become more refined with the onset of the Second World War.[93] By the early 1940s, Macdonald and other Trotskyists were not only questioning Trotsky's own claims about the "degenerated workers' state" within the Soviet Union, but were beginning to inquire about the legacy of Lenin, to learn about Trotsky's personal role in the repression of the Kronstadt uprising, and to consider whether valuable parallels might be drawn between Nazi fascism and Soviet Communism. The result of this growing disillusionment with Trotsky, Lenin, and the entire Bolshevik Revolution, accompanied by heightened fears of Nazism, led to East–West convergence theories with strong parallels to the Horkheimer Circle's thesis regarding state capitalism. The result was a series of articles and books that articulated theories of totalitarianism that led to similar concerns that the Frankfurt School had begun to explore—general fears about the nature of bureaucracy, human nature, and modernity itself.[94] Initially, Macdonald resisted the arguments formulated in James Burnham's *The Managerial Revolution,* which was the most popular and publicized American book on the topic.[95] For Burnham, who had been a longtime associate of Trotsky and a central figure within the early community of the New York Intellectuals, the book marked the beginning of his rapid move to the right side of the political spectrum. In it, Burnham repudiated his former faith in the socialist movement by arguing that a centrally planned society appeared to be a powerful alternative to capitalism and socialism. Much like the simultaneous writings of the Frankfurt School, Burnham argued that this political and economic coordination by managerial elites would include the domination of the cultural sphere and the conformity of the masses to authoritarianism. *Partisan Review* published an abbreviated synopsis of Burnham's central arguments, and then ran a series of articles that discussed the details of the "managerial model" to reexamine its implications.[96] Macdonald's contributions to this exchange are instructive for better comprehending how the issues of totalitarianism and mass culture were coming together in his own thought during the summer of 1941. Not yet willing to accept the bleak outlook of the theories of the "managerial revolution" or "state capitalism," Macdonald clung to Trotsky's analysis of fascism, Stalinism, and the future challenges facing the working-class movements. A market economy and a middle class still existed within Germany, Macdonald argued, but Germany's bourgeoisie had sought to overcome the crises of advanced capitalism by the intervention of state bureaucracy and the growth of a war economy. Hope, therefore, could still be located within the proletariat. As Macdonald wrote, "There is only one historical alternative to this development: socialism. The fate of our civilization depends on whether the working class is able to turn history into this channel in the next period."[97] Nevertheless, Macdonald grappled with the disappointing realization "that the Nazis and not the proletariat have shattered the structure of capitalism and that the result has been not the social progress anticipated by Marxists but instead war and reaction in their most hideous forms."[98]

Macdonald's optimism was both fragile and fleeting.[99] His position was based on the hope that working-class movements would be able to mount a successful opposition to the coordination of state power and authority. With the help of Erich Fromm and the Horkheimer Circle, Macdonald would discover how misplaced his hopes were. The psychological, ideological, and socioeconomic barriers were enormous, and Critical Theory would provide Macdonald and his friends with ways of comprehending these obstacles. Already by the early fall of 1941, Macdonald seemed to admit that the proletariat was not up to the challenge and that Marxian theory had to join in the battle against totalitarianism. He thus imagined a role for revolutionary theory that shared much in common with the role that the Critical Theorists had assigned to themselves. As Macdonald explained, "Marxist revolutionary thought and leadership must break with the abstractions of its post-war tradition and remold its concepts to fit the unexpected and unprecedented developments of the last two decades."[100]

By November 1941, Macdonald decided to make contact with the Institute for Social Research. Like so many other New Yorkers, it was impossible to know much about the Institute besides what one might have heard via word of mouth or read in print. Macdonald initially approached Theodor W. Adorno and expressed his desire to build an alliance and to publicize the work of the Horkheimer Circle. Macdonald, who still entertained thoughts of taking over *Partisan Review* at the time, suggested collaborating with the Institute. He proposed to publish everything that the Horkheimer Circle was willing to offer. Adorno, who was clearly surprised by his first and only meeting with Macdonald, wrote to Horkheimer in California:

I had an uncommonly encouraging lunch with MacDonald [*sic*] and one of his colleagues. His circle is so taken by our stuff that they would publish every sentence. I explained to them as sincerely as possible that collaboration with us is impossible, my thought being that these people, who really had something to do with us, were too unsympathetic to put off with excuses. They indicated thorough understanding. Best for them would be an essay from us about philosophy in today's Germany. I therefore told them about Stern [Günther Anders].[101]

Adhering to Horkheimer's strict ban on all overt political associations, Adorno rebuffed Macdonald and maintained the Institute's intellectual independence. The rejection of the offer, however, must have been carried out gracefully. Although his collaborative ambitions had been denied, Macdonald and his associates maintained a steady interest in the Institute's work. An intellectual alliance was born between the *Politics* circle and the Institute for Social Research, but it was an impersonal relationship of intellectual reception of the Horkheimer Circle's texts rather than the kind of cooperation and formal allegiance that Macdonald initially had in mind.

The most obvious instance of this reception took place in the *Politics* circle's thoughts on popular culture. As we have noted in our analysis of Clement Greenberg's "Avant-garde and Kitsch," the New York Intellectuals had developed a theory of popular culture that bore some resemblance to the work of the Horkheimer Circle. During the 1940s, however, the mass culture criticism of the *Politics* group came under the more direct influence of Critical Theory. Greenberg, the most innovative American critic of the earlier phase of pop culture criticism, had uncovered startling aspects of mass art. Unlike earlier critics, Greenberg insisted that mass culture was not something foisted on passive working- and middle-class people. Instead, the structure of commercial art suggested that it fulfilled a need for distraction that modern industrial capitalism produced. The result was an easy, formulaic art that could only offer the stimulation of new sensations. Glaringly absent from Greenberg's analysis was any appreciation for the possible connections that might exist between mass culture and totalitarian coordination. This had been one of the central arguments that Macdonald had formulated in his analysis of Soviet cinema, but Greenberg had rejected Macdonald's view, claiming that mass culture was simply used as a tool by Nazis and Stalinists. Greenberg thus denied that mass art complemented the authoritarian practices and ideals of the new totalitarian regimes. Before the reception of the Horkheimer Circle during the 1940s, the New York Intellectuals' interpretation of mass culture consequently maintained the phenomenon's isolation. Instead of integrating the topics of mass culture, Modernism, and totalitarianism into a more comprehensive social theory, as the Institute had accomplished in the 1930s, the New York critics, led by Greenberg, did not see a connection.

Macdonald's return to the topic of mass culture in the winter of 1944 indicated a shift from Greenberg's analysis and suggested the rise of a new appreciation for mass culture that came directly from the writings of the Horkheimer Circle. This first article, titled "A Theory of Popular Culture," echoed many of Greenberg's points regarding the history and structure of mass art (points that also corresponded to the thought of the Institute), but the essay also struggled to reconcile its realizations about mass culture with the phenomenon of collectivization in Germany and Russia.[102] Attempting to generalize about the social ramifications of mass culture, Macdonald disclosed a set of basic assumptions that confirmed his acceptance of Fromm's theories of conformity, Adorno's use of the concept of the commodity fetish, and Pollock's concept of state capitalism. As Macdonald wrote:

> In this new period, the competition between Popular Culture and High Culture is taking a new form: as in the business world, competition is now resulting in a merger. On all but the lowest levels—the pulps, the comics, soap opera—Popular Culture is more and more taking on the color of both varieties of the Old High Culture, Academic and Avantgarde, while these latter are increasingly watered down with Popular elements. As in politics, everything and everybody are being integrated—"coordinated" the Nazis call it—into the official culture structure . . . The masses are exploited culturally as well as economically, and we must look to Popular Culture for some clue as to the kind of response we may expect to socialist ideas. The deadening and warping effect of long exposure to movies, pulp magazines and radio can hardly be overestimated. This is not to say that this effect cannot be slowly worn away by economic and social changes, or suddenly (and temporarily) negated in some great crisis. If it were otherwise, our situation as radicals would indeed be hopeless. But this culture-pattern stamped deep

into the modern personality, much deeper than conscious political ideas, is a factor always to be reckoned with. One of the reasons for the sterility of socialist politics since the last war is its too narrow conception of politics.[103]

As this rather lengthy quotation shows, Macdonald had developed a view of mass culture that integrated it within the larger historical frameworks of totalitarianism and social regulation. As a consequence of his reliance on the Frankfurt School's integrated approach to mass culture and totalitarianism, Macdonald began to move toward a similarly transhistorical ideology critique. His article demonstrated that his appreciation for the form and function of the mass culture object had changed, as well as his new appreciation of its close affinities to the type of cultural coordination taking place in totalitarian societies. As Adorno had indicated in his article "The Fetish Character and the Regression of Listening," the coordination of mass culture operated on multiple fronts leading to aesthetic, psychological, and social conformity. Producers of mass culture appropriated any innovations they wished from high art and Modernism, a regression in aesthetic reception was under way as a result of reification and stylistic conformity within the cultural sphere, and audiences were losing their individuality as well as their artistic taste. Like the Horkheimer Circle's concept of popular culture, Macdonald's view expanded to include a new image of the masses resulting from their reception of popular culture. Instead of bored appendages of industrial processes, Macdonald came to see them as the innocent victims of ideological manipulation and intellectual stagnation. Like the imprisoned masses of Communist Russia and Nazi Germany, U.S. workers were losing the independent consciousness on which Marxian socialism had hung its hopes. Western civilization, therefore, was collectively drifting into the conformist world of the "totally administered society."

As Macdonald increasingly gave himself and the magazine over to the gloom and hopelessness of the Horkheimer Circle's position, he adopted the Hegelian notion of negation that had grown to become the centerpiece of Critical Theory during its late phase. Now that Macdonald recognized the connection between mass culture and totalitarianism, the affirmation of limited, progressive action began to seem rather absurd. Negation struck at the totality of the problem—the completeness of the nightmare that was contemporary reality. As Macdonald pointed out to a reader who had attacked the pessimism of *Politics:*

His objection that *Politics* suggests not even "the narrowest channels for action against the disaster" reveals this: for clearly narrow channels for action will be of no use against disaster on this scale. Only the broadest kind of approach will be effective if the threatening catastrophe is of such a magnitude, and the situation over here today is that this approach is only possible now intellectually, not in practice . . . Even if one is opposed to revolution, or has no faith in it, the negativistic approach has a pragmatic importance: it enables one to analyze modern society more accurately and profoundly. The revolutionary can afford to look at social processes more objectively than the realpolitiker: sacred cows don't exist for him.[104]

If the status quo was hopelessly corrupted, negation (or the "negativistic approach") represented the only alternative. In a world of complete barbarism, dissent and criticism became the only sources for hope.

Beginning with Macdonald's "Popular Culture: Field Notes" of April 1945, the *Politics* group first began to acknowledge its intellectual debt to the Horkheimer Circle.[105] In this series of brief aphoristic ruminations, Macdonald continuously drew from the Institute's critique of mass culture. From Horkheimer, he borrowed the concept of infantile regression, which mass art inflicted on its adult audiences.[106] Macdonald also approvingly directed his readers to Herta Herzog's article "On Borrowed Experience," which had appeared in the mass culture issue of the Institute's *Studies in Philosophy and Social Science*.[107] The longest and most detailed appreciation, however, was devoted to Leo Lowenthal's "Biographies in Popular Magazines," which a friend had found for Macdonald in Lazarsfeld's journal, *Radio Research*.[108] By constructing a formal examination of popular biographies, Lowenthal uncovered the same collectivist, totalitarian trends that Macdonald had noted earlier in Western civilization. Instead of celebrating those that made a positive social difference, Americans were reading the biographies of new "idols of consumption"—"takers," who "seem to stand for a phantasmagoria of world-wide social security; for an attitude which asks for no more than to be served with the things needed for reproduction and recreation; for an attitude which has lost every primary interest in how to invent, shape or apply the tools leading to such purposes of mass satisfaction."[109]

Macdonald, however, was not the only *Politics* writer to directly acknowledge the work of the Horkheimer Circle. Irving Howe also relied heavily on the writings of the Institute and proclaimed his debt in a 1948 article titled "Notes on Mass Culture."[110] Like Macdonald, Howe was becoming increasingly interested in the reception of mass art, but he did not want to follow in the footsteps of American highbrow critics. Formal evaluations of popular culture had shed little light on the ways in which the masses consumed it. Consequently, Howe had sought out new ways of sociologically and structurally understanding mass culture, and this search had led him to the Critical Theory of the Horkheimer Circle. Borrowing mainly from Adorno's article "On Popular Music," Howe recognized the primary functions and effects of mass art.[111] Many American critics had made note of mass art's relationship to leisure and the monotony of industrial labor, but Howe broke new ground (with the help of Adorno) by examining the role of standardization in contemporary popular culture.

Mass culture rejuvenated its bored and anxious audiences by promising stimulation and ease. Ironically, this was accomplished by providing them with an art of eternal sameness. The art products were easily consumed by the audience precisely because they were standardized (or, in Adorno's words, "predigested"). Mass culture thus offered an easy escape from the stressful world of industrial labor, but it structurally created a mirror image of that world.[112] Mass man escaped the boredom and repetition of his daily life by escaping into a fantasy world of more boredom and repetition. This mindless aesthetic consumption, however, was not without serious social consequences. Howe insisted that these new art forms presented terrible new dangers to the philosophical and psychological subject—dangers that had only begun to reach a final culmination in the barbarism of totalitarianism.

In a passage clearly emulating the dramatic ironies and gallows humor that typify the style and rhetoric of Critical Theory, Howe provocatively proposed interrelated theories of mass culture, Modernism, and totalitarianism that arose from his exposure to Institute writings. Not only did he articulate a view of art's negative potential that shares strong affinities with the aesthetic theories of Theodor W. Adorno and Herbert Marcuse, but he also fixed his attention on a seemingly innocuous art object only to dialectically disclose its hidden sociological relevance to contemporary society. As Howe wrote:

> Where art stirs a free and rich passage of materials from dream to experience and from experience to dream, mass culture tries to cage the unconscious.

It cannot of course succeed, but it does often manage to dissociate conscious from unconscious life. The audience therefore responds on two unin-
tegrated levels: surface consciousness ("having a good time") and suppressed
unconscious (the distorted evocation of experience by popular culture
themes). On the surface the Donald Duck and Mickey Mouse cartoons
seem merely pleasant little fictions, but they are actually overladen with the
most competitive, aggressive and sadistic themes. Often on the verge of
hysteria, Donald Duck is a frustrated little monster who has something
of the SS man in him and whom we, also having something of the SS man
in us, naturally find quite charming.[113]

Modernism represented the last bastion of autonomous, self-conscious
art. Both its roots and its reception relied on the efforts of freethinking
artists and audiences. Mass culture, by contrast, represented an art of total
control and assembly-line production. Instead of liberating the mind by
evoking "une promesse de bonheur," mass culture replicated the sociopolitical shackles of state capitalism, obliterated autonomous subjectivity,
and threatened modern man with psychological, cultural, and intellectual
totalitarianism.

Few of the other New York Intellectuals made such clear acknowledg-
ments of the Institute's influence. For many, the Horkheimer Circle simply
formed part of the stimulating atmosphere that constituted New York's
intellectual life during the 1930s and 1940s. Concerns about Modernism,
mass culture, totalitarianism, bureaucratic collectivism, and the Holocaust
were swirling about the country's great metropolis, and the Horkheimer
Circle was just one of many groups thinking about these topics. For others, the Institute for Social Research failed to catch their attention. A great
many New York writers probably never read any of the Horkheimer Circle's work, and even fewer had direct contact with the group on Morningside Heights. Without question, however, many of the same thinkers
who remained oblivious of the Institute's existence were introduced to
some of Critical Theory's central assumptions through the receptions that
had been made by other New York writers. Whether acknowledged or not,
the work of the Horkheimer Circle, as well as the influence of numerous
other émigré intellectuals, lurked behind the profusion of ink that the New
York Intellectuals devoted to making sense of the new world that was taking shape during and after the Second World War. Even the most casual

perusal of *Partisan Review, Politics, Commentary,* and *Dissent* discloses a continuous fascination with the basic set of interrelated topics that the Horkheimer Circle helped many of the New York writers to comprehend and interconnect.[114] In fact, the emerging importance and stature of the Institute among the New York Intellectuals is also demonstrated by the large number of articles that members of the Horkheimer Circle published in the main journals of New York's intellectual community during the late 1940s and 1950s.[115]

Historians are not in the business of considering what might have been. They tend to focus exclusively on what actually happened. The contacts between the New York Intellectuals and the Horkheimer Circle in many ways led to relatively little. Although both the New York Intellectuals and the Frankfurt School stood at similar crossroads at approximately the same time, neither intervened in the history of the other until it was already largely too late. They had similar interests and concerns, and they might have profoundly changed each other if the opportunity had ever materialized. Their collision could have led to so much more than it did. The two groups were largely held apart by circumstances and cultural distance. By the time that the Horkheimer Circle had overcome its timidity, the New Yorkers had already moved beyond it and had begun to make peace with the United States. Similarly, by the time the Horkheimer Circle began to engage with the thought of the New York Intellectuals, it already had one foot back in Europe.

One possible outcome that might have occurred if the two groups had developed closer contacts earlier is that the New York Intellectuals might not have abandoned radicalism as completely as most of them did. As we have seen in the case of Dwight Macdonald and the *Politics* circle, Critical Theory provided many of the pieces that were missing from the New York Intellectuals' theory of Modernism. Instead of retreating from politics into a stance of neo-aestheticism, the New York writers might have renewed their interest in Marx and in internationalism. Critical Theory offered the key that unified the interests and concerns of the New York Intellectuals. Marxism, modernism, alienation, conformity, totalitarianism, and the Holocaust were all interconnected within the thought of the Institute. Although an impact is evident, it could have been more pronounced. Still, Critical Theory's roots in Hegelianism and the Institute's stubborn insistence on publishing in German would have remained major obstacles to a cross-fertilization between the two groups. Perhaps these factors were insurmountable, but of all the coteries in America during the 1930s and 1940s, the New York Intellectuals represented an ideal audience for the Horkheimer Circle.

As far as the Horkheimer Circle is concerned, an earlier engagement with the New York Intellectuals might have facilitated a more direct confrontation between Critical Theory and Hook's Pragmatic Marxism. Although the attitudes regarding Positivism would have remained entirely irreconcilable, the members of the Institute for Social Research would have benefited immeasurably from engaging in a more serious confrontation with the democratic communication theory inherent within Pragmatism and the feelings of patriotism that infiltrated the New York Intellectual community during the height of World War II. As committed as Critical Theory remained to imagining a better and more just world, some of its basic assumptions were highly antiliberal and Mandarin. Some suggest that Franz Neumann gradually grew to appreciate this fact during his brief stint at Columbia after the war.[116] Perhaps the entire staff of the Institute would have been afforded this same opportunity if the Horkheimer Circle and the New York Intellectuals had developed closer ties during their years together in New York. Perhaps the task of integrating Critical Theory and Pragmatism would not have been left to Jürgen Habermas to accomplish.

PART III

CRITICAL THEORY AND THE
RISE OF POSTWAR SOCIOLOGY

chapter 5

THE ATLANTIC DIVIDE

Building Bridges between Anglo-American
Empiricism and Continental Social Theory

The Institute for Social Research, as part of the larger "intellectual migration," participated in a crucial moment in the history of transatlantic ideas. Prior to 1933, sociology was divided by the Atlantic Ocean into Continental and Anglo-American traditions. Although both heritages shared common origins in the social-scientific ideas of the Enlightenment, they grew apart during the nineteenth century and remained largely autonomous until the Second World War.[1] Continental sociology remained focused on the speculative issues that marked the discipline's birth, while the Anglo-American variant developed an early confidence in evolutionary models of social development and sought to model itself on the natural sciences.[2] When Hitler and the Nazis seized power in Germany and spread their brand of fascism across Europe, they forced Continental sociology's leading figures into exile. Although some remained at home and only underwent an interior retreat, the majority fled to Great Britain and the United States. By electing to uproot themselves through emigration, the social-scientific refugees physically united the formerly sundered world of sociology and enabled the rise of a hybrid approach that combined the two traditions.[3]

Long before this disciplinary unification took place, sociology, like the rest of the social sciences, emerged during the Enlightenment as a single tradition. The same cultural and intellectual forces that transformed the early-modern mind into the modern intellect drastically altered conceptions of society. Empowered by critical Reason and nurtured by a humanistic faith in progress, the public sphere that had been carved out by the Enlightenment destroyed the ancien régime and also rejected its views regarding society. Seeking a more scientific basis for the study of social phenomena, the proto-sociological philosophes departed from the ancient field of social philosophy. Writers such as Condorcet, Vico, and Montesquieu rejected the traditional notions of fixed social categories and processes that had been the common tools of social and political philosophers, and instead developed dynamic social concepts. More important, however, they grounded these concepts in their surrounding material conditions and recognized that such concepts had histories.[4] Rather than merely theorizing about the nature of social relations and imagining the "good life," the earliest Enlightenment sociologists were able to more accurately describe existing social relations and to explain the causes of social change. They came to recognize that society, as a man-made entity, was capable of being reformed. Montesquieu's writings in particular had a strong impact on the writers of the Scottish Enlightenment. Scottish philosophes such as David Hume, Adam Smith, Adam Ferguson, John Millar, and William Robertson built on the innovations of Vico and Montesquieu by reconceptualizing society as a process that was the product of economic, social, and historical forces.[5] Society, therefore, was the end result of a series of complex social interactions in which individual interests combined to form broader social patterns that constituted the building blocks of a given society.

In departing from social philosophy, the proto-sociologists of the Enlightenment established strong affinities between their emerging discipline and scientism. In rejecting the methods and legacy of social philosophy, members of the French and Scottish Enlightenments adopted antispeculative and antimetaphysical impulses.[6] Their observations and social theorizing were grounded in existing, observable social phenomena. Such attitudes and methods created an alliance between early sociology and Positivism that was formally constituted in the writings of Auguste Comte.

Although Comte's political views were quite different from those of his Enlightenment predecessors, his writings on sociology were heavily influenced by the French and Scottish philosophes. Coming a generation later and writing from the 1820s through the 1850s, in the wake of the French Revolution, Comte was far less optimistic about modernity and the excessive individualism unleashed by the Enlightenment. Instead of promoting liberation and social transformation, Comte's rational analysis of society sought progress through social order and unity.[7] Although the object of his sociology corresponded closely with the conservative political atmosphere during the age of Restoration, his theories and methods were a continuation and crowning achievement of enlightened social science. Rejecting metaphysics in favor of empirically grounded methods of observation, he struggled to explain the origin and growth of industrial society.[8] Instead of approaching the topic from the perspective of its smallest component part—the individual—Comte viewed society as a distinctly separate, irreducible entity with its own rules and operations. He bolstered this perspective by borrowing from biology. Just as a biological organism was the elemental building block of biological theory, society was the essential base of all sociological analysis. Implicitly built into this organic metaphor was the assumption that consensus and social harmony were the essential goals of social science. Just as biological health precluded an organism being divided against itself, Comte's assumptions of societal health embraced the ideal of unity. The purpose of sociological observation, consequently, was to build coherent theories and laws of society to which man had to conform.[9] In Comte's view, which represented a repudiation of enlightened humanism, people could not build a better society of their own choosing. Society's development followed its own path that was established by the inertia of social forces. Societies developed social institutions that fulfilled the essential functions required by their members. The goals of sociology were to perceive society's patterns of development, to uncover its functional networks of social institutions, and to promote people living in harmony with existing patterns and networks.

A short intellectual gap separated the work of Herbert Spencer from the sociological theorizing of Auguste Comte. Comte had already appropriated the organic model of society from biology and had formalized sociology's relationship with Positivism. Spencer continued both of these tendencies and expanded them with the help of Darwin's theory of evolution. Although Spencer was less extreme than Comte in his attitudes regarding individualism, he accepted the fact that human social development followed a path of its own that sociology could discern through careful scientific observation.[10] Like Comte, Spencer eschewed radical social transformation. Society changed by itself according to the laws of its own development. Alterations were not drastic but gradual, on the model of Darwin's theory of developmental changes within a species. In Spencer's view, societies, like organisms, went through a series of slow, progressive, evolutionary changes. Sociology's great value was to determine whether current social practices and organizations corresponded with the contemporary evolutionary stage of society.

After Comte (and his work's Darwinian refinement by Spencer), Continental sociology emerged as social scientists and philosophers, primarily in France and Germany, became embroiled in a series of debates regarding the central elements of the sociological canon that had taken shape. Competing theories of social development, such as Marxism, undermined the consensus among those seeking to discern the patterns of social change; and epistemological challenges to Positivism, launched by such German Idealists as Dilthey, Rickert, and Windelband, proposed that man-made, social reality was fundamentally different from objective, physical reality, thus requiring different analytic tools.[11] As different as the sociological writings of Durkheim, Weber, Tönnies, and Simmel are, they all grappled with the essential question posed by Comte: What is the basis for social cohesion in an increasingly atomized, modern, industrial world?

Durkheim's thought remained most consistent with the established parameters of the discipline. Like Comte, Durkheim was a Positivist who modeled his sociological analyses on the natural sciences. Durkheim also refused to reduce sociology to an extrapolation from psychological observations and analyses. Instead of seeing the individual as the basis for social science, he was interested in the integration and mediation of individuals within a society. His analytic building blocks were the "social facts" that maintained the coherence of the social whole. For Durkheim, society was a moral totality that could never be reduced to individual self-interests, as the liberals and Marxists insisted. "Social facts" were the forces that shaped human behavior. They were the laws, customs, and social obligations that morally compelled the actions of individuals. Social unity and assumptions regarding the pace and nature of change, however, could not, in Durkheim's view, be based on the rigid models imagined by Comte and Spencer. Modernity threatened social cohesion and promoted the atomization of individuals. It generated "social facts" such as anomie, which countered the organizing and unifying principles of society. Consequently, Durkheim embraced a vision of social conformity similar to Comte's, but he recognized that the general trajectory of modern, industrial society threatened this ideal.

Simmel and Tönnies, by contrast, launched a direct attack on Comte's and Durkheim's central assumptions, and the result was humanistic sociology. Both were greatly affected by the German reactions to sociological Positivism. Following in the footsteps of Dilthey, Rickert, and Windelband, Simmel and Tönnies emphasized that society was a man-made entity that was qualitatively different from the objects of the natural sciences. As a product of human creation, society required subjective analysis (*Verstehen*), which Positivism strictly forbade. Rather than developing methods based on the natural sciences, Simmel and Tönnies advocated techniques that had more in common with the cultural studies practiced in the humanities. They rejected Positivist sociology's search for objective social laws, proposing instead that society was constituted by human interactions and their complex cultural meanings.[12] Social reality could not be observed in the commonsense fashion that Comte and Durkheim had proposed. Positivism, for both Tönnies and Simmel, resulted in reified, false conceptions of the social world whose observations were meaningless unless their organizing principles were uncovered. According to Simmel, as well as Tönnies, subjective methods based on common practices in philosophy, history, psychology, and literary studies were more rigorous than the sense-certainty assumptions formulated by Comte and Durkheim. Sociology's goal had to include the interpretations of social forms and interactions. Simmel and Tönnies called for the development of sociological abstractions from the complexity of social life, seeking the coherent explication of such abstractions with the assistance of concrete phenomena. Rather than imputing a single meaning to a social interaction, Simmel and Tönnies expanded the scope of their analysis to relocate the interaction more completely within the social and historical totality. The result was an approach to sociology that did not involve the mere description of facts. Instead, their humanistic sociology generated abstract concepts of social relations that went beyond affirming evolutionary models of societal progress and cohesion.

Max Weber achieved his great notoriety in Continental sociology by synthesizing the Positivist and humanist strands of the discipline. Born and educated in Germany, Weber shared many ideas with Simmel and Tönnies. For the three German thinkers, for example, Positivist evolutionism imposed a series of deterministic assumptions on the study of society; like orthodox Marxism, it thus eliminated from culture all active and intentional elements. Both stripped sociology of human agency. Weber was a more systematic thinker than Simmel or Tönnies. By focusing his attention on human actions, Weber was able to provide a sociological vantage point that neither reified social phenomena nor atomized society into a limitless arena of social interactions. His great innovation was to recognize that actions were endowed with meaning, and the meanings were closely bound up with the structure and values of a society. The aim of sociology, in Weber's view, was to interpret social action, its causes, effects, and societal meaning. Because of the value of a rigorously scientific approach to social actions, a sociologist could not completely abandon Positivism. Comte's and Durkheim's methods were not sufficient, however. Actions had to be interpreted, and objective observation was unable to accomplish this task. A subjective element, similar to what had been proposed by the humanistic sociologists, was also required. Weber's sociology thus combined subjective empathy for the social actor with the scientific analysis of an action's means and ends. The result was an abstract social matrix of continually changing meanings and values that undergirded the actions of a society's members. Social development did not follow a single trajectory as the Positivists had assumed, but human actions were socially mediated.[13]

The issues that preoccupied the Continental sociological tradition were not foreign to the Anglo-American world before the "intellectual migration," but the early dominance of Comtean and Spencerian Positivism delayed and minimized their influx. U.S. sociology had begun to take shape after the Civil War, as in Europe, partly in response to rapid industrialization and urbanization. Like their Positivist counterparts in Europe, early practitioners of American sociology were predisposed to conservative, antimodern fears, and their strong links to the scientific passions of the Enlightenment made them theoretically similar. The first American sociologists were deeply uneasy about modernization and the changes it brought to social life in the United States. Industrialism and urbanization seemed to threaten the "ideals of frontier democracy and the personalized intimacy of agrarian society."[14] Such views corresponded closely with the sentiments of the social gospel movement, as well as with early defenders of labor and the urban poor (such as the Grangers, the Knights of Labor, and the American Federation of Labor). Consequently, American sociology combined a conservative emulation of Positivist European sociology with a progressive reformism that had little in common with the aristocratic,

Old World nostalgia that infused much of Europe's social theorizing.[15] During these formative years, the typical American sociologist came from a rural, Midwestern background and grew up in a religious environment.[16] As I noted in the discussion of Columbia University's sociology department (chapter 2), Giddings and many of the discipline's other leading figures manifested a practical, reformist passion for social work, as well as a scientific determination to make sense of modern society.

Similar reformist tendencies ran through British sociology during its early years. In an effort to meet the changing needs of the population, British legislators utilized and supported the first large-scale social surveys. Although the techniques had been pioneered in Prussia during the eighteenth century, amateur British social scientists put them to use in an effort to grapple with the "social question" during the 1890s.[17] The studies of Charles Booth, B. Seebohm Rowntree, and A. L. Bowley and A. R. Burnett-Hurst clearly demonstrated the value of survey research, particularly with such pressing problems as poverty.[18]

The survey techniques did not make it across the Atlantic until the first years of the twentieth century, but they were put to regular use following their arrival in the United States. American sociology, which had strong institutional and financial support by the turn of the century, was able to gather professionally trained and organized teams of survey researchers to study not only poverty, but such issues as taxation, education, health care, and crime as well. It is estimated that 2,800 survey projects had been carried out in the United States by 1928.[19] Such a statistic not only highlights how prevalent the methodology and its reformist goals were, but it also indicates how quickly U.S. sociology had grown and become professionalized. While Continental sociologists grappled with highly abstract speculative issues that would eventually have major epistemological repercussions within the discipline, American sociologists maintained the legacy of Positivist social science and applied many of its assumptions to survey work and the solving of social problems.

Before the First World War, then, Comte and Spencer were the main theoretical inspirations for American sociologists. They were widely read, their views widely accepted.[20] Consequently, American sociology was modeled on the natural sciences, its main goal was the uncovering of social laws, its organic image of society was derived from biology, and its concept of change was modeled on Darwin's theory of evolution. With widespread consensus on such issues, the Anglo-American branch of the discipline was free to focus on methodological innovation. The survey research, which became so common before the Great Depression, was almost entirely guided by the Positivist, evolutionary assumptions that arose from American reliance on Comte and Spencer.

There were exceptions to the dominance of Positivism and survey research, such as the community studies that arose at the University of Chicago. Robert Park and Ernest Burgess, the most visible and emulated of these exceptions, were the architects of the "Chicago School." Park had studied in Germany, where he encountered the humanistic critique of Positivism and the work of Simmel. In particular, Simmel's notion of human interaction became an important influence. Park came to the field of sociology from journalism, and he was therefore acutely aware of the many problems facing the populations of the United States' swelling cities. Borrowing from Simmel's conception of social interaction, Park pioneered an innovative method for examining human behavior in the new urban environments. The latter communities were like nothing that had existed before in the United States. As Park and Burgess explored the new urban spaces armed with the tools that Park had fashioned from Simmel, they theorized that social systems formed natural economies based on competitive cooperation.[21] Individual actors struggled for self-recognition by constructing public personas for the social environment. At the same time, their actions and interactions gave rise to the formation of social institutions, values, and folkways. Urbanism, industrialism, and immigration threw these traditional institutions, values, and folkways into turmoil. The urban landscape thus formed a crucial laboratory for examining the effects and resolutions caused by such changes. Statistical surveys of such urban communities made little sense, because they prevented the kind of close, interpretive observation that Park's theoretical model required. The community study, while not examining the same quantity of data, provided access to the kinds of qualitative details that Park and Burgess sought.[22]

By the early 1930s, when the "intellectual migration" began, many American social scientists had acquired extensive experience with large-scale social surveys and were striving to model their discipline more closely on the natural sciences. As we saw in our investigation of Columbia University, many of the country's leading figures were increasingly interested in statistics, empiricism, and the conquest of increasingly complex social problems. The theoretical assumptions of Comte and Spencer were widespread in the United States, and the impact of more speculative thinkers was minimal. Marx, Durkheim, and Weber were largely unknown, and Simmel's work, which had received a very limited and idiosyncratic reception, only affected Chicago and other Midwestern schools of sociology that emulated Park's methods. In Europe, Continental sociology had its own share of Positivists, but the majority of its practitioners were largely preoccupied with grand speculative issues. Most Continental social scientists therefore remained unaware of the empirical innovations that were being pioneered by Anglo-American sociologists.[23] The discipline on the Continent was beset by internecine theoretical feuds, which retarded efforts to professionalize, and without the same abundance of financial support from both public and private sources, Continental sociologists were unable to carry out research investigations on the same scale as Americans. The "intellectual migration" changed all of this by bringing both traditions together, but the synthesis formed a sociological canon that became tied to America's postwar hegemony. Anglo-American and Continental sociology were reunited, but the resulting merger served as a tool of American diplomacy and ideology during the Cold War.[24] The legacy of the "intellectual migration," however, did not end with the ascendancy of American empiricism and Parsonian Functionalism. In a complicated turn of events, many of the same refugee sociologists that had helped bring the two sociological traditions together also provided the ammunition that shattered the postwar amalgamation.

Before exploring the Horkheimer Circle's role in the latter series of transformations, we must be more specific about the "intellectual migration" and its impact on the field of sociology. The term can be misleading because it conjures up the image of European ideas being imported into the United States. When it comes to the history of sociology, however, the migration of ideas was definitely a two-way street. Anglo-American ideas had as great an impact on the European immigrants as the speculative Continental tradition had on Americans. Furthermore, and perhaps more important, there were Americans who played leading roles in the Atlantic unification of sociological thought. The term "intellectual migration" in no way minimizes their impact. In fact, Talcott Parsons, the leading American architect of postwar sociology, began his efforts to merge the two traditions before Hitler ever came to power. The presence of Continental refugees in the United States aided such work and perhaps created the conditions for Functionalism's successful reception after the war.

The Continental sociologists who fled to the United States functioned largely as ambassadors and translators for their branch of the discipline.[25] The exiles faced substantial obstacles—language barriers, cultural differences, and a tight job market—in the United States, and few thinkers, consequently, were able to enjoy notoriety and success there. They left their families and secure professional positions in Europe, and they entered a foreign environment that required professional savvy and careful diplomacy. As David Kettler and Gerhard Lauer have explained, American enthusiasm for the model of the German research university created a set of natural allies, but this same model of higher education provoked a more numerous cohort of critics who questioned its overspecialization and autonomy.[26] Further compounding the plight of the German émigrés was the fact that they imported Weimar feuds concerning *Bildung* and *Wissenschaft* that were grounded in a rhetoric that made such debates largely incomprehensible to American social scientists of the 1930s who were simultaneously arguing about the roles of social theory and empirical science.[27] The refugees from Germany carried heavy baggage that created rivalries among them and confounded American hosts who expected the émigrés "to shift rapidly from the old to the new context of problems."[28] It is not surprising that such pressures made some of them excessively defensive and protective. The European émigrés nevertheless provided many American social scientists with their introductions to the works of Weber, Durkheim, Simmel, Tönnies, and Mannheim, as well as to Marx and Freud.

The largest and most prominent assemblage of European social scientists was at the New School's University in Exile. Unlike the Horkheimer Circle, which maintained a fairly unified set of theoretical assumptions, the social scientists at the University in Exile came from so many disciplines and theoretical orientations that it is hard to locate a coherent "New School approach" to sociology. Alvin Johnson, the group's American founder and head, sought to include European scholars that generally shared his views. Consequently, most members of the University in Exile were politically progressive, social-democratic, anti-Marxist liberals. As for their common theoretical perspectives, there were strong preferences for empiricism, the sociological legacies of Weber and Mannheim, economic planning models, and Gestalt psychology.[29] The University in Exile sought to transcend ideology by marshaling a variety of theoretical orientations aimed at practical solutions for pressing social problems.[30] The latter approach corresponded well with American preoccupations with scientifically rigorous social science and problem solving. The New School, consequently, helped to add Weber and Mannheim to the Anglo-American canon, but it wedded such theoretical perspectives to empirical methodologies, for which American social scientists already had a hunger. A fertile ground for Functionalism was thus established in New York before Paul Lazarsfeld and Robert Merton had even begun to introduce it at Columbia.

The members of the New School established a reputation partly through their collective strength. Paul Lazarsfeld, by contrast, was a self-made sociological phenomenon, who exerted considerable impact on American sociology as a result of the empirical creativity and entrepreneurialism of his approach to social research. Lazarsfeld's popularity was enhanced by his methodological expertise. Originally trained in mathematics, he entered the field of sociology by accident. Close contacts with Viennese psychologists propelled him into the field of empirical social psychology. His famous Marienthal study, which exhibited close affinities with American survey research, brought him to the attention of the Rockefeller Foundation, and he was thus brought to the United States. Through shrewd networking with American sociologists, businessmen, and social research foundations, Lazarsfeld was able to create the Bureau for Applied Social Research—a self-sustained center for empirical studies. To some, Lazarsfeld's high-profile wheeling and dealing appeared as a political sellout,[31] a former Austro-Marxist mortgaging his great sociological talent to market researchers. To others, however, Lazarsfeld was a pioneer exploiting big business to pay for methodological innovations and research discoveries that were his hidden agendas. Viewed from any angle, however, Lazarsfeld transformed the organization and practice of social research in the United States. Together with Merton, one of Parson's most innovative disciples, Lazarsfeld built Columbia's sociology department into a model for postwar social science. Although Lazarsfeld continued to show little interest in theory, the assumptions underlying his empiricism fit comfortably with Functionalism. Both focused on human action and its mediation with social institutions.[32] Lazarsfeld provided American sociologists with new techniques to continue pursuing empirical survey research. His collaboration with Merton, however, was a major step in the consolidation of postwar sociology. With Merton's assistance, empirical research became a tool for examining social needs and the integrating (or disintegrating) functional roles played by specific social actions.

While the New School and Paul Lazarsfeld represented the heights to which refugee sociologists could climb, the majority of the other exiles generated far more modest impacts in the United States. Alexander von Schelting, Weber's star pupil, gained a teaching position at Columbia, but he never translated his celebrated commentary on his mentor's work and consequently only exerted an influence over his colleagues and students during his brief time on Morningside Heights. Hans Gerth spent years seaching for work before locating a position at the University of Wisconsin, where he gained a loyal following that briefly included C. Wright Mills. Gerth is best known, however, for translating some of Weber's writings and for introducing Mannheim's work to Madison. Kurt Wolff also struggled to find a position until he found one at Ohio State. Like Gerth, his primary notoriety arose from his translations and teachings of the Continental masters (in Wolff's case, Simmel and Mannheim). Most of the other émigré sociologists were not as fortunate in the pursuit of teaching prospects. Some sought work in secondary schools, while others tried their hand at journalism.

On the spectrum sketched above, the Horkheimer Circle stands between the contributions to the rise of a postwar sociology made by Lazarsfeld or the New School and the more isolated, interlocutory role of Gerth or Wolff. During its first years in the United States, the Institute for Social Research pursued its marriage of social philosophy and empirical research in relative isolation. Its members feared the political repercussions of academic notoriety, and they had the financial resources to enjoy the autonomy that accompanied obscurity beyond the confines of Morningside Heights. Financial setbacks, however, had an impact on the group's aims and necessitated a shift away from splendid isolation. At the same time that the Horkheimer Circle introduced its American reading public to Critical Theory, which was presented as an alternative to Anglo-American empiricism and Positivism, the Institute for Social Research adopted many of the same techniques that it was attacking. When its first qualitative, interpretive research proposals were rejected for their lack of scientific rigor, the Horkheimer Circle amended its approach and adopted a compromise between Continental theory and Anglo-American methodology. Although its synthesis did not correspond to the triumphant marriage of Functionalism and empirical research embodied by figures such as Merton and Lazarsfeld, its members returned to Germany as ambassadors of American social science.

The latter proposition undoubtedly will surprise readers already familiar with the Frankfurt School. Most scholarly accounts emphasize the consistent marginality of the Circle and the importance of isolation for the group's subversive and controversial discoveries about late capitalism and the emerging new world of total administration. The Institute for Social Research, according to such accounts, was a collection of lonely critics and radicals bucking the dominant paradigms of their age. Seeing themselves as dissenters and naysayers, they sought neither fame nor notoriety. The gravity and danger of their discoveries were so severe, we are told, that they rejected the traditional role of the social scientist. As the world sank into human barbarism, the only meaningful response was to launch a flotilla of messages in bottles that might someday be discovered by a more aware public. Such an audience, we are told, took shape with the rise of the New Left and the student movement in the 1960s.

The popular image of a "Frankfurt School" sketched above was produced by the members of the Horkheimer Circle, the historians to whom they told their story, New Left intellectuals, who saw themselves as the inheritors of Critical Theory, and the radical and critical sociologists that added the Institute for Social Research to their pantheon of predecessors. This mythic "Frankfurt School" is not, however, merely a fabrication or exaggeration. The image of the "Frankfurt School" arose because elements of its thought and history support such a likeness. The main purposes of the present and subsequent chapters are to represent more clearly than in previous accounts the Horkheimer Circle's relationship to American sociology— trying to move beyond the mythology and to see how this complex coterie of thinkers could simultaneously contribute to the emergence of American postwar social science while becoming some of its most vocal critics.

THE EARLY YEARS OF SELF-IMPOSED ISOLATION IN THE UNITED STATES

Were one to focus only on the Horkheimer Circle's first years in New York, its reputation for reclusiveness might seem warranted. By continuing research begun in Europe and concentrating on its journal, the Institute for Social Research was more isolated between 1934 and 1938 than it later was. The Horkheimer Circle collaborated with American scholars, but initially avoided the institutional integration for which its new colleagues at Columbia had hoped, instead virtually pursuing isolation in the service of a commitment to a sociological approach born in Mitteleuropa.

As new arrivals in the United States, Horkheimer and his colleagues maintained a firmer relationship to their native tradition of Continental sociology than at any other point during their exile. Instead of accepting the Positivist sociological paradigm they saw surrounding them in the United States, the Institute for Social Research remained firmly aligned with its compatriots in Germany. Displaying its debt to German Idealism, the Horkheimer Circle rejected the sense-certainty assumptions that formed the basis of Anglo-American empiricism. Like Simmel and Weber, the members of the Institute recognized that social observations required interpretation and integration within a wider understanding of societal processes. Yet, while critical of the assumptions and repercussions of empirical social science, the group did not entirely reject Anglo-American sociology. Empirical research materially grounded the Horkheimer Circle's social philosophical theorizing, but its conception of materialism had its roots in the Marxian critique of Idealism. Like Marx and Weber, its members developed an approach that could benefit from the observational rigor of empirical sociology by incorporating elements of it into their social philosophy. The initial conception of Critical Theory, which Horkheimer developed in his inaugural address in Frankfurt (which was examined at the outset of this study), represented an innovative synthesis centered on a dialectical mediation between sociology and social philosophy.

While they were examined in chapter 2 in the frame of the Frankfurt School's institutional relations with Columbia University, the research projects on authority, the family, and the German working class, as well as other empirical studies from the 1930s, deserve further scrutiny in the different and wider context of the Horkheimer Circle's position in American sociology. Far from being appendages to the theoretical writings that appeared in the *Zeitschrift für Sozialforshung,* the empirical research projects are inextricable from the social theory that the Institute had been crafting in Europe in the early 1930s. The empirical investigations, after all, arose in response to the perceived failures of orthodox Marxian expectations.

The primary issue at stake was why the working classes had not organized in a revolutionary manner against the forces of capital. By conducting empirical investigations on family dynamics, the Institute examined what its members had come to view as the key arena of socialization in bourgeois society. The premise of the investigations seemed to be that, to comprehend how the bourgeoisie, an ultimately self-destructive class, according to Marx, perpetuated itself, the Marxist as sociologist had to understand how the European family worked. Authority became a guiding concept of the investigations, as the researchers and theoreticians grew to become convinced that irrational deference to existing power undercut the rational critiques of capitalism. The empirical studies accompanied the Horkheimer Circle's first theoretical steps along the Western Marxist trajectory that had been launched in the 1920s by Lukács and Korsch, and they provide us with the first glimpses of the totally administered, one-dimensional world that eventually became the nightmare vision of the Frankfurt School.

It is clear from Horkheimer's correspondence during the group's early years in the United States that he remained deeply committed to merging empirical research and social philosophy. It is also clear that he recognized that cooperation with U.S. sociologists would require an undesired revision of this early conception of Critical Theory. American researchers were clearly interested in the empirical aspects of the group's work,[33] but the construction of a general theory of society, which had arisen from the group's dialogue with other Marxian-inspired intellectuals in Europe, could never be a goal shared by sociologists in American academia. As Horkheimer explained to Adorno in 1934:

> Unless you have greatly changed, you are still one of the very few people from whom the Institute, and the special theoretical tasks which it is trying to undertake, can expect anything intellectually. The numbers of these people and the amount of sympathy on which they are able to count at the moment are dwindling. But for the same reasons, and to the same extent that they are dwindling, the duty to hold on and to develop one's own position further becomes greater. We are the only group whose existence is not dependent on a progressive assimilation, the only group which can maintain the relatively advanced state of theory which has been achieved in Germany and advance it even further.[34]

Instead of amending the methods and goals of the Institute to assimilate with American approaches to social science, the Horkheimer Circle camouflaged the theoretical underpinnings of Critical Theory in order to pursue the ambition of constructing a comprehensive theory of bourgeois society.

When the Horkheimer Circle reassembled in New York in 1934–35, it was confronted with its American colleagues' preoccupation with empirical research, statistical surveys, and practical results. At Columbia and elsewhere, American sociology had its roots in social work. Thus, even though sociology and social work gradually grew apart, academic sociology retained a commitment to comprehending and solving social problems.[35] As we observed in the Frankfurt School's clashes with Sidney Hook and other American Pragmatists, Critical Theory could embrace neither the comparisons between the natural and social sciences that were encountered in the United States nor the utilization of a pragmatic, means–ends logic for identifying and confronting social problems.

Once in the United States, the Institute continued on the intellectual trajectory that had been established in Frankfurt, but it presented its work to new colleagues circumspectly. Social Philosophy and social theory, consequently, remained the guiding orientations of the group, and empirical social research functioned as a complement to the series of Western Marxist challenges that the Institute's theoreticians proposed. In order to appeal to American sociologists sympathizing with their plight, however, the Horkheimer Circle emphasized the elements of their approach that corresponded to American research interests and practices. In the first, self-published, introductory brochure from the International Institute of Social Research, Horkheimer and the staff presented Critical Theory especially for the consumption of their American hosts:

> As social and economic crises recur and become more gripping, the social sciences are assuming greater and greater importance for the reorganization of modern society in the sense of an adaptation of the social processes to the growing needs of humanity. To contribute to this task, the social sciences must examine the general tendencies of these processes in conjunction with practical problems. For this purpose, not only far reaching empirical knowledge is essential, but also the application of the correct methodological principles. The Institute considers therefore the European philosophy of the

eighteenth and nineteenth centuries as important for the theory of society as are political economy and statistics. The economic and technical factors of social processes interact inextricably with cultural and psychological factors. It is important to be able to understand this reciprocity and in keeping with this need, the social sciences try to comprehend, for instance, how economic development affects the cultural aspects of life and further how the economic foundations themselves are in turn affected. It is, therefore, necessary to combine economics, sociology, philosophy and psychology for a fruitful approach to the problems of the social sciences.[36]

Such an introduction to the work of the Institute for Social Research was a great departure from the formal overture provided only a few years earlier at Horkheimer's inauguration.[37] While accurate in many respects, the introductory brochure obscures the philosophical and political underpinnings of early Critical Theory. Instead of proclaiming the debts to Hegel and Marx (as Horkheimer had done in Frankfurt), this American introduction obscured the roots of Critical Theory and suggested a heritage connecting the group to the entire legacy of the Enlightenment. By presenting themselves in such a manner, the Institute could appear to be a group of social researchers sharing the same essential goals as many U.S. sociologists, namely, those of combating the effects of the Depression in the mid-1930s. Throughout the decade, the main objective of the Institute's myriad projects remained that of contributing to the formulation of a theory of contemporary society. Although American hosts might be intrigued by the empirical techniques and practical policy innovations that such studies implied, U.S. sociologists remained unaware of the Institute's larger project. Horkheimer and his colleagues were not interested in short-term solutions to the problems affecting German workers or European families. Instead, they were committed to analyzing and confronting such phenomena as symptoms of a broader crisis in world history.

The substantial size of the Institute's endowment provided Horkheimer with the financial means to protect the group from assimilation, and thus empirical research was able to continue throughout the 1930s as a significant component of the group's theoretical agenda. Unlike members of the New School and individual sociologists such as Paul Lazarsfeld, the Institute for Social Research was not forced into collaboration with American researchers by economic necessity. While most of Continental Europe's refugee social scientists sought to build contacts and a reputation within U.S. academia, the Horkheimer Circle enjoyed the luxury of working alone and preserving the integrity of its intellectual vision. It formed its own German-speaking enclave on Morningside Heights and only occasionally met with American scholars. Even though it remained thousands of miles away from the shores of Europe, its contacts with colleagues back home remained far more numerous and substantial than its encounters with American sociologists. In effect, the Institute's finances permitted the group to prolong their connections with the world of Continental sociology. Their work and its audience remained firmly grounded in the Continental milieu that had shaped the Institute. Until the outbreak of the Second World War and the subsequent spread of Nazism, the Continental tradition remained an academic alternative for the members of the Horkheimer Circle. The war—and poor investment strategies—would severely limit the Institute's options, making assimilation a virtual necessity by the end of the 1930s.

Even during its early years of economic security, however, the émigré Horkheimer Circle was not entirely isolated from the world of American sociology. We have already examined some of Fromm's early contacts with American psychologists and sociologists.[38] Because of his involvement with the empirical aspects of the group's theory building, Fromm was the most visible figure to American social researchers. The rest of the Institute, by contrast, preferred to work more closely with Horkheimer on the comprehensive theory of bourgeois society. They contributed expert interpretations of data from their particular fields of specialization, but they left the management of empirical research to Fromm and the teams of sociologists and social psychologists that he assembled.

The most noteworthy of the empirical research projects was the substantial volume *Studien über Autorität und Familie*. Although the Horkheimer Circle organized and paid for many large-scale studies during the early 1930s, it is the only completed manuscript credited solely to the Institute for Social Research. Although it appeared in German, Horkheimer and the other members of the Institute viewed *Studien über Autorität und Familie* as their intellectual debut in the United States. For its American readers, however, it presented a daunting challenge. Written in a highly stylized, German academic prose, the volume also grappled with concepts that arose out of unfamiliar, Continental conversations. English and French synopses were provided for each section, but the book could only have been appreciated by those equipped with the requisite intellectual tools. *Studien über Autorität und Familie* nevertheless received a modest number of almost unanimously favorable reviews in the Anglo-American sociological journals.[39] Howard Becker, writing for the *American Sociological Review* (the most visible and significant of these evaluations for American sociologists), proclaimed:

> It is an important and interesting book, with a manner of treating its problem quite different from current American research on the family. It will reward the effort of any American scholar who polishes up his German and reads it. The nature of the problem may perhaps be called social-psychological because the attempt is made to consider the problem of authority in the family and then to relate to wider social institutions the respect of authority which is engendered there. Attention is centered on our own Western European society as an actual productive mechanism and on the family as a means of generating individuals who can peaceably take their places in it . . . The analysis of the material is undertaken from two systematic standpoints: first from the historical, stressing the interaction of the patriarchal family form with social structure, and second the psychological, showing how specific character attitudes emerge from and function in the social order as it now exists. The treatment is characterized by the cool vision of realistic thinkers on current social life.[40]

Reviewers were primarily interested in the theoretical essays by Horkheimer, Fromm, and Marcuse that preceded the empirical studies. Few of the book's Anglo-American readers commented at length on the later sections of the text, because their findings were so numerous that they were "impossible to summarize."[41] The three theoretical essays, while establishing the historical and sociological context for the empirical findings that followed, were more representative of the sort of writing that appeared in the *Zeitschrift für Sozialforschung* than the type of integrated social research that would have captivated American readers such as Robert Lynd and other sociologists seeking broader methodologies to generate concrete answers to complex social problems.

Not surprisingly, Fromm's essay, which was the only contribution that addressed the Institute's sociological methodology, was singled out in the review literature. The Anglo-American academic world was already familiar with psychoanalysis, but few were aware of the type of revisionism that Fromm advocated or the social-scientific applications that such an approach made possible. Consequently, the reviews became an opportunity for many to evaluate Freudianism. To many reviewers, Fromm's character types represented an important sociological innovation.[42] Instead of reducing social behavior to individual psychodynamics, Fromm's approach suggested an integration of psychology and sociology that expanded far beyond the former's traditional focus on the lone social actor. Fromm proposed to use psychoanalysis to inform sociological generalizations about the Western family and the dynamics of authority fostered within it. The relations to authority functioned as "ideal types" that could then be related to broader historical and social developments. As Becker pointed out:

> This brilliant analysis by Fromm sets the stage for a development of a characterology which actually relates social institutions to individual behavior and offers an excellent example of the type of collaborative work which is possible in such an Institute as that which produced this book. Apparently here psychologists cannot maintain their frozen isolation from the demands of students of society.[43]

It seems, then, that to most Anglo-American readers of *Studien über Autorität und Familie,* Fromm's integration of psychoanalysis and sociology represented an important, original development.

It was also criticized. Not surprisingly, since American social science was not yet conversant with psychoanalysis, critiques of Fromm's essay came from European colleagues, such as Hans Speier, who had evaluated Freud's work before his arrival in the United States. Speier, a prominent member of the Gestalt-dominated New School, ridiculed Fromm's attempt to build sociologically relevant character types from psychoanalysis:

> The reviewer has been doubtful as to the value of Freudian psychology for an analysis of social phenomena. He must confess that the performance of Erich Fromm has not removed his doubts. Despite the fact that Dr. Fromm tries to rid his method of its unhistorical implications, it is more interesting to search in his study for the methodological and psychological reasons for the wholesale denial of authority as one of the fundamental phenomena of social life than to study the futility of this denial in detail.[44]

Speier proposes, further, that family authority might represent a qualitatively distinct sociological phenomenon with little bearing on political coercion and repression. His unreceptive view was untypical, however; most of *Studien über Autorität und Familie*'s readers in the United States viewed the volume (especially Fromm's essay) as a promising sign of the possible integration of Anglo-American and Continental sociology. Yet, if such readers eagerly awaited future publications by the Institute for Social Research, they would not see them until 1950, when the anti-Semitism project was completed.

Encouraged by the moderate success of *Studien über Autorität und Familie,* many friends of the Institute convinced its members to expand their investigations of authority to include data regarding the United States. Others, especially at Columbia, were interested in the unpublished research on the German working class. Horkheimer sought to satisfy such suggestions and interests, and to sustain the Institute's momentum by initiating two new projects. As Fromm continued to make headway with his analysis of the German working-class data, he also organized a study of authority among college students at Sarah Lawrence, as well as an American version of the Weimar workers' project focusing on unemployed families in Newark, New Jersey.[45] In addition to providing the Institute for Social Research with material that could be used for a comparative analysis of Europe and the United States, the studies simultaneously pursued some new approaches to old problems. The Sarah Lawrence study, for example, looked beyond the dynamics of family authority, focusing instead on young adults and their relationships with institutional authority. While *Studien über Autorität und Familie* provided an important theoretical frame for comprehending the roots of attitudes toward authority, the Sarah Lawrence study, by addressing the comparisons between family and institutional authority, met the criticisms put forward by such Institute detractors as Speier. By combining Fromm's growing appreciation of the relationships between authority in the working-class family and socioeconomic conditions, the Newark unemployment study offered an even more innovative strategy. Traditional authority systems within families were crumbling under the strains of the Depression, and these circumstances enabled Fromm to explore comparisons with the data that was gathered in Europe before the Institute's departure.

Early friends of the Institute were pleased with these developments, which suggested that the Institute was contributing significantly to American social science. In a January 1937 letter to Horkheimer congratulating the Institute on expanding its research program, for example, Robert Lynd explained:

> I have been following with interest the progress of the Institute's study of Authority in the Family in Newark, NJ. This study bids fair to make an important contribution to our all too limited knowledge of the familial sources of the authority patterns in human personality. It has just come to my attention that you are paralleling the Newark study with one or more comparable studies abroad, in Vienna and, I hope, other cities. This is precisely the sort of comparative research that we so badly need, and you have put all of us in your debt by carrying forward comparative research of this important sort.[46]

The Sarah Lawrence study and the Newark unemployment study were of great importance to the Horkheimer Circle, particularly with regard to early relations with U.S. sociologists. In addition to bringing empirical research findings to an American audience not fluent in German, the new projects represented a continuation of the Institute's commitment to the interdisciplinary analysis of authority, socialization, and socioeconomic conditions.

Exile, however, placed significant strains on the members of the Institute and greatly affected their ability to complete the projects. In part, strains arose from the difficulty of balancing the expectations of American friends with the internal goals of the Institute. As we have noted, the Horkheimer Circle's primary aim was a fully developed theory of bourgeois society. The expansion of empirical research might complement this pursuit of theory, but the *Zeitschrift für Sozialforschung* remained the primary vehicle of theoretical exposition and consequently remained the central focus of the group's inner circle. Fromm remained the major figure responsible for overseeing the empirical work, but the proliferation of political conflict in Europe and Fromm's nagging health problems created additional hurdles.

In the past, the Institute for Social Research drafted contracts with European research teams to gather its empirical data. Although Fromm designed the general configurations of the investigations, the actual research was carried out by the European subcontractors of the Institute (especially in Holland, Vienna, and Paris). With the consolidation of Nazism, data collection became impossible in Germany and Austria by 1938, a situation that was, of course, worsened by the outbreak of war in Europe the following year.[47] Nor was the Horkheimer Circle able to rely on its friends in Europe to carry out empirical work in the United States. Instead of using the Institute's staff for the research in Newark or at Sarah Lawrence, which would have sacrificed the momentum of the work on theory, Horkheimer and Pollock resorted to the same methods that had been utilized in Europe—hiring research teams in the United States to carry out the work.

Paul Lazarsfeld, Mirra Komarovsky, and Ruth Munroe happily collaborated with the Institute, enjoying the financial assistance that the work included. The Horkheimer Circle, meanwhile, was able to report to its emerging collection of American friends that the research projects were moving forward. The collaboration, of course, cost the Institute money, but it did not interfere with the theory building taking place in the pages of the *Zeitschrift für Sozialforschung.* An unforeseen cost, however, also accrued. Unlike the research carried out in Europe for *Studien über Autorität und Familie,* the intellectual property generated by the American investigations was not credited to the Horkheimer Circle. As discussed earlier in the present study, Komarovsky and Munroe published their own findings acknowledging only briefly the roles of Horkheimer, Fromm, and the Institute.[48] In the eyes of most U.S. social scientists, the Horkheimer Circle had little to do with either study. Instead, the Institute appeared to be a failure at Anglo-American research methods. Years later, after the main damage to the Horkheimer Circle's reputation had already been done, Paul Lazarsfeld acknowledged the injustice that had occurred. As he explained in a letter to Theodore Abel:

> Now as to the evaluation of their [the Institute's] scientific work. I have a strong feeling that an injustice has been done, and that our committee is called upon to make amends. I understand, for example, that you are using Mirra's study as one of the three major research contributions in your own book. Angell, in his recent SSRC bulletin, called it "the greatest methodological progress since 'The Polish Peasant.'" Everyone has now forgotten that the plan for the study was completely laid out by the Institute, and that Mirra was hired as one of several candidates to carry the study through.[49]

The Horkheimer Circle thus expanded its empirical research to appeal to an American audience, but the efforts boomeranged as it sought to protect its primary focus on the theory of bourgeois society. The hiring of American researchers allowed both projects to move forward, but outside involvement also enabled others to receive the credit. To an extent, the Horkheimer Circle got what it deserved. It understood the importance of empirical research to American sociologists, but it thought that it could satisfy its new colleagues without doing the bulk of the work itself. Had the theoretical work that the Institute's inner circle privileged over the studies been connected more closely to the empirical research and the interests of the U.S. audience, the Horkheimer Circle's strategy might not have backfired as badly as it did. Instead, the Institute pursued a theoretical endeavor that remained hidden from most Americans. Even if U.S. sociologists had been apprised of the Institute's social theory, few could have understood the early version of Critical Theory that cut against the grain of Anglo-American, social-scientific interests. The Institute had promised further research to its few American friends, but the results seemed to be the work of others not connected closely with the group. Any interest that *Studien über Autorität und Familie* might have generated in the United States had dissipated by the end of the 1930s.

THE END OF ISOLATION AND THE FIRST ATTEMPTS AT U.S. ASSIMILATION

The Institute for Social Research underwent a major transformation during the late 1930s. A drastic decrease in the Institute's endowment and the group's evolving fears regarding fascism combined to end the Horkheimer Circle's early conception of Critical Theory. In the wake of economic disaster, Horkheimer sought to address the group's financial worries by altering the structure of the Institute and by seeking full-scale collaboration with American sociologists. Consequently, he abandoned the interdisciplinary mediation between empirical research and social philosophy. The Horkheimer Circle did not, however, follow in the paths that had been established by the New School and Paul Lazarsfeld. The Institute for Social Research appealed to the Anglo-American sociological tradition, but it did not abandon its commitments to social philosophy or social theory. Ironically, at the same time that the Horkheimer Circle sought an accommodation with American sociology, Critical Theory shifted into a new phase in which Positivism and technocracy grew to be associated with the proliferation of fascistic barbarism in late-capitalist society. As the Institute for Social Research competed for grant support in the arena of "traditional theory," its theoretical concerns expanded to include the condemnation of precisely the same "traditional," Anglo-American modes of social science. Consequently, the Horkheimer Circle sought recognition within American sociology to help finance the theoretical critique of this worldview and the society that financed it.

During its first years of exile, the Institute for Social Research had been both lavish and generous with its money. It paid for the renovation of the group's headquarters on 117th Street; it provided the leadership of the group (Horkheimer and Pollock) with salaries sufficiently ample to hire domestic help; it enabled most of the Institute's inner circle to take vacations to such places as Lake Placid, Santa Fe, the California coast, the Canadian Rockies, Bar Harbor, and Cape Cod; and it enabled the Horkheimer Circle to hire an office staff that included a multilingual secretarial pool. At the same time, members of the Institute were sustained in their common theoretical efforts and rarely distracted by teaching or administrative duties. In addition to making the lives of the group's members more productive and comfortable, the available funds also sustained a sizable group of like-minded academics in Europe. In a memorandum of 1943, Pollock estimated that the Institute had spent approximately two hundred thousand dollars between 1933 and 1942 to fund the research and writing of at least 130 scholars remaining on the Continent.[50] As long as the Horkheimer Circle had adequate funds at its disposal, it was able to nurture the work of its own members and allies abroad.

The stable financial situation, however, changed drastically in 1937. Although the American economy had begun to limp out of the Depression, the Horkheimer Circle suffered the first in a series of substantial decreases in its endowment.[51] After losing approximately four hundred thousand dollars in 1937, the Institute had to dip into its principal assets for the first time in its history.[52] The following year brought no relief, as the American economy slumped back into recession. Pollock, the group's economic specialist and administrative leader, tried to manage finances through this tense period from 1937 through 1940, but he later admitted that he had let everyone down. His office gradually took on the characteristics of a Wall Street analyst's,[53] and outside financial advisers were consulted to assist

Pollock with a number of investment strategies (including residential real estate in upstate New York).[54] By the end of the 1930s, the fiscal situation had become so dire that Horkheimer began to consider radical new initiatives to guarantee the survival of at least the group's inner core.

Horkheimer's primary impulse was to jettison the Institute's empirical research, which was not what one would call cost-effective. In addition to paying Fromm and the teams of American researchers necessary for such endeavors, the Institute still had to muster the resources to pay the inner circle of theoreticians, the primary contributors to the *Zeitschrift für Sozialforschung.* Perhaps more important, Horkheimer had grown uncertain about the merits of continuing a group of studies on authority, the practical results of which were being undermined by his own political observations.[55] *Studien über Autorität und Familie* had analyzed the dissolution of patriarchal authority in the bourgeois family and its sociopolitical repercussions. Such interpretations suggested that Nazism's life span would be brief, but events in Europe throughout the 1930s were clearly disproving such predictions. Everywhere, authoritarianism seemed to be growing, not diminishing. These realizations did not simply result in dissatisfaction with the Institute's empirical efforts. Indeed, they fundamentally undermined the purposes and tasks that had been assigned to Critical Theory during its early period. In Horkheimer's eyes, the entire basis for a comprehensive theory of society needed to be rethought and perhaps empirical research functioned more as a hindrance than he had believed.

Even before he began work at the Institute for Social Research, Horkheimer had been questioning the epistemological basis of science.[56] Although his initial conception of the Institute's mission called for a mediation between social science and philosophy, his investigation of scientific logic and its repercussions continued. In a series of essays for the *Zeitschrift für Sozialforschung*—such as "Geschichte und Psychologie" (1932), "Bemerkung über Wissenschaft und Krise" (1932), "Materialismus und Metaphysik" (1933), "Zum Rationalismusstreit in der gegenwärtigen Philosophie" (1934), "Zum Problem der Wahrheit" (1935), and "Egoismus und Freiheitsbewegung" (1936)—Horkheimer delivered critiques of rationalism and the natural sciences, proposing the traditions of German Idealism and Marxian materialism as alternatives.[57] While scientific logic produced a frozen, reified worldview of objects, dialectical logic produced a dynamic understanding of the world that made room for historical change and development.

Instead of producing analyses of the world that already implied its domination by the bourgeoisie, Horkheimer dreamed of developing a major study of dialectics that would summarize all his thoughts on social philosophy and would make the case for abandoning "traditional," bourgeois science.[58]

Throughout the 1930s, Horkheimer's passion for the dialectics project grew, soon supplanting his initial aims for the Institute. Empirical social science had become increasingly expensive, and Horkheimer had begun to question its merits as he monitored the situation in Europe. Rapidly, his philosophical attitudes regarding the natural sciences began to undermine the pursuit of the Institute's program in the United States, and they became increasingly bound together with his gloomy assessment of contemporary society. The book on dialectical logic seemed to be the perfect response to all of these problems. Such a project held the promise of linking Horkheimer's epistemological concerns to the general crisis facing Western civilization. In addition to offering an alternative to the natural and social sciences of the bourgeoisie, a major treatise on dialectical logic also might enable Horkheimer to sketch the general contours of contemporary society. The financial crisis of the late 1930s, however, threatened to destroy the Institute and Horkheimer's new plans. To sustain the group and his ambitions, he was in need of a way to scale back expenses or to locate new revenue streams.[59]

The haphazard course that Horkheimer set for the Institute was shaped by the desperation and fear that accompanied the threat of financial ruin. Instead of settling on one course of action, Horkheimer pursued multiple strategies simultaneously. Because the schemes were incompatible with one another, the net effect was chaos—the slowing of social-scientific and theoretical productivity, the disappointment of former American friends and allies, and the eventual loss of vital members of the Horkheimer Circle's inner core.

As the financial crisis deepened during 1938, Horkheimer began entertaining plans to dismantle the Institute. Initially, he understood his and the Institute's goal of a comprehensive, critical theory of society as a collaborative, interdisciplinary project. When he began to envision the dialectics project, however, it had become an individual mission. He no longer desired a mediation between empirical research and social philosophy, and no longer required the specialized expertise of many of the Institute's associates. In

fact, the economic drain that staff salaries imposed on the Institute constituted a major threat to Horkheimer's personal ambitions. As he considered the obstacles and examined his options, he realized that the Weil
endowment was more flexible than he had previously believed. The bylaws
did not require the existence of a formal Institute for Social Research.
Horkheimer could, if he wished, drastically reduce the group around him
and transform the Institute into a foundation. He subsequently had a portion of the endowment's earnings set aside in a private account for himself, and he established a timetable for phasing out members of his staff.[60]
Initially, Horkheimer and Pollock insisted on a number of substantial salary
cuts, but the long-term hope was to drive away the nonessential specialists who could bring no fresh insights to the dialectics project. The reduc-
tions were simply a way to facilitate an exodus from within the group's
inner circle. In 1939, Fromm and Gumperz were approached by Pollock,
and the result was their departure from the Horkheimer Circle. Neumann,
Kirchheimer, Marcuse, and Lowenthal were notified of future cuts during
the following year, but their departure was delayed as they sought alternative sources of income. They all hoped for closer connections to Columbia University and dreamed of appointments to the Faculty of Political
Science. Columbia, however, was in no position to hire anyone permanently, which prompted the Horkheimer Circle's associates to find financial shelter with the government's new war agencies that had begun hiring
social scientists after Pearl Harbor.

The unraveling of the Horkheimer Circle's inner core did not sit well
with the few American friends that the Institute had developed during
its early years of exile.[61] To many of Horkheimer's former allies, the new
initiative seemed irrational, harsh, and unfair. Among the departures,
moreover, were the very associates of the Circle who were best known to
American scholars. While Horkheimer, Adorno, and Pollock (whose work
was largely unknown to the American reading public)[62] were spared the
new austerity measures, the other staff members (who were trying harder
to make a name for themselves in American academia)[63] were the targets
of the budget cuts.

Perhaps more important to American observers of the Horkheimer
Circle, however, was the fact that the new cuts represented serious obstacles to the continuation of empirical research. U.S. social scientists were
generally unaware of Horkheimer's theoretical goals and his plans for the

dialectics project. Even if American sociologists had known of such projects in philosophy and social theory, it is doubtful that they would have been drawn to them. Horkheimer's approach represented an emphatic return to the traditions of Continental social science. The elements of the Anglo-American approach that had complemented Continental theorizing in the initial version of Critical Theory appeared to be threatened by the new turn in the Institute's fortunes.

Despite the dismal circumstances that Horkheimer established with this series of moves, the dissolution of the Institute was not immediately carried through. Although Fromm and some peripheral members of the Horkheimer Circle broke with the group, others held on to their diminished positions as Horkheimer and Pollock unsteadily shifted course. Just as it seemed that the Institute for Social Research no longer had a future, however, Horkheimer began to support initiatives to gain grants from American research foundations. But the timing for such a new scheme was not good. Horkheimer had parted ways with the staff members most capable of aiding him in the preparation of sociological grant proposals, and, more important, he simultaneously had provoked the American friends and allies of the Institute. Both of these developments, as it turned out, presented great obstacles to the initial success of the grant proposals. The push for external funding, however, opened a new phase in the history of the Institute's reception among American sociologists.

The first proposed research initiative focused on anti-Semitism. Although the topic was paramount in the minds of Germany's intellectual refugees, American Jews, by contrast, were not as focused on it.[64] Anti-Semitism, consequently, provided an opportunity for the Institute for Social Research. If the Horkheimer Circle was able to convince American Jewish groups of the impending danger facing all Jews, there might be substantial funds available. Anti-Semitism, moreover, was increasingly bound up with the crisis of modern society as a whole, precisely the Institute's main concern. In fact, while designing the project, Horkheimer gradually discovered the significance of anti-Semitism for his own work on the dialectics project.[65] Initially, he had linked anti-Semitism with the standard monopoly-capitalist interpretation of fascism that was pervasive throughout the Weimar Left. As Horkheimer dramatically proclaimed in 1938, before the initial idea for a future research project had germinated in his mind, "But whoever is not willing to talk about capitalism should also

keep quiet about fascism."[66] This perspective shifted, however, as plans
for the anti-Semitism project went forward. While laying the foundations
for the proposal, Horkheimer and Adorno were captivated by Pollock's
concept of state capitalism, which took shape at the same time.[67] In a 1939
report to Robert MacIver and Columbia's sociology department, Pollock
succinctly explained the overlapping of ideas that was taking shape in the
group's thinking about anti-Semitism:

> In Europe, the liberal conditions of the 19th century appear as a sort of
> interlude. One of the main causes for the persecution of the Jewish minor-
> ity in the totalitarian order is the replacement of the functions of the mar-
> ket by governmental functions.[68]

After taking Pollock's new revelations about fascism into consideration,
the Jews, in a particularly dramatic fashion, came to represent the plight
of religious myth and modern man in post-Enlightenment society.[69] The
dangers facing the Jews of Europe, therefore, signaled the existence of far
more pervasive crises for Western civilization.[70]

The second series of research proposals, which focused on the Horkheimer Circle's native country, also addressed the Institute's central concerns during the late 1930s and early 1940s. As Europe and the United
States braced for the expansion of the Second World War, Horkheimer
and his colleagues recognized the value of a comprehensive study of the
years leading to the Nazi seizure of power. From the outset, the main
theme of the proposed project was the innovative insistence that Nazism
was not an aberration, but instead a continuation of socioeconomic and
cultural trends begun during the Weimar Republic (some even extending
further back into Germany's past).[71] The plan was for the project to be
divided among the members of the Institute's inner core, with each member being assigned a topic in his area of expertise: Pollock would complete
the analysis of German bureaucracy; Lowenthal would examine mass culture; Horkheimer would dissect the displacement of religion by ideology;
Marcuse would tackle the impact of the First World War on Germany's
youth; Neumann would determine the role played by labor; and Adorno
would address the broad cultural picture by writing on literature, art, and
music. Although the division of labor was reminiscent of the group's
interdisciplinary approach to the topics of authority and the family, the

proposals regarding National Socialism were far closer to the theoretical essays that had appeared in the *Zeitschrift für Sozialforschung*. Instead of mediating between empirical social science and social philosophy, the proposals returned to the speculative roots of Continental sociology. In part, the planning for "Cultural Aspects of National Socialism" provided Horkheimer and Adorno with yet another outlet to explore their thoughts for a new theory of society and its relationship to contemporary philosophy. As was the case with the proposed anti-Semitism project, the Institute's approach, with its focus on the spread of technological rationality as the ground of fascist barbarism, was again closely connected to Horkheimer's plans for the dialectics project. In anticipation of *Dialectic of Enlightenment*, the proposal for "Cultural Aspects of National Socialism" signaled a chilling warning to Western civilization. Nazism was not simply a German problem. It represented a deeper set of issues that involved the fate of the world.

By initiating the two research projects, the Horkheimer Circle became far more visible than it had been. Even before Horkheimer decided to pursue research grants, the entire group began to break out of its collective isolation. In previous years, only Fromm had established relations with American scholars beyond the confines of Morningside Heights.[72] Once the Institute could no longer be protected by its financial cushion, however, Horkheimer recognized the importance of establishing the Institute's reputation among a wider network of American scholars. In spite of the fact that the Institute's social critique had begun to shift toward mass culture and the theory of the racket society, Horkheimer hired the Phoenix News Publicity Bureau as the group's public relations firm.[73] Perhaps the Horkheimer Circle sought a glimpse of the culture industry from the inside. The declared purpose of the move, however, was to promote the reputation and accomplishments of the Institute for Social Research in the United States.[74]

While the Phoenix News Publicity Bureau publicized the Institute's image in the U.S. press in the late 1930s, members of the Horkheimer Circle simultaneously sought to break out of their collective cocoon. Relations with Columbia had been positive, if sporadic, until Erich Fromm's departure, which threatened future support from Columbia's sociologists. With the two new research proposals, Horkheimer and Pollock sought to mend fences by consulting closely with the leading members of the sociology department—Robert Lynd and Robert MacIver.[75] In addition, they re-cruited to their advisory board especially eminent members and former members of the Columbia faculty such as Charles Beard (who was a for-mer member of Columbia's history department), Edwin Borchard (who was periodically employed by Columbia's Faculty of Political Science), Philip Jessup (one of Columbia's most highly esteemed professors of inter-national law), Wesley Mitchell (one of Columbia's most famed econo-mists), Lindsay Rogers (who was a member of Columbia's Department of Government), and James Shotwell (another member of Columbia's his-tory department, who concentrated on medieval history, foreign relations, and the origins of the industrial revolution).[76] While purely a diplomatic maneuver, the choices for the advisory board do indicate further efforts to increase the visibility of the Institute.

The other school and department of sociology that was crucial to the Institute's efforts was the University of Chicago. Although Fromm had established the contacts with the social science departments there, Hork-heimer sought to develop his own ties to the country's most prominent sociology department.[77] In the fall of 1937, he introduced the work of his Circle by approaching Louis Wirth, the central figure among Chicago's social scientists, for an appraisal of the Institute's translators.[78] Although Wirth was fascinated by Critical Theory's approach to social research, the university did not offer funds. Nevertheless, faculty supporters of the Hork-heimer Circle were permitted to add their names to the Institute's Amer-ican sponsors. Wirth was one of the first to offer his name and reputation for this purpose. Joining him were other major figures from the social sci-ences at Chicago that were also approached by Horkheimer. The list of Chi-cago supporters thus grew to include Harold Lasswell (who was originally a social psychologist at Chicago but moved on to a job at the Library of Congress), Charles Merriam (who was one of Chicago's leading political scientists with close ties to the sociology department), Edward Shils (who, although transitioning from graduate student to faculty member, aided the Horkheimer Circle during the late 1930s with a report on recent devel-opments in American sociology), and Robert Maynard Hutchins (who was the president of the University of Chicago).[79]

In addition to building important institutional affiliations with the two most important sociology departments in the United States, the Institute also sought to foster relationships with other well-connected scholars who might be able to assist with the initial anti-Semitism project and the proposed analysis of Nazism.[80] At the same time, since anti-Semitism was obviously of great importance to American Jewish organizations, the Institute courted these institutions and their friends. Such efforts, of course, required adjustments to American patterns of research funding. In Europe, specialists connected to local and state governments oversaw the financing of scholarly research. In the United States, private donors and foundations were decisive.[81] Instead of negotiating the complexities of coterie politics, as had been necessary in Germany, Horkheimer now had to adopt the roles of diplomat and promoter. Members of the Institute, following the director's example, thus sought the support of prominent American Jews, such as Supreme Court Justice Louis Brandeis, as well as scholars, such as Paul Oppenheim, who had close ties to influential Jewish figures in the United States.[82]

Although the contacts with Jewish groups would lead eventually to grants from the American Jewish Committee (AJC), the Institute's initial appeals bore no fruit. In the interim, the Institute impatiently sought other allies from the private sector—most significantly, from America's psychoanalytic establishment. Since Horkheimer's inauguration as director, the Institute for Social Research had pioneered a merging of Hegel, Marx, Weber, and Freud. Although Fromm's role in forging the latter, interpretive synthesis was crucial, we have seen that he was aided in the effort by other members of the Horkheimer Circle. Although none of the associates had Fromm's expertise, nearly all of them had studied (and had undergone) psychoanalysis.

Beyond Critical Theory's affinities with Freud, Horkheimer had other reasons to seek financial aid from American psychoanalysts. Freudianism, unlike the Marxian pillar of the Institute's theory, seemed politically benign. By the time Horkheimer and his associates arrived in the United States, moreover, Freud's ideas were rapidly growing in popularity and institutional strength. Because fears of political persecution kept Horkheimer from pursuing support from the American Left, his turn to the psychoanalytic establishment seems, in retrospect, virtually inevitable.

The fact that many of the Institute's friends from Europe rapidly became influential figures among U.S. psychoanalysts only made the situation more enticing. Indeed, the influx of European analysts into the United States that began in 1933 provided the American psychoanalytic establishment with the structure and coherence that it had lacked.[83] As the psychoanalytic refugees entered the country's poorly organized ranks, they brought order and stability to the American scene. Their authority, derived from their personal contacts with Freud and their intimate knowledge of his thought, placed them at the top of the psychoanalytic networks that they endeavored to expand and solidify. The Institute for Social Research, which had nurtured Germany's psychoanalytic movement through a formal academic alliance with the Frankfurt Psychoanalytic Institute, stood to benefit from the rising fortunes of fellow émigrés.[84]

Neil McLaughlin has argued that the Horkheimer Circle's rift with Fromm was linked to the quest for financial support from the American psychoanalytic establishment.[85] During the early years of association, both Fromm and the Institute claimed an orthodox Freudian orientation grounded in the libido theory. As Fromm increasingly pioneered social-psychological research methods for the Horkheimer Circle's studies of authority and the family, however, he amended his views, ultimately adopting a revisionist position that emphasized the societal mediation of biological instincts. Although it enabled him to develop a more stable social-psychological framework, Fromm's departure from psychoanalytic orthodoxy was soon rejected by his colleagues at the Institute for Social Research. The break between the two parties did not occur, however, until the Institute was in financial trouble. Unquestionably, the rift between Horkheimer and Fromm was initially driven by economic concerns, but the Institute for Social Research maintained public attacks against its former colleague for many years. In fact, the Horkheimer Circle went to great lengths to de-emphasize Fromm's role in the development of Critical Theory. As McLaughlin compellingly suggests, more was at stake than a disagreement about theory. The unusual openness with which the Horkheimer Circle challenged Fromm was not simply intended to bolster Critical Theory. It may also have been intended to attract the attention and support of the country's orthodox psychoanalytic community. By publicly keeping up attacks against Fromm, the Horkheimer Circle appealed to potential benefactors from the ranks of the U.S. Freudians.[86]

As the Institute for Social Research finalized the break with Fromm, Horkheimer turned to the orthodox Freudians for support of the anti-Semitism project.[87] The psychoanalytic refugees, whose interest in anti-Semitism overlapped with that of the Horkheimer Circle, gave the Institute's project careful consideration. Unquestionably, the break with Fromm enabled the proposed work on the topic to be taken more seriously by the orthodox Freudians, who were wary of their revisionist counterparts in the United States. Breaking with Fromm enabled the Institute's anti-Semitism proposal to sidestep the revisionist taint. Although Ernst Simmel's Psychoanalytic Institute was still in its infancy and could not provide the necessary funds from its own fledgling budget, Simmel promoted the work of the Horkheimer Circle among his orthodox Freudian colleagues by approaching private benefactors on the Institute's behalf and by highlighting the need, within the American Psychiatric Association, for research on anti-Semitism. Although none of the efforts led to financial assistance, the aid of the psychoanalytic community promoted the reputation of the Institute and the importance of its proposed work.[88]

The Institute, then, gained much-wanted visibility and a considerable network of American friends, but the proposed studies of anti-Semitism and of Nazism's origins remained unfunded. Unquestionably, by intensifying the competition for social-science research funding, the instability of the U.S. economy did not help matters. Once the United States entered the war, however, and the economy began to stabilize and grow, money was available in greater quantities for social science, and the Horkheimer Circle finally achieved success in its search for external sources of income. In addition to the unstable socioeconomic conditions that hindered the Institute's first efforts at grant support, the Horkheimer Circle was also not adequately known and could not yet benefit from their growing list of American contacts and supporters.[89] After several years of developing a public image in the United States and building relationships with prominent American sociologists and psychoanalysts, the Horkheimer Circle placed itself in the position to earn its sizable grant from the American Jewish Committee. This networking process, however, took several years to result in this eventual achievement.

The Institute's initial failure to gain funding for the first anti-Semitism project and the proposed study of Nazism can also be attributed to the fact that they did not match well with the interests and methods of American sociologists. Instead of suggesting innovative empirical research methods, which later became central to the Horkheimer Circle's AJC-sponsored

Studies in Prejudice, the first anti-Semitism project and the Nazism project proposed a sociological approach that remained firmly rooted in the theoretical orientation of the Continental tradition.[90] U.S. grant support would require a greater accommodation with the methods and traditions of the Anglo-American sociological tradition. Until the Horkheimer Circle was willing to make such a shift in its priorities and approach, however, the group's ambitions and hopes would remain unfulfilled.

chapter 6

ASSIMILATION AND ACCEPTANCE

Studies in Prejudice

The first proposal for an anti-Semitism project was published by the Hork-heimer Circle in 1941. The piece appeared in the newly transformed version of the group's periodical, which had begun to be published in English as *Studies in Philosophy and Social Science.*[1] In part, the article represented a final effort to publicize the institute's work on this front. American Jewish philanthropies had not yet embraced the project, even though it had been in circulation among potential donors since 1939. In the meantime, the group had tried to anticipate U.S. scholarly interests by shifting away from anti-Semitism and by formulating the newly proposed investigation into the rise of German Nazism. As the war in Europe escalated throughout 1940, Horkheimer pushed forward with the Germany project and elected to simultaneously publish the anti-Semitism proposal. On the one hand, its appearance in *Studies in Philosophy and Social Science* could bolster the image of the institute in the eyes of would-be sponsors of the Germany project who would clearly note the theoretical entwinement of the two topics. On the other hand, Horkheimer may also have published the proposal because of the rapid deterioration of conditions in Europe. With the escalation of the Nazi menace, Jewish philanthropists in the United States might take a new interest in the institute's research on anti-Semitism.

Viewed in hindsight with the *Studies in Prejudice* in mind, the first draft of the anti-Semitism proposal represents a stark contrast to the project that was eventually produced. Although the initial proposal successfully illustrated the seriousness of the problem by emphasizing the modern characteristics of contemporary anti-Semitism,[2] its theoretical hypotheses failed to deliver convincing sociological or psychological interpretations of the phenomenon. Instead of uncovering the deep roots of anti-Semitism as the proposal promised, the Institute was only able to provide some provocative historical narratives and unsubstantiated character typologies. Instead of advocating an inductively rich approach to the topic that might have appealed to the methodological interests of American social scientists, the Horkheimer Circle proposed a more conceptual approach that owed its inspiration to the types of theoretical writings that had been appearing in the *Zeitschrift für Sozialforschung.*

Instead of adopting concrete observational techniques that might have enticed U.S. scholars, the Institute presented sweeping historical analyses of prejudice that bore striking conceptual resemblance to modern anti-Semitism, and it engaged in critical analyses of enlightened humanism to highlight the hypocrisies and shadow side of European modernity.[3] Without the aid and assistance of Erich Fromm, even the hypothetical character types lacked the scientific rigor that had enabled *Autorität und Familie* to gain recognition within the Anglo-American sociological tradition. The anti-Semitic character types of 1941 had no grounding in survey research or projective testing.[4] They represented Weberian "ideal types" that arose from the theoretical models of modernity that the Institute was developing. In fact, the only portion of the project that proposed any form of inductive social research was a film study that aimed to provoke semiconscious and unconscious responses to various fictional scenarios. Its aim was to uncover the varieties of anti-Semitism through a series of screenings to test audiences.[5] Plans for the film study were spearheaded by Theodor W. Adorno. After his experiences with Lazarsfeld's radio project, Adorno hoped to design an experimental methodology that would address the deficiencies he had detected in Lazarsfeld's survey techniques. Whereas Lazarsfeld had sought to quantify audience "likes" and "dislikes," Adorno recognized that mass media provided an indirect medium for provoking conscious and unconscious reactions to concrete reality, thereby enabling the Institute to study the operations of prejudice in everyday life.[6]

Although the Horkheimer Circle's approach was consistent with the general thrust of Critical Theory that had arisen from the traditions of Continental sociology and that had evolved during the first phase of American exile, it also anticipated the chilling disclosures of *Dialectic of Enlighten-ment*. The first anti-Semitism proposal arrived at a hypothetical theory of prejudice that reinforced the Institute's pessimistic assessments of Euro-pean humanism, enlightened Reason, totalitarianism, and mass culture. Instead of proposing an empirically verifiable image of the modern anti-Semite, the Horkheimer Circle's first published examination of the phe-nomenon was more concerned with locating this social threat within a broader societal critique of contemporary Western civilization. Despite the significance and importance of this work for the Institute and its theoret-ical endeavors, the anti-Semitism proposal of 1941 received little reaction from Americans. By not addressing or meeting the needs of American social scientists, the proposal represented an unusual approach to a topic of great importance—albeit a topic that remained sensitive for Jewish philanthropies. Until the Institute could adopt the "scientific" standards of American social researchers and the concerns regarding anti-Semitism reached a crisis point, the Horkheimer Circle would find little support for Critical Theory in the United States.

Horkheimer, perhaps recognizing the futility of the Institute's grant efforts, refocused his attention on the dialectics project. Heeding the advice of his doctors, he moved to the more forgiving climate of Southern Cali-fornia in April 1941.[7] Surrounded by a colony of Hollywood's German refugees, he and his wife settled in Pacific Palisades, where the plans for *Dialectic of Enlightenment* went forward.[8] In the next months, Horkheimer was joined temporarily by Marcuse and Pollock, and he was permanently reunited with Adorno. As the work moved forward with the dialectics project, the entire Institute received the news from the Rockefeller Foun-dation that the "Cultural Aspects of National Socialism" was a failure.[9] Simultaneously, it also suffered the frustration of idly waiting for posi-tive responses to the anti-Semitism project. As the proposal languished on the desks of Jewish philanthropic foundations and would-be American sponsors, Horkheimer and Pollock were again forced to move forward with plans to liquidate the Institute. At the same time, however, they entertained a desperate ploy initiated by the members of the Institute remaining behind in New York. Recognizing that their intellectual free-dom was in jeopardy, Neumann, Marcuse, and Lowenthal led an effort to secure either a future at Columbia or grant support for the anti-Semitism project.[10]

Horkheimer had been considering the possibility of closer relations with Columbia University since January 1941, and the negotiations for such an arrangement went ahead in earnest following the bad news from the Rockefeller Foundation.[11] Although some faculty within Columbia's sociology department had grown frustrated with the Institute for Social Research (most notably Robert Lynd), Neumann seemed the logical candidate to direct the delicate negotiations on Morningside Heights.[12] Unlike Horkheimer and Pollock, Neumann had made a greater effort to develop relationships with his U.S. colleagues, and his work in the fields of law, labor, and economics corresponded more closely with that of Columbia faculty than the more esoteric and exotic social philosophy practiced by the other members of the Institute. At the same time that attempts were made to convince Columbia sociologists (especially Robert MacIver) to incorporate members of the Institute into their department, Horkheimer also pressed Neumann to continue the campaign in support of the anti-Semitism project. The Institute's inner circle, after accurately assessing their position, shrewdly recognized that both efforts were closely connected. Instead of multiplying Neumann's duties and dividing his time, Horkheimer and Pollock understood that the best way to convince Columbia of the Institute's worth was to gain support for their ambitious anti-Semitism project. Neumann, consequently, revised the anti-Semitism proposal and marketed the Institute both to those in power on Morningside Heights and to those closely associated with Jewish foundations and philanthropic societies.[13]

By the end of 1941, the efforts directed by Neumann from New York were swiftly moving forward. An extensive series of negotiations had taken place between Institute members and Robert MacIver. Although Horkheimer viewed the results of these talks with his customary pessimism and reserve, MacIver had agreed in principle to a yearly rotating appointment of one Horkheimer Circle member to Columbia's faculty.[14] At the same time that Neumann led these efforts on Morningside Heights, he also tinkered with the anti-Semitism proposal and submitted new versions of it to a broader collection of Jewish philanthropies, as well as to sympathetic educational and political institutions.[15] In hindsight, the most important of these initiatives was directed at the Jewish trade unionists of New York. These efforts, which Neumann contracted out to Isaeque Graeber, eventually led to the grants awarded by the Jewish Labor Committee and the American Jewish Committee.[16]

As Neumann and Graeber pursued this broad group of potential donors, the prospects grew particularly bleak as the United States entered the Second World War. On the one hand, the war effort united the entire population of the United States in opposition to fascism—a circumstance that established an alliance between the country's Jewish and non-Jewish populations against a common enemy. Instead of Nazi anti-Semitism representing a narrowly Jewish concern, National Socialism had grown to represent a major threat to the entire nation. On the other hand, however, the war created new civic needs and philanthropic responsibilities. During the first months of 1942, Neumann and Horkheimer both arrived at the opinion that the requirements of the war effort would diminish the resources available for studying anti-Semitism. As Neumann, who convinced Horkheimer of this changed atmosphere only days after the bombing of Pearl Harbor, explained:

> The prospects are, of course, not very good at present. In the first place anti-Semitism has definitely receded into the background. In the second place many foundations will utilize their funds and abilities exclusively for the war effort . . . This view is, of course, shortsighted since there is not the slightest doubt that either during the war or certainly after it anti-Semitism will become much more powerful than ever before because it will be fused with a definitely Fascist movement. Still, there are a good number of people who see that the breathing spell which the initial war period gives to the Jews, should be utilized.[17]

Neumann thus pressed forward with his efforts, but remained guarded about the project's future. The stakes remained high and perhaps had become elevated by the expansion of hostilities, but the logistical realities of the war effort dampened the Institute's hopes. In the meantime, Horkheimer and his colleagues considered the new possibilities that the war might offer to them.[18]

The renewed push for grant support suffered a further setback in January when Neumann was hired to the new, one-year appointment that the Institute had arranged with MacIver. Neither Horkheimer nor Pollock could have been surprised by this development, but it still came as a terrible blow to their egos. Despite all of Neumann's hard work on the group's behalf, the administrators of the Institute felt that the appointment belonged to Horkheimer (or, at the very least, to Horkheimer's selection for the post, Leo Lowenthal). Although this might have been a reasonable expectation in earlier years, it was no longer tenable. Horkheimer had departed for California, he had entrusted Neumann with the Institute's business on the East Coast, and Neumann had completed and published *Behemoth,* the book that would bring him much attention and fame within U.S. academic circles. Although such achievements may have been insignificant in the eyes of Horkheimer and Pollock, Neumann's more visible stature and notoriety were acknowledged by Columbia with the awarding of this first one-year appointment.

Instead of accepting this defeat gracefully, Horkheimer bitterly used the opportunity to strike at Neumann and the New York branch of the Institute. As soon as the word of the promotion reached Los Angeles, Horkheimer and Pollock pushed ahead with a drastic series of salary cuts and firings. If a strengthened relationship with Columbia could not be possible on their own terms, they were willing to slash most of the Institute's staff to protect their control over the organization. Neumann, Marcuse, and Kirchheimer, who all were beginning to dominate the daily operations of the New York branch, would be sacrificed for the good of the administrative directors. Regardless of whether Neumann accepted the Columbia position or not, Horkheimer insisted that his salary be terminated by October 1942.[19] Despite his pleas and protestations, Neumann could not convince his colleagues to spare him. Consequently, he took the position at Columbia and at the same time sought future employment options. Fully recognizing that Columbia could only offer the position for a year, Neumann blazed a career path into government service—a trajectory that would subsequently be followed by his close friends and colleagues, Marcuse and Kirchheimer.

As Neumann concluded his affairs with the Institute and embarked upon the professional transition that would lead him into the Office of Strategic Services, he began a final campaign on behalf of the anti-Semitism project. Perhaps he moved forward with this last initiative to fulfill his obligations and commitment to the project, but perhaps he also saw the anti-Semitism project as the one olive branch that he could offer to Horkheimer. By single-handedly procuring funding, Neumann might make himself too important to the Institute and thereby force Horkheimer to keep him on the staff. Neumann and Graeber made a final appeal to the American Jewish Committee during the summer of 1942. Much to the surprise of the entire Horkheimer Circle, the proposal was finally received with great enthusiasm. As Neumann recounted to Horkheimer:

> I have just come back from a two hour conference that Graeber and I had with Mr. David Rosenblum, Chairman of the Public Relations Committee of the Anti-Defamation League and of the American Jewish Committee. The outcome is briefly this: It is likely that we shall get a grant of $10,000 for the execution of the Anti-Semitism project if this sum is matched by an equal sum supplied by the Institute . . . I am confident that we have a very big chance of getting the $10,000 and though your presence here may not be indispensable I feel, that in this situation, every step should be done to ensure a happy conclusion of our endeavors.[20]

Despite Horkheimer's typical skepticism and his misgivings about being interrupted from the dialectics project, the Institute's director did travel to New York and met with the American Jewish Committee in September. Although Horkheimer had to return to California before a final agreement could be reached, even he had to acknowledge that the project's prospects looked better than they ever had in the past.[21]

The task of arriving at a final plan for the project was consequently left to Neumann, who negotiated the details of the collaboration with the American Jewish Committee. In October 1942, Neumann again met with David Rosenblum and this time the two spoke concretely about the logistics of such an endeavor. In anticipation of a final pitch to the executive committee of the AJC, Rosenblum wanted to have an American codirector lined up and also wanted to clarify the project's fundamental research problems. Neumann, after proposing a handful of potential codirectors, ultimately settled on Robert Lynd, who particularly appealed to Rosenblum.[22] Despite Lynd's reputation as a political radical, Rosenblum saw him as precisely the kind of high-profile scholar that the AJC would appreciate.[23] The two then moved to the more substantive topic of the project's parameters and agreed that research should focus on the political function of anti-Semitism, the effect that postwar changes might have on European and American anti-Semitism, labor and anti-Semitism, and a typology of anti-Semites.[24]

Although Horkheimer praised Neumann's efforts in their personal correspondence,[25] the Institute's administrators were deeply concerned about the possible consequences of Neumann's decisions. Generally, they supported Neumann's conception of the project and its research components, but they bitterly disagreed about the choice of codirector and the consequences for the future plans of the Institute.[26] In their eyes, Neumann was attempting to carve out a permanent future for himself with the Institute at the expense of Horkheimer, Pollock, and the group's freedom as social theorists. The negotiations with the American Jewish Committee therefore went forward, but so did the plans for Neumann's termination. Recognizing the strength of Neumann's ties to both Lynd and the Institute's contacts at the AJC, Pollock prepared both parties for Neumann's upcoming departure for Washington.[27]

The American Jewish Committee and the Institute for Social Research continued their discussions regarding the anti-Semitism project throughout the autumn of 1942. Despite Horkheimer and Pollock's efforts to conclude an arrangement, the AJC preferred to move more cautiously. The size of the grant was substantial, and the leaders of the Horkheimer Circle insisted that a substantially larger financial package would be necessary to meet their goals. In addition to this question regarding the financing of the project, progress toward a final deal was also slowed by a transfer of power within the American Jewish Committee. Joseph M. Proskauer was elected as the new president of the AJC in January 1943. Unlike the Institute's former contacts, David Rosenblum and executive vice president John Slawson, Proskauer and his new administration were expected to view the project more unfavorably. Members of the Horkheimer Circle and their allies assumed that Proskauer, who was an ardent Republican, would accept the conservative and isolationist position that American Jewry had nothing to gain from publicizing the plight of Jews in Europe. Consequently, it was extrapolated that, by extension, Proskauer would oppose plans to publicize the threat of anti-Semitism in the United States. Fortunately, however, for the members of the Horkheimer Circle, Proskauer and his colleagues were not inclined to view the proposal in this manner, and a formal grant of ten thousand dollars was offered on 2 March 1943 to pay for research that would be conducted between April 1943 and April 1944.[28]

The proposal that was finally accepted by the American Jewish Committee is in stark contrast to the 1941 publication that appeared in *Studies in Philosophy and Social Science*. Although the revisions of the project did bear some resemblance to its initial articulation, the successful grant proposal highlights the extent of the Horkheimer Circle's willingness to intellectually assimilate. Instead of unabashedly maintaining the integrity and Eurocentrism of its early theoretical plans, the Institute reframed both itself and the project within an American context.

This effort at U.S. integration was evident from the outset of the new grant proposal. Unlike the earlier drafts of the anti-Semitism project that made little mention of American scholars or their work in the field, the revisions from the fall and winter of 1942 demonstrated the Institute's support from U.S. intellectuals, as well as its knowledge of recent American literature on the topic. Instead of introducing the proposal with a broad theoretical statement that expressed the group's interpretation of modern society, the successful AJC petition inserted a list of sponsors and testimonials to precede the introduction. Although few Americans had actively aided the Institute in its quest for grant support, many scholars had agreed to lend their names and reputations as part of the project's sponsoring committee.[29] The revised grant application thus made use of these names and testimonials not only to enhance the image and significance of the research propositions, but also to dispel the isolated image of the Institute in circulation among certain New York intellectual circles. The testimonials, in particular, performed the impressive function of highlighting both the importance of the project and the Institute's capabilities.[30] Especially when one considers the reputations of those being quoted, the impact on the readers from the AJC must have been significant. Here were some of the country's prominent social scientists praising both the Horkheimer Circle and its research plans.

The actual introduction to the revised grant proposal further echoed the new image of the Institute that had already been sounded in the list of sponsors and testimonials. To underscore the prominence and importance of studying anti-Semitism, the Institute no longer restricted the discussion to its own theories about prejudice and the crisis of contemporary culture. Instead, the members focused on recent American writings on anti-Semitism and suggested that the rise in interest reflected a growing appreciation for the importance of the problem.[31] American commentators, according to the Horkheimer Circle, were increasingly becoming interested in the phenomenon, because anti-Semitism was undergoing a fundamental transformation from its premodern and archaic manifestations. Although few recognized what was happening, anti-Semitism was becoming totalitarian.[32] Such a shift signaled new dangers to worldwide Jewry and justified the need for research into this frightening development.

Like the earlier proposal's distinction between premodern and modern anti-Semitism, the nontotalitarian and totalitarian conceptions of the topic enabled the Institute to connect its broader interests in the critique of contemporary society with the topic of Nazi prejudice. The use of the term "totalitarianism" enabled the Horkheimer Circle to draw from work on the dialectics project and the theory of state capitalism, and it allowed it to make a direct appeal to American fears regarding the nation's new enemies. As the members of the Institute pointed out:

> The new anti-Semitism is totalitarian. It aims not only at exterminating the Jews but also at annihilating liberty and democracy. It has become the spearhead of the totalitarian order, and the aims and function of this order can be vastly clarified by a study of anti-Semitism . . . the attacks on the Jews are not primarily aimed at the Jews but at large sections of modern society, especially the free middle classes, which appear as an obstacle to the establishment of totalitarianism. Anti-Semitism is a kind of rehearsal; when the results of the rehearsal are satisfactory, the real performance—the attack on the middle classes—takes place.[33]

The Horkheimer Circle still utilized a revised Marxian analysis to see the rise of totalitarianism as a contemporary crisis within capitalist societies. The primary threat, however, no longer jeopardized merely the working class, small businesses, and free professionals. The Horkheimer Circle broadened its rhetoric to present the totalitarian menace in terms that an American audience would appreciate. It threatened liberty, democracy, and the middle class—the very foundations of American society.

As much as the new AJC proposal represented an assimilation to American interests and institutions, some elements of the project were envisioned to remain the same. Most notably, Germany was maintained as a primary focal point. Although the project reenvisioned the anti-Semitic menace to highlight its threat to the United States, National Socialism still served as the most advanced prototype of the totalitarian danger. Consequently, the Institute suggested:

> Since German anti-Semitism is more fully developed than any other, the case of Germany supplies us with the best point of departure, the best

model for studying the social basis of anti-Semitism, its methods of propaganda, and the psychological mechanism with which it operates.[34]

Germany could function as a historical case study that might shed light on the circumstances that gave rise to totalitarian anti-Semitism, as well as possibly illuminating the potential consequences of its proliferation. Unlike the 1941 proposal, however, the Horkheimer Circle recognized the importance of moving beyond the lessons that could be taken from Germany. To meet this end, they adopted an infection model for totalitarian anti-Semitism that seemed to suggest the existence of potential parallels between Weimar Germany and the postwar conditions that were likely to exist in Europe and the United States. As the revised proposal suggested:

After the collapse of National Socialism, the new form of anti-Semitism it has created is likely to survive it and spread to countries other than Germany . . . After the war various social groups may try to regain their prewar privileges or retain their war gains. Small and middle business men will fight for the restoration of their independence; the farmers will clamor for subsidies without which many of them would be reduced to starvation; big business will try to get rid of government interference—an attempt which will certainly be opposed, as it might create a wild post-war boom followed by a dangerous depression; labor will demand full employment, more social security, a share in the management and profits. Every group will try to shift the burden of the war costs on the other groups, and in this situation it is likely that a strong "social demand" for a vigorous anti-Semitic policy will arise.[35]

It is unclear whether the readers of the revised proposal would have recognized the speculative nature of this presumption. By the early 1940s, numerous questions abounded among Americans regarding the rise of Nazism in Germany, and the suggestion that the postwar United States might follow in Weimar's path might have seemed plausible to some. This infection theory did locate the danger as a worldwide threat and thereby built a bridge between European and American concerns. This new proposition directly addressed the potential dangers facing American Jewry. The Institute simply had to incorporate the methods and standards accepted by Anglo-American social scientists to convince its readers that its research and hypotheses were sound. To serve this agenda, the Institute for Social Research greatly expanded the scope of the project and its scientific rigor.

Like the 1941 proposal, the revised investigation promised to include a study of the origins and history of anti-Semitism. The description, however, was far less impressionistic. Whereas the earlier work proposed some intriguing but tenuous hypotheses, the new appeal to the AJC promised to rigorously uncover the history of prejudice and mass persecution. Instead of identifying specific events and intellectual movements that anticipated contemporary anti-Semitism and failing to appropriately explain the basis for each, the Horkheimer Circle outlined its procedure without sharing its social-philosophical insights and expectations. The result was a coherent and concrete description of a research methodology that could be embraced by historians and social scientists in the United States. This historical analysis promised to accomplish what the earlier grant proposal had offered (a historical examination of anti-Semitic behavior and its rhetorical basis in the messages of demagogues), but it devoted itself to these topics without drawing attention to the Continental orientation of Critical Theory and thereby undermining the credibility of the project.[36]

In a similar fashion, like the 1941 proposal, the revised AJC project also sought to uncover anti-Semitic character types and their basis in common perceptions of Jews. These research goals, which represented the major psychological contribution of the enterprise, made up the other essential piece of the plan. Modeled closely on *Autorität und Familie*, the Horkheimer Circle recognized that this section of the study had the potential to generate great interest in the United States. Psychoanalysis was rapidly growing in popularity, and an innovative usage of Freudianism had the potential to appeal to a sizable scholarly audience. If the Institute could simultaneously incorporate elements of Anglo-American sociological methodology into this approach, the visibility of the Institute might be dramatically increased. Additionally, a Positivist orientation could temper some of the criticisms that might be directed at the more qualitative nature of the proposed psychoanalytic approach. Instead of separating the various aspects of the psychological study, as the 1941 article had planned, the new appeal to the AJC consolidated the analysis of anti-Semitic character types by simultaneously considering their sociological basis in contemporary reality and their political function.[37] By envisioning this multidisciplinary agenda, the Horkheimer Circle was able to market itself and its experience with this type of work. The members of the Institute pointed out that

> we must combine history, sociology, social science and psychology. Anti-Semitism is the synthesis of all reactionary features of present-day social life; it cuts across every scientific discipline and touches on every problem of our social, political and economic existence. Hence it can only be fully studied by a synthesis of all the sciences covering the various aspects of the problem. Our project aims at such a synthesis. The problem cannot be adequately attacked by juxtaposition of scholars from various fields. A mere symposium of scholars without experience in team-work would be incapable of producing an integrated study. This can be achieved only by an institution such as our Institute where scholars from different scientific disciplines have been trained over a period of years to work cooperatively.[38]

Knowing the Institute for Social Research the way its American audience did not, we must confront two great ironies emanating from this formulation. First, the type of interdisciplinary synthesis that underlay the true methodological orientation of the Horkheimer Circle was entirely inconsistent with the traditions of Anglo-American social science. The term "Critical Theory" appeared nowhere in the revised grant proposal, and the readers from the AJC would never have been able to imagine how different their conception of social-scientific synthesis was from the Hegelian orientation of the Institute. Second, the kind of cooperation that the Institute touted in this new formulation of the project was a complete fabrication. Interdisciplinary cooperation had existed throughout the early 1930s, but financial pressures had ended it. As the Horkheimer Circle harkened back to experiences with earlier projects, the director was dismantling the staff of the Institute's New York branch. How much interdisciplinary cooperation would be possible after the majority of the New York staff was working for the U.S. government?

The revised AJC grant proposal concluded with a direct appeal to U.S. social researchers and foundations. The new research program needed to appeal to the orientation and interests of potential American sponsors. The old proposal had failed to accomplish this, much like the equally unsuccessful Nazism project. Both initiatives aggressively asserted the recent theoretical and philosophical breakthroughs that had been pioneered by members

of the Institute, but this strategy could only have limited appeal among
U.S. researchers. The initial results of the dialectics project, despite its
innovative contributions to Marxian theory and social philosophy, could
never have been mistaken for Anglo-American social science. Grounded
in the speculative habits of Continental social theory and the rigors of
Hegelianism, the critique of instrumental reason had little appeal for a
U.S. audience. Likewise, Pollock's theory of state capitalism formed the
basis for the Horkheimer Circle's analysis of totalitarianism, but a study of
totalitarian anti-Semitism required more rigorous scientific standards and
needed to rely on more than an abstract socioeconomic critique of contemporary Western civilization. The Institute's members, however, were not
willing to completely abandon the sociological traditions they had brought
with them from Continental Europe. Instead of advocating a total assimilation, the group recognized the possible benefits of trying to combine
the two approaches. Realizing that it would need assistance, the Horkheimer Circle suggested that it collaborate with American specialists and
that through working together a marriage of the two sociological traditions might be successful.[39] As the members of the Institute explained:

> Such a combination of the highly developed American empirical and quan-
> titative methods with the more theoretical European methods will consti-
> tute a new approach which many scholars regard as highly promising . . .
> What will be important in the proposed tests is not the explicit opinions
> of those subjects but the psychological configurations within which these
> opinions appear. The terms which occur most frequently in free associations
> may supply us with valuable cues. It will be particularly instructive to com-
> pare the frequency curves of various subjects and socio-psychological types.
> A more precise knowledge of the emotional backgrounds of anti-Semitic re-
> actions may enable us to elaborate more differentiated psychological meth-
> ods of defense against anti-Semitic aggression.[40]

Manifesting neither epistemological intransigence nor pandering accommodation, the Horkheimer Circle arrived at a vision of social research that
would cause many enthusiastic receptions of *Studies in Prejudice*.

Historians of the Frankfurt School have struggled to make sense of this
milestone in the Institute's U.S. history. All agree that *Studies in Prejudice*
represent a major shift in Critical Theory, but the explanations for this

transition vary. Some, like Helmut Dubiel, minimize the importance of the change. Dubiel prefers to de-emphasize the empirical research projects and instead focuses on the theoretical production of the *Dialectic of Enlightenment*. At the same time that Critical Theory had abandoned its revolutionary audience and the members of the Institute were fashioning philosophical and cultural critiques largely for themselves, there was mysteriously no attempt to mediate empirical research with theory, as was the case during the group's earlier history.[41] Martin Jay, by contrast, convincingly suggests that the Horkheimer Circle grew increasingly more comfortable with empirical research as it learned more about it during the American sojourn.[42] Rolf Wiggershaus, more cautious about the meaning of the shift, proposes two possible explanations. Recognizing that anti-Semitism had grown into the focal point of the Institute's interests by the winter of 1942–43, Wiggershaus believes that material and reputational needs forced the topic of anti-Semitism into the group's theoretical work (such as the dialectics project), or the work with the AJC served as an empirical complement to the group's philosophical speculations.[43] Lewis Coser, who worked with the members of the Institute on Morningside Heights, suggests that *Studies in Prejudice* might be viewed as a reconciliation with the Institute's inherent bourgeois tendencies. All came from well-to-do German families, and they had always seen themselves as radicals in Babylonian exile. The anti-Semitism project therefore most notably suggested an abandonment of revolutionary utopianism and the temporary adoption of American liberalism.[44] Peter Hohendahl and Zoltan Tar, viewing the shift in more purely intellectual terms, emphasize the significant reorientation in sociological outlook. Whereas the Institute formerly focused on the socioeconomic underpinnings of social phenomena and the structural transformation of society, *Studies in Prejudice* marked a move toward depth psychology and ideological reeducation.[45]

Although elements of truth pervade all of these explanations, it is important not only to grapple with the intellectual dimensions of these decisions but also to look at them in relation to the circumstances exile produced for the Frankfurt School. When we consider the desperation arising from the Institute's plight at the end of the 1930s and at the beginning of the 1940s, it also may be possible that the members of the Horkheimer Circle undertook this transition more as passive participants than as the active molders of their own fate. When Pollock discovered the severity of the group's fiscal crisis, Horkheimer received a great deal of advice from many of the Institute's friends. Robert Lynd, Robert MacIver, Adlof Löwe, Paul Tillich, and many others offered suggestions and support to the refugees from Frankfurt. On the sociological front, however, Paul Lazarsfeld provided the most assistance and may have served as a role model for the Institute.[46] Although the Horkheimer Circle suffered a long string of disappointments in the United States, Lazarsfeld had a clear record of success. Lazarsfeld had arrived at the same time as the members of the Institute, but he had come with nothing. In the same time that it had taken the Horkheimer Circle to jeopardize its existence Lazarsfeld had rapidly climbed the academic ladder to a permanent post in Columbia's sociology department and had laid the foundations for the Bureau for Applied Social Research.

Despite his partly deserved reputation as a sociological mercenary and professional opportunist, Lazarsfeld developed a successful strategy for pursuing social research in the United States. Instead of creating theory for its own sake or only tackling those questions that interested him as a researcher, Lazarsfeld encouraged those around him to seek out socially relevant and methodologically acceptable topics that overlapped with one's theoretical, political, and epistemological agendas.[47] If applied successfully, this strategy could provide support from U.S. sociological foundations for topics that represented the true interests of the researcher. The revised anti-Semitism proposal that gained acceptance from the AJC in March 1943 may have been the Horkheimer Circle's application of Lazarsfeld's strategy. The successful AJC grant formulated an anti-Semitic threat that was relevant to American Jewry and envisioned a methodology that was consistent with U.S. sociological practices. In addition to rescuing the Institute's finances and reputation, the money that paid for the anti-Semitism project also provided Horkheimer and Adorno with salaries that enabled them to think more generally about the topic. Consequently, the Institute for Social Research concluded the 1940s with the successful publication of *Studies in Prejudice,* as well as the completion of its theoretical masterpiece, *Dialectic of Enlightenment.*

THE EXECUTION AND RECEPTION OF
STUDIES IN PREJUDICE

The anti-Semitism project grew rapidly over the course of the 1940s and catapulted the members of the Horkheimer Circle to prominence in the study of prejudice. Ironically, this initiative, which in the end was pursued largely for financial reasons as the project's content increasingly drifted away from the Institute's theoretical interests, marked the group's breakthrough in the United States. After several years of struggling to gain recognition in the United States, the work that garnered the Institute the spotlight was not a truly representative piece of Critical Theory. Instead, it manifested a clear accommodation with Anglo-American research methods and sought to combine these empirical techniques with the speculative traditions of Continental sociology.

The Institute's collaboration with the AJC moved swiftly. Unlike earlier Institute projects that either involved large teams of researchers or germinated over lengthy periods of time, the anti-Semitism project began on a shoestring budget and taxed the group's depleted staff. The Horkheimer Circle had devised an ambitious proposal and now had to deliver on its promises. Despite the intense expectations and the harried research schedule, the evolution of the project was steady and methodical. As much as Horkheimer always bemoaned the stratagems and duties of U.S. research directors, the sustained support and proliferation of *Studies in Prejudice* represented a testament to his managerial acumen.

From the beginning, Horkheimer hoped to continue his life and his work on the dialectics project in Los Angeles while the work for the AJC commenced. Consequently, he divided the anti-Semitism project into two parts. The first of these halves addressed the origins and history of totalitarian anti-Semitism. This portion of the project was run out of the New York offices of the Institute by Pollock and represented a continuation of the earlier work on German history, National Socialism, and state capitalism. Making use of these sociopolitical analyses of German society and culture that had been under way since the late 1930s, Pollock and his team sought to produce a history of German Nazism that emphasized the evolution of anti-Semitic policy.[48] The second half of the project, meanwhile, also maintained links to the Horkheimer Circle's past. This portion of the project was directed by Horkheimer in Los Angeles, and it sought to provide psychological insights regarding the rise of totalitarian anti-Semitism in the United States. Harking back to Fromm's work with the Institute on *Autorität und Familie,* the psychological analysis of totalitarian anti-Semitism recalled the successful marriage of psychology and sociology that characterized the Institute's early interdisciplinary research.[49] This half of the project was clearly the more important of the two, because it necessitated significant methodological and theoretical innovations. In addition to formulating an experimentally tested model for the new anti-Semitic personality, the L.A. group also sought to disclose and combat the techniques of anti-Semitic agitators. Horkheimer's half of the anti-Semitism project required the mediation between psychoanalytic theory and empirical research. This was precisely the sociological combination that interested U.S. allies and the AJC in the Institute's proposal, but it represented a serious challenge to social philosophers such as Horkheimer and Adorno.[50]

The Los Angeles team needed to swiftly begin a series of large-scale social research projects that shed light on both the anti-Semitic character and the techniques of anti-Semitic agitators, but they needed assistance. Although both Horkheimer and Adorno were quite knowledgeable about Freudianism, neither was trained in social psychology. The consequences of this lack of formal training became starkly evident in only the first months of work for the AJC. As Horkheimer disclosed in a letter to Marcuse:

> The problem of Antisemitism is much more complicated than I thought in the beginning . . . Since we have decided that here in Los Angeles the psychological part should be treated I have studied the literature under this respect. I don't have to tell you that I don't believe in psychology as in a means to solve a problem of such seriousness. I did not change a bit my skepticism towards that discipline. Also, the term psychology as I use it in the project stands for anthropology and anthropology for the theory of man as he has developed under the conditions of antagonistic society. It is my intention to study the presence of the scheme of domination in the so-called psychological life, the instincts as well as the thoughts of men. The tendencies in people which make them susceptible to propaganda for terror are themselves the result of terror, physical and spiritual, actual and potential oppression. If we could succeed in describing the patterns, according to which domination operates even in the remotest domains of the mind, we would have done a worthwhile job. But to achieve this one must study a great deal of the silly psychological literature and if you could see my notes . . . you would probably think I have gone crazy myself.[51]

The passage suggests that Horkheimer, clearly still captivated by the new view of society that the dialectics project had generated, grappled to accept the obligations imposed by the revised anti-Semitism proposal. Even as he struggled to complete the new work for the AJC, he could not relinquish his view that anti-Semitism was merely a symptom of instrumental reason and the disenchantment of the world. Although stubbornly wedded to this initial vision for the project, Horkheimer shrewdly recognized that the entire L.A. team was in over its head.[52] Instead of struggling alone, he actively sought the assistance of nearby psychological experts. As Horkheimer explained to Pollock in the spring of 1943:

> Since the program on the psychological part depends entirely on the extent to which I can count on the cooperation of universities, private psychologists and students, a.s.f. [and so forth], my first statement on a plan of operation can only follow a series of interviews with competent people around here . . . I need introductions to the people who can give me help in all my steps.[53]

By the summer, the Horkheimer Circle located such a team of collaborators—R. N. Sanford, Else Frenkel-Brunswik, and Daniel J. Levinson, who collectively came to be known as the Public Opinion Study Group.[54]

With the psychological portion of the project organized through the aid of U.S. social psychologists, the anti-Semitism project moved forward on a series of interconnected, thematic fronts. Horkheimer and Adorno, in collaboration with Sanford's Public Opinion Study Group, pursued the psychoanalytic description of the anti-Semitic character and empirically derived their findings from questionnaires and interviews; Adorno, with help from Lowenthal, analyzed the documented speeches of anti-Semitic agitators in the United States; Horkheimer, together with other members of the Los Angeles team, devised an experimental methodology for a film study;[55] and at the same time, Pollock's New York research team summarized the Institute's interpretations of totalitarian anti-Semitism by revisiting past work on the origins and implications of German Nazism. Because of the size of these separate investigations, integration was a frequent struggle. Although each section had been envisioned as a component of a greater whole, the task of overseeing and bridging the pieces was an enormous chore that became increasingly difficult as the projects grew and new research initiatives were added. Nevertheless, during the first years of collaboration with the AJC, Horkheimer imagined the final goal as a textbook on anti-Semitism and a program to combat it.[56]

Although the research proposal accepted by the AJC promised to con-clude the project in a year's time, every member of the Horkheimer Cir-cle recognized that this timetable was an impossibility. The endeavor was too vast and complex to be completed satisfactorily in such a short period. Consequently, the group undertook the project with the view that the major hurdle would be to entice the AJC to renew funding beyond the first year. As this initial phase drew to a close, Horkheimer clearly eluci-dated the Institute's private position:

> We should be very careful with apologies. If we want to make a point of practicability, we should rather state that this period of our work was mere preparation. We tried to find and test methods which, if employed on a much larger scale, could lead to the formulation of new devices for the fight against anti-semitism. We might say that an adequate synchronization of research work with practical fight can only be the outcome of a continued period of close cooperation. (I am quite aware that I insisted upon showing clearly that our work is aimed at realistic measures. Since, however, the means at our disposal were much too small, there could not be any real result in this regard. I do not think we should engage in empty assertions, or even in bringing up the issue quasi in self-defense.)[57]

Publicly, however, the Institute dealt more gingerly with the AJC. Instead of rationalizing the renewal of funding by shifting blame (as Horkheimer had done among his colleagues), the Institute repeated the successful strat-egy that had resulted in the first grant—it again muted the role of Criti-cal Theory and emphasized the potential contributions to American social science and Jewry.[58] Although the Institute had little hard data to impress the members of the AJC, it tried to emphasize the methodological and conceptual innovations that had been made. Instead of admitting failure, it successfully emphasized the potential that its work fostered.

Despite the uncertainty that surrounded this new round of negotiations, a generous extension was granted for 1944–45. This first continuation, however, represented merely the beginning of a sustained commitment from the AJC. Although this renewal also came up for review in 1945, the Institute received further extensions that enabled the eventual completion of *Studies in Prejudice.* The AJC's governing body was clearly impressed by the possibilities and implications of the Horkheimer Circle's work. This financial commitment, however, did not come without a price.

Although the Institute and its collaborators were given the opportunity to show "practicable" results, changes were imposed by those paying the bills. Seeking more institutional involvement with the project, the AJC formed a Scientific Department that became a further collaborative entity. Although Horkheimer was asked to return to New York to lead this Scientific Department, other American social scientists were also hired—most notably Samuel Flowerman.[59] In the short term, there were few consequences of this administrative change. The AJC was simply granted more control over the operations of the project that it had financially undertaken. In the long term, however, this provided the basis for controversy and conflict. The new arrangement provided the AJC and the new staffers of the Scientific Department with the ability to intervene in the project's trajectory. For Horkheimer, who was accustomed to operating as an administrative autocrat, this set of circumstances increasingly became intolerable as the project was pulled apart among its competing interests. Instead of yielding the textbook on anti-Semitism that all parties had expected, the administrative feuding contributed greatly to the final format—a series of five monographs produced by a handful of research teams that, at times, arrived at disparate conclusions.

In addition to this administrative transformation, major revisions regarding the content and shape of the project were also requested. Most notable among these was the suggestion that Nazi anti-Semitism and American anti-Semitism were not necessarily identical.[60] This struck at the heart of the Institute's concept of totalitarian anti-Semitism, which had formed the basis for its theoretical assumptions. The AJC's rejection of this principle jeopardized the work of the Institute's New York office and forced the Horkheimer Circle to engage in more focused analyses of American Jew hatred. The AJC, showing a preference for the social-psychological investigations of the L.A. group, eagerly sought more information regarding the causes and dynamics energizing anti-Semitism in the United States. The resulting reshuffling of priorities led to substantial additions to the project, such as the investigations regarding American veterans and working-class laborers.[61] These changes represent a further transformation in the Institute's crowning American achievement. Unlike the earlier revisions of the anti-Semitism project, these alterations were imposed by forces outside of the Horkheimer Circle. The effects, however, were congruent with similar shifts that the Institute had imposed earlier on itself. The recommendations of the AJC and the interventions by Americans within the newly established Scientific Department caused the presence of Critical Theory to be further expunged from *Studies in Prejudice*. Whereas the original project envisioned the entwined analyses of anti-Semitism and contemporary society, the revisions of the project resulted in a series of social-psychological studies. This is not to say that the Horkheimer Circle failed to include any of its theoretical insights, but the net result was a more thorough assimilation with American research than had been initially envisioned.

The results of this accommodation, however, well may have been worth the intellectual price. Like so many other refugee social scientists, the Horkheimer Circle received great dividends from bridging the Atlantic's severed sociological traditions. By adopting the use of English and by combining psychoanalytic theory with empirical social research, the Institute regained its financial stability and established its credentials in the world of American academia. A network of personal and professional contacts had been nurtured since the first attempts at grant support in the late 1930s. *Studies in Prejudice* greatly strengthened and expanded this network. In 1941, the Horkheimer Circle begged for assistance from Columbia faculty members such as Robert MacIver. By 1943, MacIver had become affiliated with the Institute by accepting the role of codirector for the anti-Semitism project. Similarly, Robert Lynd, who had become a hostile enemy of the Institute following the departure of Erich Fromm, returned as an ally and champion of its work after the significance of *Studies in Prejudice* became clear.[62] Even Paul Lazarsfeld, who at times ungenerously characterized the group's struggles in the United States,[63] lavished praise on Horkheimer and extended his hopes for future collaborations between the Institute and his Bureau of Applied Social Research.[64]

In addition to strengthening and reinvigorating these old relationships, *Studies in Prejudice* also created fresh ties between the Horkheimer Circle and prominent American social scientists. Many of these new associates were drawn in from the Institute's older footholds in American academia. Contacts, for example, between the Horkheimer Circle and Columbia University or the University of Chicago stretched back to the Institute's first days in the United States. As the anti-Semitism project moved forward, the number of social scientists familiar with the group from Frankfurt grew on both campuses. In the case of Columbia, Lazarsfeld's presence on Morningside Heights and his active collaboration on the Institute's labor studies made most of his staff, friends, and colleagues aware of the work of the Horkheimer Circle. This included the established and influential friends of the Bureau of Applied Social Research (such as Robert Merton, Hadley Cantril, and David Riesman),[65] as well as the junior faculty members and graduate students connected through a variety of activities to Lazarsfeld's think tank (such as C. Wright Mills, Kingsley Davis, Seymour Martin Lipset, Nathan Glazer, Lewis Coser, and Alvin Gouldner).[66]

Largely in connection with Riesman's appointment at the University of Chicago and the Institute's long-standing ties to Robert Hutchins, many of these same connections resurfaced in Hyde Park when a large number of Columbia's young talents were drawn to the college's social-science program that Hutchins had created. Teaching "Soc 2" to the university's large undergraduate population, a network of social scientists sympathetic to Continental theory took shape.[67] The group included David Riesman, C. Wright Mills, Daniel Bell, Nathan Glazer, Lewis Coser, and Benjamin Nelson, who all were familiar with the Institute from their days in New York. They were joined, however, by colleagues that had grown to learn of the Horkheimer Circle by other means. Barrington Moore, for example, became acquainted with Neumann, Marcuse, and Kirchheimer during his work for the Office of Strategic Services.[68] Others, such as Phillip Rieff, learned of the Horkheimer Circle through their new colleagues, as well as Bruno Bettelheim, Morris Janowitz, and Edward Shils's collaboration on *Studies in Prejudice*.[69] For a large number, the Institute for Social Research had been one contribution to their growing fascination with sociological theory. Knowledge of the Horkheimer Circle, consequently, not only contributed to acquaintance with Critical Theory, but it also more generally bestowed knowledge and applications of the intellectual traditions emanating from Marx, Weber, and Freud. Like other coteries of émigré social scientists, the Institute served as a conduit between curious young Americans and the legacy of the Continental tradition. From the college of social science program it was only a matter of time before this interest in the Horkheimer Circle, and more broadly in Continental sociology, had spread to the department's graduate faculty. As this leap was made, the Institute gained Everett C. Hughes as a highly significant U.S. associate. Not only did Hughes provide powerful support for the Horkheimer Circle's plans for returning to Germany, but he also orchestrated a faculty exchange between the University of Chicago and the Institute for Social Research.[70]

Harvard University's emerging departments of social science rounded out the Horkheimer Circle's growing network of institutional and personal alliances at the apex of American sociology. Although less populated with true "friends" of the Institute than was the case at Columbia and the University of Chicago, the professional contacts with Harvard cannot be overestimated. At the same time that the Horkheimer Circle emerged from its state of relative obscurity, Harvard completed its efforts to build the foundations for a world-class department of sociology. Talcott Parsons, who rose to be one of the country's foremost social theorists, and Samuel Stouffer, who established himself as one of the nation's preeminent social researchers with the publication of *The American Soldier*, both received appointments in Cambridge. Although the two failed to bridge both halves of the discipline as successfully as Merton and Lazarsfeld accomplished at Columbia, Harvard enjoyed the notoriety and prestige commensurate with the nation's other bulwarks in the field owing to the presence of both men.

The Institute's primary ally on the Harvard faculty, however, was neither Parsons nor Stouffer.[71] The first significant contact that the Horkheimer Circle developed through the anti-Semitism project was with the social psychologist Gordon Allport. Horkheimer became aware of Allport's work on American minority groups and prejudice during the winter of 1944–45.[72] Having grown accustomed to seeking out the advice of U.S. scholars working in related fields, the Institute's director wrote to Allport and arranged a meeting for February 1945. When the two got together and completed the predictable round of pleasantries, Allport took a keen interest in the psychological aspects of the anti-Semitism project. In addition to learning everything he could about the activities of the Los Angeles team, Allport recommended potential field researchers who might be available to assist the Institute. By May of the same year, this collaboration was formalized. At a meeting on 18 May, accompanied by Robert MacIver and Hadley Cantril, Allport became a codirector of the anti-Semitism project.[73]

Other Harvard social scientists, most notably Talcott Parsons, thus became admirers and friends of the Institute through a mutual interest in the topic of prejudice, as well as through the news of the group that was carried to Cambridge by Allport. With regard to Parsons, it is also likely that he learned a great deal about the Horkheimer Circle through his close collaboration with Edward Shils. Shils had been a longtime collaborator with the Institute since the 1930s, and he worked closely with Bettelheim and Janowitz on tasks connected to *Dynamics of Prejudice*. Although Shils could be severely critical of the Institute's work, he admired Horkheimer and the entire group.[74] As he pointed out in 1970, "Horkheimer is in a certain sense one of the most influential of modern social thinkers."[75] No doubt, Shils's positive assessment was not lost on his mentor and friend Talcott Parsons. Consequently, as antagonistic as Critical Theory and Functionalism appeared throughout the history of postwar sociology, Parsons added his name and reputation to the Horkheimer's Circle's list of U.S. allies from the field of social science.[76]

This notoriety and exposure, however, were not limited to academic circles. As the Horkheimer group reached the culmination of the anti-Semitism project, it publicized its work and conclusions through a number of venues that have escaped the attention of most historians. Through public lectures at Jewish colleges and local temples, the members of the Institute reached out to American Jewry to share its findings. Although simultaneously exploring plans to reopen a branch of the Institute back in Frankfurt, efforts were made to share the results of the anti-Semitism project with a more popular audience in the United States. During 1948 and 1949, Horkheimer and other associates of the Institute accepted teaching and speaking engagements primarily in Southern California.[77]

The most sustained initiative took place at the Los Angeles College of Jewish Studies, where Horkheimer organized a quartet of courses—one beginning in the fall of 1948, another in the spring of 1949, and a final duo in the fall of 1949. The first class, "Social Studies 1: Origins, Manifestations, and Motivations of Anti-Semitism," closely followed the contours of the Institute's initial plan with the AJC. In a sense, it may have most closely approximated the general textbook on anti-Semitism that the Institute had envisioned. The course examined the history of anti-Semitism (from medieval Europe to contemporary America), theoretical analyses regarding its nature, the empirical research pertaining to it, and potential methods of defense.[78] Its culmination was a radio address delivered by Horkheimer on KFMV that was produced in cooperation with the College of Jewish Studies. The talk, titled "How Research Fights Antisemitism," summarized many aspects of the course and included questions from the students of Social Studies 1.[79]

The second class, titled "Social Studies 2: Jews in Modern Culture," was offered in the spring semester of 1949 and looked at the cultural contributions of the Jews throughout Western civilization. Combining the Institute's growing preoccupation with the topics of ethnicity and aesthetics, Social Studies 2 may provide a hybrid glimpse at the group's growing self-identification with European Jewry. Perhaps acknowledging its own debts to its intellectual and cultural forerunners, the Institute sought to isolate and identify the contributions of Jewish thinkers within the broader context of European culture. After establishing the sociological position of Western Jewry throughout the history of European and American societies, the course moved through a series of units focusing on the contributions of specific Jewish thinkers in the fields of philosophy, political and social thought, law, natural science, literature, modern art, music, and business.[80]

As for the two courses that were to be offered during the fall of 1949, there are no notes or course syllabi. In fact, we only know that the courses were approved by the college. The actual class meetings may have never taken place. The first of these proposed courses was titled "The Jew in the Fine Arts," and its course description provided the following rough outline:

> Jews in cultural conflict, stressing the double aspect of the cultural differences of the Jews from other groups and of their assimilation. Interpretation of the elements of extreme progressivism on the one hand and of conformist popularity on the other. A limited number of outstanding, highly characteristic, or successful Jewish artists will be discussed in detail, e.g. painting (Pissarro, Modigliani, Chagall, Herbert Walden); music (Mahler, Schoenberg, Gershwin); literature (Sholem Aleichem, Kafka, Proust, Karl Krause).[81]

The second proposed course, "Education 3: Understanding Your Neighbors," represents what might have been the furthest departure from the work connected to the anti-Semitism project. Instead of exploring issues regarding prejudice or Jewish history, "Education 3" suggested instruction in ethical activism and religious toleration. Like the other class from the fall of 1949, our only knowledge of its proposed content comes from a flyer that accompanied the college's notice of approval. According to this only piece of evidence, "Education 3" promised to provide:

An understanding of basic religions of mankind and an appreciation of the role of religion in the general culture. A description of some of the forces which make for or prevent an understanding of the various religious and racial groups in our country.[82]

Although little is known about these lecture courses, they represent a significant phase in the Horkheimer Circle's sociological reception in the United States. The anti-Semitism project received a great deal of attention from American social scientists and scholars. At the same time, however, the members of the Institute were also attempting to make a popular impact as American citizens and Jews. As limited as this popular reception may have been, it reminds us to not lose track of the middlebrow audience that also may have been influenced by *Studies in Prejudice.*

Considering this broader range of receptions is all the more important when one takes the literary reception of *Studies in Prejudice* into account. The review literature, produced entirely by a scholarly audience, constitutes only a partial reception of these monographs. There were many who bought, read, and were affected by these books. Because, however, we have no access to the thoughts and reactions of these anonymous readers, we can do no more than speculate as to the nature of their receptions. Rethinking the role of review literature may provide us with the only insight we can gain regarding popular responses to these works. Reviewers do not simply introduce potential readers to literary products. They also establish intellectual and cultural contexts for interpreting and evaluating the significance of books. Reviews thus lay the groundwork for reception. In addition to generating publicity, they also set the parameters for which works are received. The review literature regarding *Studies in Prejudice,* consequently, may offer us more than simply the academic reception of these works. The reviews may also instruct us about the popular reception, if we see the reviewers as the interlocutors of the Institute's sociological project.

Before the publication of *Studies in Prejudice,* the environment for the project's reception was prepared by the magazine *Commentary.* From the very first issue, the magazine began to publish a series of articles that brought the work of the Horkheimer Circle to the attention of American readers.[83] Aside from passing along summaries of the Institute's findings and conveying excitement about the possibilities created by such research, the articles engaged in little criticism of the anti-Semitism project. That task could not be successfully accomplished until the entire series was published. Nevertheless, these early articles brought news of the Institute and its work to American readers. Perhaps more important, the interest of *Commentary* also established the significance of not only the problem of anti-Semitism but also the potential solutions that the Horkheimer Circle was struggling to envision.

Like the work of the Institute, *Commentary* was financially supported by the American Jewish Committee. In fact, the magazine's offices were in close proximity to the AJC's scientific department. Despite these shared conditions of patronage, the interest of the *Commentary* editors seems to have been entirely sincere. According to Nathan Glazer, who wrote a regular sociological column for *Commentary*, the journal was never requested to publicize the ongoing research of the Horkheimer Circle. Instead, he proposes that the fascination of the magazine was a fortuitous accident.[84] Archival evidence corroborates Glazer's recollections and suggests that the editor in chief, Elliot Cohen, was a friend of the Institute. In the spirit of collegiality, Horkheimer closely monitored the birth of *Commentary* and passed along his encouragement and excitement.[85] The relationship, however, went far deeper than pleasantries and friendly words of support. Cohen's letters refer to frequent talks with Horkheimer that had to subside when the latter returned to California in 1946.[86] More important, transcripts exist regarding a meeting that took place between the editors of *Commentary* and the members of the Institute's New York bureau. On 29 May 1946, Cohen, accompanied by Nathan Glazer, Clement Greenberg, and Robert Warshow, gathered with Leo Lowenthal, Paul Massing, Frederick Pollock, Felix Weil, A. R. L. Gurland, Marie Jahoda, and Adolf Löwe to discuss the lessons of Nazism and the threats posed by anti-Semitism. The transcripts suggest that Cohen and his colleagues from *Commentary* actively sought the expertise of the Horkheimer Circle on these issues.[87] The subsequent stream of articles that appeared in the magazine and drew attention to the Institute's unpublished work on the topic suggests an attempt on the part of the editors to convey this same information to the readers of *Commentary*.

By 1950, interested Americans no longer had to read secondhand accounts in *Commentary* about the research undertaken by the Institute for Social Research and the American Jewish Committee. *Studies in Prejudice* was published by Harper during the first months of 1950, and the response was extremely positive. As a collective series of projects, the set of five monographs was praised for its scientific and intellectual rigor. As J. F. Brown wrote, "even in the immediate present, the publication of this series represents what may perhaps be an epoch-making event in social science."[88] The project deployed an interdisciplinary approach (particularly the union of theoretical analysis and empirical research that united the fields of sociology, social and clinical psychology, political science, economics, and social philosophy—all of which had been woven together during earlier phases of Critical Theory, but which seemed like a major development to American reviewers), rigorously used all available methodological tools and techniques, engaged in innovative uses of Freudian theory, and shed new insights regarding the nature of prejudice.[89] The most striking feature noted in these accolades was the novelty of the Institute's approach. The reviewers, just like the readers of the Horkheimer Circle's initial grant proposals, were reassured by the Institute's use of Anglo-American empirical methods. With the project built on this solid foundation, the uses of Freudianism and the techniques borrowed from other disciplines became more acceptable. The Horkheimer Circle's intellectual assimilation yielded a product that was distinctly different from earlier examples of Critical Theory. Although members of the Institute struggled not to see this development as a dangerous accommodation, the move was perceived by Americans as a radical new fusion in sociological research. Based on the review literature, one can reasonably conclude that *Studies in Prejudice* established the methodological credentials of the Horkheimer Circle. As a result of this reception of the project, the Institute for Social Research could be recognized with Paul Lazarsfeld, the staff of the New School, and Talcott Parsons (as well as many others) as contributors to a unified postwar sociology, which overcame the intellectual divide that had once separated sociology's two trajectories.

This is not to suggest that *Studies in Prejudice* were met with universal approval. Although nearly all reviewers perceived the project in a highly positive fashion, some of the most glowing assessments were tempered with minor reservations and criticisms. In no case, however, did reviewers suggest that such problems undermined the overall achievement of the Institute. They simply called attention to various shortcomings to direct the efforts of future researchers who were sure to follow in the path blazed by the Horkheimer Circle. Among the problems most often cited, reviewers emphasized the lack of practical strategies for combating anti-Semitism and the tenuous correlation between prejudiced views and political ideologies.[90] Although the criticism regarding practicability had been a concern since early in development of the anti-Semitism project, members of the Horkheimer Circle could especially point to the F-scale and the structural analyses of anti-Semitic agitators as tools to be used in the fight against anti-Jewish prejudice. Furthermore, they were able to point out that the tools and methods pioneered by their study offered a number of future gains that could be realized with the continuation of research and further study.

The second criticism, however, regarding the shaky correlation between ethnocentrism and political mentality was a more serious issue. The Institute, together with the Sanford team, had endeavored to provide rigorously empirical scales to demonstrate the correspondence between the psychological and sociopolitical spheres. The critics, however, recognized that the construction of the scales and the handling of the questionnaires suggested that theoretical expectations shaped the trajectory of the research. This, of course, was true. The entire project, in fact, began from a series of hypotheses generated by *Dialectic of Enlightenment*. The researchers found empirical confirmation for the theories, but the limited scope of the project prevented them from carefully examining the views of "middle-scorers" (those that scored neither exceptionally high nor exceptionally low on the ethnocentrism scales). From a practical standpoint, the result of this methodological practice was a great deal of information amassed about those on the extreme fringes rather than those in the middle. More perceptive critics, such as Tamotsu Shibutani, were even able to anticipate the accusations of political bias that Edward Shils initiated in 1954. As Shibutani pointed out:

> The value-laden terminology only betrays the personal interests of the authors, which are commendable, but also introduces unnecessary complications into the study, which unfortunately defeats their purposes . . . While it may be comforting to regard those whom we dislike as pathological and lend "scientific" sanction to our condemnation, such a procedure is not always conducive to an impartial analysis and genuine understanding of the phenomenon in question.[91]

Although this line of attack was quite damaging to the project's theoretical thrust, the reviewers nevertheless still were able to celebrate the technical achievements of *Studies in Prejudice*. These criticisms only undermined the theoretical thrust of the project. The purpose and execution remained unscathed, and the door was open for future researchers.

One could, in fact, argue that the emerging controversy over political biases is precisely one of the central factors that led to the overwhelming significance of *The Authoritarian Personality*. Although the entire *Studies in Prejudice* were met with a warm reception, only *The Authoritarian Personality* enjoyed a major impact on the history of sociology. In 1973, David McKinney's *The Authoritarian Personality Studies* sampled 101 sociological projects from 1950 to 1957 that emulated the procedures and tested the hypotheses of the original study.[92] Having taken a cursory look at the sociological literature from 1957 to the present, the numbers that McKinney points to are just the tip of the iceberg. *The Authoritarian Personality* generated and continues to generate much interest among researchers in the social sciences. To some extent, this is undoubtedly owing to the promise that such a research program holds—the ability to uncover hidden prejudiced views before they surface and have consequences. Certainly, from an educational standpoint, such a tool would be of great interest to many social reformers. Nevertheless, one must also acknowledge that the other reason for this attention relates to the more controversial aspects of the project, and clearly the political implications constitute the center of this firestorm.

POSTSCRIPT—RETURNING TO GERMANY: THE "FRANKFURT SCHOOL" AND POSTWAR SOCIOLOGY

The Horkheimer Circle's relationship to American sociology did not end with the Institute's return to Frankfurt. For one thing, only Horkheimer, Adorno, and Pollock returned to the Goethe University. They consequently left most of their former associates behind. Erich Fromm, Leo Lowenthal, Herbert Marcuse, Franz Neumann, and Otto Kirchheimer all remained in the United States, and all of them maintained their contacts with their U.S. colleagues in sociology. Lowenthal, however, was the only figure who formally remained within the discipline, and even he served as a trailblazer for the emerging sociology of literature. The others built their postwar reputations in other disciplines. Marcuse and Fromm, although keenly attuned to the social sciences, returned to their former fields of philosophy and psychology, while Neumann and Kirchheimer became political scientists and theorists. All of these figures enjoyed high-profile positions in the United States through the prestige of their appointments or through the reputations they forged in print, but none of them adopted the hybrid approach to the study of society that had been adopted in *Studies in Prejudice*. Instead of participating in the postwar marriage of empirical and theoretical social research, the "permanent exiles" from the Institute adopted a variety of approaches that all shared a closer resemblance to the Critical Theory of the late 1930s. Ironically, by not being included in Horkheimer's postwar plans, these former associates may have obtained a greater degree of intellectual freedom. Rather than taking on the responsibilities of postwar German reconstruction, Marcuse, Fromm, Neumann, and Kirchheimer were not restrained by the necessities and political exigencies of a society in turmoil. As Germans struggled to come to terms with their past, they also found themselves on the front lines of the Cold War. Throughout the entire history of the Horkheimer Circle, the director drew his authority from the fact that all of the group's members associated the Institute with the material unburdening of the imagination. The postwar environment and the pressures created by the return from exile ironically seem to have reversed these conditions.

Horkheimer first began to entertain the idea of returning to Germany in 1947, when an offer arrived from the Goethe University of Frankfurt. Proceeding in his typically conservative manner, the Institute's director carefully considered the available options. As Pollock reported to the group's New York advisory board:

> Our dilemma has been accentuated by an official invitation from Frankfurt University to re-open the Institute in Frankfurt and to participate in the University's work . . . For all those who deem it probable that Germany is destined to play again a role in Europe within the visible future, it must be of some importance to build up groups, however small, among German students who will be in a position to evaluate the problems of contemporary civilization and take a stand themselves, can hardly be overestimated.[93]

The only problem with this ambition was that such an undertaking would threaten the Institute's work in the United States. Consequently, to the extent that Horkheimer entertained this option, he only envisioned the potential opening of a Frankfurt branch. In the interim, however, it would be necessary to determine how sincere and serious the offer from the Goethe

University was. Much unfinished business still existed between the Institute and the university's administration with regard to the group's hasty exodus from Germany. Institutional and personal property had been confiscated and compensation would be in order. Horkheimer, consequently, waited to make any judgments regarding the matter until he had the opportunity to travel to Frankfurt and explore the possibilities in person.

Travel plans were eventually made possible in April 1948 by the Rockefeller Foundation. The grant, arranged with the support and assistance of his Columbia colleagues,[94] enabled Horkheimer to visit Germany, where he prepared a study of the current state of the social sciences,[95] determined the material needs (books and equipment destroyed during the war) of scholars, and delivered a series of lectures at the Goethe University of Frankfurt.[96] The visit also provided Horkheimer with the ability to negotiate an arrangement with the university administration, as well as to attend the UNESCO conference in Paris where he presented his paper "The Lessons of Fascism."[97] Much to Horkheimer's surprise, the Goethe University was extremely eager to entice the Horkheimer Circle to return. The university and city offered full financial and professional restitution. For Horkheimer and Pollock, these arrangements made the hope of returning to their old lives a real possibility; and for Adorno they constituted a future in the only environment that he had ever considered home.

The postwar reconstruction of Germany also might provide the new branch of the Institute with opportunities unavailable in the United States. As exiles free from the taint of Nazism and as social scientists with valuable experience in the United States, Horkheimer and his colleagues might have the ability to shape the future West German society. Through the connections that had been nurtured over the past decade with American sociologists, the Institute might have the support to reform German social science and to enact its plans for denazification. The psychic and material rewards that might result from assuming such a position at the center of West German sociology were enormous.

These prizes, however, also included a tremendous price—the possible sacrifice of some of the autonomy and freedom that Horkheimer previously had valued so dearly. Horkheimer, Adorno, and Pollock were dimly aware of these possible consequences even before a serious offer had been made by the Goethe University. As Pollock reported after a meeting with James Shotwell:

His advice regarding the opening of a branch of the Institute in Frankfurt, Germany, was an unqualified yes. He is much concerned with the moral disintegration of Germany and believes that a group like ours could form a "cell" which might not only influence favorably the German academic environment but help to guide American occupation policies. Because of our independence, we would be in a much better position to criticize American mistakes and make suggestions for improvements. In America we would be one group among many others. In Germany our particular training in both, German and American, approaches would make our position unique.[98]

To what extent they believed in the possibility of maintaining "independence" remains unclear. In hindsight, it seems strange that Horkheimer and Pollock failed to see that such a position might cast them in the role of intellectual ambassadors from the United States. In their defense, however, one must acknowledge that the Cold War and the intellectual hegemony of postwar social science were not yet clear.

Recognizing that the American government and the international community might have an interest in bolstering the social sciences in Germany, Horkheimer became not only an advocate of foreign investiture but also a self-serving supporter of the Institute's role in this process.[99] Setting their sights on funding that might be obtained from the High Commissioner of Germany (HICOG) and American research foundations, the staff of the Institute sought to publicize their plans and the role they might play in West German reconstruction. In June 1949, American friends of the Institute publicly expressed their support for the proposed return to Frankfurt in the *American Sociological Review*.[100] In a notice composed by Horkheimer (but signed by scholars such as Gordon Allport, Hadley Cantril, Austin Evans, Everett C. Hughes, Otto Klineberg, Paul Lazarsfeld, Robert Lynd, Robert MacIver, Robert Merton, Talcott Parsons, R. N. Sanford, Herbert Schneider, James Shotwell, and Paul Tillich), the Horkheimer Circle's allies praised the group's achievements and emphasized the beneficial role that it could play in Germany. In particular, the notice emphasized the unifying function of the Institute in the field of sociology. As the signatories stated:

For a quarter of a century its greatest service to the social sciences has been in creating a link between the emphasis on theory characteristic of older European sociology and the techniques of modern empirical research.[101]

Such a cosmopolitan orientation contributed to the value of such a group in the reconfiguration of German society. In an appeal directed at the American HICOG and U.S. social-science foundations, the Institute's friends attempted to convince these agencies of the Horkheimer Circle's merits. As the notice concluded:

> The function of the revived Frankfort [sic] branch would be twofold: the planning and conduct of research projects and perhaps more significant, the instruction of a new generation of German students in modern developments in the social sciences. Thus the Institute would be able to do its share directly in achieving a deeper understanding of the social and cultural atmosphere of postwar Germany, in the interests of both the occupying countries and the Germans themselves. In our judgment, this proposal will be welcomed by everyone who appreciates the important contribution that social science can make towards a rational development of Germany's relation with the world.[102]

Following Horkheimer's lead, the Institute's friends gladly reaffirmed the niche that the returning staff sought to carve out for themselves: not only would the Institute closely monitor West German society, but also it would bring the hybrid form of postwar sociology to colleagues trapped in the legacy of Continental social theory.

In the short term, Horkheimer's campaign was a success. The Institute for Social Research returned to Germany with great fanfare, it received the generous support of the HICOG and the Rockefeller Foundation,[103] it affiliated itself with Lazarsfeld's Bureau of Applied Social Research,[104] and its staff was viewed as a living bridge to the past. In addition to its teaching duties, which primarily consisted of instructing German students in empirical methods, the Frankfurt Institute pursued an innovative group study of political attitudes.[105] In the minds of some authors, these achievements were paid for, however, with the price of further accommodation to a set of methods and agendas that were inconsistent with Critical Theory.[106] On the other hand, one could also view these developments more benignly. For one thing, the Institute's initial activities in Germany were entirely consistent with plans articulated throughout the 1940s by members of the group in their personal correspondences. Furthermore, the German postwar history of the Institute raises questions regarding the war and its impact on the Horkheimer Circle. Before the danger of the Cold War was evident, it might be possible that the Institute's views had been transformed by American exile. If this were the case, the newly adopted reverence for democracy evident in *Studies in Prejudice* might be less a case of intellectual accommodation and more a sign of ideological transformation. *Dialectic of Enlightenment* may suggest a preference for nihilism over Marxian utopianism; however, *Studies in Prejudice* may represent more than a reconciliation with American research methods—they may also signal an appreciation for the ideals of U.S. democracy. Once the Cold War policies of denazification were abandoned in favor of Soviet antagonism, however, the old reservations and cynicism undoubtedly returned. Still, we might want to entertain the possibility that the Institute's homecoming was motivated by loftier ambitions than simple careerism.

Regardless of how one interprets the activities of the Institute following its return to Germany, the old academic rivalries of the past soon reared their head. As rumors about the Institute's subversive intellectual and political orientations circulated in West Germany, other sociological teams gained grant support at Horkheimer's expense.[107] With the fruits of its schemes drying on the vine, a final sociological phase began at the Institute. Although largely beyond the scope of our study regarding the Horkheimer Circle's American reception, this final trend shaped the American perceptions of the Institute throughout the 1950s and 1960s.[108] Empirical studies were still carried out by fresh teams of researchers connected with the Institute. Although this work was overseen by Horkheimer and Adorno, the two rapidly vanished from the picture. Horkheimer became preoccupied with his duties as the rector of the Goethe University and Adorno returned to philosophical speculation. As a consequence, the empirical works of the 1950s and 1960s are generally ignored and not considered part of the "Frankfurt School" canon by most American observers. To most Americans, the sociological legacy from this period is the famed *Positivismusstreit*.[109] For those American social researchers more closely aware of the Institute's actual relationship to U.S. sociology, however, Adorno's readoption of the antiempiricist rhetoric of the 1930s and early 1940s came as a shock. As Paul Lazarsfeld commented:

> When, after the war, the majority of the Frankfurt group returned to Germany, they at first tried to convey to their German colleagues the merits of empirical social research which they observed in the United States . . .

Within a period of five years, however, the situation changed completely. Adorno embarked on an endless series of articles dealing with the theme of theory and empirical research. These became more and more shrill, and the invectives multiplied. Stupid, blind, insensitive, sterile became homeric attributes whenever the empiricist was mentioned . . . Thereafter one paper followed another, each reiterating the new theme. All have two characteristics in common. First, the empiricist is a generalized other—no examples of concrete studies are given. Second, the futility of empirical research is not demonstrated by its products, but derived from the conviction that specific studies cannot make a contribution to the great aim of social theory to grasp society in its totality. Empirical research had become another fetish concealing the true nature of the contemporary social system.[110]

Lazarsfeld's comments clearly convey the perspective of one who was aware of the Institute's entire legacy in the United States. Unlike the younger generation of radical sociologists and New Leftists, Lazarsfeld could recall the agendas of an earlier period. When viewed in its historical entirety, one must note that the Horkheimer Circle's attitude toward empirical research swung from stubborn resistance to desperate accommodation and then back again. Partly driven by ambition, the horrors of the Second World War, and the disillusioning realizations of the Cold War, these shifts are entirely comprehensible. Nevertheless, Adorno's postwar opposition to Positivistic social science has helped to camouflage an important phase in the Institute's relationship to American sociology.

PART IV

MESSAGE IN A BOTTLE

chapter 7

SPECTERS OF MARX

The Frankfurt School in the
Era of the New Left

By turning to the topic of the relationship between the Frankfurt School and the New Left, our analysis takes us in a surprising and new direction. Where previous sections of this book have explored cases in which the Frankfurt School had more substantial encounters with the United States and its various networks of public and academic intellectuals than has traditionally been assumed, these final two chapters represent the opposite phenomenon. The era of the 1960s has typically been presented as the moment during which the *Flaschenposte* (messages in bottles) finally found a sizable audience—the New Left of the 1960s. Thus, the 1960s have come to represent the time during which the Frankfurt School emerged from obscurity and became famous. As far as the United States is concerned, the member of the Frankfurt School attributed with achieving this surprising feat is Herbert Marcuse.

In the midst of the tumultuous uprisings throughout Europe in the spring of 1968, the American mass media heralded Marcuse as the "guru" and "father" of the emerging New Left, and these images stuck.[1] Regardless of whether a reporter or reviewer was an admirer or a detractor, both sides accepted the general assumption that Marcuse was the unlikely inspiration of the widespread student activism.

As Sol Stern admiringly wrote in the June 1968 edition of *Ramparts* (the Catholic journal that transformed itself into the first glossy magazine allied with the "Movement"), "When the improbable student rebellions of West Berlin, Morningside Heights and the Sorbonne broke out this spring, all agreed that Herbert Marcuse was the Marx of the children of the new bourgeoisie."[2] While Stern acknowledged the U.S. New Left's indebtedness to C. Wright Mills's writings on power, Paul Goodman's misgivings about the effects of a democratic education, and William A. Williams's shattering of Cold War myths, he characterized Marcuse's contributions to the student movement in this way: "Marcuse's importance for them derives not from any new disclosures about how society works but from his establishment of a radical philosophical perspective capable of withstanding the ideological onslaught in the name of scientific enquiry that young people are subjected to in the universities."[3]

At the same time, an early critic such as Kurt Glaser was able to pinpoint Marcuse as "the long-sought-for prophet of the New Left" in anticipation of criticism directed at both this prophet and his disciples.[4] As Glaser went on to write in his introduction of Marcuse to the readers of the *National Review*, "His [Marcuse's] current prestige with the New Left, however, derives from the more recent *One-Dimensional Man* (Boston, 1964; Berlin, 1967) and his essay 'Repressive Tolerance,' which first appeared as the last chapter in Woolf, Moore, and Marcuse, *A Critique of Pure Tolerance* (Boston, 1965) and has achieved wide circulation in Germany. 'Repressive Tolerance,' the more popular of the two writings since it is shorter and easier to read, is widely cited by both the Left and its critics as an action manifesto for street brawlers and stagers of Happenings designed to shock."[5]

The final two chapters represent an investigation into this image of Marcuse as a "guru" or "prophet" and arrive at a conclusion that may surprise some readers. Although there is no denying that Marcuse emerged as a celebrity in the late 1960s, the evidence for his widespread reception and influence within the broad ranks of the New Left in the United States is problematic. Sales of *One-Dimensional Man* were extraordinary, but one begins to question how many students actually read this complex text and thus were influenced by it. For a book of such philosophical sophistication, one would expect to find numerous writings clarifying the work of such a central intellectual figure. Such writings would surely be evident throughout the literature published by Students for a Democratic Society (or SDS) or the numerous underground newspapers and journals that spoke to and for the counterculture. The archival findings, however, yield a very different picture. There were a handful of notable exceptions—pockets of undergraduates and graduate students who became deeply inspired by Marcuse, but these groups largely used his writings to critique and to explain the crises that eventually tore America's New Left apart. As for the wider constituency, the archival record suggests that Marcuse had far less resonance and impact than is generally assumed. And therefore we are faced with a sobering possibility: that Marcuse, one of the most sophisticated critics of the culture industry, was transformed into a commodity during the height of his fame.

Marcuse himself seemed to realize the danger of his own celebrity and struggle against it. In an interview conducted with the *New York Times* in the summer of 1968, he bristled at the first question, which inquired about his feelings regarding his newfound notoriety: "I am deeply committed to the movement of 'angry students,' but I am certainly not their spokesman. It is the press and publicity that have given me this title and have turned me into a rather salable piece of merchandise . . . there are very few students who have really read me, I think."[6] When his words, transmitted through the print media, failed to have their intended effect, Marcuse began to reiterate this message to the students directly. For example, on 4 December 1968, Marcuse was invited to a lecture in New York celebrating the twentieth anniversary of the radical newspaper *The Guardian*, and began his speech with another denial of his presumed relationship with the student movement: "I am not responsible for what the *New York Times* calls me. I never claimed to be the ideological leader of the Left and I don't think the Left needs an ideological leader. And there is one thing the Left does not need, and that's another father image, another daddy. And I certainly don't want to be one."[7]

Although some admirers of Marcuse might be tempted to interpret these two chapters as historical revisionism, their origins and intentions could not be farther from this characterization. They are intended to take a careful look at both Marcuse and the American New Left during these years of turmoil. I am interested both in examining what Marcuse offered to his audiences during this era and in uncovering the topics that preoccupied the Movement that grew entangled with his own life and scholarly reputation. The New Left grew to embody something very significant for Marcuse. Although it didn't represent the revolutionary force that would sweep away advanced technological society, its passions and fears provided him with confirmation for the utopian characteristics of his critical theory. As we come to look at these relationships more closely, it appears that

Marcuse not only was not a "guru," but he may have been more influenced by the New Left than the New Left was influenced by him. Whether conscious of it or not, Marcuse developed a symbiotic relationship with the student movement during the 1960s. The "Movement" inspired him to examine the forms that resistance might take against a destructive social system that sometimes seemed insurmountable, and this led him to become active in emerging movements such as civil rights, the anti–Vietnam War front, ecology, and identity politics. At the same time, Marcuse tried to offer his advice to any segments of the New Left that were willing to listen. Although his advice was not able to save the larger antiwar movement and civil rights movement from increasing factionalism, he was able to provide graduate students and sympathetic scholars with the tools for comprehending what had gone wrong.

The goal of these chapters is not to debunk Marcuse or his work; rather, it is to liberate Marcuse from the mythology that surrounds his writings and intellectual legacy. Marcuse rightly recognized that the mass media of the 1960s had distorted his message by proclaiming him a "guru," a term that simultaneously was being used to describe mystics such as the Maharishi Mahesh Yogi and Timothy Leary. The effect of this image was to marginalize both Marcuse and his ideas and to pigeonhole his thought as a subcultural (or countercultural) phenomenon. As Marcuse's celebrity grew, the Frankfurt School was caught up within the Marcuse mystique and ensnared in the same dynamics of the culture industry, thereby distorting its work and its significance and relegating it to the subculture of the seminar room. Thus, the final portion of this book will take Marcuse and the American New Left as its focus, but its aim will be to shatter the myths surrounding the Frankfurt School more broadly and permit the *Flaschenposte* the opportunity to be freed from the subcultures to which they were relegated in the wake of 1968.

THE HORKHEIMER CIRCLE AND THE NEW LEFT

The 1960s were the most important and confusing moment in the history of the Horkheimer Circle's reception in the United States. Embraced by the New Left of both Europe and the United States, the *Flaschenposte* that had been written with little hope of reaching any audience arrived in the hands of an entirely new generation searching for answers to the problems of the Cold War and a nuclear age. To most members of the Horkheimer

Circle, the unexpected fame that they experienced in later life was soon overshadowed by disappointment with the movements with which their reputations had become entwined. The New Left was short-lived, and its self-destruction was as disturbing as it was shocking. The same generation of students that had rejected the apathy of the 1950s by embracing the anti-nuclear, civil rights, and antiwar movements saw many leaders of the New Left transformed into anti-intellectual, violent, urban guerrillas in the span of only a decade. Adorno best summed up the sentiments of nearly the entire group when he stated, "When I drew up my theoretical model, how could I have guessed that people would want to realize it with Molotov cocktails."[8] Despite the fact that most of the Horkheimer Circle's writings were precipitated by the threat of Nazism, the Institute's vision of totalitarianism provided the student movement with conceptual frameworks for dissecting contemporary society. Thus, the Critical Theory of society that was fashioned in the Weimar Republic was taken up by the New Left throughout Europe and the United States to construct a comprehensive theory of the Cold War landscape. To meet this aim, young scholars beginning in the late 1960s began to publish, translate, promote, and comment on the writings of the Horkheimer Circle. Ironically, at the moment that the Institut für Sozialforschung achieved the high point of its recognition and reception in the United States, its identity and coherence were highly problematic. In 1968, at the height of the student movement, the Horkheimer Circle existed as only a shadow of its former self. The consequent rise of Critical Theory that began in the 1960s was a theoretical reconstruction. As the historical record was assembled into a comprehensive picture of the group as it had existed in the 1930s and 1940s, the notion of a Frankfurt School was born. Ironically, it bore little more than a historical relationship to the institution existing in the late 1960s and early 1970s.

The organizational destruction and fracturing of the Horkheimer Circle was a long process that forms much of the context for the events and reception history outlined in this book. By 1968, at the height of the student movement, Theodor Adorno was the only member of the original Horkheimer Circle who still spoke officially on behalf of the Institute. When Horkheimer and Pollock both retired and moved into neighboring houses in Montagnola, Switzerland, Adorno assumed the role of director of the Institut für Sozialforschung. An entirely new staff of colleagues surrounded him, though. None of the other major figures had returned for good to Europe. No longer formally linked to the Institut für Sozialforschung, they remained in the United States and pursued careers in American academia.

In addition to the staffing differences between the new Institut für Sozialforschung in Frankfurt and the former Institute in New York, the theoretical coherence that once held the Horkheimer Circle together was now largely gone. To be sure, most of the former colleagues maintained general outlooks consistent with the Critical Theory they had created. They remained radical naysayers (as Lowenthal liked to put it, "I never wanted to play along")[9] committed to humanism and the ideal of critical reason, and their inspirations for all of these values originated from classical German thought—the heritage of Kant, the Romantics, Hegel, Marx, Schopenhauer, Nietzsche, Freud, and Weber. Over time, however, they came to disagree on both theoretical and political matters. On some issues, they were splitting hairs with one another: orthodox Freudianism versus revisionism, identity theory versus nonidentity, aesthetic utopianism versus aesthetic nihilism, and the notion of history as progress versus the concept of history as decline. For the more astute and expert recipients of Critical Theory, these matters had great bearing on the New Left and its role in Western society. For more casual observers, however, the issues that meant the most and also seemed to separate the former members involved questions of theory versus action, biological utopianism versus hopelessness, and Americanism versus anti-Americanism.

Of the core members still associated with the postwar operations of the Institute in Germany, many differences separated the exiled institution from its reconfigured existence in Frankfurt. The German homecoming carried with it new responsibilities and challenges that had not existed for the group in the United States. The Institute would, of course, undergo no more visits from the New York police or the FBI, and finances would never be as tight as they had been during the late 1930s and early 1940s. Nevertheless, Horkheimer, Pollock, and Adorno returned to a dramatically changed Germany. The fact that they were Jewish, Weimar leftists cut two ways. On the one hand, they were embraced as the living legacy of a German tradition that had largely vanished. On the other hand, they were the targets of lingering anti-Semitism and conservatism on German university campuses.[10] Similarly, although they were able to lean on American colleagues and occupation authorities for assistance, they remained tight-lipped about topics such as the escalating Cold War. To some extent, this may be a continuation of the consistent policy of political caution that Horkheimer had adopted in exile. At the same time, however, it may indicate that there was no true return from exile. The Federal Republic of Germany inhabited a perilous position during the days of the Cold War. It was the last outpost of democracy and capitalism before one reached the vast Soviet frontier. To many Germans, the state seemed little more than an American colony—entirely dependent on American military and financial aid.

When examining his correspondence, one is struck by Horkheimer's uncertainty about returning to Germany and then remaining there. In 1947, only a year before his first journey back to Europe since the beginning of the war, Horkheimer absolutely rejected the idea of any Institute member leaving the United States to work in Germany.[11] At the same moment, however, he writes of the need for a group like the Institute to bring its expertise to the study of contemporary German society. Consequently, he aimed for the reestablishment of a German branch of the Institute, but anticipated that it would be staffed by none of the core members of the Circle. By the beginning of 1948, Horkheimer had drastically changed his plans and now hoped to return to Germany to begin the task of reaching out to the nation's youth.[12] As James Schmidt compellingly indicates, the reasons for this change of heart may not have been entirely as selfless as Horkheimer suggested.[13] Prior to the final decision to return to Germany, Horkheimer had been exploring the possibility of developing a relationship between the Institute for Social Research and UCLA, and this arrangement unraveled at precisely the time that Horkheimer shifted gears and began exploring the possibilities back in Frankfurt. Nevertheless, thus began his commitment to German reeducation. One could argue that it remained his primary motivation throughout the rest of his life.[14] He worked closely with the UNESCO's studies on youth and pedagogy, he guided the Institute's postwar research toward the examination of West German political attitudes, and his activities as rector of Frankfurt University all connected with his concern about the new generation of Germans.[15]

Despite this commitment to Germany's future, Horkheimer struggled with the thought of returning to the United States. As difficult as exile had been, there were aspects of the experience that must have appealed to him a great deal. Instead of severing his ties with the United States and concentrating on his new life in Germany, Horkheimer kept his options open. He went to extraordinary lengths to maintain his U.S. citizenship, and continued to write in English, publishing a book with the Library of Congress titled *Survey of the Social Sciences in West Germany.*[16] Perhaps in part to keep one foot in the United States institutionally, Horkheimer not only helped to organize a faculty exchange program between the University of Chicago and the Goethe University of Frankfurt but was also one of the first faculty members to journey to Hyde Park. The exchange enabled him to get back into an American classroom, and also provided him with the opportunity to renew his acquaintances with his American sociological colleagues. Despite his chronic poor health and Chicago's chilly autumns, the trip was so enjoyable that Horkheimer struggled to make himself return to Europe. As he wrote to Franz Neumann's friend and colleague Helge Pross, he would have remained in the United States were it not for his obligations back in Germany.[17] In fact, had Horkheimer and Pollock not found the lovely location in Montagnola, the two almost definitely would have retired in the United States.[18]

Unlike the Institute's permanent exiles who remained in the United States, Horkheimer's postwar views may have been influenced by a surprising nostalgia for the United States that was only able to arise after returning home to Germany. The basis for the nostalgia was a profound sense of gratitude. Having witnessed the role played by the United States during World War II and the Cold War, Horkheimer took the view that the country had twice saved Europe collectively and him personally from totalitarianism.[19] As cynical and nihilistic as he could be at times, Horkheimer did not see the United States as the lesser of two evils. Although the totally administered society was troubling, it was no comparison to the blatant totalitarianism of the Communist world.[20] As much as he opposed the excesses of the Cold War and sympathized strongly with the American civil rights movement, Horkheimer could not join the opposition to the Vietnam War,[21] and his resentment of the New Left became well known. But his disdain for the student movement seems to have had more to do with his feelings for the United States than it did with his analysis of the New Left.[22] No longer peddling the standard anti-American line of the European émigré, Horkheimer became a patriot not unlike the New York Intellectuals who voiced similar views for strikingly similar reasons.

Adorno, on the other hand, felt less warmth for the United States. No doubt, exile was an intellectually important experience for him.[23] As some have suggested, life in the United States cooled his ardor for high culture, which he formerly had a tendency to fetishize.[24] Nevertheless, his sentiments toward the United States were primarily negative. Although his contribution to Fleming and Bailyn's *The Intellectual Migration* diplomatically acknowledged the personal and intellectual debt to his American exile experience, his negative feelings about the United States remained well known.[25] Adorno suffered terrible homesickness during his life as an émigré, and it wasn't merely Germany that he missed. Like so many other members of the Horkheimer Circle, Adorno came to view the United States as nearly the complete antithesis of the Europe he left behind. The United States was unreservedly modern, capitalistic, and commercial—a land of alienation, widespread conformity, and violence. It struck a discordant tone with Adorno's European, bourgeois mentality. Although biographers such as Detlev Claussen and David Jenemann are correct to note that life in the United States and the disharmony that this produced with his former life in Europe were enormously influential and largely responsible for his mature social theory, Adorno still viewed exile as a trauma.[26] The United States afforded him none of the nostalgia that the Old World provided in such abundance, but it also enabled him to grapple with a new world that he first glimpsed there and then continued to reflect upon from the German "colony" that he inhabited for the later portion of his life.[27] As he provocatively suggested in the subtitle of his collection of exile aphorisms, *Minima Moralia,* emigration damaged his life and led to intellectual transformation.[28] It would be a mistake, however, to see Adorno's views during the late 1960s as merely a reflection of his complicated attitudes toward the United States. His opinions were more complex than Horkheimer's, and far more personal than Pollock's views, which were strongly influenced by Horkheimer.

Adorno spent the 1960s immersed in a pair of projects that would overshadow his already impressive body of previous work. Unlike so many of his earlier writings, both were sustained analyses. They focused on the two entwined topics that formed the center of his intellectual constellation—philosophy and art. *Negative Dialectics,* his most sustained philosophical work, presented his positions developed over a career of thought. Completed during the rising tide of student unrest, Adorno struggled to articulate a philosophy of nonidentity and to formulate a radicalism for the new postindustrial, global era that had begun. Right on its heels, Adorno spent the final years of the 1960s occupied with the topic of art. Although unfinished at the time of his death, *Aesthetic Theory* functioned as a complement to *Negative Dialectics*. Taken together, both books represented Adorno's desire to philosophically and aesthetically explore the possibilities opened up by the concept of nonidentity. Instead of embracing the metaphysical illusions of phenomenology (a topic already raised in his critiques of Husserl and Heidegger) or the false totality conjured by Hegelian identity theory or Parsonian Functionalism, Adorno tried to preserve the freedom of philosophical and representational objects by reexamining subjectivity's relationship to the world. His philosophy and artistic preferences emphasized the role of negation in the operation of dialectics. Instead of formulating a method of conceptual construction, Adorno formulated a destructive epistemology that continually unmasked the reified constructedness of objects within late-capitalist society and imagined the recuperation of reason through aesthetics.[29]

Such exacting work left him less time to function as a public figure, although it must be noted that Adorno continued to function as a public intellectual, making him a significant influence on the emerging German New Left.[30] As the New Left arose in both the United States and West Germany, Adorno was becoming more preoccupied than ever with theory. Frankfurt's student radicals were not entirely wrong when they likened him to an ivory tower intellectual. To a large extent, he had retreated into his work and was less interested in the political struggles of the moment. Although his reclusiveness and commitment to theory turned the West German SDS against him (and him, in turn, against them), he was far more sympathetic to the student agenda than either Horkheimer or Pollock.[31] Although members of Subversive Aktion (a Situationist International–inspired West German radical group) began to attack the discrepancy between Adorno's radical thought and his political inaction as early as 1964, he was not a target of the student movement's disruptive and intimidating tactics until 1968 and 1969. Before the German New Left pushed him to the breaking point with its harassment, Adorno remained largely indifferent to it. Although he recognized the presence of his thought within the New Left's pantheon, speaking and writing for the students (as Marcuse did) threatened to jeopardize his work on *Negative Dialectics* and

Aesthetic Theory. Furthermore, the students' goals and agenda had little in common with Adorno's avant-garde forays into the philosophy and aesthetics of nonidentity. In fact, the populist tone of the student movement seemed precisely to be the sort of thinking that his current work was dedicated to opposing.

By the late 1960s, as a continual target of the Frankfurt SDS's derision and bullying, Adorno's criticisms of the New Left focused on the theory/practice dichotomy that the students emphasized. Adorno sympathized with the plight of Vietnam, but he saw the situation differently from his former colleague Marcuse and others sympathetic with student radicalism. Regardless of the atrocities taking place in Indochina, he failed to see how inhumanity justified reciprocal barbarism. As he explained to Marcuse in a letter of 1969:

> The strongest point that you make is the idea that the situation could be so terrible that one would have to attempt to break out of it, even if one recognizes the objective impossibility. I take that argument seriously. But I think that it is mistaken. We withstood in our time, you no less than me, a much more dreadful situation—that of the murder of the Jews, without proceeding to praxis . . . To put it bluntly: I think that you are deluding yourself in being unable to go on without participating in the student stunts, because of what is occurring in Vietnam or Biafra. If that is really your reaction, then you should not only protest against the horror of napalm bombs but also against the unspeakable Chinese-style tortures that the Vietcong carry out permanently. If you do not take that on board too, then the protest against the Americans takes on an ideological character . . . You object to Jürgen's [Habermas] expression "left fascism", calling it a *contradictio in adjecto*. But you are a dialectician aren't you? As if such contradictions did not exist—might not a movement, by the force of its immanent antimonies, transform itself into its opposite?[32]

Derisively, Adorno reminded Marcuse of their shared debt to dialectical logic and accused Marcuse of relinquishing his critical thought. Perhaps by being a victim of the students, Adorno was able to see them differently from Marcuse. On the one hand, Adorno's words are suggestive of the ivory tower syndrome. On the other hand, however, they called on Marcuse to remember the legacy of the Institute and the circumstances that had shaped that legacy. Adorno did not reject praxis in its entirety. He simply tried to remind his former colleague of theory's necessity. Viewed through his newly fashioned prism of the negative dialectic, Adorno's view of the student movement was far less generous or sympathetic. Adorno was obviously troubled by the reckless hypocrisy in the behavior of the New Left, but he also saw how little the students shared in common with the traditions of Critical Theory. Had he lived to see the New Left's implosion, he hardly would have been surprised by it. The Weathermen, the Red Army Fraktion, the Red Brigades—his advice to Marcuse suggests that he saw all of them coming.

Adorno's epistolary confrontations with Marcuse illustrate the intellectual differences that separated the members and former members of the Horkheimer Circle by the 1960s. The distance in attitudes corresponded partly with the geographic expanse that kept the former colleagues apart. As we have seen, returning to Europe provided Horkheimer with a perspective on the United States that he could not have gained in America. Adorno, by contrast, was less moved by loyalty to the United States than he was impacted by his own relationship to the German student movement. Had Marcuse returned, perhaps he might also have developed a different relationship to the New Left. Other figures formerly associated with the Institute, however, remained in the United States and still did not share Marcuse's views.

Although some never had the opportunity to pass judgement on the New Left, their postwar intellectual trajectories suggest that they would have shared views similar to those of Horkheimer and Adorno. By the late 1960s, two figures from the Horkheimer Circle had died. After a successful career on Columbia University's Faculty of Political Science, Franz Neumann was tragically killed in car accident in 1954 as he was making plans for a new career in Europe at the Freie Universität of Berlin. His close friend and replacement at Columbia, Otto Kirschheimer, died in 1965 at a time when the student movement remained in its infancy. It is doubtful that either would have given his support to the New Left. Although both remained committed to the pursuit of critical thought, both traveled long intellectual journeys from radical encounters with the political philosophy of Carl Schmitt in their youth to growing appreciations for American democracy in their later years at Columbia University.[33] Although neither had accepted the rest of the group's commitment to Pollock's theory of state capitalism or the tragic concept of history that would infiltrate the Circle through the late work of Walter Benjamin, their respect for America's political and legal system represented a sharp departure from their early commitments to Weimar Social Democracy and Bolshevism.

Leo Lowenthal, who essentially edited the *Zeitschrift für Sozialforschung* throughout the exile period and served as one of Horkheimer's most loyal collaborators, perhaps was most surprised about not being invited to join the reconfigured Institute back in Frankfurt after the war. A tireless worker on behalf of the group, he expected to figure in Horkheimer's future plans and was bitterly disappointed when he recognized that his efforts were not as appreciated as they should have been. He had fallen from the inner circle as Horkheimer pushed forward with *Dialectic of Enlightenment,* and his position was further undermined by the problems that had surfaced in his contributions to the anti-Semitism project for the AJC.[34] When Horkheimer finalized his decision not to begin republishing the *Zeitschrift für Sozialforschung* upon his return to Frankfurt, Lowenthal's future with the new Institute was all but determined. During the war years, Lowenthal had left the group with many of the others to work for the U.S. government in the war effort. To his disappointment, he was not able to accompany the others at the OSS. Based on his sociological background, he was asked to analyze German radio broadcasts for the Office of War Information.[35] Following the war, Lowenthal was able to use his experience to earn a position at the Voice of America studying the war's impact on American society. Through his sociological work in the field of communications research and popular culture, Lowenthal eventually was awarded a position in the sociology department at the University of California Berkeley, where he evolved into a pioneer in the sociology of literature.

When the student movement literally sprang up around him on the Berkeley campus, his initial reaction was to sympathize with it.[36] As time passed, however, his support began to erode. Much like Horkheimer, Lowenthal grew to see the New Left driven more by psychological needs than oriented toward political goals. Although his more muted support and enthusiasm for the New Left continued until the 1970 invasion of Cambodia, this single event and the students' reaction to it finally ended his support of student radicalism. As he recalled years later, "those were the days when the students wanted to 'reconstruct' the university. Well, I have to admit that I wasn't completely sold on the idea of an intra-university democracy."[37] Thus Lowenthal followed the course pioneered by many of his liberal U.S. colleagues and his former cohorts back in Frankfurt—increasing disillusionment with the New Left that reached a breaking point with the disruption of the university.

Erich Fromm, meanwhile, enjoyed a success and notoriety in the United States that was uncommon among his generation of émigrés. After departing from the Horkheimer Circle in the late 1930s, Fromm established his reputation in the United States with his classic book *Escape from Freedom* (1941). Although largely derived from his work on authority and conformity with the Institute for Social Research, most Americans did not link *Escape from Freedom* to the work of the Horkheimer Circle until the late 1960s. Fromm went on to run several psychoanalytic institutes and to serve on various professional committees. His subsequent books sold well, but their message rapidly began to change. Writing increasingly for a mass audience, Fromm's interests veered toward the existential (with his growing fascination with Eastern religions) and toward the current breed of self-help gurus who populate the world of trade publishing and talk radio. With *The Art of Loving* (1956) and *May Man Prevail?* (1960), many of his scholarly admirers felt that Fromm, in his pandering to the masses, had become irrelevant. Nevertheless, with his participation in various left-wing causes such as the antinuclear movement (the Committee for a SANE Nuclear Policy), he remained an important public figure on the academic Left. Despite the congruence between Fromm's views and those of the New Left, the student movement was largely disinterested in him. Perhaps his popular appeal made him too mainstream for a movement exploring increasingly radical methods and goals. Perhaps more to the point, Fromm was too close to the American liberal Left and did not capture the imagination of frustrated youth in the same way that a more marginal figure such as Herbert Marcuse did. Ironically, Fromm, whose vision of socialist humanism might have added a dimension of sanity to the New Left as it spun out of control by the late 1960s, was a figure that the students largely ignored.[38]

HERBERT MARCUSE:
THE UNLIKELY ORIGINS OF A "GURU"

As Max Horkheimer contemplated the return of the Institut für Sozialforschung to Germany, Herbert Marcuse continued to work for the U.S.

government—hardly the place where one would expect to find the man who would later become the so-called pied piper of the New Left.

The 1940s were a significant decade for Marcuse. Always a bit more outgoing and personable than the more reserved leaders of the Frankfurt School, Marcuse learned a great deal about Americans and the United States during his work with the Office of Strategic Services (OSS). As John Herz quipped, "the left Hegelian *Weltgeist* had found its temporary abode there in the Central European section of OSS."[39] Although Herz cautioned that Marcuse and his colleagues from the Institute for Social Research, Franz Neumann and Otto Kirchheimer, had little influence in the OSS because their superiors found their reports "too far out . . . too European," the collaboration between German and American scholars within the Central European Branch was important for all parties.[40] In addition to Marcuse, Neumann, and Kirchheimer, this office also contained other émigrés such as the historians Hajo Holborn and Felix Gilbert, the philosopher Hans Meyerhoff, and the political scientist John Herz, while the historians William Langer, Eugene Anderson, Harold Deutsch, Carl Schorske, and Leonard Krieger represented the American contingent. As Schorske recalled:

> In one of those paradoxical inversions of hierarchy that war produces, young academics like me, fresh from graduate school, often occupied positions of authority over mature scholars who adapted their ways of work less readily than the young to collective intellectual production and to the practical requirements of their government consumers. Thus I often found myself as organizer and editorial critic of intellectuals whose superiority in learning and analytic power was evident to all concerned. No one was embarrassed by the semi-carnivalesque inversion; each party was engaged in educating the other. The seniors provided the cultural substance and sometimes the methods of analyzing German developments; the juniors showed how to sharpen the focus of research projects and clarify the formulation of research results to maximize their political relevance and persuasiveness.[41]

In a similar manner, H. Stuart Hughes, who also worked with Marcuse and many of the other émigrés in both the OSS and then the State Department after the war (which had absorbed the Central European Branch of the OSS), described his time with the members of the Frankfurt School as "a third education, another postdoc . . . on top of the one I had received in wartime, and doubtless the best of the three."[42]

But what of Marcuse—what was the impact of government work in Washington on him? As Douglas Kellner convincingly argues in his introduction to the first volume of Marcuse's collected papers, the years with the OSS and the State Department were not a radical change for Marcuse. Work with the Institute had required him to examine contemporary social, political, economic, and cultural trends. Thus, Marcuse's work with the U.S. government enabled him to continue his analysis of European society. The collaborative nature of this new work environment could only have broadened the interdisciplinary experience that he had already encountered with Max Horkheimer. From his office in Washington, Marcuse and his colleagues were able to conduct formal and informal "seminars" on recent historical trends and world events. They were able to gather a wider array of resources concerning National Socialism at a time when other émigrés were only able to speculate about the situation in Germany. Similarly, they were able to witness the unfolding of the Cold War from an insiders' vantage point. Thus, Kellner is quite right in noting that "Marcuse's government work thus provided important knowledge and experiences that he would draw upon in his later work and which gave his theory empirical and historical grounding and substance."[43] His subsequent books, *Eros and Civilization, Soviet Marxism,* and *One-Dimensional Man,* were all influenced by his ideas concerning totalitarianism, which had been transformed by his years in Washington.

Marcuse's writings from this period further help to support this interpretation. Although his official contributions to the OSS and the State Department are problematic indicators of his intellectual development, nonofficial and unpublished writings from the same era bear striking similarities to subsequent works.[44] "Some Remarks on Aragon: Art and Politics in the Totalitarian Era," for example, developed several ideas that gained prominence in *Eros and Civilization.* Prompted by the Nazi horrors and the evidence of widespread collaboration and passivity, Marcuse searched for the basis for an opposition that might adequately confront the omnipresent domination evident in totalitarian society. One antidote that he saw was art—a theme that had dominated his earliest writings and a topic he returned to in his last book, *The Aesthetic Dimension.* Recognizing the dangers that the culture industry presented to revolutionary art, he wondered:

"How could art, in the midst of the assimilating mechanisms of mass culture, recover its alienating force, continue to express the great refusal?"[45] Marcuse sought the answer to this question by examining the new artworks emerging from the ranks of the French Resistance. Writers like Louis Aragon had revived beauty, love, and freedom—qualities that Marcuse later linked to Eros—to be juxtaposed against the forces of totalitarianism to highlight the plight of the human subject. As Marcuse explained, "The work of art must, at its breaking point, expose the ultimate nakedness of man's (and nature's) existence, stripped of all the paraphernalia of monopolistic mass culture, completely and utterly alone, in the abyss of destruction, despair, and freedom."[46] At the same time, Marcuse extolled the Resistance writers' nonrepressive exploration of sensual love. In a passage that sounds reminiscent of *Eros and Civilization,* he wrote: "Sensuality as style, as artistic a priori, expresses the individual protest against the law and order of repression."[47] In this unpublished essay of 1945, Marcuse already imagined the "great refusal" and had formulated the links between "sexual liberation" and the "new sensibility."

Similarly, Marcuse's unpublished "Thirty-three Theses" of 1947 anticipates another of Marcuse's late writings, *One-Dimensional Man.* By 1947, the realities of the Cold War pervaded Marcuse's daily routine and the entire atmosphere of Washington.[48] The thirty-three theses reflect Marcuse's complex awareness of the forces that had been unleashed by the rising tensions with the Soviet Union, and they also indicate that Marcuse's concept of totalitarianism had expanded to include European fascism and Soviet Communism, as well as the United States. Consequently, the theses presented the formulation of an East–West convergence theory suggesting that less separated Soviet and American society than the Cold Warriors believed. As Marcuse explained, "After the military defeat of Hitler-Fascism (which was a premature and isolated form of capitalist reorganization) the world is dividing into a neo-fascist and Soviet camp. What still remains of democratic-liberal forms will be crushed between the two camps or absorbed by them."[49] Soviet Communism had been utterly corrupted by bureaucratization,[50] the European and American proletariat was becoming integrated within the socioeconomic systems of the West,[51] and few signs of the "great refusal" seemed evident. Nevertheless, Marcuse wrote on behalf of the hopeless and told them that socialism still represented the solution.[52]

With Truman's termination of the OSS in October 1945, Marcuse made the transition to the State Department and became increasingly unhappy about his job as the reality of the Cold War settled in Washington. His prior work for the OSS had concentrated on Socialist and Communist groups within Europe. Such organizations were thought to be natural points of resistance within Nazi territories. With the coming of the Cold War, Marcuse's expertise was increasingly sought for quite a different purpose.

Marcuse's increasing disappointment and unease with his role at the State Department was not simply a matter of ideology. Never a Soviet sympathizer, he was also not a Cold War anti-Communist. What bothered him most was the exaggeration of the Communist threat. His work for the State Department sought to clear up what he saw to be the serious misunderstandings between the United States and the Soviet Union.[53] The more serious consideration regarding his government job, however, arose as his friends from the OSS departed. Marcuse and his colleagues were not typical government bureaucrats and they established an atmosphere that reflected the academic environments to which they were better accustomed. With the exodus of friends such as H. Stuart Hughes and Carl Schorske back to academia, Marcuse was isolated among a new group of professional government research analysts, and the escalation of Communist witch hunts made him uneasy. Washington was becoming an inhospitable environment to a person with sensibilities such as his. He remained, however, until 1951.

His long postwar presence at the State Department had little to do with his feelings about the job and much more to do with his prospects and circumstances. His great desire was to return to the Institut für Sozialforschung. There he might regain the intellectual freedom and camaraderie that he sought. Although Horkheimer briefly entertained the idea, he decided against it at the same time that he elected to not restart the *Zeitschrift für Sozialforschung*. Simultaneously, Marcuse's prospects in American academia looked quite bleak. Although he had endeared himself to many members of Columbia's sociology department, the only available position was offered to his friend Franz Neumann. He could seek employment at a relatively small college and publish his way toward the kind of position he wanted, but he put such plans on hold as his wife, Sophie, was diagnosed with cancer. Until she passed away in 1951, he would keep his family in Washington, where he would care for her and seek the best treatment for her deteriorating condition.

During the early 1950s, Marcuse juggled two incongruous projects that demonstrated his academic versatility. The first began in Washington, D.C., in 1950 while he was still working for the State Department. Recruited by Edith Weigert to offer a lecture series at the Washington School of Psychiatry, Marcuse formulated the basis for his book *Eros and Civilization* (1955). Work on the book, however, progressed slowly. After Sophie's death, Marcuse was awarded a Rockefeller Foundation grant to pursue a study of Marxism in the Soviet Union. The new project was inspired by his work for the State Department. His experiences over the preceding five years made him uniquely qualified to enter the expanding field of Soviet studies, but he spent his free time continuing to refine his thoughts on psychoanalysis. The Rockefeller grant enabled him to reconvene with old OSS friends at the newly founded institutes for Russian studies at Columbia and Harvard. The years 1952 and 1953 brought him back to Morningside Heights, where he was reunited with Franz Neumann and his former friends at Columbia University, while 1954 and 1955 brought him to Harvard University, where he reconnected with former OSS colleagues such as Barrington Moore and H. Stuart Hughes. Although his primary task was the completion of the manuscript on Soviet Marxism, he continued to spend his free moments exploring the relationship between Marx and Freud that formed the basis for *Eros and Civilization*. Much as he apportioned his time during his days with the OSS, Marcuse's professional life remained dedicated to foreign policy, while his private life was occupied by satisfying his other scholarly interests. The results of this nearly five-year juggling act were *Eros and Civilization* and *Soviet Marxism* (1958), as well as an appointment as professor of politics and philosophy at Brandeis University.

Eros and Civilization represented a major achievement for Marcuse. *Reason and Revolution* was an important contribution to Anglo-American interpretations of Hegel, but the tradition of German Idealism did not command as large an audience in the 1940s as psychoanalysis did in the mid-1950s. Freud's work had enjoyed a steady rise in popularity in the United States, and the Institute for Social Research profited from the success of psychoanalysis by introducing it into its sociological research. By the 1950s, however, Freudianism began to reach the pinnacle of its popularity in the United States. Its influence not only infiltrated the worlds of psychology and social science, but also had crept into the humanities.

Freud's central concepts were beginning to be utilized by literary scholars, historians, and philosophers. Marcuse, thus, was among several major figures to push psychoanalysis in revolutionary new directions and to capture the imagination of others working in the humanities.

Eros and Civilization frequently has been singled out as one of the most successful mediations between Marx and Freud ever achieved by the Frankfurt School.[54] This is not entirely true. By engaging in a dialogue with Freud's *Civilization and Its Discontents,* Marcuse used Marx's method of historical materialism to undermine Freud's central assumption—that all societies required repression and consequently suppressed natural, human happiness. At the same time, however, Marcuse's conclusions took him in a very different direction from that pioneered by Horkheimer and Adorno in *Dialectic of Enlightenment.* While Freud confirmed the bleak vision of contemporary society embraced by the Institut für Sozialforschung back in Germany, Marcuse's reinterpretation of psychoanalysis reinvigorated the concept of revolutionary change.

According to Freud, the tragedy of human civilization was the inescapable discontent of the civilized psyche. Due to material scarcity, the ego had to adopt a reality principle to control the instincts. In Marcuse's view, however, this tragic circumstance was far from inevitable. It was only the inevitable outcome within bourgeois and late-capitalist societies. Capitalism required the psychological internalization of social control and conformity. The reality principle, Freud's basis for reasonable repression of individual instincts, was a historical construct, and the capitalist reality principle was suffused with surplus repression. Bourgeois individuals submitted to more social control than necessary and surrendered too much of their autonomy. Societies were not eternally the same or absolute. Instead, they were variable. One could thus imagine alternatives.

This subversion of psychoanalysis by historical materialism, however, uncovered a more important realization for Marcuse, and this put him at odds with his former colleagues of the Horkheimer Circle.[55] While Horkheimer and Adorno embraced Freud for his tragic view of human history that tended to confirm their own bleak visions of the totally administered society, Marcuse found that the most important universal truth inherent in Freud's conception of human nature was the impulses to be free and happy. Bourgeois society required the repression of these instincts, but one could imagine alternative societies that might better correspond to the natural state of the human condition. As the other members of the Horkheimer Circle embraced a social philosophy rooted in nonidentity and negative thinking, Marcuse revived the concept of utopia by the reconfiguration of psychoanalytic anthropology. Authentic art, in his view, was a means by which people traditionally expressed utopian yearnings. By probing our natural, creative instincts (Eros), Marcuse theorized that contemporary society had the ability to realize these utopian yearnings previously only available through the aesthetic experience—a more free, pleasurable, and authentic existence. All that was required was a fundamental shift in the means of production and their social organization.

Marcuse's second monograph of the 1950s, *Soviet Marxism,* was no less controversial, but it did lack some of the creativity and Romantic optimism that filled *Eros and Civilization.* As its title suggests, *Soviet Marxism* was a political and ideological analysis of Marxism in the Soviet Union. As far as the history of the Horkheimer Circle is concerned, *Soviet Marxism* was an important moment in the group's political history. Although members and former members of the Institut für Sozialforschung had made negative but vague allusions to the USSR on numerous occasions,[56] Marcuse's book was the most open and direct confrontation with Bolshevism in the history of the group. Its stance, however, was entirely consistent with the leading figures of the Institute—Horkheimer and Adorno. While *Soviet Marxism* looked at many facets of society and politics within the USSR, its most provocative point was that the Soviet Union was moving in a parallel direction with the advanced, industrial powers of the West. At this stage in his career, Marcuse was content to merely illuminate the similarities between the two superpowers. He resisted the temptation to develop these findings, as he later would in *One-Dimensional Man.* Much of his American audience thus struggled to make sense of this dry and scholarly book.[57] On the one hand, *Soviet Marxism* was highly critical of the Soviet Union. Simultaneously, however, the book was launching comparable attacks on the United States. What his audience could not yet realize was that this represented Marcuse's first, tentative attempt at a social-political convergence theory. The two societies (both East and West) were actually moving toward each other—bureaucratic, totalitarian civilizations directly related to Horkheimer and Adorno's concept of the totally administered society.

Utilizing the method employed in so many of the studies of the Institut für Sozialforschung, Marcuse subjected Soviet society to an immanent critique. By examining its Marxian ideology in relation to the realities of Soviet society, Marcuse highlighted the contradictions. In part, his goal was to condemn the realities of Soviet life, but he also struggled to rescue Marxism by uncoupling its association with Bolshevism. His critique focused on the rise of bureaucratic conformity in Russia and the failure of socialist democracy to flourish. Hinting at his earlier sympathies with Germany's Council Movement and the populist doctrines of Rosa Luxemburg, Marcuse insisted that democracy was not an inevitable victim of Marxian revolution. To the contrary, Marxian socialism was inherently democratic. In its efforts to industrialize, the Soviet Union veered from a democratic course. By relying too heavily on government planning, a vast bureaucracy displaced the workers' control over the means of production. Although it began as a revolution from below within the soviets, Russia's backwardness forced a shift to a revolution imposed from above by bureaucratic control. Although he argued that the Stalinist terror state was withering away with the more liberal policies of Khrushchev, Marcuse saw the USSR's totalitarian tendencies increasing. The repressive mechanisms of the Bolshevik state were disappearing, but the more subtle forms of coercion and repression that were similarly prevalent in the West were on the rise.

Brandeis University provided an ideal environment for Marcuse to explore the intellectual repercussions of *Eros and Civilization* and *Soviet Marxism*. When set side by side, the two books formed an incongruous pair. Although both works emphasized the repressive dangers of contemporary society, *Eros and Civilization* sounded a strong note of optimism, while *Soviet Marxism* painted a bleak picture in which the horrors of Bolshevik society seemed comparable with the soft totalitarianism of the West. How would he reconcile these positions as the 1960s began?

Marcuse pursued this task in his classes and public speeches at Brandeis. This new university, located just outside of Boston, aggressively sought a first-rate faculty, and its administration was not afraid to hire scholars with strong credentials but unorthodox views. Although Marcuse's frank embrace of Marxism and leftist political causes periodically troubled the university's president, Abram Sacher, Marcuse was granted a great deal of freedom at Brandeis.[58] As a predominantly Jewish school, moreover, its student body, as Todd Gitlin remembers, included an unusually large number of red-diaper babies.[59] Like Madison and Berkeley, the suburban town of Waltham, Massachusetts, was a site of 1950s bohemianism and radicalism. Thus, not only was Marcuse able to develop his radical perspectives in courses such as "History of Political Theory" or "The Welfare State and the Warfare State," but he was also able to publicly seek a political and philosophical resolution to the incongruous implications that arose from *Eros and Civilization* and *Soviet Marxism.*

Some of his views deeply disturbed other members of the Brandeis faculty. Irving Howe and Lewis Coser, two of the university's most prominent voices from the Left, initially embraced Marcuse. Both knew him from his time in New York with the Horkheimer Circle, and they invited him to be a semi-regular contributor to their new magazine, *Dissent.*[60] By 1956, however, Marcuse had a serious falling out with both Howe and Coser. Although there are no written documents in the Marcuse archive to either confirm or deny the accounts of his Brandeis colleagues, Howe and Coser retrospectively recounted that the cause was Marcuse's refusal to condemn the Soviet repression in East Germany and Hungary. Howe and his friends were steadfast proponents of democratic socialism, and they perceived Marcuse's position as a defense of Stalinism.[61] The Brandeis Archives, however, shed more light on Marcuse's controversial position. Reporters Rachel Price and Ruth Feinberg published an article for the university newspaper, *The Justice,* indicating not only that Marcuse's position was more complex and nuanced than either Howe or Coser recalled, but also that members of the student audience were not outraged by his views:

The same facts can be interpreted in many ways. The way in which an analysis of the facts about Poland and Hungary led to radically different conclusions at last night's SPEAC meeting hinged upon divergent visions . . . Dr. Marcuse presented the logic of History. By asking and answering the question: Is the revolt in Hungary a revolution or a counter-revolution, he explained the activities as generating a spontaneous workers' movement against an oppressive Communistic regime. This movement, however, was joined by forces which are reactionary. Dr. Marcuse recounted the fascistic history of Catholic, agrarian Hungary, and commented that the superimposed communist government could not have imbued the revolutionaries with any Communistic, socialistic, or democratic ideals. Therefore, the revolution was, in reality, a counter-revolution which would tend to reinstate the status quo before Communist control—a status quo consisting of militarism,

large land ownership, nationalism, clericalism, and fascism . . . An analysis
of the facts led Dr. Marcuse to the conclusion that it would be ideologi-
cally impossible to side with either the Soviet intervention or the counterrevolutionary forces; he would side with "those who spoke at first but were
silenced, and who will speak again."[62]

Far from being a defense of Stalinism, Marcuse's view was consistent
with the views expressed in *Soviet Marxism*. While Marcuse had no sympathy for the Soviet invasion, his experiences in the Office of Strategic Services made it impossible for him to endorse the unqualified support of the
Hungarian uprising that Howe or Coser expressed.

Brandeis students, nevertheless, remained fond of Marcuse despite—
and perhaps because of—some of his controversial views. Although some
may have embraced him for articulating unpopular opinions during a conformist and complacent era, most were attracted to the substance of what
he offered to them. Marcuse was a difficult instructor, and his students
willingly accepted the demands he placed on them. In part, his courses
challenged Brandeis students by introducing the Continental tradition
that shaped his own thinking. Kant, Hegel, Marx, Husserl, and Heidegger
all figured prominently in his courses, which highlighted the dialectical
methods and negative thinking of Critical Theory.[63] For his best students,
Marcuse provided seminars on political philosophy and German Idealism, and he encouraged and supported them in gaining grants to study in
Frankfurt with Adorno and the other members of the Institut für Sozialforschung.[64] And he gained much from his students and his time at
Brandeis. The period in Waltham was important for the development of
his thought. One must bear in mind that Marcuse spent most of his professional life prior to his appointment at Brandeis in nonteaching roles,
and the transition to an American college campus represented a new and
invigorating change. Unlike the German universities where he had been
educated, higher education in the United States provided greater contact
between faculty and students. Marcuse grew to love this distinction. As
Peter Marcuse recalled:

> I think my father found the more informal and open atmosphere of the US
> more congenial than the more rigid and hierarchical relationships tradi-
> tionally found in Germany . . . both Horkheimer and Adorno were stiff—

what one might today call uptight—in their personal posture, Horkheimer to the point of pomposity. I remember as a little boy being told to be on my best behavior when we went to visit Horkheimer and his wife. My father simply liked the American manner more than the German.[65]

The American classroom, therefore, became a transformative environment for Marcuse. It provided him with a model for the kind of intellectual liberation that he wrote about later in connection with the New Left, and it helped him to recognize that the "great refusal" might be sitting right in front of him. Marcuse acknowledged this debt when he dedicated his essay "Repressive Tolerance" to his students at Brandeis.

During the late 1950s and early 1960s, Marcuse completed the transition from being a European thinker to being an American intellectual.[66] Although he had lived in the United States for nearly three decades, his work for the Horkheimer Circle and the U.S. government concentrated on predominantly European issues. He had assimilated aspects of American thought (particularly with regard to the social sciences), but his outlook remained European. Even his work of the 1950s represented a continuation of his earlier interests and preoccupations. *Eros and Civilization* and *Soviet Marxism* stemmed from issues with which he had been fascinated since his first years with the Institut für Sozialforschung. *One-Dimensional Man,* however, marked a departure. Although it represented a continuation of a theoretical method and perspective that remained European in both origin and orientation, Marcuse used these European methods to focus his attention on the United States. In part, this also may explain the book's appeal. Instead of disclosing the mysteries of Hegel and Freud to an English-speaking audience or examining the details of Soviet ideology and society, *One-Dimensional Man* sought to diagnose the American, Cold War condition. Although its argument could apply just as easily to Western Europe, its cultural and political landscape was dominated by the nuclear arms race (the danger of which was highlighted by the Cuban missile crisis), U.S. habits of consumption, American analytic philosophy, the unusual world of American labor, and the American mass media. The United States had become the primary target for his Critical Theory of society.

To most scholars of the Horkheimer Circle, *One-Dimensional Man* represented Marcuse's contribution to the group's theoretical conclusions that arose from Horkheimer and Adorno's *Dialectic of Enlightenment.*[67] Seeing the United States as a prophetic model for Western development, both books formulated a nightmare vision of late capitalism, in which reason had become obliterated, freedom had been surrendered, and history could finally be perceived as a steady descent into barbarism. In a sense, these books came to embody the sense of tragedy that pervaded Walter Benjamin's *Theses on the Philosophy of History,* but they charted territory that Benjamin could not have foreseen because of his untimely death. Benjamin witnessed the horrors of two world wars, and these obliterated his last remnants of hope. *Dialectic of Enlightenment* surpassed Benjamin because it more clearly diagnosed the problems set in motion by modernity, and it looked beyond the catastrophe of the two world wars by examining the emerging contours of advanced industrial society evident in the United States. *One-Dimensional Man,* however, moved beyond the territory explored by Horkheimer and Adorno. Although its basic argument was certainly similar, Marcuse again extended the historical scope of the analysis by encompassing the Cold War world. Unlike many of the other members of the Horkheimer Circle, Marcuse remained devoted to the original goal of Critical Theory. Instead of taking on administrative responsibilities or more specialized disciplinary pursuits, Marcuse continued to work toward a comprehensive theory of Western civilization. *One-Dimensional Man* represented his greatest contribution to Critical Theory's original mission.

One-Dimensional Man contends that in the Cold War era, Western societies, primarily the United States, simultaneously generate wanton waste and unimaginably destructive capabilities, as well as affluence and the perception of security. This contradiction, Marcuse argues, was exacerbated by the fact that these irrational conditions were rationalized. These societies followed logics of their own—logics that camouflaged the contradictions and dangers. To make matters worse, technological productivity had not resulted in more freedom, as Marxism had predicted. Although the citizens of Western societies felt that they enjoyed greater freedom than any people before them, Marcuse insisted that their choices were limited and preselected, provocatively distinguishing between false freedoms and needs from true ones. His readers had the freedom to choose between laundry detergents, but lacked the more empowering ability to make choices that dramatically affected their own lives or psyches.

Unlike the Communist East, the countries of the West did not enforce this paradoxical set of dangerous conditions on their populations through terror. Nevertheless, Marcuse argued, the West was trapped in a more insidious form of soft totalitarianism rooted in technology and instrumental reason. The lure of Positivism and instrumental thought, as Horkheimer and Adorno had argued, interfered with man's ability to consider anything except the status quo. Instead of seeking to understand reality, contemporary American thinkers simply described it. The distinction was significant. In Marcuse's view, the Positivist, instrumental mentality caused too many of his contemporaries to surrender their capability of seeing two-dimensionally. Instead of both perceiving the world as it was and how it might be, Western citizens became one-dimensional thinkers. Thus, they abandoned the basic critical impulse behind Western philosophy. Unable to envision the good life or to rationally evaluate contemporary society, "one-dimensional man" abandoned all interest in the past or the future and focused on the present and the mindless fulfillment of false needs through consumption.

One-Dimensional Man's bleak view of American society irked many in U.S. academic circles. At a time when so many prominent intellectuals heralded the "the end of ideology," praised the coming of "postindustrial society," and looked in wonder at America's affluent society, Marcuse's book struck a discordant note. Not only did he not join the self-congratulatory chorus of American conservatives, but also he expressed an agenda equally hostile to that of most liberals. In his eyes, the whole system was rotten. The welfare state merely stabilized and bolstered an essentially destructive socioeconomic system. *One-Dimensional Man* did appeal, however, to other dissenters who worried about recent developments in the United States and their repercussions. For many of the emerging voices of cultural dissent, Marcuse's book provided a sociostructural analysis explaining the subjective and aesthetic fallout. Thinkers such as Erich Fromm, David Riesman, and Paul Goodman were critical of the United States in the early 1960s, but their analyses focused on the psychological and emotional emptiness present among increasing segments of the population. Marcuse attacked these same conditions, but he also presented a totalizing analysis of the structural apparatus that caused them, the ideological apparatus that hid this structure, and the overall historical consequences.

One-Dimensional Man also irked the Marxists. Although Marcuse pinpointed monopoly capitalism as the structural dynamic that created one-dimensional men, he rejected most of the traditional tenets of Marxism. Unlike Marx, Marcuse insisted that technological progress was not inherently liberating. As the United States demonstrated, technical mastery engulfed all spheres of society with largely negative effects. Instead of liberating people from capitalist labor, American technological progress de-radicalized the proletariat and solidified the domination of monopoly capital. Alienation remained pervasive not only among the working class but also among white-collar workers. Nevertheless, all of these groups were more integrated within the system. The results represented an utter repudiation of Marx's expectations. Through its incorporation, the proletariat was no longer the revolutionary negation of capitalism. Furthermore, owners and management had vanished within the corporatization and bureaucratization of American monopoly capitalism. Unlike the conspiratorial "power elite" of C. Wright Mills, Marcuse insisted that the traditional targets of class resentment had grown depersonalized and diffuse. Were a significant revolutionary force available, it would struggle to seize control of the political and economic levers.

Although Marcuse's prognosis was overwhelmingly negative, he was able to pinpoint small causes for hope. As the East and the West moved beyond a developmental point of no return, there remained people within both "one-dimensional societies" who refused to play along or, in the case of the United States, were excluded from the comforts of the country's one-dimensional society. Civil rights protesters, racial minority groups, bohemian artists, intellectuals, and countercultural radicals remained outside of the smooth-functioning system that Marcuse described. Such people had the ability to push beyond the boundaries established by the one-dimensional worldview. By seeking to understand history and philosophy and by committing themselves to the theoretical challenges of the Cold War age, these nonconformists might achieve the capacity to imagine a more progressive, satisfying, and just world. Suggesting a cross-fertilization of artistic impulses and philosophical rigor, Marcuse called for a marriage of imagination and reason. Such a liberation of mind, however, remained the first and essential step toward social transformation and reorganization. One had to recognize the extent of the problem before one could ponder strategies for changing it. Finding solace in the words of Walter Benjamin,

Marcuse thus ended *One-Dimensional Man* with the paradoxical formulation: "It is only for the sake of those without hope that hope is given to us."[68] Marcuse's critical theory of Cold War society produced a frightening interpretation of the political, economic, and cultural realities of the 1960s. It uncovered the underbelly of Kennedy's Camelot. The absolute negativity of the vision, however, was precisely the source of hope for those who were willing to see it. By alerting people to the problems, Marcuse hoped to mobilize the forces for change.

chapter 8

MARCUSE'S MENTORS

The American Counterculture and the
Guru of the New Left

By now, all of us probably share a fairly common view of Herbert Marcuse when it comes to the 1960s. His name and image are linked to the emergence of the New Left in countless history and philosophy textbooks. We've seen the photographs of the solemn, old philosopher surrounded by hundreds and sometimes thousands of earnest young faces. We've heard the tales of the wall posters that appeared at the height of the student unrest in Paris's Latin Quarter and in Rome linking Marcuse to a revolutionary pantheon including the likes of Marx and Mao. Some may even be aware of the public condemnations and protests that dogged Marcuse at the end of his career at the University of California San Diego (UCSD), when he was attacked by the likes of the American Legion, California's governor Ronald Reagan, and the vice president of the United States, Spiro Agnew.[1]

Marcuse became a celebrity in the spring of 1968, and his days in the media spotlight lasted nearly as long as the movement to which his legacy has become linked. But his relationship with the New Left, particularly in the United States, is far more complex than the mainstream press of that era realized. When Marcuse's name emerged in connection with so many of the protests of 1968, the country's news organizations sought him out. They read his books and attempted to make sense of them; they attended his speaking engagements; and they tracked him down to his home in La Jolla, California. Reporters pressed him to discuss his analysis of contemporary America, to explain the basis for his profound discontent with such an affluent society, and to elaborate his positions regarding "repressive tolerance" and "counterviolence." Marcuse's responses were characteristically witty and provocative, and his views clearly shared much in common with the students protesting throughout the United States and Europe. Thus, Herbert Marcuse was dubbed a pied piper of student unrest, and a guru mythology was born.

Despite the Frankfurt School's significant contacts with American scholars and public intellectuals throughout the war years and the early Cold War, it was the reception of Marcuse during the 1960s, 1970s, and 1980s that established the academic reputation of the Frankfurt School in the United States. A casual perusal of the biographies of Marcuse and the secondary literature on Critical Theory might lead one to expect a broad and varied reception of Marcuse's thought within the writings of American student protesters and countercultural figures.[2] After all, Marcuse was a sophisticated social theorist, and one can only imagine the difficulties that his writings presented to American college students during the 1960s. This secondary literature regarding Marcuse even might cause historians to expect that a richly complex picture of the many impulses and agendas that were incorporated within the diverse world of the American New Left could be uncovered, in part, through the receptions of Marcuse available in archival sources and oral histories of the late 1960s and early 1970s. Such an analysis of these sources, however, reveals a very different result.

Marcuse's reception and influence among the New Left and the counterculture in the United States was neither as large nor as substantive as either the media of the 1960s or many subsequent historians of the New Left and Critical Theory have reported. True, there were strong pockets of reception—a group in Madison, Wisconsin, connected with the journal *Studies on the Left* produced an early and robust series of writings about Marcuse and the Frankfurt School, the early volumes of *Telos* and *New German Critique* represented some of the most sustained efforts to discuss and translate Critical Theory in North America, and there were broader cohorts of graduate students in the fields of philosophy, history, sociology, political science, and comparative literature who were deeply affected by their encounters with Marcuse and the Frankfurt School—but the typical undergraduates of the late 1960s who flocked to SDS and considered themselves countercultural were not, by and large, the protégés of Herbert

Marcuse. Students at Brandeis, UCSD, and the other campuses throughout the University of California system are clearly the exceptions to the
broader pattern, because Marcuse was among these students and was engaged with specific issues on their campuses. But the broader "Movement"
was more distanced from the Marcuse phenomenon. The typical reader
and contributor to *New Left Notes* or *Ramparts* shared much in common
with many of Marcuse's moral and political sentiments, yet they unlikely
read or discussed, and clearly did not write about, his unique brand of
Critical Theory.

Marcuse himself discerned at least part of the reason for his lack of
impact within the American New Left. Throughout his public speeches
and correspondence with members of the student movement, he bluntly
expressed his frustration with the pervasive anti-intellectual tendencies
that existed within SDS and the broader counterculture. He recognized
the challenges that his writing and analyses presented to their U.S. audiences, but he declared that education, complexity, and sophistication were
essential tools for grasping the breadth and depth of the problems that
faced American society in the 1960s and 1970s. Thus, he eschewed the
simple slogans and rhetoric that would have facilitated his reception in
favor of a more demanding and uncompromising discourse that preserved
his thoughts within the philosophical, historical, and sociological contexts
from which they arose. One needed to know something about Plato, Kant,
Hegel, Marx, Weber, and Freud (or at least be willing to educate oneself
about such demanding writers) to grasp what Marcuse had to offer. The
liberation of an individual consciousness was a complicated and challenging endeavor, but it was the essential first step in the social transformation
that Marcuse had in mind. Thus, it is not hard to see why it was the more
intellectually curious graduate students of the Vietnam era who had some
of the most profound and enduring encounters with Marcuse's Critical
Theory.

Another related reason for Marcuse's limited appeal is the actual content of his thought. The early identity of SDS was shaped by activism, and
this remained a central component of the American New Left. The early
protesters for civil rights and against the Vietnam War saw themselves as
the heirs to a rich legacy of democratic activism and thought passed on
from the likes of Thomas Jefferson, Henry David Thoreau, and C. Wright
Mills.[3] Strategy, commitment, and action thus were the dominant topics

that guided the thought of organizations such as SDS and that built the sense of community enabling activists and members of the counterculture to see themselves as a "Movement" and "beloved community."[4] Marcuse, while not objecting to protest, civil disobedience, or revolutionary action, saw theory as an equal, if not more important, ally of practice. Because of his understanding of the processes of reification and his belief that a softer but more insidious form of totalitarianism was pervasive in the West, Marcuse insisted that practice without theory was crippling and potentially dangerous.[5] Consequently, he had misgivings about the utility of the democratic tradition that inspired student organizations such as SDS. But this is not to say, as some have claimed, that Marcuse was antidemocratic. Rather, he was deeply committed to the ideals of democracy, but his misgivings had been shaped by his own experiences with Germany's failed revolution of 1919. Having witnessed the collapse of the Workers' and Soldiers' Councils, the turmoil of the Weimar Republic, and the horrors of Nazism, Marcuse was acutely aware of the problems inherent in democracy. Revolutionary practice and democratic processes were all well and good, but they accomplished nothing if people chose to be unfree. Thus, Marcuse's analysis of American and European societies delivered a blistering critique of late-capitalist liberalism yet still maintained social democracy as a political ideal (but a form of social democracy that was better able to distinguish between true and false needs, as well as between forces of construction and destruction).[6] While the American New Left remained preoccupied by activism and framed its dissent in terms that were traditionally American, Marcuse emphasized critical reason and framed his ideas in relation to both his experiences and his philosophical training—both of which were distinctly German.

Marcuse's style and content were both formidable obstacles to his reception by American audiences. His work was read and discussed, but it could never have the influence that the media of the late 1960s imagined. Certainly, in Europe the situation was distinctly different. Students from across the Continent came from an educational system and from societies that shared more in common with the history, intellectual traditions, and assumptions that shaped Marcuse's ideas. Thus, they represented a more ideal audience for his writings. But Marcuse's European popularity and impact did not mean that a similar phenomenon had taken place in the United States, as the American press had assumed.

MARCUSE AND THE NEW LEFT:
THE TRADITIONAL ACCOUNT

Although academics praised *Eros and Civilization* and *One-Dimensional Man* was widely reviewed, Marcuse remained largely unknown to Americans before 1968. Despite the visibility of these books, his activities remained relatively consistent until the end of the decade. The one exceptional change was his move to California. On the heels of *One-Dimensional Man,* Marcuse was asked to retire from his position at Brandeis. Although some insist that the decision was largely because of increasing discomfort with his politics and activism, the request was triggered by his sixty-sixth birthday. Instead of fighting the move by the Brandeis administration, Marcuse accepted a job offer from the University of California at San Diego. Southern California seemed to suit him during the final phase of his life. He enjoyed the climate, walks on the beach, and the laid-back atmosphere. As many have quipped, La Jolla represented the antithesis of both New England and Europe. Nevertheless, this highly artificial environment transformed from the desert Southwest appealed to him. Perhaps, in part, it represented the perfect atmosphere to continue his thoughts on the United States' one-dimensional society. Amid the palm trees, shopping malls, suburban sprawl, and within driving distance of Hollywood, Marcuse continued his critique of U.S. society and culture.[7]

Although his political activities and engagement had increased with the escalation of the civil rights movement and the Vietnam War, Marcuse never could have expected to become a celebrity. Philosophers such as John Dewey no longer functioned as major public figures in American society. In addition to this basic fact of U.S. media culture, he was on the wrong side of the generation gap, and he was foreign. More important, American audiences could hardly be expected to easily digest his difficult writings. Unaware of the Continental context that shaped much of his thought and unfamiliar with the intellectual legacies from which he drew inspiration, most in the United States were ill-equipped to make sense of his work. Even today, it seems unimaginable that this man with this message would captivate the attention of so many people in the United States.

Marcuse's surprising rise to social and cultural prominence was not lost on the media of the period or on the historians looking back on it. Nearly everyone who has ever written about Marcuse has struggled with the mystery of his fame. Typically, all of these accounts begin with the spring of

1968.[8] Throughout this turbulent season of unrest, young people attacked their contemporary societies and affirmed their own revolutionary pantheon on wall posters and in pamphlets. Self-consciously proclaiming themselves a New Left, the student protesters embraced many of the traditional sources of radical inspiration (Marx, Lenin, Bakunin, Sorel, and Breton). They added new figures, however, to reflect their self-appraisal as a new vanguard. Predominantly, the new additions came from Third World liberation movements (Castro, Guevara, Mao, Ho Chi Minh, and Fanon). The most noticeable exception was Herbert Marcuse. Particularly when Italian students in Rome and French students in Paris displayed placards with the names "Marx, Mao, and Marcuse," the media swarmed to uncover who Marcuse was. Much to their surprise, he was not one of the glamorous revolutionaries of the developing world. Instead, he was a complex philosopher and social theorist living in Southern California. Most recognized that Marcuse did not serve the same function as the anti-imperialist revolutionaries. While Third World activists had strategic and symbolic importance, Marcuse represented another dimension of the New Left. If the others were the practical role models, Marcuse was the ideological mentor or guru.

Once the press arrived at this conclusion, it began to survey Marcuse's work and sought interviews with him. The more the media learned, however, the more surprising his link to the students appeared. Many publicly wondered whether the students actually read his work.[9] Marcuse provided a systematic critique of late capitalism. The students, meanwhile, were galvanized by causes such as the civil rights movement, university reform, and the Vietnam War. Marcuse, therefore, was not directly related to the primary issues provoking student protest. Others, however, linked Marcuse's improbable rise to a single book, *One-Dimensional Man*.[10] Those insisting on the tight linkage between Marcuse and the New Left argued that this book provided a systemic analysis that resonated with student fears and frustrations. Marcuse's book unmasked the forces that the New Left engaged in combat, and it explained the reasons for the student movement's failures to achieve many of the changes that it sought. With the help of Marcuse, the New Left was able to embrace more radical and revolutionary programs calling for a complete transformation of Western society. As a nameless French protester explained to a perplexed member of the media, "We see Marx as prophet, Marcuse as his interpreter, and Mao as the sword."[11]

To some, determining Marcuse's reception by the New Left and his relationship to the increasingly violent student protests represented a purely
academic issue. Depending on one's political views, the solution to this
inquiry either buoyed or sank Marcuse's posthumous reputation. Among
those looking back on the New Left with nostalgia and longing, the establishment of a more clear reception only elevated the status of a man
who was labeled by some as an armchair Marxist. To others, however, who
looked on the 1960s with disgust, a clarified connection between Marcuse
and the New Left would only find him more or less culpable in the irresponsible destructiveness of the era and its continued resonance in American culture.[12] Still more, though, is at stake than simply the extent of
Marcuse's influence on student revolutionaries, and the issues involved are
more important than the historical fortunes of a deceased prophet for a
defunct movement.

Discussions of Marcuse's relationship to the student movement, whether
written in the 1960s or published more recently by historians, construct
assumptions about the New Left. These accounts presuppose a trajectory
of New Left radicalism that may not be entirely accurate. Perhaps the New
Left was less consistent and more confused in its views than commentators traditionally have presented. Furthermore, maybe Marcuse appealed
to varying degrees among various segments of the student movement.
Instead of homogenizing the entire American New Left, perhaps we are
better served by trying to locate the fissures and fault lines that divided
the movement and led to its eventual implosion. As many acknowledge,
the Weathermen were not the inevitable outcome of the New Left's ideological development.[13] By thrusting Marcuse into this picture of the forces
that formed the ideology of the New Left, isn't Marcuse's legacy subject
to similar distortions? By tightening Marcuse's connection to the thought
of the New Left, all dissidents can be transformed into apocalyptic terror-
ists of a new "modernist Marxist" variety.[14] Such formulations distort the
meaning and legacy of the New Left.

Our historical understanding of Marcuse and his legacy similarly are
contorted by assumptions about his reception among student revolutionaries. Again, members of the media and historians formulated a relatively
simplistic picture of the final years of his career. Because so many accounts
emphasize the influence and importance of *One-Dimensional Man,* this
single book overshadows Marcuse's other writings from the period.[15] The

result is that other contributions from this era, "Repressive Tolerance," *An Essay on Liberation,* and *Counterrevolution and Revolt,* are forgotten.[16] One is left with the idea that Marcuse's thought changed very little during the turbulent years of the New Left. Absent is any consideration that Marcuse's views may have developed or changed as he was caught in the spotlight. More important, any consideration that the students may have influenced Marcuse is lacking. The following sections of this chapter reexamine this reception history and relationship between Marcuse and the New Left.

THE ROOTS OF THE U.S. NEW LEFT

The roots of Students for a Democratic Society (SDS) dated back several years before the publication of *One-Dimensional Man.* Its inception, furthermore, was less closely related to the Marcusean agenda. The American New Left was not mobilized by the rejection of political Marxism, as was the case in Europe. Marcuse's neo-Marxist formulations powerfully resonated with European youth angered by the parliamentarian power politics embraced by the older generation of politicians and labor union officials, but these circumstances were noticeably absent in the United States. The Old Left in the United States did not abandon its faith in Marx as its European counterparts had—it simply vanished. The reasons were complex. In part, the Old Left collapsed as a result of World War II. The war ended the Depression and inspired a sense of patriotism that was fatal to Old Left anti-Americanism. The postwar era brought new dangers, but it was also a period of triumph for both the nation and its citizens. The United States contributed significantly in the defeat of a formidable foe, and the conclusion of hostilities marked a return of the American dream. Communism was no longer fashionable or appealing in this new environment. Furthermore, Cold War anti-Communist coercion and intimidation eroded the Old Left's political base. Between the public witch hunts and the private harassment of suspected Communists and fellow travelers, many retreated into the shadows keeping their views and politics to themselves. Others gave up on Marxism altogether. The death blow for many, however, was the revelations of Khrushchev's "secret speech" of February 1956 in which he acknowledged the atrocities of the Stalinist police state. Following this momentous event, even the most stalwart party faithful had to acknowledge that the vociferous critics of the Soviet Union had been (at the very least) partially right about the nature of the Bolshevik state.

The New Left took shape as a self-conscious antithesis to the sense of frustration, failure, and angst that still pervaded the existing pockets of the Old Left. Inspired by the events of the early 1960s, Students for a Democratic Society took shape in an atmosphere of optimism, idealism, and reformism that accompanied the election of John F. Kennedy. Instead of constructing a proletarian movement as the Old Left had done, Alan Haber (the chief architect of SDS) built a movement based on youth.[17] By promoting as broad a platform as possible, SDS sought to build bridges between the factions of the traditional Left and its liberal allies. Instead of turning away red diaper babies and other Communist sympathizers, the New Left rejected the widely popular anti-Communism of the era. While conservatives, liberals, and Social Democrats continued to emphasize the centrality of anti-Communism to their political platforms, SDS struck a pluralist tone of anti-anti-Communism. It called attention to the abuses of McCarthyism and the reckless adventurism that anti-Communism caused in U.S. foreign policy. At the same time, however, SDS also embraced the grand social visions of the liberals. To a large extent, its discontent arose in response to the liberals' dreams not going far enough—an immanent critique of liberalism. Ultimately, the catalyst that brought these young students together and galvanized such a broad constituency of the political spectrum was the civil rights movement.

Outraged by the hypocrisy of a nation pledging itself to the causes of freedom and justice and then systematically withholding them from its largest racial minority group, the core that formed Students for a Democratic Society was captivated by the nonviolent protests of black students and demonstrators across the South. The lunch-counter sit-ins, following the principles of Thoreau's civil disobedience and Gandhi's nonviolent resistance, provoked the proponents of racism and discrimination to demonstrate their prejudice and injustice against blacks. Merely by trying to assert their civil and legal rights, African-American students and their supporters forced the nation to see the stark realities of the country's racial divide. Their actions were dramatic and powerful. At the same time that the sit-ins subverted southern Jim Crow practices, they juxtaposed the aggressive racism of the Southern whites with the stubborn nobility of southern blacks. The drama transfixed the country and resonated powerfully among northeastern and Midwestern college students.

For the early architects of Students for a Democratic Society, the sit-ins confirmed the effectiveness of direct action. The actions of a small minority had the ability to capture the attention of a nation, and these actions also had the ability to educate a public largely ignorant of a particular set of problems. Strategy, not ideology, had won supporters over to the civil rights movement. Much to the later detriment of the student movement, this lesson would prove to be impossible for the New Left to unlearn. Once activists came to see practice as preferable to theory, they refused to get bogged down in the difficulties and controversies that ideology raised. Instead of addressing such issues and running the risk of turning off possible supporters, they preferred to keep their movement openly ambiguous—to let their actions speak louder than their words.[18]

The early members of SDS traveled to the South on the "Freedom Rides" and participated in the voter registration drives of the "Freedom Summers." It is impossible to overestimate the transformative nature of these experiences for the students undertaking these journeys. The rural communities, the culture of the South, the poverty—all were eye-opening encounters that broadened the views of those traveling south from largely urban or suburban, white, middle-class communities. One also can not overestimate the sense of excitement and fulfillment that accompanied civil rights work. For Todd Gitlin, one of the great chroniclers of the New Left, the "Freedom Rides" gave the movement its entire character. They provided a sense of moral seriousness; they created a common tradition, style, and culture for the New Left; and they established a community of like-minded souls committed to public action on behalf of those excluded from America's promises.[19]

The primary figure responsible for giving voice to these sentiments and for laying out the purposefully broad political orientation for Students for a Democratic Society was Tom Hayden. The Port Huron Statement, the clearest embodiment of what the New Left stood for in its early years, was largely his creation. Although many of the details of the political platform were rewritten in committees and thus bore the handiwork of many, Hayden formulated the main ideological brushstrokes in June 1962.

His inspiration was C. Wright Mills. Years later, Hayden would write his master's thesis on Mills. At the time of the Port Huron Statement, however, Mills functioned as an intellectual mentor and role model for Students for a Democratic Society. Mills had been one of the few public thinkers of the 1950s not to loudly celebrate the United States. Where others saw a triumphant nation enjoying the fruits of its victory over fascism, Mills feared the tendencies he saw around him—increasing political and economic centralization, the peacetime military buildup, the transformations caused by the escalation of bureaucratization, and the rise of mass society. From his perspective, power had changed hands in the wake of World War II. Until that point, it was held in the hands of the public, where it had been intended to reside. During the era of the Cold War, however, it had been passed on to the corporations and government interests.

If these themes sound familiar to those of the Horkheimer Circle, it is not accidental. Although a direct line of reception is difficult to establish, Mills was well acquainted with the Institute for Social Research. After arriving at Columbia University in 1943, he became familiar with the scholarly terrain of Morningside Heights. He also began a brief foray into the world of the New York Intellectuals. In his free time, he settled into the circle around Dwight Macdonald and shared the group's quasi-Trotskyist concerns about bureaucratic collectivism. Meanwhile, Mills's professional life grew to be subsumed by Paul Lazarsfeld's Bureau of Applied Social Research. Although required to carry out the kind of statistical analysis that was Lazarsfeld's hallmark, Mills hated the work and grew to despise his involvement with the Bureau.[20] Like so many other left-leaning sociologists who passed through Columbia during the 1940s, the most senior member of the department to sympathize with his politics or his scholarly interests was Robert Lynd. By the mid-1940s, the questions surrounding Mills's acquaintance with Critical Theory disappear. As James Schmidt and others have discovered, Mills was one of the scholarly reviewers recruited by Oxford University Press to assist in evaluating Horkheimer's book *Eclipse of Reason*.[21]

Any and perhaps all of these contacts would have enabled Mills to become acquainted with the Horkheimer Circle. The New York Intellectuals, particularly the group around Dwight Macdonald (as we have noted), were briefly taken with the bleak outlook of the Institute during the 1940s. It is hard to imagine the work of the Institute not coming up in discussions among Macdonald and his friends during the years that Mills was closely involved with them. Lazarsfeld also could have functioned as an interlocutor between Mills and the Frankfurt School. The Bureau for Applied Social Research had worked closely with the Horkheimer Circle on several aspects of the *Studies in Prejudice*. In fact, some of Mills's professional duties might have been tangentially or directly connected with the Institute's work on anti-Semitism. Lynd, however, seems the most likely source of Mills's connection to the Institute. Mills, like Lynd, became consumed with the study of power in the wake of World War II. Lynd's work, which was more closely inspired by Neumann and his other friends from the Institute for Social Research, led to only one publication on the topic—an appropriation of Pollock's racket theory of society.[22] Mills, on the other hand, wrote on the topic of power throughout the late 1940s and 1950s and produced three classic monographs: *The New Men of Power* (1948), *White Collar* (1952), and *The Power Elite* (1956). Although it is clear that Lynd and Mills discussed the question of power frequently during their overlapping years at Columbia, it seems inconceivable that the former would not have alerted Mills to the thought of the Horkheimer Circle in view of the powerful pull that it exerted on Lynd.

Regardless of the conduit, evidence clearly shows that Mills was an acquaintance of the Horkheimer Circle. Irving Louis Horowitz, one of Mills's most acclaimed biographers, insists that his growing awareness and interest in Marxism originated from his contact with the Critical Theorists of the Institute for Social Research.[23] Although such a claim makes for an exciting piece of intellectual history, an examination of the Institute's archives does not bear the assertion out. No incontrovertible pieces of evidence exist that show the kind of scholarly relationship that Horowitz implies. It is clear, however, that Mills was more closely associated with the Horkheimer Circle than some might realize.[24] At the same time that he warned Hans Gerth (his former mentor, who was hoping to earn a post as a researcher with the newly returned Institut für Sozialforschung in Frankfurt), Mills actively pursued a Fulbright fellowship to come to Frankfurt himself. Although his primary desire was to experience European life for an extended period of time, he was also interested in pursuing research through the Institute and in teaching a course on empirical methods in sociology.[25] Something besides the promise of a semester or two abroad may have been pulling him toward the Institute.

Although there are striking similarities between some of the work of C. Wright Mills and the Horkheimer Circle, the most that one can say is that he shared a corresponding set of fears about the prospects for Western societies. Mills, like his counterparts from Frankfurt, maintained a

Weberian perspective, and they both searched for an escape route in the Marxian tradition. The methods and specific findings of the two, however, were markedly different. Aside from the broadest theoretical harmony, Mills's studies into the nature of power in Cold War America (*The New Men of Power, White Collar,* and *The Power Elite*) bore few similarities to the Horkheimer Circle's analysis. Instead, Mills's monographs showed his digestion of the Institute's thought, and his effort to move beyond them. While Horkheimer and Adorno nearly abandoned any hope in the future and clung to their ideal of critical reason, Mills ventured far past these strains of Continental nihilism and reassembled many of the same concerns with a pronounced American accent. Instead of locating hope in a radical reexamination of Freud as Marcuse and Fromm had done, Mills found something more tangible and powerful for American readers—he returned to the ideals of American democracy set forth by Jefferson and Paine (and amplified by closer contemporaries such as John Dewey). Although some might (and did) question whether Jeffersonian democracy ever existed in the United States and whether there was a historical basis for the kind of public that Mills envisioned, his utopia was grounded in distinctly American thoughts and traditions.

For Hayden and other early supporters of SDS, Mills's formulations were a powerful influence. The Columbia sociologist had hit upon a formula that appealed directly to the broad constituency that SDS sought to hold together. His diagnosis of the problems facing the United States shared much in common with not only the Horkheimer Circle but also many other radical groups. Throughout the 1950s, intellectuals not participating in the celebrations of American victory and success emphasized the alienation, emptiness, and powerlessness that many were feeling. Mills's thought thus harmonized with a wider chorus of discontent. At the same time, he located the solution to the country's ills in an indigenous set of beliefs. The answers to the problems facing the United States no longer had to be found in Europe or Russia. They were where people least expected to find them—in their own backyards, so to speak. Furthermore, unlike Communism, Mills's utopian formula achieved a perfect balance between individual and collective responsibility. The ideal of the yeoman farmer fulfilling his individual obligations to the democratic community was a powerful image when Jefferson constructed it, and its continued resonance helps explain its popularity among the New Left. Despite the fact that

Mills greatly romanticized the notion of early American democracy, his notion of face-to-face, "participatory" (as Tom Hayden called it) democracy was his lasting political and ideological legacy to SDS.

Beyond his appeal as a thinker, Mills also represented an attractive role model to many who gravitated to SDS in the early years. Mills was the self-styled, rugged individual who formed the antithesis to the powerless masses to whom he devoted so much of his writing. Ever since his arrival at Columbia University, he had been wildly out of step with the image and atmosphere of the Ivy League. He hailed from Texas, spoke nostalgically about the Wobblies, drove a motorcycle to class, and wore a leather jacket and blue jeans. In addition to this rebel persona that anticipated so much of the cultural style of the 1960s, Mills was an outspoken advocate of experience. He needed to build his own house, clear his own land, and repair his own motorcycle. These were essential tasks that could not be left to a specialist. Mills wanted to learn from these experiences and broaden himself as an individual. In his mind, these activities were not divorced from his life as a scholar. They broadened and deepened it. In this sense, both the Mills mythology and the man himself reinforced the essential link between theory and practice that was so important to the first members of Students for a Democratic Society.

Mills—by no means the only figure in Tom Hayden's intellectual pantheon—thus exerted literal and symbolic influence on Students for a Democratic Society. He certainly equipped the group with many of the most important tools used in building their "house of theory."[26] At the same time, Mills symbolically represented the marriage of theory and practice that captivated the early members of Students for a Democratic Society. Like the SDS founder, Alan Haber, Hayden sought to merge activism with analysis, and Hayden's concept of participatory democracy provided him with a compelling notion that also afforded flexibility to the organization. In connection with what he had learned from Mills, participatory democracy evoked the notion of a political tradition that had fallen into decline in recent years. SDS merely sought to reinvigorate the country by rediscovering the roots of the nation's political traditions. At the same time, the concept and the image of Mills created a bridge between the two core constituents within the movement. Participatory democracy provided enough substance to satisfy ideologues in search of a vision, but it also provided a broad enough set of ideals to justify a multitude of political actions and strategies. It thus successfully cemented the unstable coalition of radicals and intellectuals that the organization recruited. Both could find a home within the community of SDS. During the early years, Hayden's "house of theory" was no single-family dwelling. It was built to accommodate as many recruits as possible.

At the same time that these ideas and ideals were productive during the early history of SDS, they created flaws and fault lines that would eventually lead to the disintegration of the organization. Despite Mills's rhetoric and style, his primary function was as a sociological critic. Politics was one of his passions, but he hardly aspired to lead movements or direct strategies. He was a theorist (and a provocative one at that). As far as he was concerned, it did not matter how accurate he was about the origins and history of American democracy.[27] His fundamental purpose was to alert the country to the problems that had beset it. A political movement, however, could not concentrate on simply diagnosing social, cultural, and political ailments. People would be enticed by such criticism of the status quo, but constructive alternatives would galvanize their allegiance and commitment.

For a time, participatory democracy served as this constructive agenda for SDS. Because it was so vague and flexible, it could appeal to a broad coalition, and it could justify any number of possible actions. During the early years of SDS, participatory democracy was able to set the organization into motion on multiple fronts. By simultaneously pursuing the goals of nuclear disarmament, pacifism, and the organizing of poor, urban neighborhoods, SDS was able to broaden its membership and its analysis of American society. It failed, however, to export the ideal of participatory democracy outside of the movement. While local groups of activists experimented with the ideal and built strong communal ties, they were frustrated in their inability to spread their message or experiences beyond like-minded groups of students. Furthermore, the sense of identity and commitment inspired by activism tended to create a divide between them and the intellectuals of the organization. Direct involvement with social ills made the activists feel better, but it was no substitute for permanent solutions. With the coming of the Vietnam War and the spectacular growth of SDS, the inability to realize the promise of participatory democracy created confusion, factionalism, and frustration. Within a young, developing movement, this kind of uncertainty and failure could be endured. It created a more explosive situation when the movement was enormous, deeply hostile to the government, and beset with the same problems.

REASSESSING THE RELATIONSHIP
BETWEEN MARCUSE AND THE NEW LEFT

Students for a Democratic Society entered a distinctly new phase of its history during the mid-1960s, years of exponential political growth and dramatic ideological change. The Vietnam War and the high-profile position that SDS staked out within the antiwar movement attracted vast numbers of college students and members of the growing counterculture into the ranks of the organization. Although few translated into hard-core supporters, the new volunteers could be counted on for sporadic participation in the lives of local chapters. At the same time, the events of the early 1960s drastically altered the ideological position of SDS. In the wake of the Bay of Pigs, the SDS's position of anti-anti-Communism took on a new emphasis, moving toward a quiet sympathy for the Castro regime. The parent organization of Students for a Democratic Society, the League for Industrial Democracy (LID) became increasingly uneasy with rhetoric that it interpreted as pro-Communist or fellow-traveling. LID, as well as other Old Left circles, sought to intervene and change the course of SDS. LID's fiscal threats and bullying eventually resulted in the desired rhetorical modification, but the fallout of the clash had a permanent impact on SDS. It erected an insurmountable wall between the SDS and the factions of the Old Left that supported it in its infancy, and thus commenced the radicalization of SDS. In the opinion of Todd Gitlin, the early clash with LID over anti-anti-Communism welded SDS together through the heat of political battle, but it also scarred the student organization.[28] Originally, the founders of SDS had adopted a style and stance guided by a shared vision of pluralism. As their sentiments moved them further to the left, however, pluralism was abandoned and unforeseen ideological assumptions crept into the thinking and strategies of SDS. The more such views hardened, the more participatory democracy lost its meaning and function for SDS. As SDS increasingly stopped talking about theory to appeal to a consensus of student activists, the theoretical mooring that was the basis of that consensus disintegrated.

The Cuban missile crisis, the Vietnam War, and the early setbacks of the civil rights movement further contributed to the leftward movement of views within SDS and further obliterated the illusion of pluralism. These three events undermined the last vestiges of confidence in Kennedy-era liberalism, and the positions that SDS adopted toward these issues put it at odds with former liberal allies and constituents. Kennedy's foreign policy toward Cuba and Vietnam proved him to be little different from his predecessors. He believed in anti-Communism, nuclear deterrence, and the domino theory just as his political opponents had. The final betrayal came at the Atlantic City Democratic National Convention, when the liberal–labor coalition that dominated the party betrayed the civil rights program. By refusing to recognize the political arm of the Student Nonviolent Coordinating Committee (SNCC), the Mississippi Freedom Democratic Party, the Democratic Party prevented the voices of the civil rights movement from being heard and from helping to shape the party platform. To members of the SDS who had gained their political identity through this movement, the debacle at Atlantic City was simply one more betrayal by the liberal establishment. It bolstered the growing sense of us versus them, young versus old, radical versus Old Left, SDS versus liberal.[29] These developments of the early 1960s clearly made the New Left new, but they also generated ideological and theoretical repercussions that SDS was unprepared to handle. The Port Huron Statement and its central concept of participatory democracy did not constitute the basis for a solid political platform under such changed circumstances.

The factor that eventually raised theory to a level of the utmost importance within SDS was the visibility that accompanied the Vietnam War. By 1966, Students for a Democratic Society could no longer use the idea of participatory democracy as the overarching vision for its multi-issue agenda. It sought to appeal beyond the student community and the issue of Vietnam.[30] Some SDS leaders envisioned the organization becoming a key player within the U.S. political arena.[31] Not content, therefore, to merely become synonymous with student opposition to the war, the leaders of SDS recognized that they needed to develop a clearer ideological agenda if they wished to maintain their support and to mobilize their new recruits for anything besides ending the war. They sought to take stock of the lessons learned from the confrontations that SDS experienced with liberals and the Old Left. They wished to evaluate their experiences with participatory democracy. They hoped to review their pasts as activists and to follow up with the social analysis and lessons that were supposed to accompany action.[32]

To meet such goals, the SDS national committee encouraged the formation of the Radical Education Project (REP). Designed and implemented as an independent entity within SDS, the creators of REP sought to devise an educational program for SDS that could be copied on campuses and in local chapters throughout the country. The implementation committee was composed of former SDS leaders, propagandists, and intellectuals (such as Alan Haber, Jerome Badanes, Michael Locker, Carl Oglesby, Richard Flacks, Todd Gitlin, Robert Ross, and Lee Webb), and their shared goal was to seek a common ideological perspective for the New Left. Dick Ochs perhaps summarized the hopes and goals of the implementation committee best when he expressed these words of encouragement in a letter to Alan Haber: "Your draft for a REP is a great idea and something of this sort is long overdue. I believe such systematic studies are necessary because SDS needs to recapture the intellectual dynamism which characterized its early growth."[33] What Ochs and the members of the REP implementation committee sought, however, was an improvement over the idea of participatory democracy that was inadequate for the complexities facing SDS by the mid-1960s.

The tools that REP pioneered to pursue its agenda were pamphlets, reading lists, a network of traveling speakers, and discussion groups. Instead of encouraging local chapters to devote all of their time and energy to direct actions to stop the war, REP encouraged them to seek out an understanding of the problems facing the country and the potential routes toward reform. In addition, REP wished to support and nurture "radicals in the professions." In order to make the shift from a student movement to a popular movement, SDS needed to find a way to be relevant for people after they graduated.

The prominence and successes SDS already achieved were largely driven by the moral outrage of college students. Such moral sentiments, however, failed to diagnose or address the systemic problems that many saw infecting the United States. Education, theory, and analysis were necessary to propose alternatives that made sense, to uncover strategies that could be effective, and to assemble a shared ideological vision that could transcend the issue of the Vietnam War. As Haber wrote in his draft statement for REP:

Democratic radicalism is renewing itself around a basically moral proposition that people should have the opportunity to participate in shaping the decisions and the conditions of economic, political and cultural existence, which affect their lives and destinies . . . The vitality and the idealism of the new movements are related in part to the directness of this relatively un-ideological moral position. But a left movement requires more than idealism and passion. Intellectually, it must have knowledge: it must have understanding and analysis; and it must have a social program and a prescription which translates radical vision into concrete realities. Organizationally, it must have roots and relevance to every major section of the American community: and it must catalyze and encompass insurgency in every institution or sphere of life that it would seek to transform . . . The task of the movement, now, is not only to seek immediate political objectives—locally and nationally. It must create, or coalesce anew, a generation of democrats—people, not only youth, who will maintain a radical value commitment and identity and a functional relation with the "movement." It must bring about opportunities for communication which allow us to build on another's thought, to learn from one another's experience and to reinforce one another in action.[34]

Moral outrage and direct action had been adequate for SDS in its early years, but they were inadequate to the challenges and goals facing SDS in the late 1960s. Unable to imagine an ideological ideal beyond the traditional rhetoric of participatory democracy, Haber envisioned REP as a force that could lead SDS beyond the realization of Hayden's old ideal. Haber's use of the word *radicalism,* however, signals the abrupt changes that SDS had undergone since Port Huron.[35]

Marcuse thus joined the ranks of a large pantheon of intellectuals and theorists that the REP began to promote. By no means, however, was he one of the most visible figures being studied at this early stage.[36] Although Left intellectuals were already aware of *One-Dimensional Man* and its critique of advanced industrial society, most members of SDS (who typically preferred action to theory) were unaware of it in 1966. When one takes into account the vast literature that was produced by SDS, as well as the even larger group of underground newspapers that identified with the counterculture, it is amazing how infrequently Marcuse, his ideas, or his writings are even mentioned.[37] Although Marcuse biographers insist that *One-Dimensional Man* was highly visible and influential within the U.S. New Left before 1968, few of the underground newspapers or radical periodicals of the period confirm this. In fact, Marcuse's name is rarely found in any popular New Left writings before 1968. Where he does come up, there are few engagements with his thought or attempts to report on it. Although this does not mean that a reception of Marcuse's Critical Theory was not taking place (people could have been digesting and discussing *One-Dimensional Man*), it was not taking place publicly in print in the way that one might expect after reading Marcuse's biographers and the reporters from the mass media of the era.

Trent Schroyer, for example, studied sociology and philosophy at the New School for Social Research in the late 1960s, and represents a scholar still committed to many of the intellectual and political ideals that Marcuse espoused in the late 1960s. From Schroyer's vantage point, the thought of Marcuse was pervasive. Although largely written about in more scholarly journals such as *Telos,* Schroyer believes that Marcuse's influence transcended his scholarly audience and was widespread within the broader student movement. As Schroyer recalled, people frequently spoke of Marcuse and afforded him tremendous respect.[38] Similarly, another scholar with close ties to Marcuse and his work, Jeremy Shapiro, indicated that Marcuse was omnipresent in the circles that he moved in during the 1960s and 1970s—warning that one must be careful to draw conclusions purely from the written and archival record of the era.[39]

At the same time, however, there are others with close ties to SDS that tend to confirm the findings from the written records. When Tom Hayden, for example, was asked about the reception and influence of Marcuse within the Movement, he revealed that he owned Marcuse books but didn't read much of them. In general, Hayden recalled finding Marcuse's work too pessimistic and theoretical to have much resonance in a popular movement such as SDS. In fact, Hayden queried me about how one might come to expect that Marcuse had an influence in SDS.[40]

Richard Flacks came to the University of Michigan as a graduate student in 1958 and immediately got involved with the civil rights movement and disarmament. Both led him on a collision course with the other creators of SDS in Ann Arbor. Like his friend Tom Hayden, Flacks had similar recollections of Marcuse's relationship to the student movement:

> SDS did have strong intellectual roots, but Marcuse was not among them. *One-Dimensional Man* was not I think much noticed when it first came

out—among New Left activists. "Repressive Tolerance" was. Its timing (for better or worse) was excellent since it seemed to legitimate protest aimed at disrupting the speech of "Establishment" figures. Of course around that time is when mainstream media were hyping Marcuse as a New Left father figure; I remember being amused at that coverage since it certainly didn't fit the reality of his then reputation. Once that hyping occurred his stature no doubt changed, and his stream of writings in the late 1960s certainly resonated with the moods of the Movement. My own thought at the time was not that this was the source of the ideas about resistance so much as trying to codify or legitimate ideas that were already very much being expressed within the movements.[41]

A careful examination of *Studies on the Left,* a radical journal emerging from history and sociology graduate students at the University of Wisconsin, confirms Flacks's view. Although a translation of Walter Benjamin's "The Work of Art in the Epoch of Mechanical Reproduction" appeared in only the second edition, the rest of the Frankfurt School was largely ignored. Instead, an enormous emphasis was placed on the work of C. Wright Mills and contemporary events in the American South, in American cities, in Cuba, in South America, and in Vietnam.

Todd Gitlin, another prominent sociologist, was not among the founders of SDS in Ann Arbor, but he was active in the branch of SDS at Harvard University. Gitlin was elected president of SDS in 1963. When queried about his own perspective on Marcuse's reception within SDS, Gitlin replied:

Increasingly after 1965 and especially in 1968–69, most of the SDS leadership was not terribly serious, intellectually. In their circles, I would doubt you would find many but glancing references to any intellectuals outside the Marxist-Leninist-Guevarist-Maoist orbit. Since Herbert Marcuse was theoretically so disinclined to find grounds for strategy or action, he was not terribly useful—except to confirm gloom.[42]

Despite acknowledging the impact of *One-Dimensional Man* in his own memoir of the 1960s, Gitlin's more recent view is reminiscent of the perspective of Tom Hayden. *One-Dimensional Man* was too grim—and *An Essay on Liberation,* which came out in 1969, was "too giddy."

David Wellman observed and participated in the student movement at the University of California in Berkeley, where he was a veteran of SDS and a member of its REP. Although he recalled that some activists such as Mike Davis, Ron Aronson, and Stanley Aronowitz were keenly interested in Marcuse, this was not the case for him or for most of the students that he knew. As Wellman explained:

> I'm not surprised that you haven't found much mention of Marcuse in the archival materials on the American New Left. I don't remember him being an important figure to us during the Radical Education Project. Our idea of education during that period didn't pertain to theoretical, philosophical issues but much more basic understandings of American society and how to change it. That said, I do remember people reading *One-Dimensional Man* later on . . . I can't estimate how many other people were reading it. I guess there was some interest since I recall discussing it with people in informal settings. I personally was turned-off by the book. It struck me as incredibly pessimistic and unhelpful to people trying to make change. I read him to be saying that change was impossible given the one-dimensionality of modern society and since that was what I was trying to do, the book was less than useful to me. It was an argument for why my activism was doomed to failure. I did, however, find his notion of repressive tolerance incredibly important. It gave voice to my experience in the student and civil rights movement. It gave a name to the way we were treated by people in power.[43]

Numerous other veterans of the "Movement" expressed strikingly similar memories and experiences with Marcuse's writings. Although some, such as Stanley Aronowitz, remember that *One-Dimensional Man* was much discussed, they also confirm that Marcuse's writings were too philosophical to have been of widespread interest within the American student movement.[44] Thus, the oral histories tend to confirm the written record preserved in radical publications such as *New Left Notes, Studies on the Left*, and *Ramparts*. Prior to Marcuse's emergence in the media spotlight of 1968, *One-Dimensional Man* was not a particularly significant book for members of the American New Left, and Marcuse was far from a guru. A receptive audience for his perceived pessimism and intellectual rigor was lacking within the student movement. If student radicals were familiar with Marcuse at all, activists were acquainted with his essay "Repressive Tolerance," which appeared in 1965 and generated a flurry of critiques by socialists, Social Democrats, liberals, and conservatives. Therefore, even if one was not directly familiar with Marcuse's essay, one could be aware of the many summaries and attacks of it.

In "Repressive Tolerance," Marcuse turned the concept of free expression on its head in a critique of U.S. society. To some, the fact that he was a scholar (someone who most would expect to be entirely in favor of openness and the free flow of ideas) made these formulations particularly shocking. That a democratic society, especially universities, required the freedom of speech was a cornerstone of the ideology of the United States. In spite of, and perhaps because of, its importance, Marcuse located the appropriate justifications for his case against "pure tolerance" by unleashing an analytic critique of American society that harked back to *One-Dimensional Man*. But where the latter offered hope to the hopeless through its dissection of contemporary society, "Repressive Tolerance" presented a moral and political justification for rejecting the lies and hypocrisies of the system by demonstrating the moral necessity of censorship and counterrepression. Grounding his argument in the famous Holmes decision, Marcuse shared the view that a "clear and present danger" to society justified the suspension of civil rights.[45] Marcuse differed, however, in his definition of a "clear and present danger." In his view, the United States itself during the 1960s represented such a threat. American militarism, racism, and anti-Communism were repressive and destructive. These policies and the country that sponsored them had to be opposed by responsible intellectuals and activists. Silence and respect for the freedom of speech only bolstered this corrupt and violent society. The "pure tolerance" of those obeying the demands of a free society only contributed to the atmosphere of unfreedom rampant in the United States. Such behavior only strengthened the establishment and its tyrannical policies. "Pure tolerance" had to be abandoned in favor of "liberating tolerance." As Marcuse explained, "Liberating tolerance, then, would mean intolerance against movements from the Right and toleration of movements from the Left. As to the scope of this tolerance and intolerance: . . . it would extend to the stage of action as well as of discussion and propaganda, of deed as well as of word."[46] Instead of remaining silent out of respect for the rights of those one opposed, radicals rejecting the "System" were entitled and obligated to combat it by stifling it.

Marcuse's call to action did not shirk away from the controversial topic of violence. As Marcuse argued, "The historical calculus of progress (which is actually the calculus of the prospective reduction of cruelty, misery, suppression) seems to involve the calculated choice between two forms of political violence: that on the part of the legally constituted powers (by their legitimate action, or by their tacit consent, or by their inability to prevent violence), and that on the part of potentially subversive movements."[47] While Marcuse proclaimed that the violence of the legally constituted powers tended to be regressive, he did not say the same of the violence practiced by subversive movements. No matter how often or insistently he denied his support of violence in speeches and interviews throughout the late 1960s and 1970s, he did make a strong case for counterviolence in his essay "Repressive Tolerance." The pacifist civil disobedience of the early civil rights and antiwar movements no longer made sense. Both were noble, but foolish. The United States was a brutal and violent society. Prisoners, racial minorities, women, and the people of Third World countries were all aware of this fact. All were frequently the victims of such systemic savagery. Puny acts of civil disobedience were not enough. Desperate times called for dramatic measures. Marcuse drew a distinction between the violence of the "System" and the violence of radicals in search of reform, freedom, and justice. Systemic violence could only be matched and overcome by counterviolence that was capable of eliminating it.[48] Abstract rights and abstract normativity no longer mattered. One either supported American society and its policies or one opposed them. The choice was simple so long as one was able to share Marcuse's visions of true and false, right and wrong, and just and unjust. Once one determined which side he or she was on, the traditional moral and ethical imperatives would follow. Those supporting the "System" could continue to play by its rules. Those opposed, however, had no use remaining constrained by them.

His colleagues in the academy bitterly rejected the arguments put forth in "Repressive Tolerance." To most, Marcuse's definition of freedom contradicted the views of liberalism dominant in the United States. Freedom did not mean autonomy, as Marcuse understood it. Freedom, rather, represented an "ordered system of liberties and restraints."[49] It was a framework that prevented individuals from trampling on one another. These conditions were necessary for people to achieve their greatest potential, thus benefiting the collective. On top of that, Marcuse's colleagues could not share his especially bleak view of individualism and reason within the late-industrial world of 1960s America. Whereas Marcuse saw a country sinking into greater depths of waste and brutality, they saw the United States enjoying unprecedented successes and bravely protecting the West from Communism. His peers, consequently, disparaged his venom for "pure tolerance." In fact, to many, Marcuse's faith in his evaluation of the United States made him comparable to classic totalitarians. As David Spitz wrote in *Dissent:* "Marcuse's argument is essentially, though in reverse, the argument of Dostoevsky's Grand Inquisitor."[50] Marcuse offered nothing but his own fantasies of tyranny—a dictatorship of the intellectuals.[51] Although some, such as Michael Walzer, endorsed Marcuse's critique of the United States and were able to see the distinction between the traditional "negative freedom" touted by liberals versus the Rousseauian "positive freedom" embraced by Marcuse, even these partial sympathizers were unable to share the means that Marcuse proposed.[52] They supported the ends that he sought, but they feared that Marcuse sought to replace one form of totalitarianism with another.

Student radicals, on the other hand, were ready for Marcuse's new activist message of 1965. The members of Students for a Democratic Society represented the ideal audience for Marcuse's "Repressive Tolerance." Like him, they were frustrated by the United States and their inability to change it. When they supported the civil rights movement, the liberals within the Democratic Party abandoned them; when they ventured into inner-city neighborhoods seeking to organize poor families, their vision of participatory democracy failed to catch on as they had expected; when they struggled to end the war in Vietnam, the Johnson administration escalated it. Throughout these early years of activism, SDS remained faithful to the peaceful methods of protest rediscovered during the sit-ins. By the mid-1960s, however, civil and campus authorities began to discover how to thwart passive resistance. Once authorities accepted the fact that protests would necessarily bring social disorder, they concentrated on shortening and minimizing such disruptions. By utilizing aggressive force and by engaging in harassment and intimidation, law-enforcement authorities taught activists a lesson—but the message was not the one that they expected to communicate. Instead of discouraging protest, authorities only discouraged the method of passive resistance. Once the state utilized force, the student movement reacted in kind. Now Marcuse's notion of counterviolence took on a new meaning.

Even as "Repressive Tolerance" implicitly encouraged many within the student movement to pursue more dramatic and dangerous actions, Marcuse sternly lectured SDS members on the need to explore theory and their past failures. This apparent contradiction was the crux of Marcuse's never simple relationship to the New Left. Encouraged by the sudden and dramatic rise of the New Left, Marcuse, in a short period of time, began to abandon the pessimism of *One-Dimensional Man.* The student protesters excited him, but he simultaneously remained concerned about them. After all, as much as Marcuse had pioneered a neo-Marxism that went beyond the false expectations of orthodox Marxism, he never was ready to see the student protest movements as a new revolutionary subject. Rather, the New Left represented only the first signs of a new sensibility.

When SDS contacted Marcuse at the beginning of 1965, its members emphasized the problems that had beset SDS and the peace movement. Mike Davis, who later became a noted journalist and editor for *New Left Review* and author of the acclaimed book *City of Quartz,* joined SDS during his brief month as an undergraduate at Reed College. After being expelled from college, he continued to work for SDS, initially in the New York office and then back in California. Under his own initiative, Davis contacted Marcuse in January 1965 from SDS's Los Angeles office. Davis was familiar with Marcuse's reputation, but wasn't yet familiar with his thought. Davis recalled owning a copy of *One-Dimensional Man,* but admitted:

> I tried to read *One Dimensional Man,* but understood not a word. Later I mastered *Reason and Revolution* (during dinner breaks while I was a Teamster), which opened my eyes to philosophy, but it was frankly an immense effort. Most SDSers, especially the college drop-outs like myself, had too little background in theory to really appreciate Marcuse or even understand his location in the history of Marxism. We admired him, but in the same way that people admire Einstein. Malcolm X and maybe C. Wright Mills were more our speed.[53]

Functioning as an official spokesperson for SDS, Davis explained to Marcuse that the antiwar movement was too reactive (it put forth no offensives of its own, but only responded to the government's actions), it had largely failed in its attempts to relate itself to other insurgent movements (such as civil rights and the urban poor), it neglected to link the war to other problems and conditions within U.S. society, it was unable to identify the institutional basis of American foreign policy and the popular support of the war, and it had relied too exclusively on the symbolic politics of demonstrations. Citing all of the problems that would only intensify throughout the middle and late 1960s, Davis and SDS sought Marcuse's help. They sought his advice, wished to consult him as an intellectual mentor, and hoped to recruit him as an SDS speaker.[54]

Although Davis had discussed the intellectual challenges facing SDS and the imperative need to overcome them, Marcuse remained distrustful and disappointed at the lack of theoretical sophistication in the letter and literature he received from SDS.[55] Not surprisingly, there remained a distance between the program of SDS and the Critical Theory of Marcuse. While Davis emphasized SDS's need to master the empirical social data and to gain the strategic upper hand, Marcuse remained an advocate of dialectical thought and critical reason. In fact, it is not hard to imagine Marcuse fearing that these good-hearted young people were still incapacitated by their commitment to instrumental reason and one-dimensional thought. Through no fault of their own, they had crippled their movement and cause. In a letter from the latter half of January 1965, Marcuse warned Davis:

> I detect in your report a strong anti-intellectual sentiment, almost an inferiority complex of being an intellectual and working *as* and with intellectuals. This may well be fatal to the whole movement, for this sentiment completely fails to understand the role of the intellectual today, in the one-dimensional society and totalitarian democracy. I know my Marx well enough to realize what I say. Where it is first of all the question of *knowledge,* of developing the *consciousness* of what is going on and of the possible ways of getting out of the whole, the task is an intellectual one. It, your goal of preparing for a complete reversal of established policies is compromised by the desperate efforts to build up a "mass organization" where there is no basis for a mass organization, to lean on other movements with which you have little in common, and to work with groups whose interests (for the foreseeable future) are different (if not opposed to) from yours. I believe

that the idea of "community work" (nay of "community" itself) is a pernicious concept, perhaps even a reactionary one. "Community work"—that is the sphere of the social worker, of appropriate government agencies—of the Establishment, which will sooner or later take it in hand.[56]

As this letter bluntly indicates, Marcuse maintained the views expressed in *One-Dimensional Man*, while simultaneously considering the bold call to action represented by "Repressive Tolerance." On the one hand, the letter shows in no uncertain terms that he had no faith in the approach pursued by the peace movement—he opposed its fixations on action and strategy, he failed to understand SDS's interest in the civil rights movement, and he saw the antipoverty efforts of SDS's Economic Research and Action Project as Band-Aids for a fatally wounded society (no better than the policies of the welfare state that blocked the road to revolution). But, on the other hand, he was also in the process of changing his tune. What was the point of rejecting "pure tolerance" and engaging in counterviolence to promote "liberating tolerance" if he was right about SDS? "Repressive Tolerance" was not the only sharp turn in Marcuse's thought—in fact, it was only the first. He would make a more startling shift away from the views expressed in this first recorded encounter with SDS after his rise to fame with the publication of *An Essay on Liberation*.

Had Marcuse's general views on the New Left and his particular attitudes toward SDS remained the same, one reasonably should have expected him to become increasingly more disappointed with both as the 1960s continued. Although a growing group within SDS more publicly sounded the same warnings that Marcuse had articulated in his letter of 1965, most of the activities in the REP and the orientation of its leadership remained fixated on empirical analysis and action.[57] Although Marcuse remained a steadfast opponent of simple, "Positivistic" analyses and always preferred the segments of the student movement that struggled to push forward the cause of radical theory, his attitudes toward action had undergone a dramatic change, as we have already examined in our analysis of "Repressive Tolerance." In part, Marcuse's own frustration with the war, the civil rights movement, and the continued expansion of American consumer culture may have driven him to more provocative rhetoric.

Mike Davis, however, proposes another interpretation of Marcuse's growing enthusiasm for SDS and the New Left during the late 1960s. This explanation raises a biographical dimension and offers an intriguing hint about what the New Left might have looked like for Marcuse. After Davis's first contacts with Marcuse in 1965, he had another encounter with Marcuse in 1969. Davis recalled phoning Marcuse in 1969 and being invited to the Marcuse home in La Jolla. When he arrived, he was greeted by Marcuse and his second wife, Inge. Over the course of the evening, Davis was amused by Inge's gentle teasing of Marcuse—remembering how the French students in Paris had followed him around like puppy dogs. Davis also recalled that Marcuse spoke at length about how much the events of 1968 and 1969 reminded him of his own experiences in Berlin during the Spartacist winter.[58] This resonance between past and present was also recalled by Carl Schorske. In an essay written for the centennial celebration of Marcuse's birth, Schorske recounted attending an antiwar protest with Marcuse in the spring of 1965. As riot police surrounded the column of protesters, Marcuse's attention was drawn to a group of Hell's Angels who were watching the procession move by. Intrigued by these fearsome-looking bikers, Marcuse began moving toward them for a closer look. Despite the cautioning of Schorske's wife, Marcuse "dismissed her concern with the remark that he knew how to behave; he had been in the street fighting in revolutionary Berlin."[59] In all likelihood, the resonance between contemporary politics and the formative experiences from his youth converged during the late 1960s. Regardless of how these factors came together, Marcuse's relationship to the "Movement" grew closer as the decade drew to a close. At the same time that Marcuse was touted as a celebrity of student protest by the press, he sought more direct personal and intellectual contact with the movement that people claimed he had inspired.

As the strategic barriers between Marcuse and SDS grew smaller and students within the Movement became acquainted with "Repressive Tolerance," concepts from *One-Dimensional Man* began to appear more regularly in the writings and thoughts of New Leftists. One must be careful, however, not to exaggerate this reception. Although some SDS thought began to show signs of Marcuse's impact, the vast majority of writing focused on protest actions on local campuses, SDS projects, and strategies. Only a tiny minority within SDS was concerned with theory or interested in the problems and questions posed by Marcuse. Furthermore, some of the Marcusean themes could easily be conflated with the lingering legacy of

C. Wright Mills. But the concepts of "one-dimensional society" and "one-dimensional man," "liberating tolerance," "Eros," and the "new sensibility" bore the distinct earmarks of Marcuse. Accompanying his distinctive conceptual tools were Marcuse's views on mass culture, alienation, bureaucracy, Positivism, and the "Great Refusal."[60] As REP and other intellectual factions within SDS struggled to find an ideological vision more compatible with the needs of the student movement during the mid-1960s, *One-Dimensional Man* helped articulate the frustration and confusion that so many felt. It offered a comprehensive analysis of U.S. society that confirmed the view held by many that SDS could only achieve its goals of combating poverty, racism, and the war by embracing more radical perspectives. *One-Dimensional Man* bridged these problems and disclosed them as mere symptoms of a larger systemic problem with American society.

During the same period leading up to the upheavals of 1968, Marcuse altered his relationship to SDS by cooperating with REP. In a memo written in 1967, Marcuse praised REP, but warned it to not be too ambitious. A "diffusion of effort" would only deplete the meager resources REP was offered within SDS. Marcuse judged the literary and cultural magazines proposed by some within REP to be unnecessary, as were the study guides on seminal New Left thinkers. He then went on to explain:

> In my view the vast scope of the REP testifies to a feeling of disillusionment and dissatisfaction with your actual efforts and achievements . . . Much of your project seems to be based on the assumption that education in the American colleges and universities makes all but impossible the development of critical thought . . . [Quoting from a REP pamphlet that had been sent to Marcuse] "Universities are organized and subsidized to produce graduates who will keep America rolling." But they are also producing, largely thanks to your efforts, the Free Speech Movement and all kinds of non-conformists . . . The project should frankly seek to drive home to its students the fact that it has definite political aims and definite priorities which are not identical with "things people want to do." You should in your internal discussions squarely face the problems of democracy and a democratic education. The great majority in this country do not have the slightest desire to change the system . . . This attitude rests on a very material basis, namely, this country is still capable of producing guns *and* butter, and as long as this is the case, people don't mind.[61]

As Marcuse's assessment of the United States grew more negative and his opinion of the New Left more positive, he became a stronger supporter of student activism. A clear theoretical and ideological vision was important for the student movement, but it needed to continue efforts to organize and to end the system supporting the war in Vietnam. Marcuse recommended that REP and SDS continue the protests and escalate their intensity, continue organizing seminars and other educational discussion groups, continue collecting and distributing radical political literature and bibliographies, liaison with New Left movements abroad, and discuss and formulate theoretical alternatives to the existing society.[62]

MARCUSE AND THE FRAGMENTATION OF
THE AMERICAN NEW LEFT

Marcuse may have been an unintentional prophet of the student movement, but he was never its guru. Just as SDS contributed to the shifting of his own ideas (which, as we've noted, took place between 1965 and 1966), his experiences with the New Left continued to transform his thought. The spring of 1968 represented the high point in student radicalism. At this dramatic moment, the populations of Western Europe and the United States realized that a vast number of their youth were desperately unhappy with the status quo and sought substantial domestic and international changes. Having discovered their own power and gradually having been seduced by their own reputation, the New Lefts of Europe and the United States were also transformed by 1968. The events of that year had a radicalizing effect. Student protesters achieved their first dramatic successes and realized their own capabilities. The French students of the Latin Quarter were not the only ones who began to "demand the impossible." Despite Marcuse's association with the spring of 1968, neither he nor his ideas were the source of this spectacular demonstration of discontent and opposition. The popular press was mistaken in its characterizations of Marcuse, and contemporary observers and historians have been misled by the error. The transformation of the New Left was driven by the events themselves. No single figure or set of ideas could encapsulate the feelings and possibilities that 1968 set loose. Instead, as we will see, Marcuse (like the students) seemed to be swept up in the wake and momentum generated by 1968. Thus, Marcuse in his late writings was largely reacting to the student movement in the United States and not directing it.

In his strict adherence to Hegelian logic and historical materialism, Marcuse constructed a confusing theoretical framework during the late 1960s. On the one hand, he was enthusiastic about the capabilities of the New Left. Throughout the prior history of the Horkheimer Circle, the Critical Theorist refused to speak about utopia in the same way that the Christian and Jew refrained from uttering the name of God. In Marcuse's view, the rise of the New Left in the late twentieth century was cause enough for lifting this ban. The students, African American militants, feminists, Third World revolutionaries, and hippies represented the instinctual rebellion against the repression that Marcuse had formulated during the early 1950s. At the same moment, advanced industrial society had achieved a level of development capable of making the Marxian transformation of society possible. The existence of this movement at this moment made concrete thought about utopia necessary.[63]

On the other hand, Marcuse also insisted that the New Left was only a first step toward utopia, not an end in itself.[64] The students, Black Panthers, and members of the counterculture indicated a turning point in the social and cultural development of the West. In Hegelian terms, the New Left was the determinate negation of monopoly capitalism. While the radicals' "Great Refusal" did not represent the new historical synthesis that would replace late capitalism, their actions did indicate a turning point in the world-historical continuum.

Before 1968, Marcuse neither adopted the Leninist or Maoist rhetoric of anti-imperialism nor romanticized the Third World freedom fighters. In fact, his brand of Critical Theory represented a departure from these crisis theories of monopoly capitalism. If Marcuse and the Horkheimer Circle had contributed anything to the American Left and Western Marxism, it was the idea that "late capitalism" was far more stable and entrenched than traditional Marxists had ever thought. Nearly all of the Institute's postemigration thought was devoted to this single thesis, which it attempted to demonstrate in many fields of social research. Furthermore, Marcuse held little hope for the underdeveloped world. The pressures of absorption into the East and the West were too enormous.[65] In short order, Third World countries would be as contaminated with the corrupt modes of thought as the advanced industrial world. Hope existed within the advanced industrial societies.[66] They possessed the material means to provide the essentials to all members of their populations. The problem was changing priorities, the modes of production, ownership, and mind-sets. Critical Theory, thus, represented an intellectual revolution first and foremost. The liberation of people's minds was the first step in liberating society.[67]

Following 1968, however, the older Marxian concept of imperialism crept into Marcuse's public speeches and writings.[68] In addition, he began to acknowledge the importance of Third World revolutionaries. While Marcuse noted the disjunction between revolutionary object (the industrial working class) and revolutionary subject (the students and intellectuals exhibiting the new sensibility) in the advanced economies of the West, he began to entertain the possibility of hope in the Third World (56). In *An Essay on Liberation* from 1969, Marcuse wrote:

> The two historical factors [revolutionary object and subject] do coincide in large areas of the Third World, where the National Liberation Fronts and the guerrillas fight with the support and participation of the class which is the base of the process of production, namely the predominantly agrarian and the emerging industrial proletariat. (Ibid.)

More intriguingly, Marcuse went a step further by linking the "ghetto" uprisings in the United States and "imperialist" struggles abroad in a manner not entirely dissimilar from the formulations later developed by the "Weatherman" faction of the American SDS. In an effort to explain this link, Marcuse wrote:

> The ghetto population of the United States constitutes such a force [of rebellion]. Confined to small areas of living and dying, it can be more easily organized and directed. Moreover, located in the core cities of the country, the ghettos form natural geographical centers from which the struggle can be mounted against targets of vital economic and political importance . . . The racial conflict still separates the ghettos from the allies outside. While it is true that the white man is guilty, it is equally true that white men are rebels and radicals. However, the fact is that monopolistic imperialism validates the racist thesis: it subjects ever more nonwhite populations to the brutal power of its bombs, poisons, and moneys: thus making even the exploited white populations in the metropoles partners and beneficiaries of the global crime. (57–58)

"Weatherman" mistook these circumstances as the signs of a "revolution-ary" situation, but Marcuse was more cautious. He had come to see these developments as "prerevolutionary," as opposed to the "nonrevolutionary" situation that he had discussed in works such as *One-Dimensional Man*.

Such rhetoric became dangerous and irresponsible when Marcuse began to assess the forces of counterrevolutionary opposition. Having already identified the enormity of the stakes in the New Left's confrontation with the American and Western European states, Marcuse was hesitant to put any moral or strategic restrictions on the "Great Refusal." On the contrary, he increasingly romanticized the struggle and legitimated the escalating rhetoric and methods being discussed within the New Left. As much as he sought to nurture the growth of a "new sensibility" (an intellectual revo-lution inspired by art that would liberate the imagination) (23–48), he made room for militant hostility, rage, and criminality, blurring the dis-tinctions between the various segments of the New Left (viii and 7): Third World revolutionaries and antiwar protesters, hippies and Black Panthers, and bohemian college students and the urban poor. Instead of appreciat-ing the often conflicting agendas that each group brought to the table, Marcuse tried to mold them into his own revolutionary ideal. By demon-izing the System, Marcuse sought to convince all of their victimhood and to legitimate all acts of opposition:

> An opposition which is directed, not against a particular form of government
> or against particular conditions within a society, but against a given social
> system as a whole, cannot remain legal and lawful because it is the estab-
> lished law which it opposes . . . The alternative is, not democratic evolution
> versus radical action, but rationalization of the status quo versus change.
> As long as a social system reproduces, by indoctrination and integration, a
> self-perpetuating conservative majority, the majority reproduces the system
> itself—open to changes within, but not beyond, its institutional frame-
> work. Consequently, the struggle for changes beyond the system becomes,
> by virtue of its own dynamic, undemocratic in the terms of the system, and
> counterviolence is from the beginning inherent in this dynamic. Thus the
> radical is guilty—either of surrendering to the power of the status quo, or
> of violating the Law and Order of the status quo. (66)

Critical Theory's absolute negation of late-capitalist society thus became linked to the agendas of the militant groups of the late 1960s and early

1970s. As the continuation of the war provoked increasingly desperate acts of opposition and as violence became an accepted tool of the state and its opponents, Marcuse's position linked him with the militant factions within the New Left. Thus the reception of his own work became entangled with the reputation of outlaw sects and apocalyptic extremists.

Marcuse's subsequent book, *Counterrevolution and Revolt,* appeared in 1972. By this time, SDS had fractured at its chaotic convention of 1969. While the national office was hijacked by the "Weatherman" faction, the Progressive Labor (PL) faction still sought to speak on behalf of the movement. Both factions eventually succeeded in alienating the majority of SDS's members. While PL took its inspiration from Mao and continued its endeavor of founding a worker–student alliance, "Weatherman" found role models in the Black Panthers, Régis Debray, and Che Guevara, as well as revolutionary icons from mass-media films such *Bonnie and Clyde* (1967) and *The Battle of Algiers* (1966), and sought to "bring the war home" at first with the underwhelming "Days of Rage" in Chicago and later through a bizarre bombing campaign. Marcuse, beholding the wreckage of SDS, sought to scold both PL and "Weatherman." Marcuse pronounced PL to be an "in-group" merely using empty Marxian clichés and succumbing to a "fetishism of labor."[69] At the same time, Marcuse distanced himself and voiced his caution regarding "Weatherman" and other action factions within the New Left: "Action directed toward vague, general, intangible targets is senseless; worse, it augments the number of adversaries" (53). Finally, to the broader mass of former SDS loyalists who began retreating from the "Movement" to the counterculture in 1969, Marcuse encouraged them to come back and to grow up. While he acknowledged that the "new sensibility" was a symptom of the contradictions within the establishment, he rejected the apolitical nature that individualism and collectivism were exhibiting within the counterculture (48–49). The more the mass media touted the counterculture as a lifestyle choice, the more Marcuse legitimately feared that the "prerevolutionary" nature of the Movement was endangered. He warned his young readers: "Co-option threatens the cultural revolution . . . Against this threat, the entirely premature immediate identification of private and social freedom creates tranquilizing rather than radicalizing conditions and leads to withdrawal from the political universe in which, alone, freedom can be attained" (49–50). In essence, Marcuse called on the Movement to transform its "pubertarian rebellion" into an *"esprit de sérieux"* (50).

How did Marcuse attempt to reinvigorate the Movement and to foster its maturation? Instead of curbing the excessive rhetoric within the New Left and encouraging moderation, he sought to regain consensus by demonizing the United States with the most abhorrent concept that he possessed in his intellectual arsenal—Nazism. Instead of accurately seeing SDS as responsible for its own demise, Marcuse attributed part of the problems besetting the New Left to the counterrevolutionary tactics of the state:

> The Nixon administration has strengthened the counterrevolutionary organization of society in all directions. The forces of law and order have been made a force above the law. The normal equipment of the police in many cities resembles that of the S.S.—the brutality of its actions is familiar . . . This is not a fascist regime by any means . . . civil rights are still there, and their existence is not disproved by the (correct) argument that the system can still "afford" this kind of protest. Decisive is rather whether the present phase of the (preventive) counterrevolution (its democratic-constitutional phase) does not prepare the soil for a subsequent fascist phase . . . This country possesses economic and technical resources for a totalitarian organization immeasurably greater than Hitler's Germany ever had . . . The only counterforce is the development of an effectively organized radical left. (24–28)

In the violent and desperate atmosphere of the late 1960s and early 1970s, Marcuse's final advice to the New Left was to get serious, but his rhetorical revival of the specter of fascism complicated this message. Marcuse wanted the New Left to mature. The days of isolated communes and cadres were over. These experiments had failed because they bred apathy and undermined the commitment to politics. The artificial world of the community became a substitute for sweeping social change. At the same time, the penchant for irony and silliness also had to come to an end. The dangers and stakes were too high for such undisciplined, naive behavior.

The movement had to become more self-disciplined and serious. The New Left had to appreciate the gravity of its plight and the consequences of its failure. Although Marcuse had grown to prefer Rudi Dutschke's subversive strategy of the "long march through the institutions" (55–56), his comparison of the Nixon administration and local U.S. authorities to the Nazi state did little to quash the fervor for revolutionary adventurism.

Perhaps more significantly, Marcuse became increasingly more willing to describe his utopia in more concrete terms and to link its achievement to the revolutionary overthrow of the United States and its allies:

> The fall of the capitalist superpower is likely to precipitate the collapse of military dictatorships in the Third World . . . They would be replaced, not by the national "liberal" bourgeoisie . . . but by a government of the liberation movements committed to introduce long overdue radical social and economic changes . . . Moreover in the capitalist countries themselves, the revolution would be *qualitatively* different from its abortive precursors. This difference would vary in degree, according to the uneven development of capitalism. In its most advanced tendencies, this revolution could break the repressive continuum which today still ties socialist reconstruction competitively to capitalist progress. Without this dreadful competition, socialism could overcome the fetishism of the "productive forces." (2)

Thus, Marcuse expected that the collapse of the United States would lead to socioeconomic liberation throughout the Third World, the Communist World, and among the advanced economies of the West. The "violence, ugliness, ignorance, and brutality" of the West's soft totalitarianism and the East's hard totalitarianism would be washed away by a revolution committed to peace, beauty, critical reason, and love.

In addition to highlighting Marcuse's complex relationship to the New Left, *Counterrevolution and Revolt* also provides us with a clue that may solve the mystery of Marcuse's stance in the late 1960s and early 1970s. Recalling the reminiscences of Mike Davis and Carl Schorske regarding the significance of the Spartacist winter, Marcuse lapses into a similarly nostalgic moment—suggesting that the model for this revolution and future society was something that he imagined in Berlin during the winter of 1918–19. Presenting an image strongly reminiscent of Germany's Council Movement, Marcuse wrote:

> If this political radicalization to the Left occurs, the system would be weakened and eventually disrupted in the de-centralized, de-bureaucratized way also indicated by the general conditions of monopoly capitalism: uneven development: workers' control in individual factories or groups of factories— "nests" of post-capitalist (socialist) units in the still capitalist society . . .

Such a development would recapture a seminal achievement of the revolutionary tradition, namely the "councils" ("soviets," *Räte*) as organizations of self-determination, self-government (or rather preparation for self-government) in local popular assemblies. Their revival is indicated not only by the historical obsolescence of bureaucratic mass parties but also by the necessity to find, as their historical heirs, new adequate sources of initiative, organization, and leadership . . . The councils will be organs of revolution only to the degree to which they represent the people *in revolt.* They are not just there, ready to be elected in the factories, offices, neighborhoods—their emergence presupposes a new consciousness: the breaking of the hold of the Establishment over the work and leisure of the people. (44–45)

Although he remained pessimistic about the prospects for the future, Marcuse remained loyal to his conception of a biological transformation of man and continued to see the intellectual adoption of a "new sensibility" as the chief goal of revolution (70–71). But he had made an important shift from social theory to political opposition. Marcuse did not lead the student movement down this path. Rather, they led the way for him. In the final analysis, this touted "guru" of the New Left was a better student than he was a teacher. As he observed the New Left during the late 1960s, he found himself reminded of events and possibilities that he witnessed in his youth. He had beheld the seemingly stable authority of the *Kaiserreich* crumble in an instant, creating the possibility for something new and liberating to take its place, and he hoped that such a utopia might be realized in the late 1960s. After bearing witness to the Freikorps's repression of the Spartacists, it is not surprising that Marcuse foresaw similar dangers lurking in the shadows—the key difference was that this was another era and another generation that bore fewer similarities to 1919 than he may have thought.

Before 1968, Marcuse was far less influential within the U.S. New Left than the media and his biographers described, and he certainly was not a guru until the media proclaimed him to be one. SDS arose from distinctly different sources, such as experiences with the civil rights movement and a dream of reinvigorating American democracy inspired by such figures as C. Wright Mills. Following 1968, Marcuse's association with the New Left contributed to the difficulties that many students experienced in attempting to appropriate his thought and to follow his advice. Although SDS was created around the idea of radical, participatory democracy, Marcuse raised disturbing questions about precisely this idea. Although his notion of a reconfigured America was democratic, he struggled to locate the basis for such a transformation. Distrustful of the American masses and their corruption by advanced industrial society, he abandoned faith in any historical precedents or contemporary phenomena. He placed little trust in the autonomous individual in late-capitalist society, which functioned as the foundation for both democracy and liberalism. Although "free" people democratically exercised their rights in the United States, too many opted to be unfree and opted to promote "unfreedom." Instead of seeking a historical development beyond this political contradiction, Marcuse revived the biological conclusions that arose from *Eros and Civilization.* Envisioning a cataclysmic end to existing American society, he formulated man's natural inclination for unrepressed freedom, joy, and pleasure. Starting over again and rebuilding in harmony with our instinctual core, Marcuse imagined his utopia. While the New Left might have been muddled in its thinking and confused in some of its methods, it generally shared many of Marcuse's goals, and the New Leftists represented evidence of his biological ideal. The existence and growth of the student movement confirmed his analysis. The students embodied Marcuse's dream of a revolution fought in the name of pleasure, joy, and play. While many commentators on the New Left struggled to understand the rise of such a powerful force of discontent within a society of vast plenty, Marcuse proclaimed that the conditions of affluence were the precise cause of the discontent. The students, dissatisfied with their material abundance, were reacting to the alienation, waste, and destructiveness that they saw around them. Marcuse, thus, may have been the New Left's prophet, but he was not its guru.

In fact, as the 1960s came to a close, he proved to be a better observer (or student) than he was a mentor. He neither set the waves of student protest in motion nor shaped U.S. student opinion on a large scale once the New Left was on the rise. Instead, he recognized the significance of the Movement and the events that he was witnessing, and he sought to counsel the New Left as it grew and tried to articulate a new agenda for the late 1960s. The New Left meant more to him than he meant to the New Left. By granting him a power and an agency that he did not wield in the 1960s, Marcuse and his thought have been frozen in time—fused to a Movement that came to an end and that many seek to cast into the dustbin of history.[70]

conclusion

THE FRANKFURT SCHOOL'S
AMERICAN LEGACY

The fate of Marcuse's work and reputation discussed at the conclusion of the last chapter is an important consideration when grappling with the reception of the entire Horkheimer Circle during the 1970s and 1980s in the United States. Although an older generation of American social scientists and intellectuals had been acquainted with the Institute for Social Research since the war, a new generation felt that it had discovered the Institute's work and recognized its significance. Marcuse's co-option by the American mass media of the 1960s made him a celebrity and simultaneously marginalized his message by depicting him in the guise of a "guru." Nevertheless, as we are continuously reminded today in the era of reality television, celebrity is not created without numerous unintended consequences. Celebrity has the ability to both empower and disempower those caught up in its dynamism. The preceding chapter tended to emphasize the negative consequences of fame. Yet, it is important to keep in mind that if Marcuse's name had never been splashed across the pages of newspapers and glossy magazines and if he had never been interviewed on television, his work might not have gained as much attention as it did within the U.S. academy—which was much better equipped to comprehend it, to criticize it, and to build upon it than were the broader ranks of the student movement.

In the months following the ill-fated SDS convention of 1969 that saw the organization split into factions, a book titled *Critical Interruptions* appeared. An editor at the New York publishing firm of Herder and Herder, fascinated by the New Left and the Marcuse media phenomenon, contacted Paul Breines for a book idea regarding Marcuse and the New Left. Breines had come to the attention of the publishing house through an essay he contributed to *Antworten auf Herbert Marcuse,* a book that was edited by Jürgen Habermas for Suhrkamp Verlag. Breines's essay, "Marcuse and the New Left in America," introduced German student radicals, among whom Marcuse's work was more widely known, to the circumstances facing the Movement in the United States and the paradox of Marcuse's relationship to the New Left. He wrote:

> To be sure, *One-Dimensional Man* and the *Repressive Tolerance* essay, let alone his early works, remain unread by large portions of the Left; only a very small percentage has, or cares to have, more than the vaguest comprehension of the philosophical tradition in which Marcuse stands . . . Given this, the fact is that he is the most widely discussed thinker within the American Left today.[1]

The contradiction inherent in the characterization was and remains obvious. What kind of discussions could Marcuse's writings have generated if Breines was correct in his judgment that Marcuse's books and essays remained largely unread? Breines's explanation was not unlike those offered by Marcuse in relation to this odd phenomenon:[2] "in the past three years significant sectors of the new Left have found in *One-Dimensional Man,* and Marcuse's subsequent work, a critique which comprehends their private and political experience while it lays bare the underlying tendencies in the society in which they live. Of equal importance within this development is the increasingly active role Marcuse has taken in relating himself and his work to the new Left."[3]

The book project Breines suggested to Herder and Herder was a collection of essays written by young intellectuals sympathetic with the New Left and reflecting on the relevance of Marcuse to the Movement. By the time work on the book, *Critical Interruptions,* commenced, SDS had splintered and the future of the American New Left suddenly seemed especially unclear. The spirit of this moment pervades every essay in the book. Some contributors, such as Shierry Weber (Nicholson) and Jeremy Shapiro, conducted critical engagements with Marcuse's work in an effort to reintepret the newly discovered challenges facing the radical subject.[4]

Other contributors, such as William Leiss and John David Ober, attempted to clarify misconceptions regarding Critical Theory and Marcuse's own writings.[5]

The two most sobering essays, however, were contributed by Russell Jacoby and by Breines himself. In Jacoby's view, the hope that Marcuse offered to the hopeless had been extinguished by the social forces Marcuse's theory had illuminated: "That his [Marcuse's] own works have so quickly become victims of the forces they exposed, testifies to the truth of his analysis—and to the strength of the forces. The 'culture industry,' with an unerring instinct for growth potential, cashes in on radical thought, stock-piling critical theory for private use, as if to stun possible practitioners into inactivity by the accumulated reserve."[6] Jacoby bore witness to the co-option of Marcuse's writings, but also to the marketing of the counterculture's radical chic. His proposed solution was to revive Horkheimer's call for a critical theory that was presented in a language "not easily understood"—thus a move toward the principles of avant-garde form and philosophical content (such as nonidentity) that had been the hallmarks of Adorno's late contributions to Critical Theory.

Breines shared Jacoby's concerns regarding the power of commodification,[7] but also attempted to ground his observations more explicitly in the events that had just taken place within SDS. Anticipating interpretations that Marcuse later articulated in *Counterrevolution and Revolt*, Breines pointed to the destructive effects that the revival of "Old Left" concepts and rhetoric had generated. In the quest for a revolutionary ideology, SDS returned to Lenin and reimagined itself as a vanguard. This was in sharp contrast to what Breines perceived to be the original nature of the U.S. New Left. As he explained:

The Movement has been precisely a movement: a process, a piercing-through the shells of advanced capitalism and traditional socialism, a not-yet and a to-be. It has been a project of discovering and inventing liberatory forms of expression, experience, organization, and struggle in a system of technically prefabricated and administered life . . . Beneath and within this project has been a drive toward the *coherence* of critical theory. And right now it appears that the severity of the need for coherence combined with the Movement's long-standing hostility to "theory" (and theorists) as a bad trip, identical to the asphyxiating fragments of non-thought and programmed incoherence met in classrooms and textbooks, is finally turning against the Movement itself.[8]

Acknowledging the anti-intellectualism that had always concerned the Critical Theorists about the New Left, Breines saw that such tendencies had led SDS directly to the barren and authoritarian realm of the commissar. Rather than continuing the quest for nonrepressive individuals and communities, student radicals had backtracked into the naive self-certainty of "Old Left" Marxism and Leninism. To combat this development, Breines called on the New Left to accept the surrealistic and utopian challenges Marcuse presented in *An Essay on Liberation*.[9]

The various impulses evident in *Critical Interruptions* were prophetic of the intellectual receptions and engagements with Critical Theory that took place throughout the 1970s and 1980s. The academic reception of the Horkheimer Circle took place amid the ruins of the Movement. While the political, action factions of the New Left tore the Movement apart with their terroristic fantasies about "bringing the war home," the intellectuals allied with the student movement generated widespread scholarly interest in the Frankfurt School.

Telos, a new journal founded in 1968 by Paul Piccone at the University of New York at Buffalo, grew to become one of the most productive publications in which the investigations begun in *Critical Interruptions* continued. Piccone's personal intellectual obsession was with Marxian phenomenology, but the journal became anything but a reflection of its founder's fascination with Husserl. Piccone was a versatile philosopher, and he envisioned a journal that would reflect the variety of his own social and theoretical interests. More important, Piccone recognized that the problems plaguing the Left would require a broad theoretical effort and necessitate contributions from a range of different theoretical approaches.[10] As Piccone announced in his first editorial statement, "*Telos* is committed to philosophical synthesis . . . We are concerned to offer alternatives to the many forces operating to further the existing fragmentation of knowledge and human existence."[11] In practice, this would mean that articles regarding phenomenological Marxism could be investigated alongside a book review of Adorno's *Jargon of Authenticity*—something that would have horrified both Heidegger and Adorno but that gratified the editors of *Telos*. Thus, as far as the Frankfurt School was concerned, some issues of *Telos* were devoted to rethinking particular aspects of Critical Theory, others were dedicated to translating and clarifying largely unknown dimensions of Critical Theory, and still others were committed to the application of Critical Theory in an effort to interpret contemporary reality.

Despite the fact that *Telos* looked well beyond the Critical Theory of Herbert Marcuse, his engagement with the New Left of the 1960s shaped the *Telos* agenda. As Piccone recalled:

> Under the influence of Marcuse's immensely popular *One-Dimensional Man*, *Telos* began to selectively dig up buried texts (which have long since become well-known in academic circles) in the effort to develop the New Left critique of technologic domination and reification by vindicating a subjectivity becoming increasingly unattainable in a society well on the way of becoming, in Adorno's words, "totally administered." We began to search for forgotten and repressed texts we had occasionally seen mentioned in passing or referred to in stray footnotes.[12]

Piccone's recollection is telling because it calls attention to the fact that, even among intellectuals engaged in the archaeological recovery of Critical Theory, the search through the ruins had been set into motion by Marcuse and his complex relationship to radical politics during the 1960s. In the same way that the members of the Horkheimer Circle found inspiration in the writings of Hegel and the young Marx to sift through the wreckage of the failed revolutions of 1918–19, young American intellectuals gravitated to Critical Theory to make sense of the debris of the New Left.

In 1973, a major milestone took place in the American reception of Critical Theory. Martin Jay's book *The Dialectical Imagination* was published, and it accomplished something entirely novel for the Horkheimer Circle—it connected the dots and communicated the complexities of Critical Theory to a wide reading audience. The small archaeological expeditions carried out by *Telos* had sought and found small artifacts, but Jay's goal was more ambitious. He succeeded in recapturing the life and work of an entire intellectual coterie that had ceased to exist at the end of the 1940s. American intellectuals had been aware of the existence of the Institut für Sozialforschung, but they never had realized the full history of the institution or, more important, how the writings of its members could be understood together. The book's acclaim and success were a testament to Jay's skills as an intellectual historian. He was able to present the contributions of the Institute in a coherent, clear, and accurate manner.

Jay's book was not written for partisans of the Movement or their critics. Despite the fact that the high drama of the New Left formed the backdrop throughout much of his research, his goal was less explicitly political and certainly less doctrinaire. As he explained, "Temperamentally unsuited to militant activism, I always maintained a certain skeptical distance from the maximalist tendencies of the New Left and had resisted joining any particular faction of 'the movement.'"[13] Instead, Jay saw his goal as "conveying the palpable sense of excitement and promise I felt in unearthing and trying to sort out so radically unfamiliar and challenging a corpus of work . . . The book was written . . . in the hope of facilitating [the reception and appropriation of that work], but without inviting the uncritical dogmatism that characterized so many other embraces of Marxist theory."[14]

As Jay noted nearly twenty-five years after the publication of *The Dialectical Imagination,* his aims were realized beyond his most "grandiose fantasies." The Frankfurt School has emerged as the focus of intense contemporary and historical interest.[15] Generally, curiosity about the New Left carved out a large marketplace for all manner of leftist theory—anarchism, socialist humanism, and, of course, Marxism (including the full array of Marxian permutations, such as neo-Marxism, Western Marxism, and Structuralist Marxism). The success of *The Dialectical Imagination,* however, helped to generate more curiosity surrounding Marcuse and his former colleagues from the Horkheimer Circle. Ambitious young sympathizers with the New Left thus had an unusual opportunity to fill this new and urgent demand. Without having to disguise or hide their intellectual and political orientations, such scholars made their way into universities to address the issues of the day, and their works were eagerly published by university presses and trade houses seeking to capitalize on the New Left/ Marcuse phenomenon. Unlike any other generation of leftist intellectuals in the United States, the generation of the 1960s was quickly accepted and legitimated. Although they wrote and lectured about an intellectual tradition critical of most aspects of U.S. society, scholars of the Frankfurt School were invited into the establishment, earning chairs at such prestigious universities as Harvard, Yale, Princeton, Cornell, Columbia, Duke, the University of California at Berkeley, and the University of Chicago.

"The long march through the institutions," which Rudi Dutschke and Herbert Marcuse envisioned, was accomplished, but, surprisingly, it was by invitation.

Within the large niche that the marketplace created for such scholars, the contributions to intellectual history, philosophy, and sociology were substantial. They surveyed the intricate terrain of Continental thought and accomplished a task that no members of the Horkheimer Circle were able to achieve in their lifetime—equipping an American audience with the tools necessary to appreciate Critical Theory on its own terms. Members of the Institute had transcended their isolation in the United States by appealing to an American audience, but the results were assimilated versions of Critical Theory. The U.S. scholars of the Frankfurt School, by contrast, generated a renaissance in the Horkheimer Circle's forerunners by providing Americans with new appreciations of Kant, Hegel, Marx, Weber, Freud, and Lukács. In the transatlantic history of ideas, perhaps no period was as fruitful for the importation of German social, philosophical, and cultural thought into the United States as the period following the demise of the New Left. Unlike the the situation of the intellectual migrants of the 1930s and 1940s, the conditions were ideal and the interlocutors were abundant for the transatlantic passages of the 1970s and 1980s.

Initially, the work of many U.S. Frankfurt School scholars bore resemblances to Paul Breines's efforts in *Critical Interruptions*. They relied on Critical Theory to reflect on the New Left and/or to explain its self-destruction.[16] In an effort to rescue the Horkheimer Circle from the taint of the Weathermen and other left-wing terrorist organizations, Critical Theory's American adherents deployed the Institute's critiques of authoritarianism, conformity, mass culture, and anti-intellectualism to explain the failures of the student movement and the resilience of "late capitalism." According to such accounts, neither Marcuse nor Critical Theory had led the student, antiwar, and civil rights movements astray. The New Left derailed itself. As many Frankfurt School supporters pointed out, the movements within the New Left had never really been terribly new. The legitimate roots of the New Left were not Western Marxism or neo-Marxism, as some members of the press and academy contended.[17] Although the New Left tried to draw a sharp line between itself and the Old Left, the two shared more in common than even many partisans of the 1960s cared to think.

For other scholars during the 1970s and 1980s, the Critical Theory of the Frankfurt School was used to support the "identity politics" that arose out of the New Left's destruction. As the student movement was pulled apart along its unstable seams, the delicate threads that once bound together civil rights activists, antiwar protesters, anti-imperialists, feminists, and early proponents of gay liberation were torn asunder. In the process, the New Left's counterculture gave way to more particularist agendas that some have aptly identified as the "quest for the ideal self."[18] Although few would deny that identity politics has not come without the price of factionalism, its supporters would emphasize the rich "democratization of selfhood" that began in the wake of the 1960s—an ideal that shares much in common with SDS's original goal of participatory democracy. The Frankfurt School, however, was only one of the inspirations for the series of theoretical cross-fertilizations that would take place in the field of cultural studies. Scholars, borrowing the Horkheimer Circle's analysis of late capitalism, poststructuralism's concepts of the discourse effect and the decentered self, and the Birmingham School's notions about culture, have struggled to arrive at interdisciplinary and intertheoretical understandings of social groups and practices. Such analyses have problematized more traditional notions of consciousness, race, class, and gender and paved the way for new understandings of power, meaning, and cultural dynamics.[19]

Despite the growth and success of a unified Atlantic culture, the American reception of Critical Theory was transformed in the process. Discussions of Critical Theory became less practical and more theoretical. Paul Piccone noted the same interest in Critical Theory, but questioned whether this scholarly reception possessed a shadow side. As he wrote in 1988:

> Two decades later Western Marxism and Critical Theory have become legitimate subdisciplines right next to the likes of feminism, black studies and post-structuralism, while whatever ruins of continental ideas have managed to survive the post-WWII Americanization of the European mind are now part and parcel of every American university's curriculum—but with unintended results. Far from precipitating the projected qualitative change in cultural life, a substantial de-provincialization of social consciousness and a more democratic and participatory political reality, Western Marxism, Critical Theory and radical philosophy in general have smoothly blended into

the otherwise bland, jargon-ridden and hopelessly conventional framework they originally challenged.[20]

A tangible bitterness and nostalgia runs through Piccone's recollections from 1988, and some of his despair was unquestionably personal. Denied tenure at Washington University, he had abandoned the academy and dedicated his career to whatever independent course he charted with *Telos*. Nevertheless, it is striking to consider how rapidly the legacy of the Frankfurt School disappeared from the public intellectual arena and how quickly it found a home within the academy. The latter shift in Critical Theory's reception during the 1970s and 1980s again points to the profound impact that Marcuse's celebrity had on the legacy of the Frankfurt School.

The receptions of Marcuse and the Frankfurt School were entangled with each other in the United States. As both were caught in the glare of the media spotlight, each was transformed into something different from what it had been. We have already examined some of the mythology that arose in connection with Marcuse's fame. In Marcuse's case, the cultural industry cut two ways. On the one hand, he could be praised by the partisans of 1968 for being the guiding force of their rebellion. On the other hand, he could be held accountable for numerous social and cultural ills by neoconservative critics of the Movement. Thus, writers such as Roger Kimball and Daniel Flynn could hold Marcuse responsible for the negative consequences of the sexual revolution and the counterculture;[21] propagandists against the "left academy," such as David Horowitz, Alan Kors, and Harvey Silvergate, could blame Marcuse for "political correctness";[22] and cultural conservatives, such as Alan Bloom, could hold Marcuse responsible for postmodernism's relativism.

The term "Frankfurt School" was first used in Germany by Franz Oppenheimer to describe himself and his colleagues at the University of Frankfurt.[23] Karl Mannheim later assumed this mantle at the University of Frankfurt, and Horkheimer was only too happy to see the term reborn when he and Adorno returned from exile. It was a sign of their prominence and significance in West German sociology. After the war and the Institute's return to Germany, the term was revived amid Adorno's participation in the "Positivist dispute" with Karl Popper. By the late 1960s, the term "Frankfurt School" was regularly used in the media and by the West German student Left to refer to the entire first and second generation of the Institute (thus, not only was the entire Horkheimer Circle lumped together, but Habermas was also included in this popular image). After 1968 and Marcuse's emergence in the American media, the term "Frankfurt School" crossed the Atlantic and became entangled with Marcuse's presumed relationship to the student movement.

Despite the fact that many of the American scholars studying Critical Theory in the United States had grown disillusioned with the student movement of the late 1960s and were using the thought of the Frankfurt School to interpret the problems evident in the New Left, they did not or could not combat the links that the popular media had established between Marcuse and the "Frankfurt School." This is not to say that the designation Critical Theory is incoherent or that the "Frankfurt School" is a meaningless term. I raise the issue to call attention to the fact that the Frankfurt School was a far less homogeneous circle of intellectuals than is widely believed. Martin Jay's *The Dialectical Imagination* can be seen as an attempt to combat such a perception. Jay selected the subtitle "A History of the Frankfurt School and the Institute for Social Research"— highlighting the distinction between the mythic "Frankfurt School" that accompanied Marcuse's rise to fame and the Institute for Social Research that had a more complex and contentious history.

Central to the image of a "Frankfurt School," I want to propose, was the experience of alienation that accompanied exile. It is not surprising that this aspect of the Institute's history captured the imagination of so many of its American commentators. Alienation and skepticism toward the United States had been a hallmark of the Movement since its inception. Thus, the crucial experience of the "Frankfurt School" émigrés could be understood as a more generalized phenomenon among the new generation that sought to learn from the Horkheimer Circle's experiences. Although there is no denying the fact the emphasis on the concept of alienation was common to nearly all of the members of the Institute, the emphasis on the isolation of the Critical Theorists helped to shroud the more active and robust engagement with U.S. society and culture that the "Frankfurt School" underwent in exile.

From the moment of the Frankfurt School's arrival, a sustained engagement with the United States began. No matter where the Critical Theorists settled after the war, they had been changed by their encounter with the United States and would consistently acknowledge this debt. Although the Frankfurt School's reception and impact among U.S. intellectuals and the broader public remained more limited, the Institute was a significant part of the broader migration of German thought to North America. Horkheimer and his Circle's emigration enabled them to participate in some American debates on social theory and politics that had begun before the Frankfurt intellectuals arrived and would continue after many of them had returned to Germany.

The academic debates that agitated the scholarly networks that the Frankfurt School entered revolved around the nature of social science: should the social sciences be modeled on the empirical methods and epistemological assumptions of the natural and physical sciences, or should the social sciences be guided by the methods and epistemological assumptions of the humanities? This is a debate that began long before the Frankfurt School arrived in the United States, and it continues as radical sociologists confront the methods and assumptions of empirical sociologists.

Before leaving Germany, the Frankfurt School had developed a method for integrating the two approaches through the use of empirical methods that were informed and guided by Hegel's dialectical logic, Marx's historical materialism, and immanent critique. Upon arriving in the United States, the Critical Theorists soon discovered that their methods and tools were significantly different from those used by American sociologists. American empirical research was guided more by pragmatic, ends-oriented considerations directed at assessing or addressing immediate social problems. In the few cases in which grand theory such as that of Talcott Parsons was formulated in the United States, it was developed to formulate and describe the integrated operations of the status quo rather than to interrogate it. Although their experiences with American science and empiricism grew to form the basis for the Critical Theorists' assaults against Positivism and Functionalism, they were never absolute opponents of empirical methods. In fact, as a result of its efforts to introduce the most advanced American empirical techniques to German citizens, the Frankfurt School was a notable early contributor to the restoration of West German sociology. As long as empiricism does not take the status quo for granted and assists the social theorists in questioning existing society, empiricism remains a useful tool of the critical sociologist.

In addition to its effects on more formal, academic discourses regarding science, empiricism, and epistemology, the Frankfurt School also left its mark on a series of broader, public intellectual controversies. The latter debates generally revolved around three interrelated issues: mass culture, the concept of totalitarianism, and the role of the intellectual in contemporary society.

Popular culture was a topic that had occupied cultural conservatives and Marxists throughout the United States and Europe prior to the 1930s, but the steady rise of mass-produced art forms during the early twentieth century generated a new focus for cultural and social criticism. To some, mass culture promoted cultural standardization, conformity, and the impoverishment of art and the human imagination. To others, it represented a benign force no more dangerous than preindustrial forms of popular culture. Early defenders of mass culture, such as Edward Shils and Daniel Bell, argued that it was more consistent with the cultural values of a democratic society than the elite forms of high culture. To the critics of mass art, such as the members of the Frankfurt School, the cultural and philosophical regimentation of mass society raised provocative parallels to the relatively new concept of totalitarianism that had been used to describe Fascist Italy, Nazi Germany, and Communist Russia. Thus, Critical Theory's nightmare visions of the "totally administered society" represented a cultural Marxist application of the totalitarian model to the advanced-capitalist, liberal state. Such Western states developed "democratic" systems of social, psychological, political, and cultural coordination resulting in the perfection of barbarism, destructiveness, and systematic waste, which remained camouflaged by illusions of pluralism, technical progress, and material prosperity.

The links between mass culture and totalitarianism transformed the role of the intellectual by altering traditional views of liberation. Revolutionary action could not precede the work of intellectuals, because action guided by a corrupted rationality led only to new regimes and forms of barbarism. Thus, the work of the intellectual was the work of the partisan—and theory represented the first step toward progressive social change. As a result of his horror regarding advanced industrial society, but also as a result of his enthusiasm regarding the surprising vigor of the discontent he witnessed, Marcuse took a leap of faith with the student movement. It was a leap that many intellectuals took with him, but it was a leap that could not be embraced as heartily by his former colleagues from the Frankfurt School. Rather than continuing to work as a critic on the boundaries of the system, Marcuse took a stand with the civil rights protesters, the anti-war activists, the women's movement, and the Third World in the name of liberation and change. Indeed, his 1965 essay "Repressive Tolerance," with its language of counterviolence and counterrepression, can be seen as having played a role in the radical movement's tailspin and dissolution during the 1970s. Marcuse's *Counterrevolution and Revolt,* published in 1972, shows him to be speaking still from within the radical movement, while distancing himself from its increasingly visible self-destructive impulses. In retrospect, one can condemn or admire Marcuse's leap of faith; many people have done both. The present study has taken a different path. It has traced the ways in which Marcuse's political itinerary vividly discloses the questions that occupied the Frankfurt School since its early years: Does political commitment entail dangers that are fatal for the work of Critical Theory? And is it desirable, or even possible, for intellectuals to remain on the margins as critical observers?

Perhaps the most vivid and poignant metaphor that the Horkheimer Circle developed in exile was the image of the message in a bottle. On 29 June 1940, Horkheimer wrote a letter to Salka Viertel, in which he famously stated: "In view of everything that is engulfing Europe and perhaps the whole world our present work is of course essentially destined to being passed on through the night that is approaching: a kind of message in a bottle."[24] The question regarding the addressees of this message (or messages, if one takes into account the fact that each member of the Horkheimer Circle was formulating them differently) has already arisen in our discussion of Marcuse. The messages were cast into the sea for a future readership to discover. But the image distorts the reality by creating the illusion that a readership and audience had not already encountered the messages before the war had even commenced in Europe. The present study has been dedicated to correcting the romantic view that Critical Theory was born in a bottle. Although it was born in Germany, the Frankfurt School spent its formative years in the United States, the impact of which I have tried to trace.

NOTES

INTRODUCTION

1. Douglas Kellner, "The Frankfurt School Revisited: A Critique of Jay's *The Dialectical Imagination*," *New German Critique* (winter 1975): 131–32.

2. Rolf Wiggershaus, *The Frankfurt School: Its History, Theories, and Political Significance* (Cambridge: MIT Press, 1994), 13.

3. Malik Verlag of Berlin, a press that published many theoretical books of the Left such as Georg Lukács's *Geschichte und Klassenbewusstsein*, benefited from the generosity of the Weils, as did such artists as Georg Grosz.

4. See Karl Korsch, *Marxism and Philosophy*, trans. Fred Halliday (New York: New Left Books, 1970); and Georg Lukács, *History and Class Consciousness: Studies in Marxist Dialectics*, trans. Rodney Livingstone (Cambridge: MIT Press, 1990).

5. Paul Breines, "Praxis and Its Theorists: The Impact of Lukács and Korsch in the 1920s," *Telos*, no. 11 (1972): 70.

6. Martin Jay, *The Dialectical Imagination: A History of the Frankfurt School and the Institute of Social Research* (Berkeley: University of California Press, 1996), 8–9; and Wiggershaus, *The Frankfurt School*, 16–19.

7. Wiggershaus, *The Frankfurt School*, 21.

8. Wiggershaus includes a detailed biographical sketch of Grünberg, as well as important details regarding his appointment as director of the Institut für Sozialforschung (ibid., 21–23).

9. See Christophe Butterwegge, *Austromarxismus und Staat: Politiktheorie und Praxis der österreichischen Sozialdemokratie zwischen den beiden Weltkriegen* (Marburg: Verlag Arbeit und Gesellschaft, 1991); and Gerald Mozetič, *Die Gesellschaftstheorie des Austromarxismus: geistesgeschichte Voraussetzung, Methodologie und soziologisches Programm* (Darmstadt: Wissenschaftliche Buchgesellschaft, 1987).

10. Based on his correspondence with Felix Weil, Jay reports that the Senkenberg Museum of Natural History offered space to the Institute during the first months of its existence (before their own building was completed). See Jay, *The Dialectical Imagination*, 10.

11. Carl Grünberg, "Festrede gehalten zur Einweihung des Instuts für Sozialforschung an der Universität Frankfurt a.M. am 22 Juni 1924," in *Frankfurter Universitäts-Reden XX* (Frankfurt: University of Frankfurt, 1924).

12. Wiggershaus, *The Frankfurt School,* 29.

13. A publishing firm, the Marx-Engels Publishing House, was formed by the Institut für Sozialforschung. In addition to publishing several volumes of the Marx-Engels *Gesamtausgabe* (Collected Works), it also produced two volumes of the journal *Marx-Engels Archiv.*

14. Wiggershaus, *The Frankfurt School,* 31–32.

15. Henryk Grossmann, *Das Akkumulations- und Zusammenbruchsgesetz des kapitalistischen Systems* (Leipzig: Hirschfeld, 1929); Friedrich Pollock, *Die planwirtschaftlichen Versuche in der Sowjetunion 1917–1927* (Leipzig: Hirschfeld, 1929); and Karl Wittfogel, *Wirtschaft und Gesellschaft Chinas* (Leipzig: Hirschfeld, 1931).

16. For the most complete account of Max Horkheimer's life and the evolution of his early thought, see John Abromeit, "The Dialectic of Bourgeois Society: An Intellectual Biography of the Young Max Horkheimer, 1895–1937" (PhD dissertation, University of California at Berkeley, 2004).

17. Horkheimer and Pollock even formalized their commitment and friendship by signing the first in a series of formal contracts between each other.

18. Max Horkheimer, *Dawn and Decline: Notes 1926–1931 and 1950–1969,* trans. Michael Shaw (New York: Seabury Press, 1978).

19. Wiggershaus, *The Frankfurt School,* 36–37.

20. Abromeit, "The Dialectic of Bourgeois Society," 75–78.

21. Max Horkheimer, "The Present Situation of Social Philosophy and the Tasks of an Institute for Social Research," in *Between Philosophy and Social Science: Selected Early Writings,* trans. G. Frederick Hunter, Matthew S. Kramer, and John Torpey (Cambridge: MIT Press, 1995), 1–14.

22. Ibid., 9–10.

23. Friedrich Pollock, "Zur Marxschen Geldtheorie," *Archiv für Geschichte des Sozialismus und der Arbeiterbewegung,* vol. 13 (1928), 203.

24. Despite his forays into other disciplines such as political science, psychology, and intellectual history, his primary orientation remained philosophical.

25. Barry Kātz, *Herbert Marcuse and the Art of Liberation: An Intellectual Biography* (London: Verso, 1982), 28.

26. This same concern was addressed later in Marcuse's career through his synthesis of Marx and Freud.

27. Kātz, *Herbert Marcuse and the Art of Liberation,* 66.

28. Herbert Marcuse, *Hegels Ontologie und die Grundlegung einer Theorie der Geschichtlichkeit* (Frankfurt: Klostermann, 1932).

29. Jürgen Habermas, *Autonomy and Solidarity,* ed. Peter Dews (New York: Verso, 1992), 220.

30. Stefan Müller-Doohm, *Adorno: A Biography,* trans. Rodney Livingstone (London: Polity, 2005), 17.

31. Ibid., 95–109.

32. Adorno juggled the *Habilitationsschrift* with composing and writing music criticism. Although his research helped him to familiarize himself with the vast literature on psychoanalysis, his academic supervisor, Hans Cornelius, privately suggested that he withdraw the *Habilitation,* proclaiming that the work lacked originality. See ibid., 98–103.

33. Wiggershaus, *The Frankfurt School,* 111–12.

34. Ibid., 113–16.

35. Later, Fromm worked many of his findings into a historical study, but he never published it during his lifetime. However, it was uncovered from the archives and posthumously published in 1980. See Erich Fromm, *The Working Class in Weimar Germany: A Psychological and Sociological Study,* ed. Wolfgang Bonss, trans. Barbara Weinberger (Cambridge: Harvard University Press, 1984).

36. Friedrich Pollock, "Die gegenwärtigen Lage des Kapitalismus und die Aussichten einer planwirtschaftlichen Neuordnung," *Zeitschrift für Sozialforschung,* vol. 1, no. 1 (1932): 8–27; and Friedrich Pollock, "Bemerkungen zur Wirtschaftskrise," *Zeitschrift für Sozialforschung,* vol. 2, no. 3 (1933): 321–54.

37. Erich Fromm, "The Method and Function of an Analytic Social Psychology," in *The Crisis of Psychoanalysis: Essays on Freud, Marx, and Social Psychology* (New York: Henry Holt, 1970), 138–62; Erich Fromm, "Psychoanalytic Characterology and Its Relevance for Social Psychology," in ibid., 163–87; and Max Horkheimer, "History and Psychology," in *Between Philosophy and Social Science,* 111–28.

38. Theodor W. Adorno, "On the Social Situation of Music," *Telos,* no. 35 (spring 1978): 128–64; and Leo Lowenthal, "On Sociology of Literature," in *Literature and Mass Culture* (New Brunswick, N.J.: Transaction, 1984), 243–55.

39. Jay, *The Dialectical Imagination,* 31.

40. Institut für Sozialforschung, *Studien über Autorität und Familie. Forschungsberichte aus dem Institut für Sozialforschung,* ed. Max Horkheimer (Paris: Alcan, 1936).

41. In fact, Alcan remained the Institute's publishing house until the fall of France.

1. NEW YORK TRANSIT

1. Lewis Feuer, "The Frankfurt Marxists and the Columbia Liberals," *Survey,* vol. 25, no. 3 (summer 1980): 156–76. Subsequent references are given in the text.

2. Martin Jay, "Misrepresentations of the Frankfurt School," *Survey,* vol. 26, no. 2 (spring 1982): 131–41.

3. Lewis Feuer, "The Social Role of the Frankfurt Marxists," *Survey,* vol. 26, no. 2 (spring 1982): 150–70.

4. R. Gordon Hoxie et al., *A History of the Faculty of Political Science: Columbia University* (New York: Columbia University Press, 1955), 21.

5. Ibid., 60–61.

6. Ibid., 286–87.

7. See Leo Davids, "Franklin Henry Giddings: Overview of a Forgotten Pioneer," *Journal of the History of the Behavioral Sciences,* vol. 4, no. 1 (January 1968): 62–72.

8. Hoxie et al., *A History of the Faculty of Political Science,* 290.

9. Ibid., 290–92.

10. Robert MacIver, *As a Tale That Is Told: The Autobiography of R. M. MacIver* (Chicago: University of Chicago Press, 1968), 83.

11. Ibid., 98–99.

12. "Memorandum on the Social Science Needs of Columbia University," written and circulated during 1928–29, *Samuel McCune Lindsay Papers,* Columbia University Rare Book and Manuscript Library, box 46.

13. Ibid.

14. Ibid.

15. "Minutes, Department of Social Science Faculty Meeting," 14 November 1932, *Samuel McCune Lindsay Papers,* box 46. MacIver appealed to the university administration throughout the 1930s in an effort to alleviate the personnel restraints imposed on the department. In a series of memorandums written during 1936, MacIver warned that the staff was inadequate to uphold Columbia's reputation in the social sciences. See Robert MacIver, "Memoranda from the Department of Social Science," 13 June 1936 and 21 November 1936, *Columbia University Archives* (formerly known as the Columbiana Collection), file folder 351/18.

16. "Minutes, Department of Social Science Faculty Meeting," 14 November 1932, *Samuel McCune Lindsay Papers,* box 46.

17. MacIver, *As a Tale That Is Told,* 106–7.

18. Ibid., 110.

19. Ibid., 115.

20. See Rolf Wiggershaus, *The Frankfurt School: Its History, Theories, and Political Significance* (Cambridge: MIT Press, 1994), 143; and Martin Jay, *The Dialectical Imagination: A History of the Frankfurt School and the Institute of Social Research, 1923–1950* (Berkeley: University of California Press, 1996), 37–39.

21. This list was compiled from a series of correspondences between Leo Lowenthal and Julian Gumperz during the final six months of 1933 and the first five months of 1934, *Leo Lowenthal Archiv,* folder 332, documents 36–48, Stadt und Universitätsbibliothek, Frankfurt am Main. Hereafter cited in the text as *LLA,* with folder and document numbers.

22. Daniel Burston, *The Legacy of Erich Fromm* (Cambridge: Harvard University Press, 1991), 17–18.

23. Wiggershaus, *The Frankfurt School,* 143.

24. Burston, *The Legacy of Erich Fromm,* 18.

25. "Memorandum for Dr. Kurt Rosenfeld," *Erich Fromm Papers,* microfilm reel 2 (originally indexed as box 2, folder 4), New York Public Library, Manuscripts and Archives Division. Hereafter cited in the text as *EFP,* with microfilm reel numbers.

26. Fromm's travel itinerary for the winter of 1933–34 included visits to these individuals in Chicago, as well as meetings with Benjamin Stolberg (a German-speaking journalist in New York), Florence Cook (an acquaintance of Fromm's from Philadelphia), Betsy Libbey (a contact that Fromm labeled a "liberal" who was connected with the Family Society), Lloyd Warner (a Boston friend of Libbey's who was also connected with Harvard's Peabody Museum), and Conrad Hilton (a freelance writer from Boston whom Fromm dubbed a "radical liberal"). The itinerary was found in the *Max Horkheimer Archiv,* box VI, folder 8, documents 332–36, Stadt und Universitätsbibliothek, Frankfurt am Main. Hereafter cited in the text as *MHA,* with box, folder, and document numbers.

27. Letter from Erich Fromm to Donald Slessinger dated 26 October 1934, *EFP,* microfilm reel 2 (originally indexed as box 2, folder 5).

28. Letters from Gumperz to Horkheimer dated 11 March 1932 and 22 March 1932 from the *LLA,* folder 332, documents 145 and 149.

29. Letter from Horkheimer to Leverett Lyon, director of educational activities and public relations for the Brookings Institution dated 16 March 1932 from the *LLA,* folder 332, document 146.

30. Letter from Pollock to Gumperz dated 30 June 1933 from the *LLA,* folder 332, document 244.

31. Letter from Pollock to Gumperz dated 25 January 1933 from the *LLA*, folder 332, document 211.

32. Feuer made this accusation about Robert MacIver's ability with German in his article "The Frankfurt Marxists and the Columbia Liberals," 157; and the same claim was asserted by Lewis Coser regarding Robert Lynd during an interview with Coser in Cambridge, Massachusetts, 6 May 1999.

33. Many of the scholars that eventually made up the New School were bitter rivals of the Horkheimer Circle. Finding the Institute's Hegelian Marxism too esoteric, they preferred Social Democratic Party (SPD) reformism. See the letter from Horkheimer to Joachim Radkau dated 9 June 1969 from *Max Horkheimer Gesammelte Schriften, Band 18*, ed. Gunzelin Schmid Noerr (Frankfurt: Fischer Taschenbuch Verlag, 1996), 735–36. Hereafter cited in the text as *MHGS*, with volume and page numbers.

34. Much of Lorwin's biographical material comes from an undated, untitled autobiography and numerous curricula vitae. See the *Lewis Lorwin Papers*, box 15 labeled "Manuscripts: Reports and articles (1929–1936)," Columbia University Rare Book and Manuscript Library, Butler Library.

35. Lewis Lorwin, "Oral History," interview by Donald Shaughnessy, Columbia Oral History Project, December 1960–March 1961, 54.

36. See Lewis Lorwin, *The Women's Garment Workers: A History of the International Ladies' Garment Worker's Union* (New York: B. W. Huebsch, 1924).

37. Lorwin, "Oral History," 106. Subsequent references are given in the text.

38. Letter from Pollock to Gumperz dated 28 November 1932 from the *LLA*, box 332, document 199.

39. Letter from Gumperz to Pollock dated 1 December 1932 from the *LLA*, box 332, document 200.

40. Letter from Gumperz to Pollock dated 8 February 1933 from the *LLA*, box 332, document 214.

41. Letter from Horkheimer to Pollock dated 25 July 1934 from the *MHA*, box VI, folder 31, document 38; and a letter from Lorwin to Horkheimer dated 7 March 1934 from *MHGS*, vol. 15, 135–40.

42. Lorwin, "Oral History," 151–52.

43. Ibid., 206–7.

44. See Feuer, "The Frankfurt Marxists and the Columbia Liberals," 157–64.

45. Letter from Lewis Corey to Robert Lynd dated 12 December 1950 from the *Robert Lynd Papers*, microfilm reel 1, Library of Congress, Manuscript Division.

46. Robert Lynd, "Possibilities of Cooperation among Research Institutions," from the *Robert Lynd Papers*, microfilm reel 2.

47. Lynd reemphasized and elaborated on many of these same points in a faculty seminar within Columbia's sociology department. This presentation, which was given at the home of Robert MacIver on 15 May 1932, was titled "Sociology as Social Research" and is found among the *Robert Lynd Papers*, microfilm reel 1. The format of the notes does not readily permit quotation, but the most significant points of correlation between Lynd's conception of social research and the Frankfurt School's can be summarized as follows: the recognition of sociology's close alliance with social reform and problem solving, the realization that the most serious social problems have no simple answers, a clear comprehension of the dangers arising from theoretical and methodological researcher biases, and,

perhaps most important, a disinclination to privilege "pure science" or quantitative methods over the theoretical and philosophical process of generalization.

48. Max Horkheimer, "The Present Situation of Social Philosophy and the Tasks of an Institute for Social Research," in *Between Philosophy and Social Science: Selected Early Writings,* trans. G. Frederick Hunter, Matthew S. Kramer, and John Tropey (Cambridge: MIT Press, 1995), 9–10.

49. Robert Lynd, "Memorandum on the Study of Changing Family Patterns in the Depression," 14 March 1933, *Robert Lynd Papers,* microfilm reel 2.

50. Ibid.

51. Ibid.

52. Robert Lynd, "Memorandum to Messrs. MacIver, Boas, and Lindsay," 1 May 1933, *Robert Lynd Papers,* microfilm reel 2.

53. Ibid.

54. "The Constitution of the International Society of Social Research," prepared by Mitchell, Taylor, Capron and Marsh (offices were located at 20 Exchange Place, New York, New York), signed and ratified by Horkheimer and Pollock in Geneva on 25 February 1934. Found in *The Columbia University Archives,* file folder 549/7.

55. "Notes for a Talk," dated 1934, from the *MHA,* box IX, folder 52, document b. Gumperz's name is written at the top of the page in Horkheimer's handwriting. The subsequent quotes in this chapter are from this speech.

2. FAILURE AND THE MYTHOLOGIES OF EXILE

1. Richly detailed accounts of this collaboration appear in the following books, although each draws quite different conclusions regarding the failures of the relationship and the significance of Adorno's contribuitions to Lazarsfeld's Radio Research Project: Christian Fleck, *Translantische Bereicherungen: Zur Erfindung der empirischen Sozialforschung* (Frankfurt am Main: Suhrkamp, 2007), 264–352; Robert Hullot-Kentor, "Second Salvage: Prolegomenon to a Reconstruction of *Current of Music,*" in *Things beyond Resemblance: Collected Essays on Theodor W. Adorno* (New York: Columbia University Press, 2006), 94–124; and David Jenemann, *Adorno in America* (Minneapolis: University of Minnesota Press, 2007), 1–104.

2. Rolf Wiggershaus, *The Frankfurt School: Its History, Theories, and Political Significance,* trans. Michael Robertson (Cambridge: MIT Press, 1994), 165–68.

3. Ibid., 230–32.

4. The disappointment and frustration that Neumann suffered while in England led him to adopt a more Marxian position, which became evident in his scholarly writings. See ibid., 224–25.

5. This is a massive topic that is highly complex, but well documented in English. See Susan Buck-Morss, *The Origin of Negative Dialectics: Theodor W. Adorno, Walter Benjamin, and the Frankfurt Institute* (New York: Free Press, 1977); Eugene Lunn, *Marxism and Modernism: An Historical Study of Lukács, Brecht, Benjamin, and Adorno* (Berkeley: University of California Press, 1982); and Richard Wolin, *Walter Benjamin: An Aesthetic of Redemption* (Berkeley: University of California Press, 1994).

6. Horkheimer and Adorno liked to refer to the Institute's work as a "message in a bottle" (*Flaschenpost*).

7. The Institute's two advisers in Columbia's sociology department, Robert Lynd and Robert MacIver, kept encouraging the Horkheimer Circle to reorient itself and to reach

out to a wider American readership. See the letter from Horkheimer to Pollock dated 30 May 1941 in *MHGS*, vol. 17, 45–49.

8. Charles Beard, "The Social Sciences in America," *Zeitschrift für Sozialforschung*, vol. 4, no. 1 (1935); and Margaret Mead, "On the Institutionalized Role of Women and Character Formation," *Zeitschrift für Sozialforschung*, vol. 5, no. 1 (1936).

9. Letter from Horkheimer to Nicholas Murray Butler dated 14 March 1936, *MHGS*, vol. 15, 483–85.

10. Ibid.

11. Institut für Sozialforschung, *Studien über Autorität und Familie* (Paris: Alcan, 1936). For an analysis of American reactions and reviews of the book, see chapter 6 and its discussion of the relationships between Critical Theory and American sociology.

12. Max Horkheimer, "Egoism and the Freedom Movements: On the Anthropology of the Bourgeois Era," in *Between Philosophy and Social Science: Selected Early Writings*, trans. G. Frederick Hunter, Matthew S. Kramer, and John Torpey (Cambridge: MIT Press, 1995), 49–110; Max Horkheimer, "Beginnings of the Bourgeois Philosophy of History," in ibid., 313–88.

13. In this section of the study and elsewhere, Fromm had attacked Freud's overemphasis on the role of paternal authority within family dynamics and the Oedipal conflict. Fromm also claimed, as he had been arguing for years, that socioeconomic factors played a crucial role in ego development and psychic life. In fact, Fromm had been arguing for a long time that it was possible to conceive of a society that was more rational because of its basis in the ego rather than in the irrational, authoritarian domain of the superego that Freud emphasized.

14. Erich Fromm, *Escape from Freedom* (New York: Avon Books, 1941).

15. Leonard Krieger, *The German Idea of Freedom: History of a Political Tradition* (Boston: Beacon Press, 1957).

16. Herbert Marcuse, "Der Kampf gegen den Liberalismus in der totalitären Staatsauffassung," *Zeitschrift für Sozialforschung*, vol. 3, no. 2 (1934): 161–95.

17. Martin Jay, *The Dialectical Imagination: A History of the Frankfurt School and the Institute of Social Research, 1923–1950* (Berkeley: University of California Press, 1996), 126–30; Wiggershaus, *The Frankfurt School*, 154–55.

18. Mirra Komarovsky, *The Unemployed Man and His Family: The Effect of Unemployment upon the Status of the Man in Fifty-nine Families* (New York: The Dryden Press for the Institute for Social Research, 1940).

19. Erich Fromm, "Fromm—S.L. Experimental Program," *EFP*, microfilm reel 17 (box 17, files 1–4).

20. Letter from Horkheimer to Nicholas Murray Butler, 18 March 1937, *MHGS*, vol. 16, 91–94.

21. Letter from Horkheimer to Nicholas Murray Butler, 2 April 1938, *MHGS*, vol. 16, 419–23.

22. Ruth Munroe, *Teaching the Individual* (New York: Columbia University Press, 1942).

23. Letter from Beatrice Doerschuk to Erich Fromm dated 9 March 1939, *EFP*, microfilm reel 1.

24. Munroe, *Teaching the Individual*, 20.

25. Theodore Abel from his unpublished diary "Journal of Thoughts and Events," 23 January 1935, *Theodore Abel Papers*, box 1, journal volume 2, Columbia University Rare Book and Manuscript Library, Butler Library.

26. Herbert Marcuse and Jürgen Habermas, "Theory and Politics: A Discussion with Herbert Marcuse, Jürgen Habermas, Heinz Lubasz, and Telman Spengler," trans. Leslie Adelson, Susan Hegger, Betty Sun, and Herbert Weinryb, *Telos*, no. 38 (winter 1978–79): 129–30.

27. Letter from Lowenthal to Horkheimer, 2 August 1940, *MHGS*, vol. 16, 747–52.

28. Heavily redacted evidence of these investigations is contained in the files of the Federal Bureau of Investigation, Washington, D.C. See FBI subject files on Theodor Adorno (file numbers 100-106126-12, 100-106126-24, and 100-106126-30), Erich Fromm (file number 105-112622), Max Horkheimer (file number 61-7421), and Herbert Marcuse (file number 121-24128).

29. Letter from Lynd to Horkheimer, 19 July 1934, *MHA*, box I, file 5, document 269.

30. Letter from Horkheimer to Pollock, 25 July 1934, *MHA*, box VI, file 31, document 38.

31. Letter from Lynd to Horkheimer, 29 April 1935, *MHA*, box I, file 17, document 247.

32. See *Samuel Lindsay Papers*, boxes 59–64, Columbia University Rare Book and Manuscript Library, Butler Library. These boxes contain all of the case reports that comprised some of the raw data from the Newark unemployment project. Many of the case studies are covered with handwritten comments by Lindsay.

33. Robert MacIver, *Society—A Textbook of Sociology* (New York: Farrar and Rinehart, 1937); and Robert MacIver, *Leviathan and the People* (Baton Rouge: Louisiana State University Press, 1939).

34. Robert MacIver, *As a Tale That Is Told: The Autobiography of R. M. MacIver* (Chicago: University of Chicago Press, 1968), 136.

35. Horkheimer saved the talking points from one of these gatherings led by Robert Lynd on the topic "The Role of Sociology among the Social Sciences," *MHA*, box I, folder 5, document 261.

36. Abel reports a discussion of National Socialism that was led by Pollock in his unpublished diary "Journal of Thoughts and Events," 15 March 1936, *Theodore Abel Papers*, box 1, journal volume 3; and he reports a discussion of sociology and psychoanalysis that was led by Erich Fromm, found in box 2, journal volume 4.

37. An excellent example of this was the arrival of Franz Neumann. Although Horkheimer was visiting the Paris bureau of the Institute for Social Research, he insisted that Pollock not "forget to introduce Neumann punctually in MacIver's seminar." See letter from Horkheimer to Pollock, 20 September 1937, *MHGS*, vol. 16, 236.

38. Letter from Lowenthal to Horkheimer, 26 November 1941, *MHGS*, vol. 17, 220–23.

39. This was extremely ironic and unlikely, when one considers how frequently Fromm traveled away from New York to combat his constant bouts of tuberculosis.

40. Fromm's visibility was not just limited to Morningside Heights. He developed many important contacts with U.S. sociologists during the 1930s. Among the most significant of these were productive relationships with John Burgess and Harold Lasswell of the University of Chicago, and Ross Stagner of the American Psychoanalytic Society. See letter from John Burgess to Fromm, 18 October 1934, *EFP*, microfilm reel 1; letters from Fromm to Harold Lasswell, 6 February 1936 and 21 November 1936, *EFP*, microfilm reel 1; and letters from Ross Stagner to Fromm, 22 May 1938 and 2 June 1938, *EFP*, microfilm reel 2.

41. Lynd and his wife, Helen, became so fond of and impressed with Fromm that they hired him to be Helen's therapist. The psychoanalysis lasted four years, and it did result in the curing of Helen Lynd's writer's block. See Helen Lynd, "Oral History," interview by Mrs. Walter Gellhorn, Columbia Oral History Project, 1973, 27–28.

42. An excellent example was Lee Deets, who struggled with a project on Hutterite communities. Lynd, who feared that Deets was failing to appreciate the psychodynamics within the communities, sent him to Fromm. The subsequent meeting between the two led to invitations for Fromm to be a featured speaker before Columbia's Sociology Club. See letter from Robert Lynd to Fromm, 26 October 1936, and letter from Lee Deets to Fromm, 30 November 1936, *EFP*, microfilm reel 1.

43. The 1940–41 Course Catalogue for Columbia's Faculty of Political Science listed Erich Fromm as a lecturer on the social science department roster.

44. Daniel Bell, interview with the author, Cambridge, Massachusetts, 3 November 1997.

45. Ibid.

46. Robert MacIver, of course, came from Scotland and was educated both there and in England. Alexander von Schelting, who was a visiting instructor during the 1930s, was another major European figure in the department. Von Schelting was one of Max Weber's prized pupils and helped introduce the work of his mentor to eager graduate students at Columbia.

47. Letter from Philip Hayden from the registrar's office of Columbia University to Horkheimer, notifying him of his appointment as an extension instructor, 1 July 1936, *MHA*, box I, folder 5, document 237.

48. Gunzelin Schmid Noerr suggests that the courses were not taught owing to limited enrollment during the academic years 1943–44 and 1947–48. He also cites archival evidence suggesting that the subject matter and title may have occasionally varied during the 1940s, reflecting the Institute's growing interest in the fight against fascism and anti-Semitism. There are, for example, outlines for reconfigured courses titled "The Social Psychology of Mass Movements" (offered during 1941–42 and found in the *MHA*, box IX, folder 35) and "Totalitarianism and the Crisis of European Culture" (offered during the fall of 1945 and found in the *MHA*, box IX, folder 36a). *MHGS*, vol. 19, 220–22. Columbia's extension catalogs, however, do not reflect these changes in title or subject matter. Extension course catalogs were consulted from 1936–37 to 1947–48, *Columbia University Archives* (formerly known as the Columbiana Collection), and the courses were offered every year with the same title and virtually the same description.

49. Max Horkheimer, untitled final lecture for "Authoritarian Doctrines and Modern European Institutions," 12 May 1937, *MHA*, box IX, folder 33, document 9a.

50. Ibid.; and interview with Daniel Bell, 3 November 1997.

51. Horkheimer, untitled final lecture for "Authoritarian Doctrines and Modern European Institutions," 12 May 1937.

52. Max Horkheimer, undated lecture titled "Authority and Society Introduction," *MHA*, box IX, folder 33, document 1c.

53. Max Horkheimer, lecture titled "II" from the *MHA*, box IX, folder 33, document 2a.

54. The names listed are Alice W. Field, Theodore Geiger, Geraldine B. Farley, Anna Hartoch, Joan Kiesler, Mousheng H. Lin, Erwin L. Malone, Caroline Newton, Leo Rosanes, Ruth A. Disbrow, Nermiu M. Menemencioglu, Marshall L. Page, Deborah Ritt, Doris F. Smith, Milton Moss, Emanuel Maier, Ernst G. Schachtel, Arthur L. Svenson, Theodore Grabelsky, Eleanor N. Winograd, Julius E. Kuczma, Melville Brown, Konrad Bekker, Gerhart H. Saenger, Joachim Schumacher, Anna L. Michaelis, Daniel Thorner, Martha Buist, Robert Hulse, Alfred Seidemann, Isidore Sherman, Benjamin H. Hellman, Meyer S. Barash,

Gerard Degae, Edwin Strauss, Harriet Werner, and David Samalin. See *MHA*, box I, folder 5, documents 107–18, 133–45, 157–66, 175, and 221–22.

55. Interview with Daniel Bell, 3 November 1997.

56. See Gunzelin Schmid Noerr, ed., *MHGS*, vol. 19, 220–22, for a list of the specific seminar topics that were collectively carried out by the Institute for Social Research. The archives indicate that seminars were conducted on the following topics: 1936–37, "Selected problems in the history of Logic, with reference to the basic concepts of the social sciences," and "On Hegel's *Logic*"; 1937–38, a continuation of "Selected problems in the history of Logic, with reference to the basic concepts of the social sciences," and "On Hegel's *Phenomenology*"; fall 1939, "Spinoza's *De Emendatione Intellectus*"; 1941–42, "On Dialectics"; fall 1942, "On the concept of culture"; and 1945–46, "National Socialism and Philosophy."

57. Interview with Daniel Bell, 3 November 1997.

58. Ibid.

59. Ibid.

60. Pollock estimated that the Institute donated nearly two hundred thousand dollars to other scholars between 1933 and 1942. See Wiggershaus, *The Frankfurt School*, 249.

61. Ibid., 249–50.

62. Ibid., 261–64.

63. Some commentators have defended Fromm's theoretical consistency, suggesting that the other members of the Institute were the ones that had changed. The Horkheimer Circle adopted an increasingly pessimistic and nihilistic attitude toward social change that was at odds with Fromm's optimism (see Daniel Burston, *The Legacy of Erich Fromm* [Cambridge: Harvard University Press, 1991], 210–14); however, other historians of the Horkheimer group point to Fromm's increasing fascination with Freud's renegade pupil Sandor Ferenczi as a likely source of the conflict. By modeling a form of Freudian revisionism on the methods and ideas of Ferenczi, Fromm de-emphasized sexuality and constructed a naive social utopianism based on the notion of matriarchal authority. According to Horkheimer and the other Institute members, analysis could not abandon its commitments to either the materialism of the human sexual drives or the essential function of the reality principle (see Jay, *The Dialectical Imagination*, 88–106; and Wiggershaus, *The Frankfurt School*, 265–71).

64. Undoubtedly, the fact that Fromm spent so little time in New York also contributed to Horkheimer's unease and suspicions.

65. Letter from Horkheimer to Pollock, 4 June 1934, quoted from Wiggershaus, *The Frankfurt School*, 162.

66. Erich Fromm, "Memorandum for Dr. Rosenfeld," undated, *EFP*, microfilm reel 2 (previously indexed as box 2, folder 4).

67. Ibid.

68. Ibid.

69. Ibid.

70. Wiggershaus, *The Frankfurt School*, 271.

71. Lynd remained a strong ally, offering assistance and advice regarding Fromm's masterpiece *Escape from Freedom*. Fromm met with Lynd throughout the writing of this book, and even came up with the title as a result of one important communication between the two. See letter from Fromm to Lynd, 1 March 1939, *EFP*, microfilm reel 1.

72. Letter from Pollock to Horkheimer, 18 September 1941, *MHGS, Band 17*, letter 589, 177–80; and letter from Horkheimer to Pollock, 3 October 1941, *MHGS, Band 17*, letter 592, 191–98.

73. Lewis Coser, interview with the author, 6 May 1999; and Nathan Glazer, interview with the author, 21 January 1999, Harvard University, Cambridge, Massachusetts.

74. Helen Lynd, "Oral History," Columbia Oral History Project, 252.

75. Letter from Marcuse to Horkheimer, 15 October 1941, from Herbert Marcuse, *Technology, War, and Fascism,* ed. Douglas Kellner, trans. Benjamin Gregg (New York: Routledge, 1998), 231–32, and found in the original German in *MHGS,* vol. 17, 199–201.

76. Ibid.

77. Paul Lazarsfeld, "An Episode in the History of Social Research: A Memoir," in *The Intellectual Migration: Europe and America, 1930–1960,* ed. Donald Fleming and Bernard Bailyn (Cambridge: Harvard University Press, 1969), 328–29.

78. Ibid., 329.

79. Paul Lazarsfeld, "Oral History," interview by Joan Gordon, Columbia Oral History Project, November 1961–August 1962, 97–98.

80. Institute for Social Research, "Report on the Activities of the International Institute for Social Research for the Year 1939," *MHA,* box IX, folder 59a, document 4.

81. Ibid.

82. Letter from Robert Lynd to Horkheimer, 8 May 1939, *MHA,* box I, folder 17, document 232.

83. Institute for Social Research, "Minutes from a Meeting of the Advisory Board for the International Institute for Social Research," 22 April 1940, *MHA,* box IX, folder 59a, document 3.

84. Institute for Social Research, "Report on the Activities of the International Institute for Social Research for the Year 1939," *MHA,* box IX, folder 59a, document 4.

85. The evolution and history of this project, as well as a more general consideration of the Horkheimer Circle's contribution to American interpretations of Nazism, are examined in detail in chapter 6.

86. Letter from Eugene Anderson to Neumann, 5 May 1941, *MHA,* box I, folder 1, document 137.

87. Institute for Social Research, "Memorandum on the proposed incorporation of the Institute for Social Research into Columbia University," 7 January 1942, *MHA,* box II, folder 5, document 220–25. This memo reflected the conclusions that had arisen from more informal discussions throughout 1941.

88. Letter from Lowenthal to Horkheimer, 1 May 1941, *MHGS,* vol. 17, 30.

89. Letter from Horkheimer to Pollock, 30 May 1941, *MHGS,* vol. 17, 45–46.

90. Paul Lazarsfeld, "William E. Wiener Oral History Library of the American Jewish Committee," interview by Ann K. Pasanella, Columbia Oral History Project, February–April 1975.

91. Robert MacIver, "Enduring All Systems of Thought," *Survey Graphic,* vol. 28, no. 8 (August 1939): 496–97.

92. Robert Lynd, *Knowledge for What? The Place of Social Science in American Culture* (Princeton, N.J.: Princeton University Press, 1948), 18–19.

93. MacIver, *As a Tale That Is Told,* 137–38.

94. MacIver, "Enduring All Systems of Thought," 496.

95. Ibid., 497.

96. Ibid.

97. Robert Lynd, "Intelligence Must Fight," *Survey Graphic,* vol. 28, no. 8 (August 1939): 498–99.

98. The bitterness of this feud is tangible in Abel's diaries from the period. Although MacIver was a staunchly moral man, the diaries suggest that he sought to undermine Lynd and Lazarsfeld. See Theodore Abel, "Diary of Thoughts and Events," *Theodore Abel Papers,* box 1, journal vols. 3 and 4.

99. Letter from Marcuse to Horkheimer, 17 October 1941, *MHGS,* vol. 17, 201–4.

100. Ibid.

101. Letter from Horkheimer to Adorno, 14 September 1941, *MHGS,* vol. 17, 168–74.

102. Ibid.

103. Letter from Pollock to Horkheimer, 18 September 1941, *MHGS,* vol. 17, 177–80.

104. Letter from Horkheimer to Pollock, 13 October 1941, *MHGS,* vol. 17, 191–98.

105. Ibid.

106. Letter from Horkheimer to Lowenthal, 25 January 1942, *MHGS,* vol. 17, 247–48.

107. This step had been considered throughout the fall in the event of Columbia's rejection of the lectureship (see letter from Horkheimer to Adorno, 14 September 1941, *MHGS,* vol. 17, 168–74); it was instituted after Neumann's appointment. As soon as the decision arrived from the university, the Institute notified Neumann that he would lose his Institute salary if he took the job (see letter from Horkheimer to Lowenthal, 25 January 1942, *MHGS,* vol. 17, 247–48). Neumann attempted shift the blame to Robert Lynd. He insisted that Lynd was trying to strike at the Institute by creating discord within its ranks (see letter from Neumann to Horkheimer, 28 January 1942, *MHA,* box VI, folder 30, documents 439–42).

108. The project was accepted by the AJC during the summer of 1942 (see letter from Neumann to Horkheimer, 21 August 1942, *MHA,* box VI, folder 30, documents 325–26).

109. Letter from Horkheimer to Lowenthal, 31 October 1942, *MHGS,* vol. 17, 365–72.

110. This topic is examined in detail in chapter 6 and its discussion of the Frankfurt School's reception among U.S. sociologists.

111. Letter from Robert MacIver to Frank Fackenthal, 10 June 1944, *Columbia University Archives,* file 549/7.

112. Letter from Friedrich Pollock to Frank Fackenthal, 10 December 1943, *Columbia University Archives,* file 549/7.

113. Letter from Lazarsfeld to Theodore Abel, 5 February 1946, *MHA,* box II, folder 5, document 149.

114. Memorandum from Paul Lazarsfeld to Robert Merton, 4 February 1946, *MHA,* box II, folder 5, document 149.

115. Minutes of the Faculty of Political Science, 1940–49, meeting of the Committee on Instruction, 22 April 1946, *Columbia University Archives.*

116. Columbia Sociology Department, "Evaluation of the Institute for Social Research," *MHA,* box II, folder 5, document 149.

117. Letter from Lazarsfeld to Horkheimer, 21 May 1946, *MHA,* box II, folder 5, document 149.

118. Letter from Horkheimer to Lazarsfeld, 10 June 1946, *MHA,* box II, folder 5, document 149.

119. Letter from Lynd to George Peagram, 8 April 1948, *Columbia University Archives,* file 378/14.

3. JOHN DEWEY'S PIT BULL

1. Thomas Bender, *New York Intellect: A History of Intellectual Life in New York City, from 1750 to the Beginnings of Our Own Time* (Baltimore: Johns Hopkins University Press, 1987).

2. William Barrett, *The Truants: Adventures among Intellectuals* (New York: Anchor Press, 1982), 58.

3. See Martin Jay, "The Frankfurt School in Exile," *Permanent Exiles: Essays on the Intellectual Migration from Germany to America* (New York: Columbia University Press, 1986), 28–61; Alan Wald, *The New York Intellectuals: The Rise and Decline of the Anti-Stalinist Left* (Chapel Hill: University of North Carolina Press, 1987); Howard Brick, *Daniel Bell and the Decline of Intellectual Radicalism* (Madison: University of Wisconsin Press, 1986); Neil Jumonville, *Critical Crossings: The New York Intellectuals in Postwar America* (Berkeley: University of California Press, 1991); Gregory Sumner, *Dwight Macdonald and the Politics Circle* (Ithaca, N.Y.: Cornell University Press, 1996); Harvey M. Teres, *Renewing the Left: Politics, Imagination and the New York Intellectuals* (New York: Oxford University Press, 1996); Hugh Wilford, *The New York Intellectuals: From Vanguard to Institution* (New York: Manchester University Press, 1995).

4. Russell Jacoby, *The Last Intellectuals: American Culture in the Age of Academe* (New York: Noonday Press, 1987).

5. The correspondence between Hook and Horkheimer can be located in the *MHA*, box I, folder 11, documents 203–8.

6. Max Horkheimer, "The Rationalism Debate in Current Philosophy," in *Between Philosophy and Social Science: Selected Early Writings,* trans. G. Frederick Hunter, Matthew S. Kramer, and John Torpey (Cambridge: MIT Press, 1995), 217–64; Sidney Hook, "Experimental Logic," *Mind,* vol. 40, no. 160 (October 1931): 424–38.

7. Years later Hook recalled the events and some of their details, but he incorrectly dated them. Although Hook remembered the meetings as occurring in 1938, the archival materials from the Horkheimer archive indicate that these encounters took place in 1936 and 1937. For Hook's recollection of these events, see Sidney Hook "The Institute for Social Research—Addendum," *Survey,* vol. 25, no. 3 (summer 1980): 177–78; but for the archival records regarding these meetings, see Horkheimer's letter to Emil J. Walter, 14 April 1938, *MHGS,* vol. 16, 431–33. For the most complete historical account of these encounters, see Hans-Joachim Dahms, *Positivismusstreit. Die Auseinandersetzungen der Frankfurter Schule mit dem logischen Positivismus, dem amerikanischen Pragmatismus und dem kritischen Rationalismus* (Frankfurt am Main: Suhrkamp Verlag, 1994), 69–96.

8. Sidney Hook, "Dialectic and Nature," *Marxist Quarterly,* vol. 1, no. 2 (April–June 1937): 253–84.

9. Hook's feuds with the Communist Party, with the various factions within the Trotskyist movement, with the Socialist Party, with the critics of McCarthyism in academia, and with the New Left were long and bitter. When the occasion of the Sidney Hook centennial took place in 2002 at the Graduate Center of CUNY, it fittingly resulted in enormous controversy when Cornel West's invitation to participate in the proceedings prompted John Diggins to consider pulling out of the event (in the end, he did not—but Irving Kristol, Gertrude Himmelfarb, and Hilton Kramer did choose to sit out).

10. Nathan Glazer, "Concerning Sidney Hook," in Matthew J. Cotter, ed., *Sidney Hook Reconsidered* (Amherst, Mass.: Prometheus Books, 2004), 247–55.

11. During a lecture of 1917, Freud observed that the most venomous disputes erupt between parties that share more in common. Because each side sees so much of itself in the other, each fixates on the differences and magnifies them. See Sigmund Freud, "The Taboo of Virginity," in the *Standard Edition of the Collected Works of Sigmund Freud,* vol. 11 (London: Hogarth Press, 1957), 193–208.

12. For an excellent analyses of Deweyan Pragmatism and its historical context within the era of the 1930s, see John Patrick Diggins, *The Promise of Pragmatism: Modernism and the Crisis of Knowledge and Authority* (Chicago: University of Chicago Press, 1994); James Kloppenberg, *Uncertain Victory: Social Democracy and Progressivism in European and American Thought, 1870–1920* (New York: Oxford University Press, 1986); H. S. Thayer, *Meaning and Action: A Critical History of Pragmatism* (Indianapolis: Hackett, 1981); and Cornel West, *The American Evasion of Philosophy: A Genealogy of Pragmatism* (Madison: University of Wisconsin Press, 1989). For similarly concise and clear analyses of Critical Theory and its historical origins, see Martin Jay, *The Dialectical Imagination: A History of the Frankfurt School and the Institute of Social Research, 1923–1950* (Berkeley: University of California Press, 1996), and Rolf Wiggershaus, *The Frankfurt School: Its History, Theories, and Political Significance,* trans. Michael Robertson (Cambridge: MIT Press, 1994).

13. Sidney Hook, *Towards the Understanding of Karl Marx: A Revolutionary Interpretation* (Amherst, Mass.: Prometheus Books, 2002). Christopher Phelps, in the "Historical Introduction" to this newly reprinted edition, illustrates that this early phase of Hook's career can best be termed Leninist—which is to say that Hook was seeking to reexamine Marx's legacy in order to produce a justification for revolutionary action. With time, this early position vanished. Eventually, Hook came to embrace Marxian Revisionism, which he had rejected with scorn in *Towards the Understanding of Karl Marx.*

14. Sidney Hook, "A Personal Impression of Contemporary German Philosophy," *Journal of Philosophy,* vol. 27, no. 6 (March 13, 1930): 141–60.

15. Ibid., 148; and for a more general discussion of Hook's evaluation of German philosophy, see Christopher Phelps, *Young Sidney Hook: Marxist and Pragmatist* (Ithaca, N.Y.: Cornell University Press, 1997), 133–39.

16. This was a judgment that was similarly reached by the Horkheimer Circle and contributed to its analysis of Pragmatism.

17. Phelps, *Young Sidney Hook,* 28.

18. Jumonville, *Critical Crossings,* 20.

19. Brick, *Daniel Bell and the Decline of Intellectual Radicalism,* 34–35.

20. Diggins, *The Promise of Pragmatism,* 235–38; and Robert B. Talisse, "Politics without Dogmas: Hook's Basic Ideals," in Cotter, *Sidney Hook Reconsidered,* 26–36.

21. Jumonville, *Critical Crossings,* 20–22.

22. John Abromeit, "The Dialectic of Bourgeois Society: An Intellectual Biography of the Young Max Horkheimer, 1895–1937," PhD dissertation, University of California at Berkeley, 2004.

23. Max Horkheimer, "Notes on Science and the Crisis," in Max Horkheimer, *Critical Theory: Selected Essays* (New York: Continuum, 1989), 3–9.

24. Ibid., 3.

25. In addition to Paul Mattick's review (which is discussed below), less confrontational reviews regarding Pragmatism also appeared. See Herbert A. Bloch's review of John Dewey's *Liberalism and Social Action* from the *Zeitschrift für Sozialforschung,* vol. 5, no. 1 (1936): 119–20; and E. M. David's review of Ralph Barton Perry's *The Thought and Character of William James* from the *Zeitschrift für Sozialforschung,* vol. 5, no. 2 (1936): 270–72.

26. The review can be seen as an anticipation of the more developed arguments that Mattick would make in his pamphlet-length attack against Hook. See Paul Mattick, *The Inevitability of Communism* (New York: Polemic Publishers, 1935).

27. Max Horkheimer, "On the Problem of Truth," in *Between Philosophy and Social Science*, 177–215.

28. Ibid., 180.

29. Ibid., 180–81.

30. Ibid., 180.

31. Diggins, *The Promise of Pragmatism*, 139–41.

32. This selective and strategic use of William James bolsters the case made by Hans Joas in a pair of articles dealing with the general reception of Pragmatism in Germany and the more specific reception of Pragmatism by the Frankfurt School. In both essays, Joas argues that William James (for good and for bad) shaped the German reception of Pragmatism. James was accessible but perhaps careless in his formulations. Thus, Germans developed the general perception that Pragmatism equated truth with utility. Horkheimer relies on this same general assumption and combines it with formulations by Max Scheler's *Die Wissenformen und die Gesellschaft* that helped him make the connection between Pragmatism and Logical Positivism by reformulating the former as an instrumental rationality of action. See Hans Joas, "An Underestimated Alternative: America and the Limits of Critical Theory" and "American Pragmatism and German Thought: A History of Misunderstanding," in *Pragmatism and Social Theory* (Chicago: University of Chicago Press, 1993), 79–93 and 94–121.

33. Horkheimer, "On the Problem of Truth," 195.

34. Herbert A. Bloch's review of John Dewey's *Liberalism and Social Action* appeared in the *Zeitschrift für Sozialforschung*, vol. 5, no. 1 (1936): 119–20.

35. Hook's initial contact and correspondence was discussed earlier in this chapter.

36. John Dewey, *Reconstruction of Philosophy* (New York: Henry Holt, 1920).

37. Horkheimer, "On the Problem of Truth," 195.

38. Ibid., 196.

39. Marshak would later receive his PhD in physics from Cornell University. Marshak was a member of the Manhattan Project, a Nobel Prize nominee, and the president of CCNY during the late 1960s. Dubbed a "loyal American" following an interrogation during the McCarthy era, Marshak nevertheless was a lifelong activist for the cause of world peace.

40. Robert Marshak's review of Horace M. Kallen and Sidney Hook, eds., *American Philosophy Today and Tomorrow,* and J. H. Muirhead, ed., *Bernard Bosanquat and His Friends,* appearing in the *Zeitschrift für Sozialforschung*, vol. 5, no. 2 (1936): 269–70.

41. The correspondence between Hook and Horkheimer can be located in the *MHA,* box I, folder 11, documents 203–8; also see Hook, "Experimental Logic," 424–38.

42. Ibid., 426.

43. Ibid., 437.

44. The evolution of Hook's dialectical logic and the refinement of his critique of Hegel are evident in a series of articles that he published from the late 1920s through the mid-1930s. See Sidney Hook, "What Is Dialectic? I," *Journal of Philosophy,* vol. 26, no. 4 (February 14, 1929): 85–99; Sidney Hook, "What Is Dialectic? II," *Journal of Philosophy,* vol. 26, no. 5 (February 28, 1929), 113–23; Sidney Hook, "The Contemporary Significance of Hegel's Philosophy," *Philosophical Review,* vol. 41, no. 3 (May 1932): 237–60; Sidney Hook, "The Marxian Dialectic," *New Republic,* vol. 74, no. 955 (March 22, 1933): 150–54; and Sidney Hook, "Dialectic and Nature," *Marxist Quarterly,* vol. 1, no. 2 (April–June 1937): 253–84.

45. See Moishe Postone, "Critique, State, and Economy," in Fred Rush, ed., *The Cambridge Companion to Critical Theory* (New York: Cambridge University Press, 2004), 181–90.

46. Otto Neurath, "Inventory of the Standard of Living," *Zeitschrift für Sozialforschung,* vol. 6, no. 1 (1937): 140–51.

47. John O'Neill and Thomas Uebel, "Horkheimer and Neurath: Restarting a Disrupted Debate," *European Journal of Philosophy,* vol. 12, no. 1 (April 2004): 75–105.

48. They were not entirely misguided in noting the parallels between a Logical Positivist like Neurath and a Pragmatist like Hook. Over the course of the 1930s, Hook's attention was split between his Pragmatic reinterpretation of Marxism and the refinement of his ideas about experimental logic. Hook, consequently, was intrigued by figures from the Vienna Circle such as Otto Neurath. Neurath, unlike some of the more formal logicians, was interested in the application of scientific logic within the social sciences—a topic that would have appealed to Hook's interests at the time.

49. These critiques would emerge in two essays from 1937. See Max Horkheimer, "The Latest Attack on Metaphysics" and "Traditional and Critical Theory," in *Critical Theory,* 132–87 and 188–243.

50. Letter from Max Horkheimer to Otto Neurath, 24 November 36, *MHGS,* vol. 15, 743–44.

51. Letter from Max Horkheimer to Theodor W. Adorno, 22 October 1936, *MHGS,* vol. 15, 688–89.

52. Horkheimer, "The Latest Attack on Metaphysics," 159.

53. Horkheimer, "Traditional and Critical Theory," 213.

54. Hook, "Dialectic and Nature," 263.

55. Ibid., 281.

56. Hook, "The Institute for Social Research—Addendum," 177.

57. Ibid.

58. Ibid.

59. Ibid., 177–78.

60. Sidney Hook, "The New Failure of Nerve," *Partisan Review,* vol. 10, no. 1 (January–February 1943): 2. Subsequent references are given in the text.

61. John Dewey, "Anti-Naturalism in Extremis," *Partisan Review,* vol. 10, no. 1 (January–February 1943): 35–36.

62. Phelps, *Young Sidney Hook,* 75–77.

63. Ibid., 214.

64. Sidney Hook's review of Herbert Marcuse's *Reason and Revolution, New Republic,* vol. 105 (July 21, 1941): 91.

65. Ibid.

66. Diggins, *The Promise of Pragmatism,* 390–91; and, for a published account of the conference's main papers, see *Science, Philosophy, and Religion: A Symposium* (New York: Conference on Science, Philosophy and Religion, 1941).

67. From an undated biographical statement found in the *Norbert Guterman Papers,* box 10, Columbia University Rare Book and Manuscript Library.

68. Norbert Guterman, "Neither-Nor," *Partisan Review,* vol. 10, no. 2 (March–April 1943): 134–42.

69. Ibid., 142.

70. Horkheimer originally wrote his retort to Hook in the midst of the controversy, but editorial problems and his busy schedule with the anti-Semitism project greatly delayed *Eclipse of Reason.*

71. A draft of the lectures was also titled "Society and Reason," dated February/March 1944, from the *Max Horkheimer Archiv,* box IX, file 36, document 6a. For a superb account of the origins of these lectures and the ensuing book, see James Schmidt, "*The Eclipse of Reason* and the End of the Frankfurt School in America," *New German Critique,* vol. 34, no. 1 (winter 2007): 47–76.

72. Max Horkheimer, "Conflicting Panaceas," in *Eclipse of Reason* (New York: Continuum, 1992), 58–91. Subsequent references are given in the text.

73. See chapter 1 for a complete discussion of Feuer's essay and the controversy it generated. Also see Hook, "The Institute for Social Research—Addendum," 177–78.

74. Sidney Hook, "Reflections of the Frankfurt School," in *Marxism and Beyond* (Totoway, N.J.: Rowman and Allanheld, 1983), 120–29. Subsequent references are given in the text.

75. See Jumonville, *Critical Crossings,* 24; and Phelps, *Young Sidney Hook,* 168–69.

76. Daniel Bell, "The Theory of Mass Society: A Critique," *Commentary,* vol. 22, no. 1 (July 1956): 75–83; and Edward Shils, "Daydreams and Nightmares: Reflections on the Criticism of Mass Culture," *Sewanee Review,* vol. 65, no. 4 (autumn 1957): 587–608.

77. See Lewis Feuer, "The Frankfurt School Marxists and the Columbia Liberals," *Survey,* vol. 25, no. 3 (112) (summer 1980): 156–76; Lewis Feuer, "The Social Role of the Frankfurt Marxists," *Survey,* vol. 26, no. 2 (115) (spring 1982): 150–70; and Daniel Bell, interview with the author in Cambridge, Massachusetts, 3 November 1997.

78. Ludwig Marcuse, "European Anti-Americanism," *Partisan Review,* vol. 20, no. 3 (May–June 1953): 314–20.

79. Francis Goffing, "The American and European Minds Compared: An Essay in Definition," *Commentary,* vol. 28, no. 6 (December 1959): 506–14.

80. This theme will be explored in greater detail in the next chapter, which examines the European and American sociological traditions.

81. David Hollinger, "Science as a Weapon in *Kulturkämpfe* in the United States during and after World War II," *Isis,* vol. 86 (1995): 442.

82. Ibid., 444.

83. Letter from Edmund Wilson to Dwight Macdonald, 10 September 1938, *Partisan Review Papers,* box 1, file 20.

4. CROSSTOWN TRAFFIC

1. See chapters 1 and 2 for a more detailed discussion of the circumstances surrounding these concerns, as well as the documentary evidence that confirms the basis of these fears.

2. Although it might be tempting to attribute the Horkheimer Circle's behavior in the United States solely to the personalities of the members, the evidence clearly suggests that the circumstances of exile drove the group to isolate itself. The pre- and postemigration history of the Horkheimer Circle strongly indicates that neither the institution nor its members were hermits. By contrast within the context of European society, the Institut für Sozialforschung always maintained a prominent position within the world of German scholarship.

3. Letter from Max Horkheimer to the C. R. B. Educational Foundation, 26 December 1937, *MHA,* box I, folder 19, document 94.

4. Letter from Max Horkheimer to Friedrich Pollock, 28 November 1943, *MHGS,* vol. 17, 506–10.

5. Daniel Bell, interview with the author in Cambridge, Massachusetts, 3 November 1997.

6. Georg Rusche and Otto Kirchheimer, *Punishment and Social Structure* (New York: Russell and Russell, 1968).

7. Martin Jay, *The Dialectical Imagination: A History of the Frankfurt School and the Institute of Social Research, 1923–1950* (Berkeley: University of California Press, 1996), 149.

8. A myriad of clippings and excerpts from the reviews of *Punishment and Social Structure* can be found among the *Otto Kirchheimer Papers,* box 2 ("Compositions" folder) from the German Émigré Collection at SUNY, Albany. According to Kirchheimer's records, the book was reviewed in the *Survey,* the *Herald-Tribune,* the *Annals,* the *American Sociological Review, Social Forces,* the *American Bar Association Journal,* the *Washington University Law Quarterly,* the *Jail Association Journal, Federal Probation,* the *Sociological Review,* the *Harvard Law Review,* the *American Historical Review,* and the *Commonwealth Review.* All of these reviews were extremely positive and credited the book with a uniquely innovative historical, socioeconomic approach to an analysis of the penal system.

9. Daniel Bell, interview with the author, 3 November 1997.

10. Daniel P. Tompkins, "The World of Moses Finkelstein: The Year 1939 in M. I. Finley's Development as a Historian," in Michael Meckler, ed., *Classical Antiquity and the Politics of America: From George Washington to George Bush* (Waco, Tex.: Baylor University Press, 2006), 95–125.

11. Daniel Bell, interview with the author, 3 November 1997. According to Bell, Nelson was an important instructor at City College. Nelson, together with Finkelstein, exerted a powerful influence on some of the New York Intellectuals studying history at City College in the late 1930s.

12. Letter from Max Horkheimer to the C. R. B. Educational Foundation, 26 December 1937, *MHA,* box I, folder 19, document 94.

13. Daniel Bell, interview with the author, 3 November 1997.

14. The "Society and Reason" lecture series grew out of Horkheimer's collaboration with Adorno on *Dialectic of Enlightenment.* The lectures, which were given under the auspices of Columbia's philosophy department, were such a great success that Horkheimer decided to convert them into a monograph—this effort resulted in the birth of *Eclipse of Reason.* For the details of this evolution, see letter from Benjamin Nelson to Leo Lowenthal, 21 March 1944, from the *MHA,* box II, folder 11, documents 296–97; and, for the best historical account of the genesis of *Eclipse of Reason,* see James Schmidt, "*The Eclipse of Reason* and the End of the Frankfurt School in America," *New German Critique,* vol. 34, no. 1 (winter 2007): 47–76.

15. The confrontation was prompted by a paper that Herbert Marcuse gave at the German Sociological Society's 1964 conference at Heidelberg. Marcuse, who had ultimately sought to draw attention to the dangers of Positivism within the field of sociology, had pointed out the tragic constellation of historical forces contained in the work of Max Weber—in particular, Weber's flirtations with German nationalism. Nelson, seeking to defend the sociological methodology of Weber, attacked Marcuse (calling him an "Existentialist neo-Marxist") for implying that the legacy of Weber somehow resulted in Nazism and the concentration camps. Nelson's criticisms were later carried by the *New York Times* (3 January 1965) as a letter to the editor. This negative publicity prompted Theodor Adorno, who was directing the Institut für Sozialforschung back in Frankfurt at the time, to defend both Marcuse and the Institute. Adorno, in his own letter to the editors, insisted that some

of Weber's thought did warrant such criticisms, and he castigated Nelson for so loosely deploying the term "neo-Marxist." See Benjamin Nelson, "Comments on Herbert Marcuse's Essay on Max Weber," in the *Herbert Marcuse Archiv*, document 249.03, Stadt und Universitätsbibliothek, Frankfurt am Main; and letter from Theodor Adorno to the editors of the *New York Times* (26 March 65), in the *Herbert Marcuse Archiv*, document 1004.23. For a more complete account of the 1964 German Sociology Conference in Heidelberg and the debates about Max Weber and sociology more generally, see Uta Gerhardt, "Worlds Come Apart: Systems Theory versus Critical Theory. Drama in the History of Sociology in the Twentieth Century," *American Sociologist*, vol. 33, no. 2 (summer 2002): 5–39.

16. Jay, *The Dialectical Imagination*, 335n.

17. Theodore Abel, from his unpublished diary, "Journal of Thoughts and Events," *Theodore Abel Papers*, box 1, journal vol. 2, Columbia University Rare Book and Manuscript Library, Butler Library.

18. Theodor W. Adorno, "Scientific Experiences of a European Scholar in America," trans. Donald Fleming, in Donald Fleming and Bernard Bailyn, eds., *The Intellectual Migration: Europe and America, 1930–1960* (Cambridge: Harvard University Press, 1969), 350–51.

19. Daniel Bell, interview with the author, 3 November 1997.

20. Ibid.

21. Ibid.

22. Institute for Social Research, *Ten Years on Morningside Heights: A Report on the Institute's History, 1934–1944* (New York: Institute for Social Research, 1944). Although an obscure mimeographed document, this history became one of the Horkheimer Circle's primary means of formally introducing itself to American academics during the 1940s. In recent years, it has served as a major document for all historians and archivists of the "Frankfurt School" because it details many of the activities of the group during its first decade of exile. The claim regarding the authorship of the essay was made by Coser himself (Lewis Coser, interview with the author in Cambridge, Massachusetts, 6 May 1999).

23. Bernard Rosenberg, "An Interview with Lewis Coser," in Walter W. Powell and Richard Robbins, eds., *Conflict and Consensus: A Festschrift in Honor of Lewis A. Coser* (New York: Free Press, 1984), 27–52.

24. Lewis Coser, interview with the author, 6 May 1999.

25. Nathan Glazer, "From Socialism to Sociology," in Bennet Berger, ed., *Authors of Their Own Lives: Intellectual Autobiographies by Twenty American Sociologists* (Berkeley: University of California Press, 1990), 190–209.

26. Ibid.; and Nathan Glazer, interview with the author, 21 January 1999.

27. Ibid.

28. See letter from Irving Howe to Leo Lowenthal, 9 February 1948, *MHA*, box IV, folder 22, documents 154–57.

29. William Phillips, *A Partisan View: Five Decades of the Literary Life* (New York: Stein and Day, 1983), 105.

30. Letter from William Phillips to Erich Fromm, 17 May 1944, *Partisan Review Papers*, box 1, file 6, Howard Gotlieb Archival Research Center, Boston University.

31. Letter from Erich Fromm to William Phillips, 18 July 1944, *Partisan Review Papers*, box 1, file 6.

32. Letter from Erich Fromm to Philip Rahv, 2 January 1948, *Partisan Review Papers*, box 1, file 6.

33. Letters from Herbert Marcuse to Philip Rahv, 13 November 1955 and 26 January 1956, *Partisan Review Papers*, box 4, file 3.

34. Letter from Jürgen Habermas to Caroline Rand Herron (a managing editor of *Partisan Review*), 28 October 1968, *Partisan Review Papers*, box 27, file 2; and letter from Leo Lowenthal to William Phillips, 2 November 1971, *Partisan Review Papers*, box 30, file 1.

35. Letter from Leo Lowenthal to Max Horkheimer, 4 August 1944, *MHGS*, vol. 17, 583–87.

36. This topic will be explored in more detail in chapter 6.

37. Nathan Glazer, "*Commentary:* The Early Years," in Murray Friedman, ed., *Commentary in American Life* (Philadelphia: Temple University Press, 2005), 38–51; and Nathan Glazer, interview with the author, 21 January 1999.

38. Nathan Abrams, "America Is Home: *Commentary* Magazine and the Refocusing of the Community of Memory, 1945–1960," in Friedman, *Commentary in American Life*, 9–37.

39. Elliot E. Cohen, "An Act of Affirmation: Editorial Statement," *Commentary*, vol. 1, no. 1 (November 1945): 1–3.

40. Letter from Max Horkheimer to Elliot E. Cohen, 21 March 1946, *MHA*, box II, folder 5, document 36.

41. Letter from Elliot Cohen to Max Horkheimer, 8 April 1946, *MHA*, box II, folder 5, document 35.

42. Abrams, "America Is Home," 9–37.

43. Franz L. Neumann, "Re-educating the Germans: The Dilemma of Reconstruction," *Commentary*, vol. 3, no. 6 (June 1947): 517–25.

44. A. R. L. Gurland, "Why Democracy Is Losing in Germany: Behind the Recent Elections," *Commentary*, vol. 8, no. 3 (September 1949): 227–37.

45. Leo Lowenthal, "Heine's Religion: The Messianic Ideals of the Poet," *Commentary*, vol. 4, no. 2 (August 1947): 153–57.

46. Ibid., 153–54.

47. Ibid., 154.

48. The literature on the formation of Critical Theory is vast. The accounts that have most informed my own analysis are John Abromeit, "The Dialectic of Bourgeois Society: An Intellectual Biography of the Young Max Horkheimer, 1895–1937," PhD dissertation, University of California at Berkeley, 2004; Seyla Benhabib, *Critique, Norm, and Utopia: A Study of the Foundations of Critical Theory* (New York: Columbia University Press, 1986); Helmut Dubiel, *Theory and Politics: Studies in the Development of Critical Theory*, trans. Benjamin Gregg (Cambridge: MIT Press, 1985); Jay, *The Dialectical Imagination;* Moishe Postone, *Time, Labor, and Social Domination: A Reinterpretation of Marx's Critical Theory* (New York: Cambridge University Press, 2003); Moishe Postone, "Critique, State, and Economy," in Fred Rush, ed., *The Cambridge Companion to Critical Theory* (New York: Cambridge University Press, 2004), 165–93; Fred Rush, "Conceptual Foundations of Early Critical Theory," in Rush, *The Cambridge Companion to Critical Theory*, 6–39; Albrecht Wellmer, *Critical Theory of Society*, trans. John Cummings (New York: Herder and Herder, 1971); and Rolf Wiggershaus, *The Frankfurt School: Its History, Theories, and Political Significance*, trans. Michael Robertson (Cambridge: MIT Press, 1994).

49. For examples, see Leo Lowenthal, "Zur gesellschaftlichen Lage der Literatur," *Zeitschrift für Sozialforschung*, vol. 1, nos. 1–2 (1932): 85–102; Leo Lowenthal, "Conrad

Ferdinand Meyers heroische Geschichtsauffassung," *Zeitschrift für Sozialforschung,* vol. 2, no. 3 (1933): 34–62; Leo Lowenthal, "Die Auffassung Dostojewskis in Vorkriegsdeutschland," *Zeitschrift für Sozialforschung,* vol. 3, no. 3 (1934): 343–82; Leo Lowenthal, "Das Individuum in der individualistischen Gesellschaft. Bemerkung über Ibsen," *Zeitschrift für Sozialforschung,* vol. 5, no. 3 (1936): 321–63; Theodor W. Adorno, "Zur gesellschaftlichen Lage der Musik," *Zeitschrift für Sozialforschung,* vol. 1, no. 3 (1932): 356–78; Theodor W. Adorno [Pseudonym: Hektor Rottweiler], "Über Jazz," *Zeitschrift für Sozialforschung,* vol. 5, no. 2 (1936): 235–59; Walter Benjamin, "Zum gegenwärtigen gesellschaftlichen Standort des französischen Schriftstellers," *Zeitschrift für Sozialforschung,* vol. 3, no. 1 (1934): 54–78; Walter Benjamin, "Probleme der Sprachsoziologie," *Zeitschrift für Sozialforschung,* vol. 4, no. 2 (1935): 248–68.

50. Walter Benjamin, "L'Œuvre d'art à l'époque de sa reproduction mécanisée," *Zeitschrift für Sozialforschung,* vol. 5, no. 1 (1936): 40–68. Two versions of this essay have been translated by Harvard University Press; see Walter Benjamin, "The Work of Art in the Age of Its Technological Reproducibility: Second Version," in Howard Eiland and Michael W. Jennings, eds., *Walter Benjamin Selected Writings: Volume 3, 1935–1938* (Cambridge: Belknap Press, 2002), 101–33; and Walter Benjamin, "The Work of Art in the Age of Its Technological Reproducibility: Third Version," in Howard Eiland and Michael W. Jennings, eds., *Walter Benjamin Selected Writings: Volume 4, 1938–1940* (Cambridge: Belknap Press, 2003), 251–83.

51. Herbert Marcuse, "Über den affirmativen Charakter der Kultur," *Zeitschrift für Sozialforschung,* vol. 6, no. 1 (1937): 54–94; and, in English, "The Affirmative Character of Culture," in Herbert Marcuse, *Negations: Essays in Critical Theory* (Boston: Beacon Press, 1969), 88–133.

52. Theodor W. Adorno, "Über den Fetischcharakter in der Musik und die Regression des Hörens," *Zeitschrift für Sozialforschung,* vol. 7, no. 3 (1938): 321–56; and, in English, "On the Fetish Character in Music and the Regression of Listening," in Andrew Arato and Eike Gebhardt, eds., *The Essential Frankfurt School Reader* (New York: Continuum, 1993), 270–99.

53. Friedrich Pollock, "State Capitalism: Its Possibilities and Limitations," *Studies in Philosophy and Social Science,* vol. 9, no. 2 (1941): 200–225; and Friedrich Pollock, "Is National Socialism a New Order?" *Studies in Philosophy and Social Science,* vol. 9, no. 3 (1941): 440–55.

54. Pollock's theory of state capitalism was echoed by Horkheimer in several essays from the same time period. See Max Horkheimer, "Die Juden und Europa," *Zeitschrift für Sozialforschung,* vol. 8, nos. 1–2 (1939): 115–37; Max Horkheimer, "The End of Reason," *Studies in Philosophy and Social Science,* vol. 9, no. 3 (1941): 366–88; and Max Horkheimer, "Autoritärer Staat," in *Walter Benjamin zum Gedächtnis* (New York: Institute of Social Research, 1942).

55. Rolf Wiggershaus, *The Frankfurt School: Its History, Theories, and Political Significance* (Cambridge: MIT Press, 1994), 280–91.

56. Postone, "Critique, State, and Economy," 165–93.

57. Max Horkheimer and Theodor W. Adorno, *Dialectic of Enlightenment,* trans. Edmund Jephcott (Stanford, Calif.: Stanford University Press, 2002).

58. This concept is borrowed from Lewis Coser and is being used for the same purpose that he intended—to distinguish between the highbrow radicalism that gave rise to Western Marxism and the proletarian/trade-unionist radicalism that filled the ranks of the

German Communist and social-democratic parties during the interwar years. The New York Intellectuals similarly saw a chasm separating themselves from the U.S. Communist Party.

59. Although many historians of the New York Intellectuals touch on this specifically Jewish dimension to the embrace of Modernism, it is developed most comprehensively by Alexander Bloom and Terry Cooney. See Alexander Bloom, *Prodigal Sons: The New York Intellectuals and Their World* (New York: Oxford University Press, 1986); and Terry Cooney, *The Rise of the New York Intellectuals: Partisan Review and Its Circle* (Madison: University of Wisconsin Press, 1986).

60. Paul Gorman, *Left Intellectuals and Popular Culture in Twentieth-Century America* (Chapel Hill: University of North Carolina Press, 1996), 13–28.

61. Ibid., 37–48 and 109–32.

62. Ibid., 53–76.

63. Ibid., 111–15.

64. William Phillips and Philip Rahv, "Editorial Statement," *Partisan Review,* vol. 1, no. 1 (February–March 1934).

65. William Phillips (using the pen name "Wallace Phelps") and Philip Rahv, "Problems and Perspectives in Revolutionary Literature," *Partisan Review,* vol. 1, no. 3 (June–July 1934): 3–10.

66. Ibid.

67. William Phillips (using the pen name "Wallace Phelps") and Philip Rahv, "Criticism," *Partisan Review,* vol. 2, no. 7 (April–May 1935): 16–25.

68. Ibid.

69. Gorman, *Left Intellectuals and Popular Culture in Twentieth-Century America,* 123–26.

70. Phillips, *A Partisan View,* 51.

71. Ibid., 44–45.

72. Irving Howe, "The New York Intellectuals: A Chronicle and a Critique," *Commentary,* vol. 46, no. 4 (October 1968): 31.

73. William Phillips, "What Happened in the 30's," *Commentary,* vol. 34, no. 3 (September 1962): 211.

74. By seeking to appear apolitical through its behavior and Aesopian language, the Horkheimer Circle affected the way that others viewed it. Instead of being out in the open like other émigrés and radicals of the 1930s, the Institute censored its members and avoided overtly political activities in an attempt to exist in isolation. Motives of self-preservation clearly outweighed political considerations, but in the minds of other public intellectuals who could not remain neutral about the debates raging over Social Fascism, the Moscow purge trials, Trotsky, and the Nazi–Soviet pact, silence was interpreted as a political stance.

75. Although members of the Institute remained in the United States and occasionally participated in these U.S. debates about mass culture (most notably Leo Lowenthal and Herbert Marcuse), the Frankfurt School generally retreated from the field.

76. Echoing the previous views that had been articulated by many of the other New York Intellectuals, Macdonald believed that Modernism represented the polar opposite of mass art. While Stalinism and commercial capitalism constructed cultures that were anti-intellectual and regimented, Modernism still embodied an aesthetic realm of freedom, authenticity, and pure consciousness. For this reason, the mass culture of Soviet Russia and the United States was particularly hostile to the avant-garde.

77. Dwight Macdonald, "The Soviet Cinema: 1930–1938," *Partisan Review*, vol. 5, no. 2 (July 1938): 37–50; and Dwight Macdonald, "The Soviet Cinema: 1930–1938, Part II," *Partisan Review*, vol. 5, no. 3 (August–September 1938): 35–62.

78. Philip Rahv, "Twilight of the Thirties," *Partisan Review*, vol. 6, no. 4 (summer 1939): 175–80.

79. Gorman, *Left Intellectuals and Popular Culture in Twentieth-Century America*, 152.

80. Greenberg initially sent a letter to Macdonald attacking his assumptions about the Russian peasants. The Soviet cinema series had contained a passing comment in which Macdonald speculated on the appeal of Stalinist art and concluded that this arose from the peasants' lack of "previous cultural exposure." Greenberg insisted that the ruling classes (in both the East and West) had always imposed their cultural standards on the rest of society from its very top to the bottom. The situation in Russia was nothing startlingly new. Conditions in the West, however, with mass art suggested something radically new. The hegemony of elite culture and its biases were directly under attack by commercial mass culture. See Florence Rubenfeld, *Clement Greenberg: A Life* (New York: Scribner's, 1997), 51.

81. The only available archival sources that shed any light on the matter are Greenberg's letters to Harold Lazarus contained within the *Clement Greenberg Papers*, the Getty Research Institute for the History of Art and the Humanities, Special Collections, Series I (Correspondences), box 2, folder 5; and Series I (Correspondences), box 3, folders 1 and 2.

82. Rubenfeld, *Clement Greenberg*, 56; and Nathan Glazer, interview with the author in Cambridge, Massachusetts, 21 January 1999.

83. Clement Greenberg, "Avant-garde and Kitsch," *Partisan Review*, vol. 6, no. 5 (fall 1939): 35. Subsequent references are given in the text.

84. Adorno, "Über den Fetischcharakter in der Musik und die Regression des Hörens," 321–56; for the English translation, see Adorno, "On the Fetish Character in Music and the Regression of Listening," 270–99.

85. Ibid., 325–33 (of the German original) and 274–80 (of the English translation).

86. Michael Wreszin, *A Rebel in Defense of Tradition: The Life and Politics of Dwight Macdonald* (New York: Basic Books, 1994), 95–104; and Gregory D. Sumner, *Dwight Macdonald and the Politics Circle* (Ithaca, N.Y.: Cornell University Press, 1996), 12–13.

87. Phillips, *A Partisan View*, 123.

88. Howe, "The New York Intellectuals: A Chronicle and Critique," 32.

89. For evidence of the reception of Erich Fromm's *Escape from Freedom*, see Dwight Macdonald, "A New Dimension," *Common Sense*, vol. 11, no. 1 (January 1942): 29; and Lewis Coser (using the pen name Louis Clair), "Why the Resistance Failed: An Outline," *Politics* 3 (April 1946): 116–18. For evidence of the reception of the Institute's views regarding Nazism (including a sophisticated grasp of the polarity between Pollock's theory of state capitalism and Neumann's monopoly capitalist interpretation), see C. Wright Mills, "Locating the Enemy: The Nazi Behemoth Dissected," *Partisan Review*, vol. 9, no. 5 (September–October 1942): 432–37; and Dwight Macdonald, "Political Notes: Nazi Economics Again," *Partisan Review*, vol. 9, no. 6 (November–December 1942): 479–82.

90. For the special issue regarding mass culture, see Institute for Social Research, *Studies in Philosophy and Social Science*, vol. 9, no. 1 (1941), which included the following articles: Paul F. Lazarsfeld, "Remarks on Administrative and Critical Communications Research"; T. W. Adorno, "On Popular Music"; Harold D. Lasswell, "Radio as an Instrument of Reducing Personal Insecurity"; Heta Hertzog, "On Borrowed Experience: An Analysis of Listening to Daytime Sketches"; William Dieterle, "Hollywood and the European Crisis";

and Charles A. Siepmann, "Radio and Education." For the special issue regarding Nazism, see Institute for Social Research, *Studies in Philosophy and Social Science*, vol. 9, no. 2 (1941), which included the following articles: Friedrich Pollock, "State Capitalism"; A. R. L. Gurland, "Technological Trends and Economic Structure under National Socialism"; Otto Kirchheimer, "Changes in the Structure of Political Compromise"; Max Horkheimer, "Art and Mass Culture"; and T. W. Adorno, "Spengler Today."

91. See Dwight Macdonald's review of Erich Fromm's *Escape from Freedom* titled "A New Dimension," 29.

92. Ibid.

93. Abbott Gleason, *Totalitarianism: The Inner History of the Cold War* (New York: Oxford University Press, 1995), 44–71.

94. Howard Brick, *Daniel Bell and the Decline of Intellectual Radicalism* (Madison: University of Wisconsin Press, 1986), 30–36.

95. James Burnham, *The Managerial Revolution* (New York: John Day, 1941).

96. James Burnham, "The Theory of the Managerial Revolution," *Partisan Review*, vol. 8, no. 3 (May–June 1941): 181–97; Dwight Macdonald, "The End of Capitalism in Germany," *Partisan Review*, vol. 8, no. 3 (May–June 1941): 198–220; Paul Mattick, "How New Is the 'New Order' of Fascism?" *Partisan Review*, vol. 8, no. 4 (July–August 1941): 289–310; and a series of letters on the topic from Victor Serge, Marceau Pivert, and Dwight Macdonald that were gathered and titled "'What Is Fascism?' The Discussion Continued," *Partisan Review*, vol. 8, no. 5 (September–October 1941): 418–30.

97. Macdonald, "The End of Capitalism in Germany," 201.

98. Ibid., 202.

99. By the early autumn of 1941, he was ready to concede that Burnham was correct in his analysis of Stalinism and that the Soviet Union was suffering from more than merely the effects of a "degenerated workers state." He acknowledged that Stalin's bureaucratic regime was "essentially the same" as the "politico-economic nature of the Nazi regime." See Dwight Macdonald's contribution to "'What Is Fascism?' The Discussion Continued," 429.

100. Ibid., 430.

101. Although the editors of the *MHGS* fail to recognize that the "MacDonald" mentioned in Adorno's letter was Dwight Macdonald, the context strongly suggests this link. The name "MacDonald" is mentioned in conjunction with Robert Warshow, as well as the world of magazine publishing in New York City. At the time that Adorno wrote the letter, Dwight Macdonald was involved in the slow process of breaking with *Partisan Review*, and he seriously considered the formation of a more highbrow, overtly political magazine. The Horkheimer Circle, of which he was clearly aware by this point, may well have been a group that he aspired to publish in English. Last, and perhaps most important, the peculiar wording of the letter suggests a connection to Dwight Macdonald. After speaking of how encouraging the lunch with "MacDonald" was, Adorno proclaims that these people, "who really had something to do" with members of the Institute, needed to be rebuffed as clearly and succinctly as possible because they were too "unsympathetic." What does Adorno mean when he calls the group around "MacDonald" unsympathetic? Clearly, he does not mean personally or professionally. The lunch was encouraging, and "MacDonald" really had something to do with the Horkheimer Circle. "Unsympathetic," consequently, must be in reference to the political orientation of "MacDonald" and his friends. Dwight Macdonald's Trotskyism would clearly have frightened Horkheimer and been viewed

unsympathetically. See the letter from Adorno to Horkheimer, 10 November 1941, *MHGS,* vol. 17, 212.

102. Dwight Macdonald, "A Theory of Popular Culture," *Politics,* vol. 1, no. 1 (February 1944): 20–23.

103. Ibid., 21–22.

104. Dwight Macdonald, "'Here Lies Our Road!' said Writer to Reader," *Politics,* vol. 1, no. 8 (September 1944): 250.

105. Dwight Macdonald, "Popular Culture: Field Notes," *Politics,* vol. 2, no. 4 (April 1945): 112–16.

106. Ibid., 112.

107. Ibid., 113.

108. Ibid., 113–14.

109. Ibid., 114.

110. Irving Howe, "Notes on Mass Culture," *Politics,* vol. 5, no. 2 (spring 1948): 120–23.

111. Ibid., 120.

112. Ibid., 121.

113. Ibid.

114. The New York Intellectuals' output on the topics of Modernism, mass culture, totalitarianism, alienation, conformity, and the Holocaust is too massive to analyze or even to list. Most of the writings are fairly repetitive—recalling and developing points that had been made at different times by various members of this community of writers. Among the theoretical highlights, see Daniel Bell, "The Face of Tomorrow," *Jewish Frontier,* vol. 11, no. 6 (June 1944): 15–20; Daniel Bell, "A Parable of Alienation," *Jewish Frontier,* vol. 13, no. 11 (November 1946); Nathan Glazer, "The 'Alienation' of Modern Man: Some Diagnoses of the Malady," *Commentary,* vol. 3, no. 4 (April 1947): 378–85; Arnold Green, "Why Americans Feel Insecure: The Sense of Alienation Is Not Exclusively Jewish," *Commentary,* vol. 6, no. 1 (July 1948): 18–28; Clement Greenberg, "The Situation at the Moment," *Partisan Review,* vol. 15, no. 1 (January 1948): 81–84; Clement Greenberg, "The Decline of Cubism," *Partisan Review,* vol. 15, no. 3 (March 1948): 366–69; Clement Greenberg, "The Plight of Our Culture," *Commentary,* vol. 15, no. 6 (June 1953); Clement Greenberg, "Work and Leisure under Industrialism: The Plight of Our Culture: Part II," *Commentary,* vol. 16, no. 1 (July 1953): 54–62; Will Herberg, "Personalism against Totalitarianism," *Politics,* vol. 2, no. 12 (December 1945): 369–74; Irving Howe, "The Lost Young Intellectual: A Marginal Man, Twice Alienated," *Commentary,* vol. 2, no. 4 (October 1946): 361–67; Irving Howe, "This Age of Conformity," *Partisan Review,* vol. 21, no. 1 (January–February 1954): 7–33; Dwight Macdonald, "The Root Is Man," *Politics,* vol. 3, no. 4 (April 1946): 97–115; Dwight Macdonald, "The Root Is Man: Part Two," *Politics,* vol. 3, no. 7 (July 1946): 194–214; Dwight Macdonald, "Masscult and Midcult," *Partisan Review,* vol. 27, no. 2 (spring 1960): 203–33; Dwight Macdonald, "Masscult and Midcult: II," *Partisan Review,* vol. 27, no. 4 (fall 1960): 589–631; C. Wright Mills, "The Powerless People: The Role of the Intellectual in Society," *Politics,* vol. 1, no. 3 (April 1944): 68–72; C. Wright Mills, "On Knowledge and Power," *Dissent,* vol. 2, no. 3 (summer 1955): 201–12; William Phillips, "The American Establishment," *Partisan Review,* vol. 26, no. 1 (winter 1959): 107–16; Harold Rosenberg, "The Herd of Independent Minds: Has the Avant-Garde Its Own Mass Culture?" *Commentary,* vol. 6, no. 3 (September 1948): 244–52; Arthur Steig, "Popular Culture: Jazz, Clock and Song of Our Anxiety," *Politics,* vol. 2, no. 8 (August 1945): 246–47; and

Robert Warshow, "The Legacy of the 30's: Middle-Class Mass Culture and the Intellectuals' Problem," *Commentary*, vol. 4, no. 6 (December 1947): 538–45.

115. Erich Fromm, "The Psychology of Normalcy," *Dissent*, vol. 1, no. 2 (spring 1954): 139–43; Erich Fromm, "The Human Implications of Instinctual 'Radicalism,'" *Dissent*, vol. 2, no. 4 (autumn 1955): 342–49; Erich Fromm, "Communications: A Counter-Rebuttal," *Dissent*, vol. 3, no. 1 (winter 1956): 81–83; Gurland, "Why Democracy Is Losing in Germany," 227–37; Otto Kirchheimer, "Franz Neumann: An Appreciation," *Dissent*, vol. 4, no. 4 (autumn 1957): 382–92; Leo Lowenthal, "Terror's Atomization of Man," *Commentary*, vol. 1, no. 3 (January 1946): 1–8; Lowenthal, "Heine's Religion," 153–57; Herbert Marcuse, "The Social Implications of Freudian 'Revisionism,'" *Dissent*, vol. 2, no. 3 (summer 1955): 221–40; Herbert Marcuse, "Communications: A Reply to Erich Fromm," *Dissent*, vol. 3, no. 1 (winter 1956): 79–81; Herbert Marcuse, "Notes on the Problem of Historical Laws," *Partisan Review*, vol. 26, no. 1 (winter 1959); Herbert Marcuse, "Language and Technological Society," *Dissent*, vol. 8, no. 1 (winter 1961): 66–74; Neumann, "Re-educating the Germans," 517–25; and Franz Neumann, "Anxiety in Politics," *Dissent*, vol. 2, no. 2 (spring 1955): 133–43.

116. H. Stuart Hughes, "Franz Neumann between Marxism and Liberal Democracy," in Donald Fleming and Bernard Bailyn, eds., *The Intellectual Migration: Europe and America, 1930–1960* (Cambridge: Harvard University Press, 1969), 446–62; and Peter Gay, who knew Neumann very well at Columbia, strongly agreed during an interview with the author in New York, 12 November 1997.

5. THE ATLANTIC DIVIDE

1. See H. Stuart Hughes, *The Sea Change: The Migration of Social Thought, 1930–1965* (New York: McGraw-Hill, 1977).

2. See Daniel Breslau, "The American Spencerians: Theorizing a New Science," in Craig Calhoun, ed., *Sociology in America: A History* (Chicago: University of Chicago Press, 2007), 39–62.

3. See Stephen Park Turner and Jonathan H. Turner, *The Impossible Science: An Institutional Analysis of American Sociology* (Newbury Park, Calif.: Sage, 1990); Edward Shils, "Tradition, Ecology, and Institution in the History of Sociology," *Daedalus*, vol. 99, no. 4 (fall 1970): 760–825; Franco Ferrarotti, "Preliminary Remarks on the Interaction between American and European Social Science," *Social Research*, vol. 43, no. 1 (spring 1976): 25–45; Urs Jaeggi, "Developmental Interaction between American and German Sociology," *Social Research*, vol. 43, no. 1 (spring 1976): 62–76; Richard Münch, "American and European Social Theory: Cultural Identities and Social Forms of Theory Production," *Sociological Perspectives*, vol. 34, no. 3 (1991): 313–35; and Uta Gerhard, "Introduction," in Uta Gerhard, ed., *German Sociology* (New York: Continuum, 1998), xv–xvii.

4. See Alex Callinicos, *Social Theory: A Historical Introduction* (Cambridge: Polity, 1999), 10–38; Robert A. Dentler, *Practicing Sociology: Selected Fields* (Westport, Conn.: Praeger, 2002), 2–5; and Alan Swingewood, *A Short History of Sociological Thought* (London: Macmillan, 1984), 7–14.

5. Callinicos, *Social Theory*, 20–24; and Swingewood, *A Short History of Sociological Thought*, 18–24.

6. Swingewood, *A Short History of Sociological Thought*, 30.

7. Dentler, *Practicing Sociology*, 5–7; and Swingewood, *A Short History of Sociological Thought*, 31–35.

8. Callinicos, *Social Theory,* 65–66; and Swingewood, *A Short History of Sociological Thought,* 41–42.

9. Callinicos, *Social Theory,* 65–66; and Swingewood, *A Short History of Sociological Thought,* 46.

10. Spencer, reflecting the views of his fellow liberals in Great Britain, maintained great faith in the individual. He saw society as the aggregate of individual interests, and he linked progress to the unfettered pursuit of individual self-interest. See Breslau, "The American Spencerians," 46–50; and Callinicos, *Social Theory,* 108–11.

11. Gerhard, "Introduction," ix; and George E. McCarthy, *Objectivity and the Silence of Reason: Weber, Habermas, and the Methodological Disputes in German Sociology* (New Brunswick, N.J.: Transaction, 2001), 39–61.

12. G. Duncan Mitchell, *A Hundred Years of Sociology* (Chicago: Aldine, 1968), 106–11; and Swingewood, *A Short History of Sociological Thought,* 134–35.

13. See Swingewood, *A Short History of Sociological Thought,* 142–46; Mitchell, *A Hundred Years of Sociology,* 84–101; and Fritz Ringer, *Max Weber's Methodology: The Unification of the Cultural and Social Sciences* (Cambridge: Harvard University Press, 1997).

14. Roscoe Hinkle and Gisela Hinkle, *The Development of Modern Sociology: Its Nature and Growth in the United States* (New York: Random House, 1954), 2.

15. Leon Bramson, *The Political Context of Sociology* (Princeton, N.J.: Princeton University Press, 1961).

16. Ibid., 3.

17. Mitchell, *A Hundred Years of Sociology,* 127–28.

18. Ibid., 129–39.

19. Ibid., 140–43.

20. Hinkle and Hinkle, *The Development of Modern Sociology,* 4–5; and Breslau, "The American Spencerians," 50–60.

21. Hinkle and Hinkle, *The Development of Modern Sociology,* 155–57; and Neil Gross, "Pragmatism, Phenomenology, and Twentieth-Century Sociology," in Calhoun, *Sociology in America,* 195–97.

22. Although Park was the most emulated among the figures that didn't fit the Positivist mold, there were others who were similarly prominent—for example, Lester Frank Ward, the reformist father of laissez-faire sociology, Charles Horton Cooley, the proto-Pragmatist, and Thorstein Veblen, the institutionalist.

23. See Paul Lazarsfeld, "Interview with Ms. Joan Gordon (1961–1962)," Columbia University Oral History Project; and Paul Lazarsfeld, "An Episode in the History of Social Research: A Memoir," in Donald Fleming and Bernard Bailyn, eds., *The Intellectual Migration: Europe and America, 1930–1960* (Cambridge: Harvard University Press, 1969), 270–337.

24. Steven Seidman, *Contested Knowledge: Social Theory in the Postmodern Era* (Cambridge: Blackwell, 1994), 93–94; Jerzy Szacki, *History of Sociological Thought* (Westport, Conn.: Greenwood Press, 1974), 502; and Stephen Park Turner and Jonathan H. Turner, *The Impossible Science: An Institutional Analysis of American Sociology* (Newbury Park, Calif.: Sage, 1990), 167–71.

25. Lewis Coser, *Refugee Scholars in America: Their Impact and Their Experiences* (New Haven: Yale University Press, 1984), 85–86.

26. See David Kettler and Gerhard Lauer, "The 'Other Germany' and the Question of Bildung: Weimar to Bonn," in David Kettler and Gerhard Lauer, eds., *Exile, Science, and Bildung: The Contested Legacies of German Émigré Intellectuals* (New York: Palgrave, 2005), 2–6.

27. Ibid., 6–13.

28. Ibid., 6.

29. Peter Rutkoff and William B. Scott, *New School: A History of the New School for Social Research* (New York: Free Press, 1986), 86–88.

30. Anthony Heilbut, *Exiled in Paradise: German Refugee Artists and Intellectuals in America from the 1930s to the Present* (Berkeley: University of California Press, 1997), 83–88.

31. Coser, *Refugee Scholars in America*, 110–11; and Heilbut, *Exiled in Paradise*, 95.

32. Coser, *Refugee Scholars in America*, 117.

33. See chapter 1 for a discussion of Columbia's perceptions of the Horkheimer Circle, and the university's ambitions for inviting its members to Morningside Heights.

34. Letter from Horkheimer to Adorno, 16 November 1934, *MHGS*, vol. 15, 265–67; this particular passage comes from Rolf Wiggershaus, *The Frankfurt School: Its History, Theories, and Political Significance*, trans. Michael Robertson (Cambridge: MIT Press, 1994), 158.

35. See Breslau, "The American Specerians," 43–46; and Patricia Lengermann and Gillian Niebrugge, "Thrice Told: Narratives of Sociology's Relation to Social Work," in Calhoun, *Sociology in America*, 63–114.

36. Institute for Social Research, "International Institute of Social Research: A Short Description of Its History and Aims," printed brochure (New York: International Institute of Social Research, 1935), from the *MHA*, box IX, folder 51a, document 2.

37. See Max Horkheimer, "The Present Situation of Social Philosophy and the Tasks of an Institute for Social Research," in *Between Philosophy and Social Science: Selected Early Writings*, trans. G. Frederick Hunter, Matthew S. Kramer, and John Torpey (Cambridge: MIT Press, 1995), 1–14.

38. See chapter 2 for this discussion of Fromm's early activities and contacts in the United States.

39. Howard Becker, "Review of *Autorität und Familie*," *American Sociological Review*, vol. 1, no. 2 (April 1936): 302–5; George Lundberg, "Review of *Autorität und Familie*," *Social Forces*, vol. 15, no. 1 (October 1936): 134–35; Clifford Kirkpatrick, "Review of *Autorität und Familie*," *Annals of the American Academy of Political Science*, vol. 188 (November 1936): 364; Hans Speier, "Review of *Studien über Autorität und Familie*," *Social Research*, vol. 3, no. 4 (November 1936): 501–4; T. H. Marshall, "Review of *Authority and the Family*," *Sociological Review*, vol. 29, no. 1 (January 1937): 1–19; and Leonard S. Cottrell, "Review of *Studien über Autorität und Familie*," *Philosophical Review*, vol. 46, no. 6 (November 1937): 670–72.

40. Becker, "Review of *Autorität und Familie*," 302.

41. Ibid., 305; and Marshall, "Review of *Authority and the Family*," 2.

42. Becker, "Review of *Autorität und Familie*," 304; Kirkpatrick, "Review of *Autorität und Familie*," 364; Marshall, "Review of *Authority and the Family*," 7–12; and Cottrell, "Review of *Studien über Autorität und Familie*," 670–72.

43. Becker, "Review of *Autorität und Familie*," 304.

44. Speier, "Review of *Studien über Autorität und Familie*," 503.

45. See chapter 2 for detailed analyses of these research projects.

46. Letter from Robert Lynd to Horkheimer, 26 January 1937, *MHA*, box I, file 17, page 245.

47. Although some controversy surrounds the Institute's decision not to publish the German working-class project, most commentators agree that the inability to continue

collecting data was a serious blow to the investigation. Fromm's findings were unquestionably a source of discomfort and debate within the Horkheimer Circle, but it is not clear whether this was the reason for the Institute's abandonment of publication plans. See Wolfgang Bonss, "Critical Theory and Empirical Social Research: Some Obervations," in Erich Fromm, *The Working Class in Weimar Germany: A Psychological and Sociological Study,* trans. Barbara Weinberger (Cambridge: Harvard University Press, 1984), 1–33; Stephen E. Bronner, "Fromm in America," in *Of Critical Theory and Its Theorists* (Cambridge: Blackwell, 1994), 207–33; Helmut Dubiel, *Theory and Politics: Studies in the Development of Critical Theory,* trans. Benjamin Gregg (Cambridge: MIT Press, 1985), 11–15; Neil McLaughlin, "Origin Myths in the Social Sciences: Fromm, the Frankfurt School, and the Emergence of Critical Theory," *Canadian Journal of Sociology,* vol. 24, no. 1 (winter 1999): 109–39; Martin Jay, *The Dialectical Imagination: A History of the Frankfurt School and the Institute for Social Research* (Berkeley: University of California Press, 1996), 116–17; and Wiggershaus, *The Frankfurt School,* 170–75.

48. Mirra Komarovsky, *The Unemployed Man and His Family: The Effects of Unemployment upon the Status of the Man in Fifty-nine Families* (New York: Dryden Press, 1940); and Ruth Munroe, *Teaching the Individual* (New York: Columbia University Press, 1942).

49. Letter from Paul Lazarsfeld to Theodore Abel, 5 February 1946, *MHA,* box II, file 5, document 149.

50. Memorandum on certain questions regarding the Institute for Social Research from Pollock to "P. T." dated 1943, *MHA,* box IX, file 258.

51. Letter from Horkheimer to Adorno, 13 October 1937, *MHGS,* vol. 16, 240–41.

52. Wiggershaus, *The Frankfurt School,* 249–50.

53. Ibid.

54. James Schmidt, "*The Eclipse of Reason* and the End of the Frankfurt School," *New German Critique,* vol. 34, no. 1 (winter 2007): 52.

55. Ibid., 247.

56. Horkheimer's first analysis of the sciences represents an intriguing anticipation of his contributions for *Dialectic of Enlightenment.* Already at this early phase of his career, Horkheimer had forged the link between natural science and the domination of nature. See Max Horkheimer, "Beginnings of the Bourgeois Philosophy of History," in *Between Philosophy and Social Science,* 313–88; and see John Abromeit, "The Dialectic of Bourgeois Society: An Intellectual Biography of the Young Max Horkheimer, 1895–1937" (PhD dissertation, University of California at Berkeley, 2004), which systematically develops this interpretation of Horkheimer's intellectual development.

57. See Max Horkheimer, "History and Psychology," in *Between Philosophy and Social Science,* 111–28; "Notes on Science and the Crisis," in Max Horkheimer, *Critical Theory: Selected Essays,* trans. Matthew J. O'Connell (New York: Continuum, 1989), 3–9; "Materialism and Morality," in *Critical Theory,* 10–46; "The Rationalism Debate in Contemporary German Philosophy," in *Betweeen Philosophy and Social Science,* 217–64; "On the Problem of Truth," in *Between Philosophy and Social Science,* 177–215; and "Egoism and Freedom Movements," in *Between Philosophy and Social Science,* 49–110.

58. Wiggershaus, *The Frankfurt School,* 177–91.

59. Ibid., 248–50.

60. Ibid., 261–63.

61. See chapter 2 for the reaction at Columbia University's sociology department.

62. Prior to the 1940s, Horkheimer's name would have only been associated with the Institute and its *Studien über Autorität und Familie*. His numerous contributions to the *Zeitschrift für Sozialforschung* were largely unknown. Pollock and Adorno were even less recognizable within the sphere of American academia. Pollock's scholarly pursuits slowed a great deal as he accepted more administrative tasks during the late 1930s, and he produced nothing with which American social scientists would have been familiar. Adorno, meanwhile, was the newest arrival in the United States, and the only reputation that he had built outside of the Institute was that of a difficult, German "mandarin" who had failed in his collaborative role with Paul Lazarsfeld's radio research project.

63. Erich Fromm, as we have seen, received much attention for his innovative psychoanalytic approach to social research. His contribution to *Studien über Autorität und Familie* was the central focus in much of the review literature, and his continued work on the topics of authority, the family, and socioeconomic conditions involved many prominent U.S. sociologists and psychologists. Not long after his departure from the Horkheimer Circle, Fromm published *Escape from Freedom* (1941), which firmly established his reputation as a leading intellectual in the United States. Herbert Marcuse, while more closely connected with the social philosophical work of the Institute, was one of the more amiable figures of the group. His relationships with members of Columbia's sociology department were so close that he was often assigned various diplomatic tasks by Horkheimer and Pollock. Although his real fame was not achieved until the 1960s, Marcuse established himself in the United States with *Reason and Revolution* (1941). Franz Neumann, like Marcuse and Fromm, also developed close ties to Columbia's Faculty of Political Science. In fact, he was the sociology department's first choice when a temporary adjunct position was created for a single representative from the Horkheimer Circle (see chapter 2 for the details). Again, like the other victims of the budgetary ax, Neumann also achieved a major academic success in the United States almost immediately after his departure from the Institute. His comprehensive analysis of the Third Reich, *Behemoth* (1942), rapidly became one of the classic texts on the Nazi state. Leo Lowenthal, although he spent a longer period of time establishing academic credentials, also became a close associate of American social scientists. Required by Horkheimer to stay behind in New York, Lowenthal supplemented his salary by working for Paul Lazarsfeld on the studies of popular culture connected with the Office of Radio Research (later the Bureau for Applied Social Research). This subsequently opened doors for Lowenthal to enter the Office of War Information and later to head up the research division for the Voice of America. The many contacts that he developed over these years with U.S. sociologists eventually led to an appointment at UC Berkeley, where he blossomed and became a major pioneer in the sociology of literature.

64. Letter from Horkheimer to Juliette Fauvez, 25 April 1939, *MHGS*, vol. 16, 596–97.

65. Wiggershaus, *The Frankfurt School*, 275; and Anson Rabinbach, *In the Shadow of Catastrophe: German Intellectuals between Apocalypse and Enlightenment* (Berkeley: University of California Press, 1997), 184–85.

66. Max Horkheimer, "Die Juden und Europa," *Zeitschrift für Sozialforschung*, vol. 8, nos. 1/2 (1939): 115; for the English translation, see "The Jews and Europe," in Stephen Eric Bronner and Douglas Kellner, eds., *Critical Theory and Society*, trans. Mark Ritter (New York: Routledge, 1989), 78.

67. Pollock's theory of state capitalism was completed at the same time that the first proposals for an anti-Semitism project were formulated. Both were first published in the *Studies in Philosophy and Social Science* in 1941. See Institute for Social Research, "Research

Project on Anti-Semitism," *Studies in Philosophy and Social Science,* vol. 9, no. 1 (1941): 124–43; and Friedrich Pollock, "State Capitalism: Its Possibilities and Limitations," *Studies in Philosophy and Social Science,* vol. 9, no. 2 (1941): 200–225.

68. Friedrich Pollock, "Report on the Present Activities of the International Institute for Social Research," 7 December 1939, *MHA,* box IX, file 57, document 1b.

69. Letter from Horkheimer to Juliette Fauvez, 25 April 1939, *MHGS,* vol. 16, 596-97.

70. The earliest proposal for the anti-Semitism project appeared as "Research Project on Anti-Semitism," *Studies in Philosophy and Social Science,* vol. 9, no. 1 (1941): 124–43. The focus and tone of this first proposal are unquestionably more similar to the interpretations of anti-Semitism found in the *Dialectic of Enlightenment* than those found in *Studies in Prejudice,* the eventual realization of the proposal.

71. The successive drafts of these research proposals remain unpublished, but they are discussed in detail by several Frankfurt School historians. For the primary source material, one must consult "The Collapse of German Democracy and the Expansion of National Socialism," 15 September 1940, *MHA,* box IX, file 169, document 100; "Studies in German Society and Culture," January 1941, *MHA,* box IX, file 170, document 3c; and "Cultural Aspects of National Socialism," 24 February 1941, *MHA,* box IX, file 170, document 3a. As for the discussions of these proposals in the secondary literature, see Jay, *The Dialectical Imagination,* 169; Roderick Stackelberg, "Cultural Aspects of National Socialism: An Unfinished Project of the Frankfurt School," *Dialectical Anthropology,* vol. 12, no. 2 (1988): 253–60; and Wiggershaus, *The Frankfurt School,* 273–78.

72. See chapter 2 for a more detailed discussion of Fromm's contacts with U.S. social scientists.

73. Letter from Horkheimer to Nicholas Murray Butler, 1 December 1938, *MHGS,* vol. 16, 516–17.

74. Although little remains known about the Phoenix News Publicity Bureau, this early PR firm does appear in the history of the Museum of Modern Art (or MoMA). MoMA hired the Phoenix News Publicity Bureau in 1931 to attract national exposure for the museum. By 1933, the relationship came to an end following a reception for an exhibition of Maurice Stern's paintings from a recent trip to Bali. The Phoenix News Publicity Bureau arranged for newsreel cameras to be present at an Indonesian-themed party in which Stern's wife appeared and danced in native costume. As Clayton Funk recounted, MoMA's "more conservative museum members objected angrily" to the media circus. Subsequently, MoMA severed its relationship with the Phoenix News Publicity Bureau and created an internal publicity department. See Clayton Funk, "The 'Art in America' Radio Programs, 1934–1935," *Studies in Art Education,* vol. 40, no. 1 (autumn 1998): 37.

75. The Institute asked Lynd to codirect the original anti-Semitism project proposed during 1939. See the letter from Robert Lynd to Horkheimer, 8 May 1939, *MHA,* box I, file 17, document 232. Lynd also made extensive editorial suggestions for "Cultural Aspects of National Socialism." See Memorandum titled "Lynd's suggestions for re-writing of German Project," 5 August 1940, *MHA,* box I, file 17, document 221. MacIver, meanwhile, was also consulted extensively on both projects. Although there is not the same evidence of collaboration during this early phase of the two projects, MacIver was one of the central figures on the Institute's advisory board, and he later accepted a role as one of the early codirectors of *Studies in Prejudice.* See "Minutes from a meeting of the New York Advisory Board for the International Institute of Social Research," 22 April 1940, *MHA,* box IX, 59a, 3 and box IX, 59a, 4.

76. See note 75 regarding the Institute's advisory board, and see any of the Institute's official stationery from the 1940s listing its U.S. sponsors. Also see R. Gordon Hoxie et al., eds., *A History of the Faculty of Political Science, Columbia University* (New York: Columbia University Press, 1955).

77. In fact, Fromm had initially wanted the Institute for Social Research to accept an offer of formal affiliation with the University of Chicago. Much to his disappointment, Horkheimer chose to align with Columbia primarily because of New York's closer proximity to Europe.

78. Letter from Horkheimer to Louis Wirth, 27 October 1937, *MHA,* box I, file 27, 155–56.

79. Again, see any copy of the Institute's official stationery from the 1940s, and the names of these Chicago scholars appear among the American sponsors of the Horkheimer Circle. Also see the correspondence between Horkheimer and Charles Merriam, 25 March 1941 and 29 May 1941, *MHA,* box I, file 18, documents 336 and 337; see the letter from Horkheimer to Lasswell, 1 April 1941, *MHA,* box I, file 16, document 86; see the correspondence between Charles Merriam and the Horkheimer Circle, 1 July 1940, 30 July 1940, and 25 March 1941, *MHA,* box I, file 18, documents 337, 340, and 343; see Edward Shils, "Memorandum regarding American sociological developments," dated 1938, *MHA,* box I, file 22, documents 372–78; and see the correspondence between Horkheimer and Robert Maynard Hutchins, 7 January 1939 and 23 January 1939, *MHGS,* vol. 16, 602–3.

80. The Institute built personal alliances with the following scholars as it pursued both projects: Sidney Fay, the chairman of Harvard's Bureau of International Research (see correspondence between Horkheimer and Fay, 20 May 1939 and 2 July 1941, *MHA,* box I, file 7, document 229 and box I, file 7, document 227); members of the New School, such as Max Ascoli, Hans Speier, Arthur Feiler, and Adolph Löwe (see the correspondence file between Horkheimer and the New School from the *MHA,* box I, file 19, documents 147–243); Leon C. Marshall, professor at American University (see Pollock's letter to the Rockefeller Foundation, 29 April 1941, *MHA,* box I, file 21, document 253); Max Lerner, who aided Neumann on the Germany project's labor section (see Pollock's letter to the Rockefeller Foundation, 29 April 1941, *MHA,* box I, file 21, document 253); Felix Frankfurter, professor at the Harvard Law School (see the letter from Horkheimer to Frankfurter, 31 May 1941, *MHA,* box I, file 7 document 412); Meade Earle, connected with the Princeton Institute for Advanced Study and later head of the American Committee for International Studies (see the correspondence between Horkheimer and Earle during 1940 and 1941 from the *MHA,* box I, file 7, documents 1–7); C. C. Eckhart, professor of history at the University of Colorado-Boulder (see the correspndence between Horkheimer and Eckhart from 1940 from the *MHA,* box I, file 7, documents 12–18); as well as Alfred Cohn, Stephen A. Duggan, and William A. Nielson (listed as part of the official sponsoring committee for the Germany project; from the *MHA,* box IX, file 170, document 18g).

81. Letter from Horkheimer to Katherina von Hirsch, 14 July 1939, *MHGS,* vol. 16, 615–16.

82. Letter from Franz Neumann to Justice Louis Brandeis, 18 June 1940, *MHA,* box I, file 3, document 318. As for Paul Oppenheim, he was a private scholar in the history of science and a fellow émigré who settled at Princeton. He lived in Princeton, New Jersey, and became an active participant within the community of refugee scholars who lived there. He also, however, was a cousin of Max Warburg and had some powerful friends at the

American Jewish Committee. See letter from Horkheimer to Neumann, 13 August 1941, *MHGS*, vol. 17, 126.

83. Coser, *Refugee Scholars in America*, 20–21 and 42–54.

84. Jay, *The Dialectical Imagination,* 88.

85. McLaughlin, "Origin Myths in the Social Sciences," 109–39.

86. Ibid., 126–34.

87. Letter from Ernst Simmel to Horkheimer, 8 May 1939, *MHGS*, vol. 16, 602–3.

88. Ibid.

89. Horkheimer was clearly aware of the Institute's limited reputation in the United States. In fact, his initial contacts with many U.S. foundations included preemptive excuses and explanations for the group's isolation in the United States. For one of the best examples, see the letter from Horkheimer to Edward S. Greenbaum of the American Jewish Committee, 18 June 1940, *MHGS*, vol. 16, 719–22.

90. A comparison of the theoretically oriented first draft of the anti-Semitism proposal and the empirically bolstered second draft will be reserved for the next chapter. At that point, the Continental underpinnings of the initial proposal will be uncovered, and the accommodation with American research methods will be presented. With regard to the Horkheimer Circle's well-known struggles with its American advisers over the theoretical and methodological approaches to the Nazism project, see Stackelberg, "Cultural Aspects of National Socialism," 253–60. Eugene Anderson, the codirector for the Nazism project (who later led the Central European division of the Office of Strategic Services' Research and Analysis Branch and was consequently the supervisor of Neumann, Marcuse, and Kirchheimer), repeatedly tried to convince the Horkheimer Circle to scale back the social philosophical rhetoric of the proposed "Cultural Aspects of National Socialism." In Anderson's view, the Institute was making a bold proposition—that a historical continuity existed between the Weimar Republic and the Third Reich. The Horkheimer Circle, however, did not make a clear case in support of this assertion, and instead provocatively proclaimed it as a theoretical truth underlying Germany's transition to Nazism. What Anderson suggested was a thorough sociological analysis of the period that could support the general theoretical thrust of the Institute. Thus, Anderson sought to de-emphasize the Institute's classically Continental approach to the problem of Nazism and tried to get the Institute to adopt an Anglo-American analysis of the phenomenon.

6. ASSIMILATION AND ACCEPTANCE

1. See Institute for Social Research, "Research Project on Anti-Semitism," *Studies in Philosophy and Social Science,* vol. 9, no. 1 (1941): 124–43.

2. Ibid., 124–25.

3. Ibid., 125–33.

4. Ibid., 133–42.

5. Ibid., 142–43.

6. See David Jenemann, *Adorno in America* (Minneapolis: University of Minnesota Press, 2007), 128–47.

7. There is little doubt that Horkheimer also had psychological and professional motives for moving to California. As the Institute suffered setback after setback, the impulse to retreat emotionally and geographically must have been tempting. Nevertheless, Horkheimer did have a long history of cardiovascular problems (angina being the most frightening of them). See the letter from Horkheimer to Pollock, 27 May 1934, *MHGS,*

vol. 5, 124–25; and Stefan Müller-Doohm, *Adorno: A Biography* (London: Polity, 2005), 260.

8. Rolf Wiggershaus, *The Frankfurt School: Its History, Theories, and Political Significance* (Cambridge: MIT Press, 1994), 291–92.

9. The news from the Rockefeller Foundation was received 28 April 1941. See the letter from Joseph H. Willits to Horkheimer, 28 April 1941, *MHA*, box IX, file 170, document 180.

10. Wiggershaus, *The Frankfurt School,* 293.

11. See chapter 2 for the details of these plans and the ensuing negotiations.

12. See the letter from Pollock to Horkheimer, 18 September 1941, *MHGS,* vol. 17, 177–80.

13. See the letter from Horkheimer to Pollock, 27 April 1941, *MHGS,* vol. 17, 25–26; letter from Horkheimer to Pollock, 30 May 1941, *MHGS,* vol. 17, 45–46; letter from Horkheimer to Neumann, 2 August 1941, *MHGS,* vol. 17, 119–20; letter from Horkheimer to Neumann, 13 August 1941, *MHGS,* vol. 17, 126; letter from Horkheimer to Adorno, 28 August 1941, *MHGS,* vol. 17, 146; letter from Horkheimer to Adorno, 14 September 1941, *MHGS,* vol. 17, 168–74; and letter from Pollock to Horkheimer, 1 October 1941, *MHGS,* vol. 17, 181–82.

14. Although MacIver raised this possibility and also suggested a regular seminar led by the Institute for Social Research, Horkheimer continued to doubt the sincerity of the offers and feared opposition from his group's enemies. Furthermore, Horkheimer seemed to worry about the prominent executive role that Neumann was inheriting. Recognizing his colleague's administrative skills and goodwill at Columbia, Horkheimer also feared that Neumann might become the primary beneficiary of these efforts rather than Pollock and himself. See the letter from Horkheimer to Pollock, 13 October 1941, *MHGS,* vol. 17, 191–98.

15. These included the Good Will Fund of Boston, the Esco Fund of New York, the Jewish Teachers Community Chest, the Falk Foundation of Pittsburgh, B'Nai B'Rith of Lowell, as well as complex lobbying efforts at Cincinnati University, Hebrew Union College, and among the Jewish trade unions in New York. See the letter from Neumann to Horkheimer, 20 December 1941, *MHA,* box VI, file 30, 1–3. As far as Neumann's revised version of the proposal is concerned, see Institute for Social Research, "A Research Project on Anti-Semitism," 10 November 1941, *MHA,* box IX, 92, 7a.

16. Graeber was an American sociologist with long-standing interests in the topic of anti-Semitism. After reading the Institute's research proposal in *Studies in Philosophy and Social Science,* Graeber contacted the Horkheimer Circle and volunteered to assist in locating funding. Graeber, who touted his many connections with U.S. Jewish foundations, was offered commissions for any grants that were awarded to the Institute as a result of his efforts. See Schmid-Noerr's description of Graeber that appears as footnote 1 accompanying Horkheimer's letter to Neumann, 13 August 1941, *MHGS,* vol. 17, 129. Also, for Neumann's assessment of Graeber's role in promotion of the anti-Semitism project, see Neumann's letter to Horkheimer, 20 December 1941, *MHA,* box VI, file 30, 1–3.

17. See Neumann's letter to Horkheimer, 20 December 1941, *MHA,* box VI, file 30, 1–3.

18. In the short term, the Horkheimer Circle recognized that Americans would need to learn a great deal about Germany. At first it considered the possibility of the Institute attempting to serve this function, but it later opted for individual members of the group to provide this service through working within government agencies. Simultaneously,

Horkheimer also recognized a possible long-range strategy. Assuming that the United States and its new allies were triumphant, plans would need to be in place for undoing the damage in Germany that had been caused by the Nazis. The Institute could get a head start on these problems and later spearhead allied efforts at denazification. See the letter from Horkheimer to Marcuse, 24 December 1941, *MHGS*, vol. 17, 235–37. At the same time that these war-related plans went forward, Horkheimer also scaled back the plans for *Studies in Philosophy and Social Science* and insisted that it be published as a yearbook. Although this represented a drastic change to the journal's form, the content remained rigorous and innovative. The edition that Horkheimer envisioned for 1942 was to articulate the Institute's emerging "racket theory of society." The concept had its origins in Pollock's notion of state capitalism, but this new conception of monopoly capital had been expanded to include analyses of the cultural and psychological changes accompanying the rise of this new economic system. See Horkheimer and Adorno's "Memorandum über Teile des Los Angeles Arbeitsprogramms, die von den Philosophen nicht durchgeführt werden können," 1942, *MHA*, box VI, file 32, document 1; see Adorno's "Reflexionen zur Klassentheorie," 1942, in *Theodor W. Adorno Gesammelte Schriften*, vol. 8, ed. Rolf Tiedemann (Frankfurt am Main: Suhrkamp Verlag, 1972), 381; see Horkheimer's "On the Sociology of Class Relations," 1943, *MHA*, box IX, file 16; and see Pollock's "Die Rackets und der Geist," 1942, *Friedrich Pollock Archiv*, box XXIV, file 7, Stadt und Universitätsbibliothek, Frankfurt am Main.

19. See the letter from Horkheimer to Lowenthal, 25 January 1942, *MHGS*, vol. 17, 246–48.

20. See the letter from Neumann to Horkheimer, 21 August 1942, *MHA*, box VI, file 30, 325–26.

21. See the letter from Horkheimer to Adorno, 17 September 1942, *MHGS*, vol. 17, 330–32.

22. Neumann's initial list included Robert Lynd, Louis Wirth, Kimball Young, Harold Lasswell, John Dollard, Salo Baron, and Louis Finkelstein. See the letter from Neumann to Horkheimer, 17 October 1942, *MHA*, box VI, file 30, 322–23.

23. Neumann claimed to have warned Rosenblum about Lynd's political reputation, and he reported that Rosenblum replied: "as long as a man was not a party communist he was all right with him the more so since in his view the problem of anti-Semitism could only be attacked by a man with left views who is willing to go to the roots of the problem" (ibid.).

24. Ibid.

25. See the letter from Horkheimer to Neumann, 24 October 1942, *MHA*, box VI, file 30, 320.

26. Horkheimer and Pollock did not want to work closely with Lynd on the anti-Semitism project. Lynd had been highly critical of the Institute since the departure of Fromm, and they feared the potential renewal of his ire that might result from possible differences of opinion regarding the execution of the proposed project. Furthermore, from an administrative standpoint, Lynd's appointment as codirector might diminish Horkheimer's control of the theoretical content of the project, as well as Pollock's command over its scientific research. See Horkheimer's letter to Lowenthal, 8 November 1942, *MHGS*, vol. 17, 378–80.

27. See the letter from Pollock to Horkheimer, 9 November 1942, *MHA*, box VI, file 33, 98–100. Pollock's effort did pay off in the long run. Although the Institute was forced

to keep Neumann on the staff for a few months longer than expected, Pollock managed to disentangle the political theorist from the future plans for the anti-Semitism project. Additionally, Lynd declined the offer to be codirector of the project. It is unclear to what extent Neumann's departure had an impact on Lynd's decision. Publicly, Lynd insisted that he was forced to turn down the position because he was too busy with other work. Nevertheless, once Lynd was no longer involved, Horkheimer asked Robert MacIver to serve as codirector, which Lynd's rival gladly accepted.

28. See Wiggershaus, *The Frankfurt School*, 355–56.

29. The "sponsoring committee" was composed of an impressive but motley array of prominent U.S. scholars and other public figures. It included Leroy Allen, Salo W. Baron, Charles A. Beard, Hadley Cantril, Morris R. Cohen, Maurice R. Davie, Herman Feldman, Carl J. Friedrich, Harold D. Lasswell, Alfred McClung Lee, Max Lerner, Robert Lynd, Robert MacIver, Karl Menninger, Julian Morgenstern, Reinhold Niebuhr, G. Ashton Oldham, Robert E. Park, Arthur M. Schlesinger, James T. Shotwell, T. V. Smith, Maxwell Stewart, E. T. Talbert, and Paul Tillich. See "Committee of Sponsors for the Project on Anti-Semitism" found in Institute for Social Research, "A Research Project on Anti-Semitism," *MHA*, box IX, file 92, document 7a.

30. The testimonials were gathered from the Institute's correspondence with Charles Beard, Stephen Duggan, Harold Lasswell, Alfred McClung Lee, Max Lerner, Robert M. MacIver, G. Ashton Oldham, James T. Shotwell, Maxwell S. Stewart, and Paul Tillich. They included comments like the following: from Harold Lasswell: "Few topics are more urgent than this and few institutions are of equal competence to your own for the successful prosecution of research. Your Institute is distinguished for careful study of individual and cultural processes and is admirably equipped to bring out the full complexity of the inter-relationships involved"; from Alfred McClung Lee: "In my estimation, such a study would contribute significantly to our knowledge of this disturbing area of social tension and conflict. The better equipped we are with realistic analyses of antisemitism the better will Americans and others be able to combat the growth of this social malady. The project outline, modified as I understand it has been since publication in a preliminary form, I think represents a satisfactory starting outline for the proposed investigation. I hope that it will be possible for the Institute for Social Research to carry this work forward in the near future"; and from Robert M. MacIver: "I regard that project as exceedingly timely. I have no fear that the results of this investigation will be anything except beneficial. I know that your group has excellent opportunities for conducting it as well as the scholarly ability and the desire to make it a faithful presentation of the facts." See "Excerpts from Testimonials," in Institute for Social Research, "A Research Project on Anti-Semitism," *MHA*, box IX, file 92, document 7a.

31. The Horkheimer Circle cited articles published in 1941, such as D. W. Petregorsky, "Anti-Semitism: The Strategy of Hatred," *Antioch Review*, vol. 1 (fall 1941); Michael Straight, "The Anti-Semitic Plot," *New Republic*, vol. 105, no. 2 (September 22, 1941); Benjamin Akzin, "The Jewish Question after the War," *Harpers Magazine*, no. 1096 (September 1941); Albert J. Nock, "The Jewish Problem in America," *Atlantic*, vol. 167, no. 6 (June–July 1941); James Marshall, "The Anti-Semitic Problem in America," *Atlantic*, vol. 168, no. 2 (August 1941); Arthur H. Compton, "The Jews: A Problem or an Asset," *Atlantic*, vol. 168, no. 4 (October 1941); and Miriam Syrkin, "How to Solve the Jewish Problem," *Common Ground*, vol. 2, no. 1 (fall 1941). See "An Introductory Statement," in Institute for Social Research, "A Research Project on Anti-Semitism," *MHA*, box IX, file 92, document 7a, 1–2.

32. Abbott Gleason, in his fascinating history of the term "totalitarianism," points out that the concept had only arrived in the United States from Europe during the late 1920s. Primarily exported from Italy and Germany, where the word had been in use since the early years of the interwar period, the concept rapidly caught on in the United States. By the end of 1941, when the country entered the Second World War, "totalitarianism" had become a widespread idea in the United States. The Horkheimer Circle had been using the concept since the early 1930s (Gleason pinpoints Marcuse's "Der Kampf gegen den Liberalismus in der totalitären Staatsauffassung," *Zeitschrift für Sozialforschung*, vol. 3, no. 2 [1934]: 161–95 as the first deployment of this concept by the Frankfurt School), but its escalating use of the term may further suggest a conscious appeal to potential American allies and sponsors. In a further effort to be contemporary, the framers of the final anti-Semitism proposal may have prominently used the concept of "totalitarianism" to modify their image of contemporary anti-Semitism. Clearly, the Institute only had Nazi anti-Semitism in mind, and it explicitly highlighted the fact that similar Jewish scapegoating was entirely absent in the Soviet Union. Nevertheless, it still evoked the concept of "totalitarianism" even though its history of U.S. usage had established fuzzy symmetries among German Nazis, Russian Bolsheviks, Italian Fascists, and even American "New Dealers." See Abbott Gleason, *Totalitarianism: The Inner History of the Cold War* (New York: Oxford University Press, 1995), 13–71.

33. Institute for Social Research, "A Research Project on Anti-Semitism," 2–6.

34. Ibid., 3.

35. Ibid., 17–24.

36. Ibid., 8–9.

37. The first grant proposal separated each of these complementary components into distinct investigations. Thus, the 1941 article called for a study of "Types of Present Day Anti-Semites" (the psychological research study of anti-Semitic character types), "The Jews in Society" (the sociological research study examining the basis for Jewish stereotypes), and "Foundations of National Socialist Anti-Semitism" (the political research regarding the governmental function of anti-Semitism). See the Institute for Social Research's "Research Project on Anti-Semitism," 133–42. The revised AJC grant, on the other hand, called for the sociological and political components of the research to supplement the psychological investigation into anti-Semitic character types. At the same time that the Institute planned to gather evidence regarding the varieties of contemporary anti-Semitism, it planned to locate the sociological conditions and political motivations connected with specific character types. The new proposal therefore set similar goals to the first but broadened and strengthened the evidentiary basis for the psychological analysis. See Institute for Social Research, "A Research Project on Anti-Semitism," *MHA*, box IX, file 92, document 7a.

38. See the Institute for Social Research's "A Research Project on Anti-Semitism," *MHA*, 14.

39. Ibid., 31.

40. Ibid., 31–32.

41. Helmut Dubiel, *Theory and Politics: Studies in the Development of Critical Theory*, trans. Benjamin Gregg (Cambridge: MIT Press, 1985), 106.

42. Martin Jay, *The Dialectical Imagination: A History of the Frankfurt School and the Institute for Social Research* (Berkeley: University of California Press, 1996), 221–24.

43. Wiggershaus, *The Frankfurt School*, 320–21.

44. Lewis Coser, *Refugee Scholars in America: Their Impact and Their Experiences* (New Haven: Yale University Press, 1984), 97.

45. Peter Uwe Hohendahl, *Prismatic Thought: Theodor W. Adorno* (Lincoln: University of Nebraska Press, 1995), 41–44 and 52; and Zoltan Tar, *The Frankfurt School: The Critical Theories of Max Horkheimer and Theodor W. Adorno* (New York: John Wiley and Sons, 1977), 102–12.

46. Early during the Institute's collaboration with the American Jewish Committee, strategies for managing the project and cooperating with American sponsors were discussed, and Lazarsfeld was touted as the appropriate role model for the Horkheimer Circle. As Pollock explained in an internal memorandum, "I am told that that is the way how the Social Science Research Council, the Rockefeller Foundation and project directors, who know their job like Lazarsfeld, prepare the extension of projects." See Pollock's "Memorandum re: Antisemitism Project," 29 October 1943, *MHA*, box VI, file 34, 146–47.

47. See Jennifer Platt, *A History of Sociological Research Methods in America, 1920–1960* (New York: Cambridge University Press, 1996); Terry Nicholas Clark, "Clientism and Universalism: Columbia Sociology under Lazarsfeld and Merton," *Tocqueville Review*, vol. 17, no. 2 (1996): 183–205; Vittorio Capecchi, "Paul F. Lazarsfeld: A Link between American and European Methodology," *Quality and Quantity*, vol. 12, no. 3 (September 1978): 239–54; and Allen H. Barton, "Paul Lazarsfeld and Applied Social Research: Invention of the University Applied Social Research Institute," *Social Science History*, vol. 3, nos. 3–4 (October 1979): 4–44.

48. The underlying assumption justifying this half of the project—that Nazi anti-Semitism represented a new sociological form of prejudice that would threaten Western civilization if it spread beyond the confines of Central Europe—was consistent with the Institute's earliest thoughts regarding an anti-Semitism project. See the report on the anti-Semitism project, 16 April 1943, *MHA*, box IX, file 43, document a; and see Wiggershaus, *The Frankfurt School*, 361–62.

49. This similarity was not lost on the Horkheimer Circle's contemporaries. Paul Lazarsfeld, who saw clear similarities to the work of Fromm, requested that his staff at the Bureau of Applied Social Research reexamine *Autorität und Familie* and make note of its similarities to *The Authoritarian Personality*. Not surprisingly, Lazarsfeld's staff noted striking parallels between the two projects. It remains unclear, however, why Lazarsfeld called for this review. See Bo Anderson's memo titled "Some Notes on *The Authoritarian Personality* and *Autorität und Familie*," 31 May 1958, *Paul Lazarsfeld Papers*, Columbia University Rare Book and Manuscript Library, Butler Library, box 20, file 13.

50. See the report on anti-Semitism, 16 April 1943, and Wiggershaus, *The Frankfurt School*, 357–60.

51. See the letter from Horkheimer to Marcuse, 17 July 1943, *MHA*, box VI, file 27a, 12–13.

52. As Horkheimer admitted to Pollock in the summer of 1943, "I am in the first place not a social scientist but a philosopher—and, what is worse, a philosopher of an old school of thought, not very popular in social science." See the letter from Horkheimer to Pollock, 9 June 1943, *MHA*, box VI, file 33, 469–73.

53. See the letter from Horkheimer to Pollock, 20 March 1943, *MHA*, box VI, file 33, 244–46.

54. See the letter from Horkheimer to Pollock, 19 May 1943, *MHA*, box VI, file 33, 505–7; and Wiggershaus, *The Frankfurt School*, 359–60.

55. The film study called for subjects to view a playground scenario in which a child was beaten viciously by classmates. In only some versions of the film was the victim

depicted as stereotypically Jewish. The study proposed to surreptitiously examine the subjects' reactions and responses and to see whether these differed depending on the perceived ethnicity of the victim.

56. See the letter from Horkheimer to Pollock, 19 November 1943, *MHGS*, vol. 17, 496–500; and Horkheimer's letter to Morris D. Waldman, 30 December 1943, *MHGS*, vol. 17, 520–30.

57. See the letter from Horkheimer to Pollock, 28 November 1943, *MHGS*, vol. 17, 506–10.

58. See the Institute for Social Research's "Project on Antisemitism: Report to the American Jewish Committee on the first year of the project ending March 15, 1944," *MHA*, box IX, file 119, document a; and Wiggershaus, *The Frankfurt School*, 363–66.

59. By 1946, health concerns forced Horkheimer to return to Los Angeles. Although far from the AJC's offices, he sought to maintain his position within the Scientific Department and stubbornly sought to retain control over the anti-Semitism project. Flowerman, however, grew to fill the void created by Horkheimer's departure. By the final years of the anti-Semitism project, he became Horkheimer's rival. The two clashed over the content, research methods, and publication of *Studies in Prejudice*. As these relations rapidly deteriorated, the alliance between the Institute and the AJC collapsed. Forced to compromise, neither party was satisfied with the final product of their lengthy collaboration. Even the publication of the five monograph series could not alleviate the tension between the two sides. Instead of celebrating the warm reception received by *Studies in Prejudice*, Flowerman and Horkheimer bitterly jockeyed with each other for the responsibility, credit, and accolades.

60. See the letter from Horkheimer to Philip Klein, 24 July 1944, *MHGS*, vol. 17, 572–73.

61. The veterans study, although directed by the Institute and the AJC, was carried out in Chicago by Bruno Bettelheim, Morris Janowitz, and Edward Shils. See Bruno Bettelheim and Morris Janowitz, *Dynamics of Prejudice: A Psychological and Sociological Study of Veterans* (New York: Harper, 1950). The labor study, by contrast, was conducted by members of the Horkheimer Circle. The result was a controversial portrait of working-class Americans that suggested the existence of widespread prejudice. As intriguing as the results were, the Institute failed to present the study either coherently or compellingly. After hiring a series of editors to rescue the troubled manuscript, the Institute opted to not publish it. See "Anti-Semitism among American Labor," *MHA*, box IX, file 146, document 1 (in four bound volumes). A final addition arose from the interviews being conducted with mental health experts, which had been a part of the anti-Semitism project from the beginning. As these interviews went forward, questions arose regarding correlations between anti-Semitism and mental illness. Probing the dynamics of this parallel thus became an additional component of the project. This last piece of *Studies in Prejudice* was undertaken by Marie Jahoda, an old friend of the Institute from Vienna (also an ex-wife of Paul Lazarsfeld), and Nathan Ackerman. See Nathan W. Ackerman and Marie Jahoda, *Anti-Semitism and Emotional Disorder: A Psychoanalytic Interpretation* (New York: Harper, 1950).

62. As Lynd's wife Helen recalled years later, "Bob was really not a Marxist student. And a great deal of his views of society and Socialism were influenced by Franz Neumann and that group that came over with him." See Helen Lynd, "Oral History," interviewed by Mrs. Walter Gellhorn, Columbia Oral History Project, 1973, 254–55.

63. At the beginning of 1946, Lazarsfeld told his colleagues at Columbia about the "idiocy of the Institute group" with regard to its past isolation in the United States. See the

letter from Lazarsfeld to Theodore Abel, 5 February 1946, attached to the Institute's dossier regarding its evaluation by Columbia's sociology department, *MHA,* box II, file 5, document 149.

64. Only one year and five months later, with the completion of *Studies in Prejudice* in sight, Lazarsfeld had dramatically changed his tone. Now he insisted: "I mentioned before that I was very much impressed by some chapters of the Berkeley Study [*The Authoritarain Personality*] . . . It is, I think, the first time that a solution has been found for combining the ideas of your group with the tradition of empirical research . . . The tests, themselves, showed that your assumptions were correct. As a result, you win two important points at the same time: the study contributes real factual discoveries and at the same time shows the value of theoretical thinking for empirical research . . . Now, on the intellectual side, very great progress has been made, but at the moment, the Institute is no clearcut administrative body. This again seems to me a real danger. Obviously, the effects of the new publications would be much greater if they were to emanate from a clearly defined administrative center. What plans have you in this respect? I would think that any affiliation, even with a small university, would be desireable." See the letter from Lazarsfeld to Horkheimer, 19 July 1947, *MHGS,* vol. 17, 845–50.

65. The *MHA* and *LLA* illuminate some aspects of these relationships through the correspondences that existed between these scholars and the Horkheimer Circle. See the Merton-Horkheimer Correspondence from the *MHA,* box II, file 11, documents 249–50, and box III, file 10, documents 198–203; and the Merton-Lazarsfeld Correspondence from the *LLA,* box A282, documents 1–17. Also see the Riesman-Horkheimer Correspondence from the *MHA,* box V, file 141, documents 16–22; and the Lowenthal-Riesman Correspondence from the *LLA,* box A721, documents 1–141. Also see Horkheimer's essay "The Lessons of Fascism," in Hadley Cantril, ed., *Tensions That Cause Wars* (Urbana: University of Illinois Press, 1950), 209–42.

66. Lewis Coser described this Columbia milieu in an interview with the author in Cambridge, Masachussets, 6 May 1999. Also see Irving Louis Horowitz, *C. Wright Mills: An American Utopian* (New York: Free Press, 1983), 76–113; Howard Brick, *Daniel Bell and the Decline of Intellectual Radicalism* (Madison: University of Wisconsin Press, 1986); and Maurice R. Stein, "Alvin W. Gouldner: The Dialectic of Marxism and Sociology during the Buffalo Years," *Theory and Society,* vol. 11, no. 6 (November 1982): 889–97.

67. See Andrew Abbott and Emanuel Gaziano, "Transition and Tradition: Departmental Faculty in the Era of the Second Chicago School," in Gary Alan Fine, ed., *A Second Chicago School? The Development of a Postwar American Sociology* (Chicago: University of Chicago Press, 1995), 221–72.

68. See Dennis Smith, *Barrington Moore: Violence, Morality and Political Change* (London: Macmillan, 1983), 53–76; and Barry M. Kātz, *Foreign Intelligence: Research and Analysis in the Office of Strategic Services, 1942–1945* (Cambridge: Harvard University Press, 1989), 10 and 137–64.

69. See Dennis Smith, *The Chicago School: A Liberal Critique of Capitalism* (New York: St. Martin's Press, 1988), 184–210.

70. Taking advantage of the ties between Chicago's sociology faculty and the staff of the Institute for Social Research, Hughes and Horkheimer both participated in a faculty exchange, spending semesters at each other's institutions. See Horkheimer's notes from his University of Chicago seminar titled "Society and Value" given during the fall semester of 1957 from the *MHA,* box VIII, file 43, document a; for the product of Hughes's visit to

Frankfurt, see Everett C. Hughes, "Good People and Dirty Work," *Social Problems,* vol. 10, no. 1 (summer 1962): 3–11; and see Helena Znaniecka Lopata's account of the exchange from her "Postscript" to Fine, *A Second Chicago School?*, 366–67. Also see Horkheimer's accounts of the Frankfurt–Chicago faculty exchange in his letter to Maidon Horkheimer, 14 August 1954, *MHGS,* vol. 18, 268–73; his letter to Adorno, 24 August 1954, *MHGS,* vol. 18, 274–76; his letter to Adorno, 3 February 1957, *MHGS,* vol. 18, 378–80; and his letter to Helge Pross, 21 February 1957, *MHGS,* vol. 18, 381–82.

71. Isacque Graeber, who collaborated with Neumann and the Institute to gain the support of the American Jewish Committee, was familiar with Talcott Parsons in the early 1940s. In fact, Parsons contributed an essay on the topic of anti-Semitism to the book that Graeber edited, *Jews in a Gentile World.* See Talcott Parsons, "The Sociology of Modern Anti-Semitism," in Isacque Graeber and Steuart Henderson Britt, eds., *Jews in a Gentile World* (New York: Macmillan, 1942), 101–22.

72. See Gordon Allport's report "A Tentative and Partial Manual for Police Training on the Subject of Police and Minority Groups," *MHA,* box II, file 1, 130–63.

73. See Horkheimer's letter to Gordon Allport, 3 May 1945, *MHA,* box II, file 1, document 123.

74. Shils was one of the most outspoken American sociological critics of the Institute's leftist assumptions about authoritarainism and mass culture. See Edward Shils, "Authoritarianism: 'Right' and 'Left,'" in Richard Christie and Marie Jahoda, eds., *Studies in the Scope and Method of "The Authoritarian Personality"* (Westport, Conn.: Greenwood Press, 1981), 24–49; and Edward Shils, "Daydreams and Nightmares: Reflections on the Criticism of Mass Culture," *Sewanee Review,* vol. 65, no. 4 (autumn 1957): 587–608.

75. See Edward Shils, "Tradition, Ecology, and Institution in the History of Sociology," *Daedalus,* vol. 99, no. 4 (fall 1970): 760–825.

76. Parsons threw his support squarely behind the Institute's attempt to return to Frankfurt.

77. Besides the teaching engagements at the College of Jewish Studies that will be looked at subsequently, there is evidence of two other community-oriented speaking engagements. One took place at Los Angeles City College's religious conference titled "Combating Group Tensions: A Seminar in Inter-group Relations." This series of seminars met every Tuesday throughout October and November of 1948. Horkheimer's seminar was conducted on 2 November 1948 and was titled "Psychological Aspects of Prejudice." Because Horkheimer improvised much of this talk, all we possess regarding its content is the description that was submitted for the seminar flyer. According to this document, Horkheimer promised to discuss "the relation of prejudice to individual emotional instability, the role of the unconscious in inter-group prejudice, and the psychological effects upon the possessor of hatreds and upon his objects." See the Los Angeles City College flyer titled "Combating Group Tensions: A Seminar in Inter-group Relations," *MHA,* box X, file 4, document 2. Another talk was delivered at the Soto-Michigan Jewish Community Center on 10 November 1948. The talk, again, was part of a series of lectures—this time dealing with the topic of anti-Semitism. Horkheimer's lecture was titled "Psychology of Hatred," and we have no lecture notes that indicate what he might have included in this talk. See the flyer advertising the Soto-Michigan Jewish Community Center series titled "A Look at Anti-Semitism," *MHA,* box X, file 5, document 2.

78. See Horkheimer's syllabus from "Social Studies 1: Origins, Manifestations, and Motivations of Anti-Semitism," *MHA,* box X, file 6, document 1.

79. See the transcript of the program titled "Broadcast: College of Jewish Studies. KFMV, Sunday December 12, 1948," *MHA,* box X, file 6a, document 6.

80. See Horkheimer's syllabus titled "Social Studies 2: Jews in Modern Culture," *MHA,* box X, file 8, document 1.

81. See the memorandum from Rabbi Phineas Smaller to Horkheimer, 7 September 1949, *MHA,* box II, file 5, documents 105–6.

82. Ibid.

83. See James Rorty, "American Fuehrer in Dress Rehearsal," *Commentary,* vol. 1, no. 1 (November 1945): 13–20, for a report on some early findings connected with *Prophets of Deceit;* Leo Lowenthal, "Terror's Atomization of Man," *Commentary,* vol. 1, no. 3 (January 1946): 1–8, for a psychological and ideological analysis of totalitarian terrorism and its objectification, alienation, and coercion of the modern individual; Samuel H. Flowerman and Marie Jahoda, "Polls on Anti-Semitism: How Much Do They Tell Us?" *Commentary,* vol. 1, no. 6 (April 1946): 82–86, for a discussion of polling techniques and their possible applications to the topic of prejudice; Nathan Glazer, "The Social Scientists Dissect Prejudice: An Appraisal of Recent Studies," *Commentary,* vol. 1, no. 7 (May 1946): 79–85, for a discussion of several works regarding prejudice that emphasized the research of the AJC and the recent publication of Else Frenkel-Brunswik and R. Nevitt Sanford's article "Some Personality Factors in Anti-Semitism" in the *Journal of Psychology* (October 1945); Samuel H. Flowerman and Marie Jahoda, "Can We Fight Prejudice Scientifically? Toward a Partnership of Action and Research," *Commentary,* vol. 2, no. 6 (December 1946): 583–87, for a report on a Public Relations Workshop that sought practical programs from social-scientific evidence provided by initiatives like the AJC project; Jerome Himelhoch, "Is There a Bigot Personality? A Report on Some Preliminary Studies," *Commentary,* vol. 3, no. 3 (March 1947): 277–84, for one of the first serious investigations of the preliminary findings from *The Authoritarian Personality* based on the essays published in the little-known book edited by Ernst Simmel, *Anti-Semitism: A Social Disease* (New York: International Universities Press, 1946), which contained the essays "Sociological Background of the Psychoanalytic Approach" by Horkheimer, "The Anti-Semitic Personality: A Research Report" by Frenkel-Brunswik and Sanford, and "Anti-Semitism and Fascist Propaganda" by Adorno; and Arnold M. Rose and Siegfried Kracauer, "The Dark Ground of Prejudice: Discussing Some Psychological Factors," *Commentary,* vol. 3, no. 6 (June 1947): 583–87, for an investigation of the social conditions giving rise to anti-Semitism that also draws on the theoretical analyses of the Institute that were first published in Simmel, *Anti-Semitism: A Social Disease.*

84. This information was conveyed in an interview between Glazer and the author in Cambridge, Massachusetts, 21 January 1999.

85. See the letter from Horkheimer to Elliot Cohen, 21 March 1946, *MHA,* box II, file 5, document 36.

86. For good examples of this, see Elliot Cohen's letters to Horkheimer, 8 April 1946 and 13 March 1947, *MHA,* box II, file 3, 35 and 33–34.

87. See the transcript titled "Record of Meeting: *Commentary* and Institute of Social Research," 29 May 1946, *MHA,* box IX, file 125, document a.

88. See J. F. Brown's review of *Studies in Prejudice* in *The Annals of the American Academy of Political and Social Science,* vol. 270 (July 1950): 175–77.

89. Ibid. See Thomas Mann's review of Massing's monograph *Rehearsal for Destruction* from the *New York Times Book Review* (11 December 1949), 3, for Mann's assessment of the

entire series; Harry R. Bredemeier's review of *The Authoritarian Personality* in *Public Opinion Quarterly*, vol. 14, no. 3 (fall 1950): 571–74; R. A. Schermerhorn's review of *The Authoritarian Personality* in *Social Forces*, vol. 29, no. 3 (March 1951); and Joseph H. Bunzel's review in the *American Sociological Review*, vol. 15, no. 4 (August 1950): 571–73.

90. For those that emphasized the absence of a positive strategy for combating Anti-Semitism, see Bunzel's review in the *American Sociological Review* (August 1950). And for those that questioned the correlation between anti-Semitism and political beliefs, see Nathan Glazer, "The Authoritarian Personality in Profile: Report on a Major Study of Race Hatred," *Commentary*, vol. 9, no. 6 (June 1950): 578–83; Schermerhorn's review from *Social Forces* (March 1951); and Tamotsu Shibutani's review of *The Authoritarian Personality* from the *American Journal of Sociology*, vol. 57, no. 5 (March 1952): 527–29.

91. See Shibutani's review from the *American Journal of Sociology* (March 1952).

92. See David W. McKinney, *The Authoritarian Personality Studies: An Inquiry into the Failure of Social Science Research to Produce Demonstrable Knowledge* (The Hague: Mouton and Co., 1973), 267–74.

93. See Pollock's draft for a letter to the New York advisory board members, 11 January 1947, *MHA*, box I, file 5, 123–27.

94. See the letter from Robert MacIver to Frank Fackenthal, 6 April 1948, *Columbia University Archives*, file 351/19; the letter from Robert Lynd to George Peagram, 8 April 1948, *Columbia University Archives*, file 378/14; and the letter from Paul Lazarsfeld to Robert Merton, 19 June 1948, *MHA*, box II, file 10, 275–77, in which Lazarsfeld claims that the Bureau for Applied Social Research served as Horkheimer's official sponsor for the grant from the Rockefeller Foundation.

95. See Max Horkheimer, *Survey of the Social Sciences in Western Germany* (Washington, D.C.: Library of Congress, 1952).

96. See the letter from Robert Lynd to George Peagram, 17 April 1948, *Columbia University Archives*, file 378/14.

97. See Wiggershaus, *The Frankfurt School*, 397–400; and Max Horkheimer, "The Lessons of Fascism," in Hadley Cantril, ed., *Tensions That Cause Wars* (Urbana: University of Illinois Press, 1950), 209–42.

98. See the memorandum by Pollock titled "Visit to Prof James Shotwell on January 3, 1947," *MHA*, box VI, file 35, 434–35.

99. For Horkheimer's assessment of the condition of German social science, see his "Memorandum concerning the need for American assistance in the promotion of social science research in Western Germany," *MHA*, box II, file 8, 25–27.

100. See "Proposal for the Reopening of the Institute for Social Research at the University of Frankfort *[sic]* on Main," *American Sociological Review*, vol. 14, no. 5 (October 1949): 681–82.

101. Ibid.

102. Ibid.

103. See the letter from Horkheimer to Frederick Lane, 27 November 1951, *MHA*, box V, file 141, 130–31; and the letter from Joseph H. Willits to Horkheimer, 31 December 1951, *MHA*, box V, file 141, 126.

104. See Lazarsfeld's memorandum titled "Foreign Research Service of the Bureau of Applied Social Research," 27 April 1950, *Paul Lazarsfeld Papers*, Rare Book and Manuscript Library, Columbia University, box 6, file 18.

105. See the Institute's report to the UNESCO, 5 April 1951, *MHA*, box IX, file 272,

document 1; also see Friedrich Pollock, ed., *Gruppenexperiment. Ein Studienbericht* (Frankfurt am Main: Europäische Verlags-Anstalt, 1955).

106. See Wiggershaus, *The Frankfurt School*, 433.

107. See Horkheimer's letter to the UNESCO, 20 March 1951, *MHA*, box IX, file 272, document 2; the letter from Horkheimer to Marcuse, 26 March 1951, *MHGS*, vol. 18, 200–202; and the letter from Horkheimer to Lowenthal, 13 April 1951, *MHGS*, vol. 18, 203–8.

108. There are a number of valuable accounts of the Horkheimer Circle's postwar sociological enterprise. See Clemens Albrecht et al., *Die intellektuelle Gründung der Bundesrepublik. Eine Wirkungsgeschichte der Frankfurter Schule* (Frankfurt am Main: Campus Verlag, 1999); Volker Meja, Dieter Misgeld, and Nico Stehr, eds., *Modern German Sociology* (New York: Columbia University Press, 1987); J.-M. Vincent, "Les métamorphoses de la sociologie allemande après 1945," *Cahiers Internationaux de Sociologie*, vol. 107 (1999): 263–88; and Wiggershaus, *The Frankfurt School*.

109. See Theodor W. Adorno et al., *The Positivist Dispute in German Sociology*, trans. Glyn Adey and David Frisby (London: Heinemann, 1976).

110. See Paul Lazarsfeld, "Critical Theory and Dialectics," *Paul Lazarsfeld Papers*, box 36, 112–14.

7. SPECTERS OF MARX

1. "One-Dimensional Philosopher," *Time*, vol. 91, no. 12 (March 22, 1968): 38–40.

2. Sol Stern, "The Metaphysics of Rebellion," *Ramparts*, vol. 6, no. 12 (June 1968): 55.

3. Ibid., 57.

4. Kurt Glaser, "Apostle of Chaos: Marcuse and the German New Left," *National Review*, vol. 20, no. 26 (July 2, 1968): 652.

5. Ibid.

6. "Marcuse Defines His New Left Line," *New York Times Magazine*, vol. 118, no. 40 (October 27, 1968): 29.

7. Herbert Marcuse, "On the New Left," in Douglas Kellner, ed., *The New Left and the 1960s: Collected Papers of Herbert Marcuse*, vol. 3 (New York: Routledge, 2005), 122.

8. Adorno as quoted in the *Süddeutsche Zeitung* (26–27 April 1969), 10.

9. See Leo Lowenthal, "I Never Wanted to Play Along: Interviews with Helmut Dubiel," in Martin Jay, ed., *An Unmastered Past: The Autobiographical Reflections of Leo Lowenthal* (Berkeley: University of California Press, 1987), 15–159.

10. The most infamous instance occurred during a faculty meeting in Frankfurt at which Adorno's appointment to full professor was discussed. The historian Helmut Ritter accused the university of "favoritism," proclaiming that a scholar only needed to be "a Jew and protégé of Horkheimer" to achieve success in Frankfurt. See Stefan Müller-Doohm, *Adorno: A Biography*, trans. Rodney Livingstone (London: Polity, 2005), 368–69.

11. One should exercise some caution with this letter, because it is unlikely that Horkheimer would have admitted his true intentions to his rival at the AJC, Flowerman. Nevertheless, other letters and recent research confirm the view that Horkheimer, Adorno, and Pollock undertook the return to Germany with a certain amount of trepidation—suggesting that the thoughts in this letter might be both honest and diplomatic. See the letter from Max Horkheimer to Samuel H. Flowerman, 15 February 1947, *MHGS*, vol. 17, 787–89. Also see Detlev Claussen, *Theodor W. Adorno: Ein letztes Genie* (Frankfurt am Main: S. Fischer Verlag, 2003), 213–15.

12. See the letter from Max Horkheimer to Ruth Nanda Anshen, 28 January 1948, *MHGS*, vol. 17, 916–17.

13. James Schmidt, "*The Eclipse of Reason* and the End of the Frankfurt School in America," *New German Critique*, vol. 34, no. 1 (winter 2007): 51.

14. Although Wiggershaus emphasizes Horkheimer's professional and financial ambitions, and Peter Stirk points to his increasing conservatism, Horkheimer also devoted much of his postwar energy to the study and reeducation of German youth. I don't mean to dispute either characterization of Horkheimer's behavior after his return to Frankfurt. Indeed, he was frequently opportunistic (as he had been in the United States), and he exhibited views that could only be characterized as conservative compared to his earlier career. See Rolf Wiggershaus, *The Frankfurt School: Its History, Theories, and Political Significance* (Cambridge: MIT Press, 1994); and Peter M. Stirk, *Max Horkheimer: A New Interpretation* (Lanham, Md.: Barnes and Noble Books, 1992).

15. For Horkheimer's own explanation of these connections, see his letter to John A. Blatnik, 10 April 1954, *MHGS*, vol. 18, 261–64.

16. Max Horkheimer, *Survey of the Social Sciences in West Germany: A Report on Recent Developments* (Washington, D.C.: Library of Congress, 1952).

17. Letter from Horkheimer to Helge Pross, 21 February 1957, *MHGS*, vol. 18, 381–82.

18. See memorandum between Friedrich Pollock and Max Horkheimer, November 1955, *MHGS*, vol. 18, 327–28.

19. See Wolfgang Kraushaar, ed., *Frankfurter Schule und Studentenbewegung: Von der Flaschenpost zum Molotowcocktail, 1946–1995*, vol. 1 (Hamburg: Rogner & Bernhard, 1998), 251–53; and Wolfgang Kraushaar, ed., *Frankfurter Schule und Studentenbewegung: Von der Flaschenpost zum Molotowcocktail, 1946-1995*, vol. 2 (Hamburg: Rogner & Bernhard, 1998), 229–30.

20. See Max Horkheimer, *Dawn and Decline: Notes 1926–1931 and 1950–1969*, trans. Michael Shaw (New York: Seabury Press, 1978), 230.

21. See Horkheimer's letter to Henry Carsh, 2 April 1968, *MHGS*, vol. 18, 688–89.

22. Horkheimer believed that the New Left was not a legitimate revolutionary movement. Student radicals were only motivated by Oedipal fantasies and sought to unleash their aggression against their parents' generation. Rather than functioning as a progressive, constructive force, the New Left represented destructiveness. See Horkheimer, *Dawn and Decline*, 234.

23. See David Jenemann, *Adorno in America* (Minneapolis: University of Minnesota Press, 2007), 179–91.

24. See Martin Jay, "Adorno in America," in *Permanent Exiles: Essays on the Intellectual Migration from Germany to America* (New York: Columbia University Press, 1986), 123–24.

25. See Theodor Adorno, "Scientific Experiences of a European Scholar in America," in Donald Fleming and Bernard Bailyn, eds., *The Intellectual Migration: Europe and America, 1930–1960* (Cambridge: Harvard University Press, 1969), 338–70.

26. In the views of both Claussen and Jenemann, it was the sociological and extraterritorial vantage point that U.S. exile provided to Adorno that enabled him to develop into the genius that he became. See Claussen, *Theodor W. Adorno*, 247–48 and 310–11; and Jenemann, *Adorno in America*, xvii–xxviii.

27. Nearly every biography of Adorno or work on the Horkheimer Circle mentions Adorno's problems with exile. For perhaps the best account, see Jay, "Adorno in America," 120–37.

28. Theodor Adorno, *Minima Moralia: Reflections from Damaged Life,* trans. E. F. N. Jephcott (New York: Verso, 1993).

29. For an excellent account of Adorno's late work, see Robert Hullot-Kentor, *Things beyond Resemblance: Collected Essays on Theodor W. Adorno* (New York: Columbia University Press, 2006), 32–44.

30. Jeremy Shapiro studied in Frankfurt during the early 1960s and vividly recalled the peculiar contradiction that existed between the emerging student Left and Adorno. As a result of Adorno's public utterances and reputation within West Germany, Frankfurt had become a destination for left-leaning students. No doubt many hoped to study and become the protégés of Adorno, but Adorno was aloof and inaccessible. This contradiction and the dashed hopes that it engendered no doubt fueled the steady growth of frustration between the idealistic student leftists gathering around Adorno in Frankfurt and eventually led to the public displays of hostility by the end of the 1960s (interview with Jeremy Shapiro in Cambridge, Massachusetts, 6 July 2007).

31. Adorno's complicated relationship with the Frankfurt SDS has been carefully documented. See Krauschaar's three-volume book series *Frankfurter Schule und Studentenbewegung.* It has also been recounted in rich biographical detail: see Claussen, *Theodor W. Adorno,* 313–401; and Müller-Doohm, *Adorno,* 448–80.

32. See Theodor Adorno's letter to Herbert Marcuse, 5 May 1969, "Introduction to Adorno/Marcuse Correspondence on the German Student Movement," ed. and trans. Esther Leslie, *New Left Review,* no. 233 (January–February 1999): 123–36.

33. For the best account of Neumann's political moderation, see H. Stuart Hughes, *The Sea Change: The Migration of Social Thought, 1930–1965* (New York: McGraw-Hill, 1977), 100–119; and for the best account of Kirchheimer's career, see John H. Herz and Erich Hula, "Otto Kirchheimer: An Introduction to His Life and Work," in Otto Kirchheimer, *Politics, Law, and Social Change: Selected Essays of Otto Kirchheimer,* ed. Frederic S. Burin and Kurt L. Shell (New York: Columbia University Press, 1969), ix–xxxviii.

34. Irving Howe had to be hired at the last minute to get *The Prophets of Deceit* into a publishable manuscript. See chapter 4's discussion of Howe's relationship to the Institute for Social Research.

35. The work in popular culture and modern media did not bore Lowenthal. He simply longed to be working for the OSS with his former colleagues and interesting young Americans such as H. Stuart Hughes, Carl Schorske, and Leonard Krieger. See Leo Lowenthal, *An Unmasterable Past: The Autobiographical Reflections of Leo Lowenthal,* ed. Martin Jay (Berkeley: University of California Press, 1987), 81–82.

36. Lowenthal enthusiastically supported Berkeley students in their opposition to the House Committee on Un-American Activities (HUAC) in 1960, as well as the Free Speech Movement (and its connection to the civil rights struggles) in 1964 (ibid., 151).

37. Ibid., 152.

38. See Allan Patience, "Erich Fromm—Socialist Humanist: Psychoanalysis and the Softer Origins of the New Left," *Meanjin Quarterly,* vol. 32, no. 3 (September 1973): 304–13.

39. These remarks come from taped interviews conducted with John Herz by John M. Spalek, 19 September 1980 and 24 October 1980, *John H. Herz Papers,* item 16, box 16, German and Jewish Intellectual Émigré Collection, M. E. Grenander Department of Special Collections and Archives, University Libraries, University at Albany, State University of New York.

40. Ibid. One should perhaps be careful with Herz's retrospective characterization. Some histories of the Central European Branch of the OSS present slightly different pictures. See Barry Kātz, *Foreign Intelligence: Research and Analysis in the Office of Strategic Services, 1942–1945* (Cambridge: Harvard University Press, 1989), 32–90.

41. Carl Schorske, "Encountering Marcuse," in John Abromeit and W. Mark Cobb, eds., *Herbert Marcuse: A Critical Reader* (New York: Routledge, 2004), 253.

42. H. Stuart Hughes, *Gentleman Rebel: The Memoirs of H. Stuart Hughes* (New York: Ticknor and Fields, 1990), 194.

43. Douglas Kellner, "Introduction," in Herbert Marcuse, *Technology, War, and Fascism: Collected Papers of Herbert Marcuse,* vol. 1 (New York: Routledge, 1998), 24.

44. For obvious reasons, the contents of these writings addressed the needs of the U.S. government and didn't always reflect Marcuse's intellectual interests. Furthermore, all of the reports from the Central European Branch of the OSS were collective labors. Therefore, although Marcuse might have been the lead researcher for a project, the finished text bore many intellectual fingerprints that are impossible to single out.

45. Herbert Marcuse, "Some Remarks on Aragon: Art and Politics in the Totalitarian Era," in Marcuse, *Technology, War, and Fascism,* 202.

46. Ibid., 203.

47. Ibid., 204.

48. See Hughes, *Gentleman Rebel,* 195–204.

49. Herbert Marcuse, "Thirty-three Theses," in Marcuse, *Technology, War, and Fascism,* 217.

50. Ibid., 218–19.

51. Ibid., 217–22.

52. Ibid., 223–27.

53. See Barry Kātz, *Herbert Marcuse and the Art of Liberation: An Intellectual Biography* (London: Verso, 1982), 130–34.

54. See David Ingram, *Critical Theory and Philosophy* (New York: Paragon, 1990), 93–105; Kātz, *Herbert Marcuse and the Art of Liberation,* 145–57; Douglas Kellner, *Herbert Marcuse and the Crisis of Marxism* (Berkeley: University of California Press, 1984), 154–96; and Morton Schoolman, *The Imaginary Witness: The Critical Theory of Herbert Marcuse* (New York: New York University Press, 1984), 229–88.

55. Adorno was so upset about Marcuse's interpretation of Freud that he made it impossible for his former colleague to publish the book in German through the Institut für Sozialforschung. See Wiggershaus, *The Frankfurt School,* 498.

56. Perhaps the most famous was Max Horkheimer's "The Authoritarian State," in which he draws little distinction between the planned economies of state capitalism and socialism. Instead, Horkheimer embraced an ill-defined notion of Germany's old Council Movement that arose with the collapse of the *Kaiserreich.* See Max Horkheimer, "The Authoritarian State," in Andrew Arato and Eike Gebhardt, eds., *The Essential Frankfurt School Reader* (New York: Continuum, 1993), 95–117.

57. For some of the highlights in the review literature, see Paul Kescskemeti, "Review of *Soviet Marxism,*" *American Political Science Review,* vol. 53 (March 1959): 187–89; Sidney Monas, "Review of *Soviet Marxism,*" *American Sociological Review,* vol. 25, no. 2 (April 1960): 286–87; C. E. Black, "Review of *Soviet Marxism,*" *Annals of the American Academy of Political and Social Science,* no. 320 (November 1958): 161–62; L. Stern, "But Is It Marxist," *Dissent,* vol. 6, no. 1 (winter 1959): 88–93; C. B. Macpherson, "Review of *Soviet Marxism,*"

Political Science Quarterly, vol. 74, no. 2 (March 1959): 152–54; and Alex Inkeles, "Attitudes to History," *Partisan Review,* vol. 25, no. 4 (fall 1958): 619–21.

58. See Abram L. Sacher, *A Host at Last* (Waltham, Mass.: Copigraph, 1976).

59. Todd Gitlin, *The Sixties: Years of Hope, Days of Rage* (New York: Bantam Books, 1993), 53 and 93.

60. See chapters 3 and 4 and their account of the Horkheimer Circle and the New York Intellectuals.

61. This account is based on an interview with Lewis Coser by the author in Cambridge, Massachusetts, 6 May 1999. Also see Irving Howe, *A Margin of Hope: An Intellectual Autobiography* (San Diego: Harcourt Brace, 1982), 188.

62. Rachel Price and Ruth Feinberg, "Coser, Marcuse, Sachs: Present Diverging Views on Revolutions," *Justice* (November 7, 1956): 4, found in the Robert D. Farber University Archives and Special Collections Department, Brandeis University.

63. See William Leiss, John David Ober, and Erica Sherover, "Marcuse as Teacher," in Kurt H. Wolff and Barrington Moore Jr., eds., *The Critical Spirit: Essays in Honor of Herbert Marcuse* (Boston: Beacon Press, 1968), 421–25.

64. For one of the best firsthand accounts of Marcuse as a teacher at Brandeis, see Angela Davis, *Angela Davis: An Autobiography* (New York: Random House, 1974), 133–36.

65. Peter Marcuse, "Herbert Marcuse's 'Identity,'" in Abromeit and Cobb, *Herbert Marcuse,* 251.

66. Ibid., 250.

67. For perhaps the most compelling case made for this perspective, see Wiggershaus, *The Frankfurt School,* 609–14.

68. Herbert Marcuse, *One-Dimensional Man: Studies in the Ideology of Advanced Industrial Society* (Boston: Beacon Press, 1964), 257.

8. MARCUSE'S MENTORS

1. Cf. Paul Alexander Juutilainen, director, *Herbert's Hippopotamus: A Story about Revolution in Paradise* (1996).

2. See John Bokina, "Marcuse Revisited: An Introduction," in John Bokina and Timothy J. Lukes, eds., *Marcuse: From the New Left to the Next Left* (Lawrence: University Press of Kansas, 1994), 1–24; W. Mark Cobb, "Diatribes and Distortions: Marcuse's Academic Reception," in John Abromeit and W. Mark Cobb, eds., *Herbert Marcuse: A Critical Reader* (New York: Routledge, 2004), 163–64; Morris Dickstein, *Gates of Eden: American Culture in the Sixties* (New York: Penguin, 1989), 69–88; David Held, *Introduction to Critical Theory: Horkheimer to Habermas* (Berkeley: University of California Press, 1980), 13 and 73; H. Stuart Hughes, *The Sea Change: The Migration of Social Thought, 1930–1965* (New York: McGraw-Hill, 1975), 180–82; Martin Jay, *The Dialectical Imagination: A History of the Frankfurt School and the Institute of Social Research, 1923–1950* (Berkeley: University of California Press, 1996), xii–xiii, xxix, 284, and 287–88; Barry Kātz, *Herbert Marcuse and the Art of Liberation* (London: Verso, 1982), 168; Douglas Kellner, "A Marcuse Renaissance?" in Bokin and Lukes, *Marcuse,* 245; Douglas Kellner, *Critical Theory, Marxism, and Modernity* (Baltimore: Johns Hopkins University Press, 1989), vii, 137–38, and 157; Douglas Kellner, *Herbert Marcuse and the Crisis of Marxism* (Berkeley: University of California Press, 1984), 1–5, 280–81, and 300–301; Rolf Wiggershaus, *The Frankfurt School: Its History, Theories, and Political Significance,* trans. Michael Robertson (Cambridge: MIT Press, 1994), 1 and 622.

3. James Miller, *Democracy Is in the Streets: From Port Huron to the Siege of Chicago* (Cambridge: Harvard University Press, 1994), 51 and 85.

4. Interview by the author with Mike Davis via e-mail, 20 June 2007.

5. See Herbert Marcuse, "The Problem of Violence and the Radical Opposition," in *Five Lectures: Psychoanalysis, Politics, and Utopia*, trans. Jeremy J. Shapiro and Shierry M. Weber (Boston: Beacon, 1970), 83–94; Herbert Marcuse, "Liberation from the Affluent Society," in Douglas Kellner, ed., *The New Left and the 1960s: Collected Papers of Herbert Marcuse*, vol. 3 (New York: Routledge, 2005), 76–86; and Herbert Marcuse, "The Failure of the New Left?" in Kellner, *The New Left and the 1960s*, 183–91.

6. See Herbert Marcuse, "Repressive Tolerance," in Robert Paul Wolff, Barrington Moore Jr., and Herbert Marcuse, eds., *A Critique of Pure Tolerance* (Boston: Beacon, 1969), 95–137; and Herbert Marcuse, "Democracy Has/Hasn't a Future and a Present," in Kellner, *The New Left and the 1960s*, 87–99.

7. Again, for a superb account of Marcuse in San Diego, see Juutilainen, *Herbert's Hippopotamus*.

8. For some of the major accounts in the popular press, see Sol Stern, "The Metaphysics of Rebellion," *Ramparts*, vol. 6, no. 12 (June 1968): 55–60; Kurt Glaser, "Marcuse and the German New Left," *National Review*, vol. 20, no. 26 (July 2, 1968): 649–54; Herbert Gold, "California Left: Mao, Marx, et Marcuse!" *Saturday Evening Post*, vol. 241, no. 21 (October 19, 1968): 56–59; Irving Kristol, "The Improbable Guru of Surrealistic Politics," *Fortune*, vol. 80, no. 1 (July 1969): 191–94; Edmund Stillman, "Marcuse: The Prophet of the New Left, Our Era's Prime Advocate of Violence, Is Here Assassinated," *Horizon*, vol. 11, no. 3 (summer 1969): 26–31. For some of the major biographical accounts of this same phenomenon, see Kātz, *Herbert Marcuse and the Art of Liberation*, 162–92; Kellner, *Herbert Marcuse and the Crisis of Marxism*, 276–319; and Jean-Michel Palmier, *Marcuse et la nouvelle gauche* (Paris: Éditions Pierre Belfond, 1973).

9. This suspicion arose most predominantly among Marcuse's critics (particularly, the New York Intellectuals) but was echoed by Marcuse himself, who was at times uncomfortable with being backed into the role of spokesman for the New Left. For examples of his critics posing this theory, see James Burnham, "Sock it to US, Herbert," *National Review*, vol. 20, no. 46 (November 19, 1968): 1158; Allen Graubard, "One-Dimensional Pessimism: A Critique of Herbert Marcuse's Theories," *Dissent*, vol. 15, no. 3 (May–June 1968): 216–28; David L. Bromwich, "The Counter-Culture and Its Apologists: Lysergic Götterdämmerung," *Commentary*, vol. 50, no. 6 (December 1970): 55–59; and also see "Marcuse Defines His New Left Line," *New York Times Magazine* (October 27, 1968): 29–31, 87–92, 97–100, and 109.

10. This is more the case with historians looking back on the Marcuse phenomenon. See Kātz, *Herbert Marcuse and the Art of Liberation*, 168; and Kellner, *Herbert Marcuse and the Crisis of Marxism*, 242 and 280.

11. See "One-Dimensional Philosopher," *Time*, vol. 91, no. 12 (March 22, 1968): 38.

12. See Allan Bloom, *The Closing of the American Mind: How Higher Education Has Failed Democracy and Impoverished the Souls of Today's Students* (New York: Simon and Schuster, 1987), 78, 147–48, and 226; Daniel J. Flynn, *Intellectual Morons: How Ideology Makes Smart People Fall for Stupid Ideas* (New York: Crown Forum, 2004), 14–31; David Horowitz, *The Professors: The 101 Most Dangerous Academics in America* (Washington, D.C.: Regnery, 2006), xxxvi–xxxvii; Roger Kimball, *Experiments against Reality: The Fate*

of Culture in the Postmodern Age (Chicago: Ivan R. Dee, 2000), 242–43; Roger Kimball, *The Long March: How the Cultural Revolution of the 1960s Changed America* (San Francisco: Encounter Books, 2000), 15, 157, 168, and 171–72; Leszek Kolakowski, *Main Currents of Marxism: The Breakdown,* vol. 3, trans. P. S. Falla (New York: Oxford University Press, 1987), 396–420; Alan Charles Kors and Harvey A. Silvergate, *The Shadow University: The Betrayal of Liberty on America's Campuses* (New York: Harper, 1999), 14–19, 25, 30–31, 68, 71, 372–73.

13. See Todd Gitlin, *The Sixties: Years of Hope, Days of Rage* (New York: Bantam Books, 1993); and Miller, *Democracy Is in the Streets.*

14. See Paul Berman, "The Passion of Joschka Fischer: From the Radicalism of the '60s to the Interventionism of the '90s," *New Republic,* vol. 225, nos. 9–10 (August 27 and September 3, 2001): 36–59.

15. See Kātz, *Herbert Marcuse and the Art of Liberation,* 168; and Kellner, *Herbert Marcuse and the Crisis of Marxism,* 242 and 280.

16. And this list only covers the major publications of the late 1960s and early 1970s. Marcuse also gave countless lectures and published numerous articles in periodicals throughout the period of student unrest.

17. See Miller, *Democracy Is in the Streets,* 23.

18. Ibid., 38–40.

19. See Gitlin, *The Sixties,* 26–28.

20. Irving Louis Horowitz, *C. Wright Mills: An American Utopian* (New York: Free Press, 1983), 76–109.

21. James Schmidt, "*The Eclipse of Reason* and the End of the Frankfurt School in America," *New German Critique,* vol. 34, no. 1 (winter 2007): 64.

22. Robert Lynd, "Our Racket Society," *Nation* (August 25, 1951): 150–52.

23. Horowitz, *C. Wright Mills,* 131 and 139.

24. In a letter to Hans Gerth from the winter of 1952, Mills discouraged his former friend from being pushed around by the Institute for Social Research. Gerth, apparently, was desperately hoping for a research post back in Frankfurt with the Horkheimer Circle, and Mills warned him to be careful: "I don't know these particular guys, except of course thru Leo Lowenthal, and I've met Horkheimer. But don't be so damn easy with them." See C. Wright Mills, *Letters and Autobiographical Writings,* ed. Kathryn Mills and Pamela Mills (Berkeley: University of California Press, 2000), 166–70.

25. See the letter from C. Wright Mills to Max Horkheimer, 15 December 1952, *MHA,* box V, file 115, 221–22; and Max Horkheimer's reply to Mills, 30 January 1953, *MHA,* box V, file 115, 218.

26. The phrase and the realization both come from James Miller. See Miller, *Democracy Is in the Streets,* 78–105.

27. Some, such as James Miller, suggest that Mills was well aware of how inaccurate his historical construct was. Richard Hofstadter, who overlapped in Columbia's history department, almost certainly must have alerted Mills to this fact. See ibid., 88.

28. Gitlin, *The Sixties,* 125.

29. Ibid., 151–62.

30. See "National Secretary's Report," *New Left Notes,* vol. 1, no. 22 (June 17, 1966): 1, 3, and 4.

31. See Steve Baum and Bernard Faber, "From Protest to Politics," *New Left Notes,* vol. 1, no. 33 (September 2, 1966): 9–12.

32. See Paul Buhle, "Clear Lake: New Answers or New Tactics?" *New Left Notes,* vol. 1, no. 36 (September 23, 1966): 1, 3, and 5.

33. Letter from Dick Ochs to Al Haber, 11 April 1966, *Students for a Democratic Society Papers,* microfilm reel #28, no. 107, titled "Radical Education Project (REP), 1966–1970."

34. Alan Haber, "Radical Education Project—Draft for Discussion and Comment," *New Left Notes,* vol. 1, no. 10 (March 25, 1966).

35. See Allen Greene, "For a Revolutionary Ideology," *New Left Notes,* vol. 1, no. 39 (October 14, 1966): 1–2 and 6–8.

36. Marcuse was mentioned with other left-leaning intellectuals in early REP literature (also discussed were William A. Williams and Art Waskow). See "Radical Education Project," *New Left Notes,* vol. 1, no. 2 (January 28, 1966): 3. Until 1968, his name appears in almost no other REP literature. The notable exception was the Boston REP's summer seminars on socialist ideology and imperialism. See "Boston SDS Holds Summer Seminars" and "Boston REP Proposal," *New Left Notes,* vol. 1, no. 32 (August 24, 1966): 28, 30. REP published no pamphlets tackling Marcuse's thought, and it did not add his writings to the REP reading lists until 1968.

37. In addition to examining the contents of *New Left Notes* (the primary periodical of SDS), counterculture journals such as *Ramparts* and underground newspapers from the 1960s and 1970s (from a microfilm collection titled *Underground Newspapers, 1963–1975,* compiled by the Alternative Press Syndicate and prepared by the Micro Photo Division of Bell and Howell) were also studied.

38. Telephone interview by the author with Trent Schroyer, 5 July 2007.

39. Interview with Jeremy Shapiro in Cambridge, Massachusetts, 6 July 2007.

40. Interview by the author with Tom Hayden in Heidelberg, Germany, 20 May 2005.

41. Interview by the author with Richard Flacks via e-mail, 20 August 2003.

42. Interview by the author with Todd Gitlin via e-mail, 21 August 2003.

43. Interview by the author with David Wellman via e-mail, 11 September 2003.

44. Interview by the author with Stanley Aronowitz via e-mail, 26 September 2003; interview by the author with Rick Ayers via e-mail, 23 August 2003; interview by the author with Paul Buhle via e-mail, 23 August 2003; interview by the author with Robert Gottlieb via e-mail, 25 August 2003; interview with Tom Hayden in Heidelberg, Germany, 20 May 2005; and interview with Bernardine Dohrn in Heidelberg, Germany, 22 May 2005.

45. Marcuse, "Repressive Tolerance," 109.

46. Ibid.

47. Ibid., 107.

48. Ibid., 102–3.

49. David Spitz, "Pure Tolerance: A Critique of Criticisms," *Dissent,* vol. 13, no. 5 (September–October 1966): 521.

50. Ibid., 520–21.

51. Ibid., 522.

52. See Michael Walzer, "Communications: On the Nature of Freedom," *Dissent,* vol. 13, no. 6 (November–December 1966): 725–28.

53. Interview by the author with Mike Davis via e-mail, 19 June 2007 and 20 June 2007.

54. See the letter from Mike Davis to Herbert Marcuse, 14 January 1965, *Herbert Marcuse Archiv,* file 1458, document 4, Stadt und Universitätsbibliothek, Frankfurt am Main.

55. Davis had written: "the question of 'Vietnams' will only be resolved by social change of a revolutionary nature and by us. But, no work being done in areas like economic re-conversion, organizing impacted areas, etc. Ergo, very little analytic dialogue within the movement. Very little research attempting to build theories and models of American 'imperialism–neo-colonialism,' or the complex of domestic economic pressures, ideological commitments, military strategies, etc. that create our foreign policy or policies. Little knowledge of how far the peace movement can go as a domestic social movement or connect with those movements already being built" (ibid.).

56. See Herbert Marcuse's letter to Mike Davis, undated, *Herbert Marcuse Archiv*, file 1458, document 5.

57. See Dick Flacks, "Whatever Became of the New Left?" and Don Mckelvey, "Intellectual Elitism and the Failure of Teaching," *New Left Notes*, vol. 1, no. 30 (August 12, 1966): 1 and 3. Already by November of 1966, members of REP's implementation committee were bemoaning the fact that graduate students had taken control over most of the SDS seminars on theory and political education—they were boring the undergraduates and driving people away. The one saving grace was the fact that while the undergraduate supporters had lost their desire to pursue theory, they were excited by their involvement in empirical fact finding and investigative research (linking military programs to colleges and universities, etc.). See Jim Jacobs's letter to Greg Calvert, 28 November 1966, *Students for a Democratic Society Papers*, microfilm reel #28, no. 107 (Radical Education Project, 1966–70). During the same period, SDS made the first movement from passive protest to militant resistance. Instead of the traditional strategy of engaging in symbolic acts intended to provoke political opponents, members of SDS shifted course and set their sights on disrupting the military-industrial complex and the institutions supporting it. See Carl Davidson, "Toward Institutional Resistance," *New Left Notes*, vol. 2, no. 39 (November 13, 1967): 1, 3–4.

58. Interview by the author with Mike Davis via e-mail, 19 June 2007 and 20 June 2007.

59. Carl Schorske, "Encountering Marcuse," in Abromeit and Cobb, *Herbert Marcuse*, 256–57.

60. See Paul Booth, "Facing the American Leviathan: Our Managed Culture," and Steven Baum and Bernard Faber, "From Protest to Politics," *New Left Notes*, vol. 1, no. 33 (September 2, 1966): 6–8 and 9–12; Steve Golin, "Student Boredom," *New Left Notes*, vol. 1, no. 38 (October 7, 1966): 3–4; Dick Howard, "Reactionary Radicals," *New Left Notes*, vol. 1, nos. 40–41 (October 28, 1966): 1–2, 4, and 9; "Beyond the Beloved Community," *New Left Notes*, vol. 1, no. 45 (November 25, 1966): 1, 3, and 8; Robert Gottlieb, Gerry Tenney, and David Gilbert, "Toward a Theory of Social Change in America," *New Left Notes*, vol. 2, no. 20 (May 22, 1967): 3–6; "Marcuse," *New Left Notes*, vol. 2, no. 23 (June 12, 1967): 2.

61. See the memo from Marcuse to members of REP that is undated from the *Herbert Marcuse Archiv*, file 1458, document 8.

62. Ibid.

63. See Herbert Marcuse, *An Essay on Liberation* (Boston: Beacon Press, 1969), 3–6.

64. Ibid., ix.

65. Herbert Marcuse, *One-Dimensional Man: Studies in the Ideology of Advanced Industrial Society* (Boston: Beacon Press, 1964), 45–48; also see the text of a speech that Marcuse delivered at a conference of the German Sozialistischer Deutscher Studentenbund (SDS)

in May 1966 reprinted as "Vietnam—Analyse eines Exempels," in Wolfgang Kraushaar, ed., *Frankfurter Schule und Studentenbewegung: Von der Flaschenpost zum Molotowcocktail, 1946–1995* (Hamburg: Rogner & Bernhard, 1998), vol. 2, 205–9.

66. Marcuse, "Liberation from the Affluent Society," 86.

67. See Marcuse, *One-Dimensional Man,* 203–57; and Marcuse, "Liberation from the Affluent Society," 81–82

68. See Marcuse, *An Essay on Liberation,* 80. Subsequent references are given in the text.

69. Herbert Marcuse, *Counterrevolution and Revolt* (Boston: Beacon Press, 1972), 38. Subsequent references are given in the text.

70. See Jürgen Habermas, "The Different Rhythms of Philosophy and Politics: For Herbert Marcuse on his 100th Birthday," in Herbert Marcuse, *Towards a Critical Theory of Society: Collected Papers of Herbert Marcuse,* vol. 2, ed. Douglas Kellner (New York: Routledge, 2001), 234–38.

CONCLUSION

1. Paul Breines, "Marcuse and the New Left in America," in Jürgen Habermas, ed., *Antworten auf Herbert Marcuse* (Frankfurt am Main: Suhrkamp Verlag, 1968), 137. Breines had grown up with the Movement as a college student at the University of Wisconsin. He had traveled south on the Freedom Rides and was an undergraduate associate of *Studies on the Left.* As a graduate student, Breines became drawn to Western Marxism—particularly the writings of Karl Korsch, Georg Lukács, and Herbert Marcuse. Although this made him a bit of a maverick among the Madison New Left, he was by no means alone in his interests in European social theory. By the late 1960s, Breines was completing his doctoral dissertation but also was reflecting on the state of the Movement. The combination of his scholarly interests and his vantage point on the American student movement made him an ideal candidate to contribute to Habermas's book.

2. See "Marcuse Defines His New Left Line," *New York Times Magazine* (October 27, 1968): 29–31, 87–92, 97–100, and 109; and Herbert Marcuse, "On the New Left," in Douglas Kellner, ed., *The New Left and the 1960s: Collected Papers of Herbert Marcuse,* vol. 3 (New York: Routledge, 2005), 122–27.

3. Breines, "Marcuse and the New Left in America," 144–45.

4. See Shierry M. Weber, "Individuation as Practice," and Jeremy J. Shapiro, "One-Dimensionality: The Universal Semiotic of Technological Experience," in Paul Breines, ed., *Critical Interruptions: New Left Perspectives on Herbert Marcuse* (New York: Herder and Herder, 1970), 22–59 and 136–86.

5. See William Leiss, "The Critical Theory of Society: Present Situation and Future Tasks," and John David Ober, "On Sexuality and Politics in the Work of Herbert Marcuse,"in Breines, *Critical Interruptions,* 74–100 and 101–35.

6. Russell Jacoby, "Reversals and Lost Meanings," in Breines, *Critical Interruptions,* 60–61.

7. Paul Breines, "From Guru to Spectre: Marcuse and the Implosion of the Movement," in Breines, *Critical Interruptions,* 1–3.

8. Ibid., 10.

9. Ibid., 20–21.

10. Paul Piccone, "20 Years of *Telos,*" *Telos,* no. 75 (summer 1988): 13.

11. "Editorial Statement," *Telos,* no. 1 (spring 1968).

12. Piccone, "20 Years of *Telos,*" 6.

13. Martin Jay, "Preface to the 1996 Edition," in *The Dialectical Imagination: A History of the Frankfurt School and the Institute of Social Research* (Berkeley: University of California Press, 1996), xiv.

14. Ibid.

15. Ibid.

16. For some notable examples, see Stanley Aronowitz, *The Crisis in Historical Materialism: Class, Politics, and Culture in Marxist Theory* (New York: Praeger, 1982); Stephen Eric Bronner, *Of Critical Theory and Its Theorists* (Cambridge: Blackwell Publishers, 1994); Russell Jacoby, *Dialectic of Defeat: Contours of Western Marxism* (New York: Cambridge University Press, 1981); Fredric Jameson, *Late Marxism: Adorno, or, the Persistence of the Dialectic* (New York: Verso, 1990); Barry Kātz, *Herbert Marcuse and the Art of Liberation* (London: Verso, 1982); Douglas Kellner, *Herbert Marcuse and the Crisis of Marxism* (Berkeley: University of California Press, 1984); Douglas Kellner, *Critical Theory, Marxism, and Modernity* (Baltimore: Johns Hopkins University Press, 1989); Christopher Lasch, *The Culture of Narcissism: American Life in an Age of Diminishing Expectations* (New York: Warner Books, 1979); Joseph McCarney, *Social Theory and the Crisis of Marxism* (New York: Verso, 1990); and Paul Robinson, *The Freudian Left: Wilhelm Reich, Gez Roheim, Herbert Marcuse* (New York: Harper and Row, 1969).

17. See Jillian Becker, *Hitler's Children: The Story of the Baader-Meinhof Terrorist Gang* (Philadelphia: Lippincott, 1977); Paul Berman, "The Passion of Joschka Fischer: From the Radicalism of the '60s to the Interventionism of the '90s," *New Republic,* vol. 225, nos. 9–10 (August 27 and September 3, 2001): 36–59.

18. See Peter Clecak, *America's Quest for the Ideal Self: Dissent and Fulfillment in the 60s and 70s* (New York: Oxford University Press, 1983).

19. See Ben Agger, *Cultural Studies as Critical Theory* (Washington, D.C.: Falmer Press, 1992); Ben Agger, *Gender, Culture, and Power: Toward a Feminist Postmodern Critical Theory* (Westport, Conn.: Praeger, 1993); Seyla Benhabib and Drucilla Cornell, eds., *Feminism as Critique: Essays on the Politics of Gender in Late-Capitalist Societies* (Cambridge: Polity Press, 1987); Seyla Benhabib, *Situating the Self: Gender, Community, and Postmodernism in Contemporary Ethics* (New York: Routledge, 1992); John Bokina and Timothy J. Lukes, *Marcuse: From the New Left to the Next Left* (Lawrence: University Press of Kansas, 1994); Mary Jo Buhle, *Feminism and Its Discontents: A Century of Struggle with Psychoanalysis* (Cambridge: Harvard University Press, 1998); Drucilla Cornell, *At the Heart of Freedom: Feminism, Sex, and Equality* (Princeton, N.J.: Princeton University Press, 1998); Nancy Fraser, *Unruly Practices: Power, Discourse, and Gender in Contemporary Social Theory* (Minneapolis: University of Minnesota Press, 1989); Randall Halle, *Queer Social Philosophy: Critical Readings from Kant to Adorno* (Urbana: University of Illinois Press, 2004); Guyton B. Hammond, *Conscience and Its Recovery: From the Frankfurt School to Feminism* (Charlottesville: University of Virginia Press, 1993); David Ingram, *Rights, Democracy, and Fulfillment in the Era of Identity Politics: Principled Compromises in a Compromised World* (Lanham, Md.: Rowman and Littlefield, 2004); Harry Kunneman and Hent de Vries, eds., *Enlightenments: Encounters between Critical Theory and Contemporary French Thought* (Kampen, the Netherlands: Kok Pharos, 1993); Charles Mills, *From Class to Race: Essays in White Marxism and Black Radicalism* (Lanham, Md.: Rowman and Littlefield, 2003); Patricia J. Mills, *Woman, Nature, and Psyche* (New Haven: Yale University Press, 1987); Jeffrey T. Nealon and Caren Irr, eds., *Rethinking the Frankfurt School: Alternative Legacies of Cultural Critique* (Albany: State University of New York Press, 2002); Lucius Outlaw, *Critical Social*

Theory in the Interests of Black Folks (Lanham, Md.: Rowman and Littlefield, 2005); Lucius Outlaw, "Toward a Critical Theory of Race," in Bernard Boxill, ed., *Race and Racism* (New York: Oxford University Press, 2001), 58–82; William S. Wilkerson and Jeffrey Paris, eds., *New Critical Theory: Essays on Liberation* (Lanham, Md.: Rowman and Littlefield, 2001). There are many other examples, and the literature is steadily growing.

20. Piccone, "20 Years of *Telos*," 4.

21. See Roger Kimball, *The Long March: How the Cultural Revolution of the 1960s Changed America* (San Francisco: Encounter Books, 2000), 157–72; and Daniel J. Flynn, *Intellectual Morons: How Ideology Makes Smart People Fall for Stupid Ideas* (New York: Crown Forum, 2004), 14–31.

22. See David Horowitz, *The Professors: The 101 Most Dangerous Academics in America* (Washington: Regnery, 2006), xxxvi–xxxvii; and Alan Charles Kors and Harvey A. Silvergate, *The Shadow University: The Betrayal of Liberty on America's Campuses* (New York: Harper, 1999), 68, 71, and 372–73.

23. In 1928, speaking in London, Oppenheimer portrayed German sociology as a struggle between a "Frankfurt School" under his leadership and a "Cologne School" under Leopold von Wiese. The incident is cited and briefly discussed in David Kettler and Volker Meja, *Karl Mannheim and the Crisis of Liberalism: The Secret of These New Times* (New Brunswick, N.J.: Transaction, 1995), 119. The citation is Franz Oppenheimer, "Tendencies in Recent German Sociology," *Sociological Review*, vol. 24, nos. 1–3 (1932): 1–13, 125–37, 249–260.

24. Letter from Max Horkheimer to Salka Viertel, 29 June 1940, from *MHGS*, vol. 16, 726.

INDEX

Abel, Theodore, 72, 75, 146, 213. *See also* Columbia University

Adorno, Theodor W., xv, xvii, 80, 98, 180–82, 205, 218, 220, 259, 271–72, 290, 337–38, 372n101, 378n62, 392n10, 395n55; *Aesthetic Theory,* 275–77; on art, 28–29, 159–61, 174–75, 185, 275–76; collaborations with Horkheimer, 61–62, 81, 162–64, 228–29, 244–45; *Dialectic of Enlightenment* (dialectics project), 81–82, 118, 128, 130, 162–64, 217–21, 229, 240–42, 262, 286, 291–92, 377n56; employment with Lazarsfeld, 62, 145–46, 228, 354n1; on exile, 275, 393n26, 393n27; on mass culture, 160–61; *Negative Dialectics,* 275–77; on the New Left, 271, 276–78, 394n30, 394n31; "On Popular Music," 185; "On the Fetish Character in Music and the Regression of Listening," 160–61, 174–75, 183; personal history, 23–25; Positivism dispute, 262–63, 343; on the United States, 262, 275; on the Vietnam War, 277

aesthetics, xvii–xviii, xix, 3, 28–29, 99, 159–61, 164–77, 185, 252, 272, 276, 282–83, 287, 368n49, 369n50. *See also* Critical Theory; New York Intellectuals

alienation, 99, 106, 160, 164, 294, 308, 325, 336, 344. *See also* Critical Theory; Marxism; New York Intellectuals; New Left

Allport, Gordon, 250, 260. *See also* anti-Semitism project; *Studies in Prejudice*

American Communist Party, 102, 138, 148, 165–69, 303, 361n9

American Jewish Committee (AJC), 91, 101, 145, 153–58, 223, 225, 230, 232–35, 238–39, 241–48, 251, 254, 381n89, 387n59; Scientific Department, 247. *See also* anti-Semitism project; *Studies in Prejudice*

American Psychiatric Association, 225

Anderson, Eugene, 88, 281, 379n71, 381n90. *See also* Institute projects: Germany project

Anglo-American sociology, xix–xx, 191, 196–208, 211, 214, 218, 226, 229, 235, 238–40, 243, 247–48, 255, 257, 260–61, 345, 374n3

anti-Semitism project, 87–88, 91, 142, 145, 151, 153–56, 219–20, 223–26, 229, 231–35, 241–63, 307, 379n75, 382n15, 386n55, 387n59; first proposal, 88, 227–29, 378n67, 379n70, 385n37; Los Angeles Branch, 243–45, 247, 250; New York Branch, 229–32, 243, 245, 247; revised

405

proposal, 230, 234–42, 244–46, 384n29, 384n30, 384n31, 385n32, 385n37, 386n48. *See also* Berkeley Public Opinion Study Group; *Studies in Prejudice*

Atlantic culture, xv–xvii, 341–42, 344–47

Atlantic history, xv–xvii, 1–2, 134–39, 191

Austro-Marxism, 9–12, 48, 103, 201, 349n9

Barrett, William, 98–99. *See also* New York Intellectuals

Becker, Howard, 209–10

Bell, Daniel, 77–78, 80–81, 101, 134, 147–51, 249, 346. *See also* New York Intellectuals

Bender, Thomas, 98

Benjamin, Walter, 24–25, 354n5, 98, 159, 279, 294–95; personal history, 63–64; "Theses on the Philosophy of History," 292; "The Work of Art in the Age of Its Mechanical Reproducibility," 160

Berg, Alban, 24

Berkeley Public Opinion Study Group, 245, 255. *See also* anti-Semitism project; *Studies in Prejudice*

Breines, Paul, 335–38, 341, 401n1; *Critical Interruptions*, 335–38, 341; "Marcuse and the New Left in America," 336

bureaucratic collectivism, 179, 186, 306

Burgess, Ernest, 198

Burnham, James, 101, 176, 179; *The Managerial Revolution*, 179–80

Butler, Nicholas Murray, 35, 40, 70–71. *See also* Columbia University

Cantril, Hadley, 86, 249, 250, 260

Chicago Psychoanalytic Institute, 44

City College New York (CCNY), 142, 147, 366n11; and "Alcove 1," 147–48, 150–51

civil rights movement, 304–5, 319, 323, 328; Freedom Rides, 305; impact on SDS, 304–5, 311–12, 316, 320, 322; Student Nonviolent Coordinating Committee (SNCC), 312. *See also* Students for a Democratic Society

Claussen, Detlev, 275, 393n26

Cohen, Elliot, 101, 153–58, 254. *See also* *Commentary*; New York Intellectuals

Cold War, xix, 133, 199, 258, 260–63, 268, 270–72, 274, 282–85, 291–95, 303–4, 306

Columbia University, xix, 3, 35–37, 141–42, 188, 218; Nicholas Murray Butler, 35; MacMahon Committee, 91–93. *See also* Columbia University's sociology department; Frankfurt School

Columbia University's sociology department, 197, 201–2, 284, 306; aims, 40–43, 352n15; history, 37–40; invitation to the Frankfurt School, 35–37, 60; negotiations with the Frankfurt School, 89–94, 230–32, 382n14; relations with the Frankfurt School, 64–66, 72–77, 218–19, 221–22, 248–49, 388n65, 388n66. *See also* Frankfurt School

Commentary, 101, 153–58, 187; Elliot Cohen, 101, 153–58, 254; Nathan Glazer, 150, 153, 254; publicity for *Studies in Prejudice*, 153–56, 253–54, 390n83; relations with the Frankfurt School, 153–58

commodity fetishism, 160–61, 171, 175, 182. *See also* Critical Theory; Marxism

Comte, Auguste, 126, 192–99

conformity, 99, 101, 123, 130–31, 171, 178, 182–83, 286, 341. *See also* Critical Theory; New York Intellectuals

Continental sociology, xix–xx, 191, 194–204, 207–8, 211, 218, 221, 226, 228, 235, 238–40, 243, 247–49, 260–61, 345, 374n3

Coser, Lewis, 101, 148, 176, 241, 289, 367n22, 369n58; relationship with Dwight Macdonald, 149–50; relationship with the Frankfurt School, 149, 249. *See also* *Dissent*; New York Intellectuals

cosmopolitanism, xix, 135–36, 154, 157–58, 165, 260–61. *See also* Frankfurt School; New York Intellectuals

counterculture, 268, 270, 297, 330, 337, 342–43. *See also* New Left

critical reason, 27, 106, 109, 111, 115, 127, 136–37, 163–64, 229, 272, 293, 299, 308, 322. *See also* Critical Theory; Enlightenment

303, 330–33, 337, 347; criticisms of
the New Left, 298, 321–23, 330; on
democracy, 288–90, 299, 318–19,
325–26, 329, 332–34; early personal
history, 22–23; enthusiasm for the New
Left, xx, 269–70, 277–78, 323–27, 329,
334, 346–47; on Eros, 283, 287; *Eros and
Civilization,* 152, 282–83, 285–89, 291,
300, 308, 334, 395n55; *An Essay on
Liberation,* 303, 316, 323, 328, 338;
European reception, 299, 301, 303, 324,
326; the Great Refusal, 283, 291, 325,
327, 329; and the guru myth, xx, 267–
70, 296–303, 317, 324, 326, 333–35,
396n2, 397n8, 398n14, 399n37; on the
Hungarian revolution, 289–90; on
Imperialism, 327–29; on Marxism, 285,
288, 294, 303, 321, 327–29; on the new
sensibility, 283, 325, 328–30, 333; *New
York Times Magazine* interview, 269;
One-Dimensional Man, 268, 282–83,
287, 291–95, 300–303, 314–18, 321, 323–
25, 329, 336, 339; praxis, 298–99, 318–19,
322–23, 325–26, 329–30, 333, 346–47;
Reason and Revolution, 126–27, 378n63,
285; "Repressive Tolerance," 291, 303,
316–21, 323–24, 336, 347; significance of
1968, xx, 296–97, 300–301, 326, 328;
significance of the Spartacist winter, 23,
288, 299, 324, 332–33; "Some Remarks
on Aragon," 282–83; *Soviet Marxism,*
282, 285, 287–91, 395n57; on the Soviet
Union, 283–85, 287–90, 332; "Thirty-
three Theses," 283; on totalitarianism,
68, 160, 282–85, 287–88, 293, 299,
331–32, 346–47; at the University of
California, San Diego, 296, 298, 300; as
a U.S. intellectual, 291, 300; on utopia,
286–87, 327, 332–34; on violence, 319,
321, 329–30
Marcuse, Ludwig, 135
Maritain, Jacques, 124–25
Marshak, Robert, 114, 363n39
Marx, Karl, 5, 27, 81, 102, 105–6, 108, 131,
178, 200, 207, 223, 249, 268, 272, 290,
294, 298, 301, 341
Marx-Engels Institute, 12, 350n13

Marxian revisionism, 105, 110
Marxian theory of value, 110, 175
Marxism, 5, 7–8, 11, 15–17, 99–102, 104–5,
125–26, 133–34, 157, 164, 167–77, 180,
187, 285, 288, 294, 303, 307–8, 321,
329, 340; alienation, 106, 160, 344;
commodity fetishism, 160–61, 171, 175,
182; dialectical logic, 65, 106, 115, 119–
22, 345; dialectical materialism, 105–6,
110–11, 115, 119–21; historical materialism, 106–8, 115–16, 118–19, 143, 159, 162,
216, 286, 327, 345; immanent critique,
65, 107, 115–16, 159, 162, 287–88, 345
mass culture, 99, 123, 134, 151, 158, 160–62,
164–87, 229, 325, 341, 346, 370n75,
370n76. *See also* Critical Theory; New
York Intellectuals
Massing, Paul, 254
Mattick, Paul, 110–11, 116, 362n26
McLaughlin, Neil, 224–25
Merton, Robert, xix, 249, 260; collaboration with Lazarsfeld, 201–2, 250. *See
also* Columbia University's sociology
department
metaphysics, 104, 107–8, 111–12, 115,
135–38. *See also* Critical Theory; Hook,
Sidney
Mills, C. Wright, 176, 202, 249, 268, 294,
298, 305–10, 316, 325, 333, 398n24. *See
also* Students for a Democratic Society
modernism, 99–101, 164–77, 185. *See
also* Frankfurt School; New York
Intellectuals
monopoly capitalism, 130–31, 161, 219–20,
294
Moore, Barrington, 249, 285
Muenzenberg, Willi, 36
Munroe, Ruth, 71–72, 213

Nagel, Ernest, 103, 116, 125
National Review, 268
naturalism, 113–14. *See also* Hook, Sidney
Nazism: significance for the Frankfurt
School, 29–30, 31–32, 43, 88, 115–16, 123,
137, 141, 153–58, 160–64, 177, 208,
213–16, 219–21, 236–37, 243, 245, 247,
254, 271, 299, 331, 371n90, 382n18;

participatory democracy, 309–12, 314, 320, 334, 342; Port Huron Statement, 305–6; and Progressive Labor (PL), 330; Radical Education Project (REP), 313–14, 317, 325–26, 399n36, 400n57; Weatherman, 302, 328–30

Studies in Prejudice, 87–88, 91, 142, 145, 151, 153–56, 219–20, 223–26, 241–63, 307, 382n15, 386n55, 387n59; anti-Semitic character and its similarities to Fromm's authoritarian character, 238, 243, 386n49; *Anti-Semitism and Emotional Disorder,* 387n61; *The Authoritarian Personality,* 256–57; *Dynamics of Prejudice,* 249, 251, 387n61; *Prophets of Deceit,* 151; *Rehearsal for Destruction,* U.S. reception, 248, 253–63. *See also* anti-Semitism project; Berkeley Public Opinion Study Group

Studies on the Left, 297, 316–17

survey research, 197–98, 201

Tar, Zoltan, 241

Telos, 297, 315, 338–39, 343. *See also* Piccone, Paul

Third World, 301, 319, 327–29, 332

Thoreau, Henry David, 298, 304

Tillich, Paul, 13, 98, 242, 260

Tönnies, Ferdinand, 195–96, 200. *See also* Continental sociology

totalitarianism, 68, 99, 115–16, 125, 130–31, 135–39, 158, 161–64, 168, 170–71, 178–87, 220, 229, 236–37, 240, 243, 245, 247, 271, 274, 282–85, 287–88, 293, 299, 320, 331–32, 346–47, 385n32. *See also* Critical Theory; Gleason, Abbott; New York Intellectuals

totality, 107–8, 115–16, 120, 122, 183–84. *See also* Critical Theory; Hook, Sidney

Trotskyism, 101, 126, 147–50, 168, 176, 179–80, 306

University of California, Los Angeles, 273

University of Chicago, 44, 47, 145, 222, 380n77, 380n79; Department of

Sociology, 39, 41, 198–99, 248–50; faculty exchange with the University of Frankfurt, 250, 388n70; Horkheimer as visiting professor, 274

University of Frankfurt, 8, 10–12, 25, 97–98, 258–59, 262

U.S. anti-Communism, 100–101, 137–38, 168–69, 177, 284, 303–4, 312

Vienna Circle, 103, 116

Von Schelting, Alexander, 202. *See also* Columbia University's sociology department

Walzer, Michael, 320

Warshow, Robert, 101, 254. *See also* New York Intellectuals

Weber, Max, 81, 115, 145, 195–96, 199–202, 204, 223, 249, 272, 298, 308, 341, 366n15

Weil, Felix, 6–13, 16–17, 254

Weil, Hermann, 7–9

Weimar modernism, 5–6

Weimar Republic, xviii, 4–6, 27, 137, 156, 200, 237, 271, 299

Wellman, David, 317. *See also* Students for a Democratic Society

Western Marxism, 7–8, 25–26, 105–8, 131, 205–6, 327, 340–41. *See also* Critical Theory; Hook, Sidney; Korsch, Karl; Lukács, Georg

West German Sociology, xx, 259–63, 343, 392n108

Wiggershaus, Rolf: *The Frankfurt School,* 2–3, 241

Williams, William A., 268

Wilson, Edmund, 138–39

Wirth, Louis, 222

Wittfogel, Karl, 7, 12, 60

Wolff, Kurt, 202

Zeitschrift für Sozialforschung, 22, 27–29, 60, 65, 80, 110–14, 144–45, 151, 204, 209, 212, 216, 221, 227–28, 284; modifications in the United States, 65–66, 151, 171, 177–78, 371n90, 382n18